Sports Illustrated™

THE STORY OF

Hockey

IN 100 PHOTOGRAPHS

CONTENTS

2002 TO 2025 | *The Modern Era* 141

1882 to 1949

Beginnings

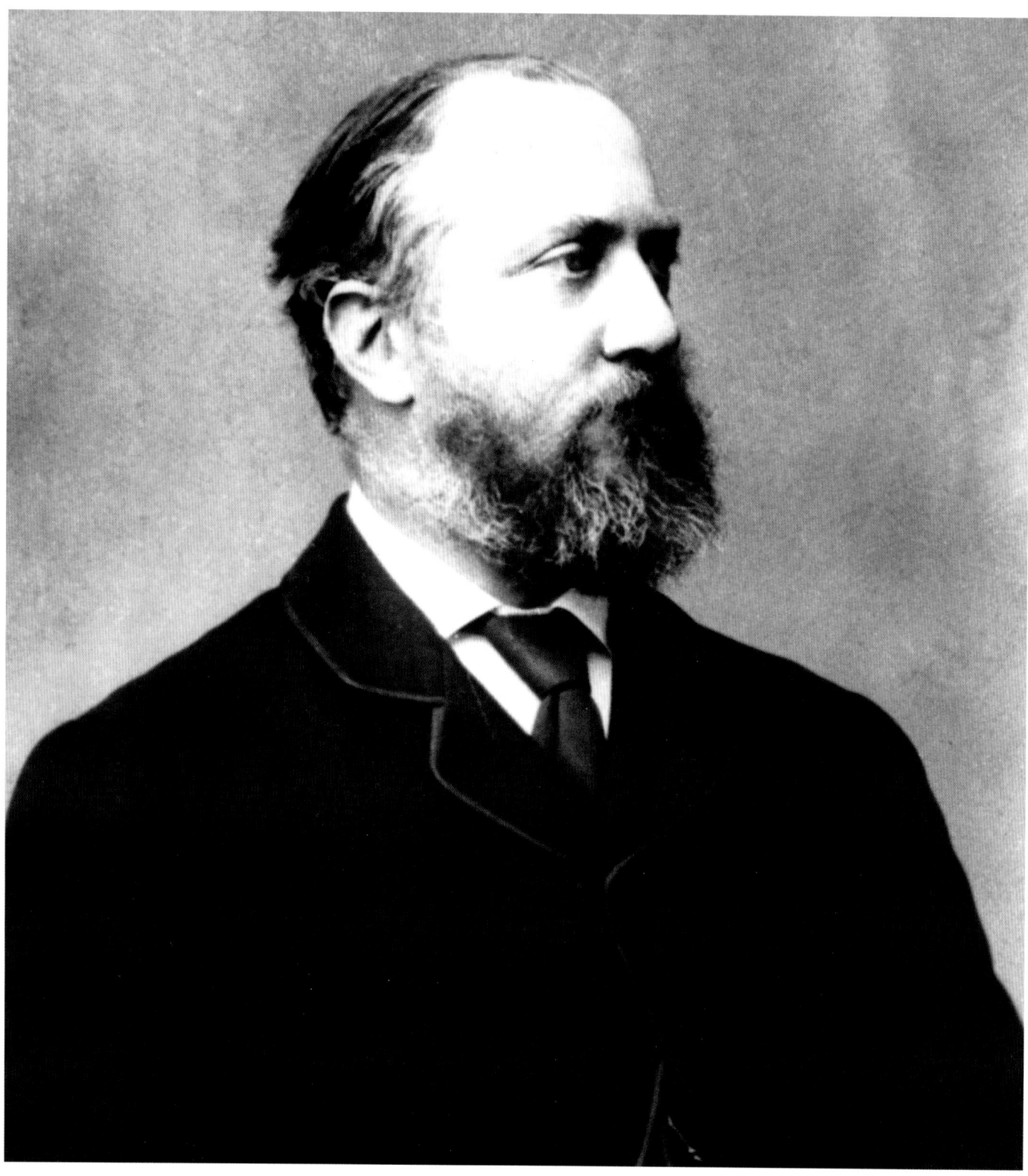

LORD STANLEY'S CUP

Circa 1892

SIR FREDERICK ARTHUR Stanley, Baron of Preston, attended his first hockey game in 1889. The governor general of Canada was visiting the Montreal Winter Carnival when he and his entourage stepped inside the Victoria Skating Rink, where the first indoor hockey match had been played 14 years earlier. The sudden appearance of the British Crown's personal representative required an immediate halt to the action. The band played "God Save the Queen," the subjects of Victoria's empire applauded and the game went on.

Lord Stanley liked what he saw. He had an outdoor rink built on the grounds of his official residence in Ottawa, where he tried skating himself. Two of his sons, Arthur and Algernon, joined teams, as did his teenage daughter Isobel. Stanley was regularly seen at Ottawa's downtown arena, in his rinkside box, watching the capital's top club.

The governor general could not attend the banquet celebrating Ottawa's league championship in 1892, so he sent a congratulatory letter—along with a pledge: he would donate a trophy "which could be held from year to year by the leading club in Canada." Later that year, the "Dominion Challenge Trophy," a cup made of silver and nickel, arrived from London.

Originally, any amateur team could challenge the holder of the Stanley Cup. Challenges took place multiple times each winter, with clubs from small towns like Rat Portage, Ontario, and New Glasgow, Nova Scotia, competing for the trophy. In 1906, professional teams were allowed to challenge for the Cup, and by 1915, the champions of the two pro leagues, in the East and West, played an annual series to decide the trophy's winner. In 1917, the best team in the western league, the Seattle Metropolitans, became the first American team to claim the Cup.

Since 1926–27, the Stanley Cup has been the championship trophy of the National Hockey League. Canadiens goalie Ken Dryden lifted it six times as a player. He described its unique aura in his book *The Game:* "When players today win a championship, in a timeless gesture of triumph, they throw their hands above their heads. And in sports, nothing fits better between a player's hands than the Stanley Cup. It is perfect."

Photograph by BRUCE BENNETT STUDIOS

THE MILLIONAIRES

Circa 1913

IN THE FIRST two decades of professional hockey, an alphabet soup of leagues swirled in Canada and the northern parts of the United States. Travel costs prevented the formation of a single pro league, so different associations competed for top players, all in hope of claiming the Stanley Cup.

Frank Patrick, the handsome young man seated front-row center in this photograph, founded the most influential of these early leagues, the Pacific Coast Hockey Association, which operated from 1911 to 1924. Bankrolled by their father's timber fortune, Frank and his brother Lester owned the league's teams, built the arenas, wrote the rules, distributed the players and also played and coached—Frank for the Vancouver Millionaires, Lester for the Victoria Aristocrats.

Before the Patricks launched their league, there had been no hockey in the mild winter climate of British Columbia. The brothers had to be creative in building the sport. The first innovation was where the games were played. Constructed in Vancouver and Victoria, the league's arenas were the first indoor rinks in Canada to have artificial ice. The Patricks also introduced the blue line and the forward pass, and they removed the position of rover, dropping the number of a team's skaters from six to five.

Most influential was the brothers' scheme for keeping fans interested at the end of the season: a series of games between the league's top two finishers, with the winner challenging the best team from the eastern league for the Stanley Cup. This invention of postseason playoffs transformed not only hockey but all North American sports.

After starting their league, the Patrick brothers issued a challenge for the Cup. Lester's Victoria team won in 1925, the last time a team outside the NHL held hockey's most coveted prize. Frank took the trophy in 1915 with the Millionaires, who earned their name from the high-priced talent the brothers lured. The team's top scorer was Fred Taylor (back row, second from right), who pocketed $1,800 for the season. While playing in Ottawa, he had earned his famous nickname, Cyclone. Frank Patrick gave him a different moniker in Vancouver, a word that was another Patrick invention: superstar.

Photograph by STUART THOMSON/CITY OF VANCOUVER ARCHIVES

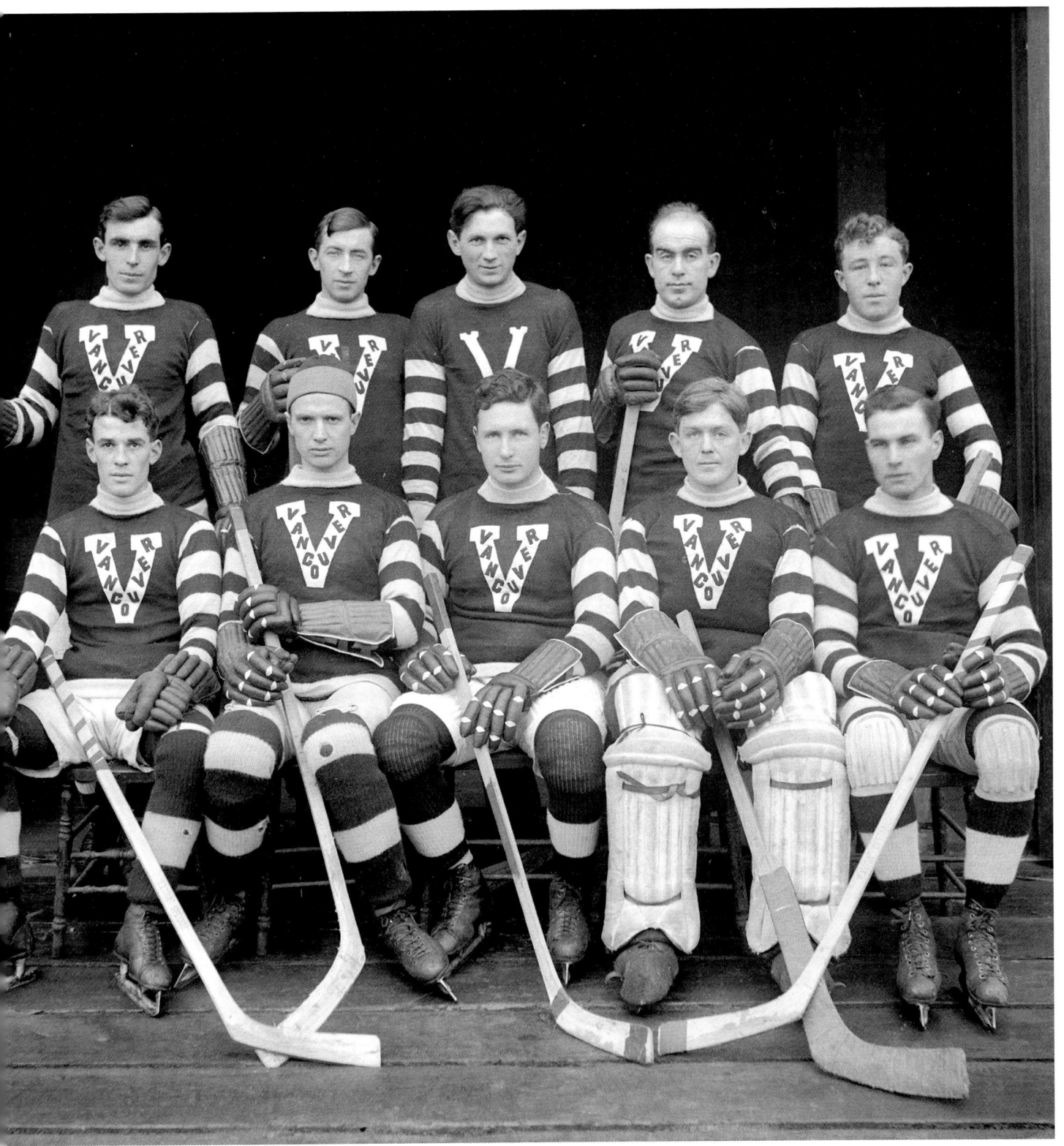

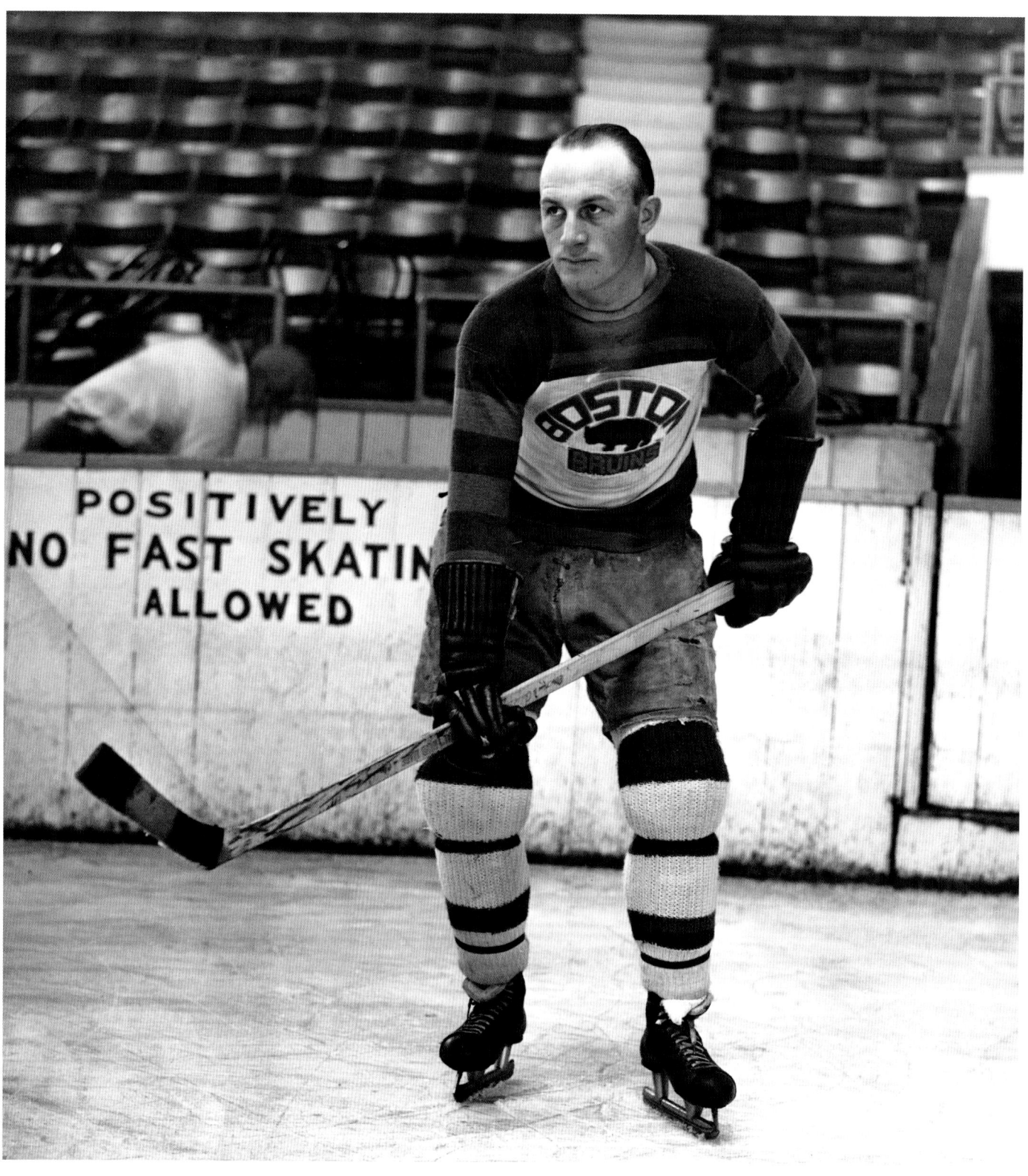

THE SHOWMAN

BOSTON ARENA, BOSTON | *Circa 1920s*

IF HOWIE MORENZ was the Babe Ruth of hockey, then Eddie Shore was the sport's Ty Cobb: equal parts relentless, ruthless and remarkably skilled. One reporter observed that spectators turned out when Shore's Boston Bruins came to town in the hope "that he will some night be severely killed."

Shore's toughness was legendary. To be sure, he helped inflate the legend. In his telling, he was born in the back of an oxcart on the road to Regina. Shore told reporters he had refused anesthetic when a doctor repaired his ear, nearly severed in a fight. The Bruins defenseman needed a clear eye to watch in a mirror, so as to give the doctor instructions. "I made him change the very last stitch," Shore said. "If I had not done that, he'd have left a scar."

The stitches on Shore's ear were his first in the NHL. (The fight had been with a teammate in his rookie training camp.) He tallied 978 stitches in his career, nearly matching his 1,099 penalty minutes.

The farm boy from Saskatchewan was also a showman. He goaded opposing players and fans like a pro wrestling heel. For a time, Shore skated onto the ice before road games wearing a bullfighter's cape. A valet would skate behind and then unveil the star defenseman in his brown-and-gold sweater, to howls from the enemy crowd. Shore even entertained teammates with his saxophone on long train rides. Coach Art Ross put an end to the recitals. Shore was a virtuoso on the ice, but he could produce little more than squawks from his horn.

The legend of Eddie Shore only grew after retirement, during his years as owner of the minor-league team in Springfield, Massachusetts. He made teams practice in the dark to cut down utilities costs and forbade players from having sex, to preserve their strength. One of his lasting innovations as team owner came not in hockey but figure skating. Joining with other owners, the consummate entertainer created a traveling ice show featuring former champions. The hard-nosed player known as Old Blood and Guts was also inventor of Ice Capades.

Photograph by GEORGE RINHART/CORBIS

THE PIONEERS

CROYDON AERODROME, LONDON, ENGLAND | *February 14, 1931*

WOMEN PLAYED HOCKEY from the very beginning. In turn-of-the-century Canada, teams were organized by schools and churches. The game grew especially during World War I, as men went off to the battlefields of Europe and companies hired women to fill jobs. Employers started hockey teams to give these young female workers a healthy evening activity.

The enterprising Frank Patrick was the first to see there was money to be made in women's hockey. In 1921, the founder of the Pacific Coast Hockey Association launched the Vancouver Amazons, a team that barnstormed throughout the Pacific Northwest. By the end of the Roaring Twenties, fans were filling the Montreal Forum to watch showdowns between the champions of the Ontario and Quebec women's leagues.

Women's hockey was also part of the sport's boom in Europe during the 1930s. Each winter, the top men's club in Canadian amateur hockey traveled through Europe, playing teams in England, France, Germany, Czechoslovakia and Switzerland. Huge crowds turned out for each stop on the tour, which culminated with the annual world championship, always held in Europe and always won by the Canadians.

During this time, women's leagues launched in England and France. The stylish women in the photo were France's top club, the appropriately named Droit au But—Straight to the Goal. Arriving in London for a four-game tour, they went on to top teams from London and Manchester in winter 1931. The tour drew enough attention in French newspapers that when an English team arrived in Paris later that year, 10,000 spectators filled the arena. The home team gave them a show, defeating the visiting Sussex Ladies 6–0. Paris papers heralded Jacqueline Mautin as the best player in women's hockey after her five-goal performance.

In both Europe and North America, women's leagues eventually disappeared in the harsh climate of the Great Depression. At the same time, women's hockey was swept aside by the cultural phenomenon of Sonja Henie. The Norwegian figure skater turned movie star launched a worldwide figure-skating boom. After Henie, more girls took to the ice in white figure skates rather than black hockey skates.

Photograph by HULTON-DEUTSCH COLLECTION/CORBIS

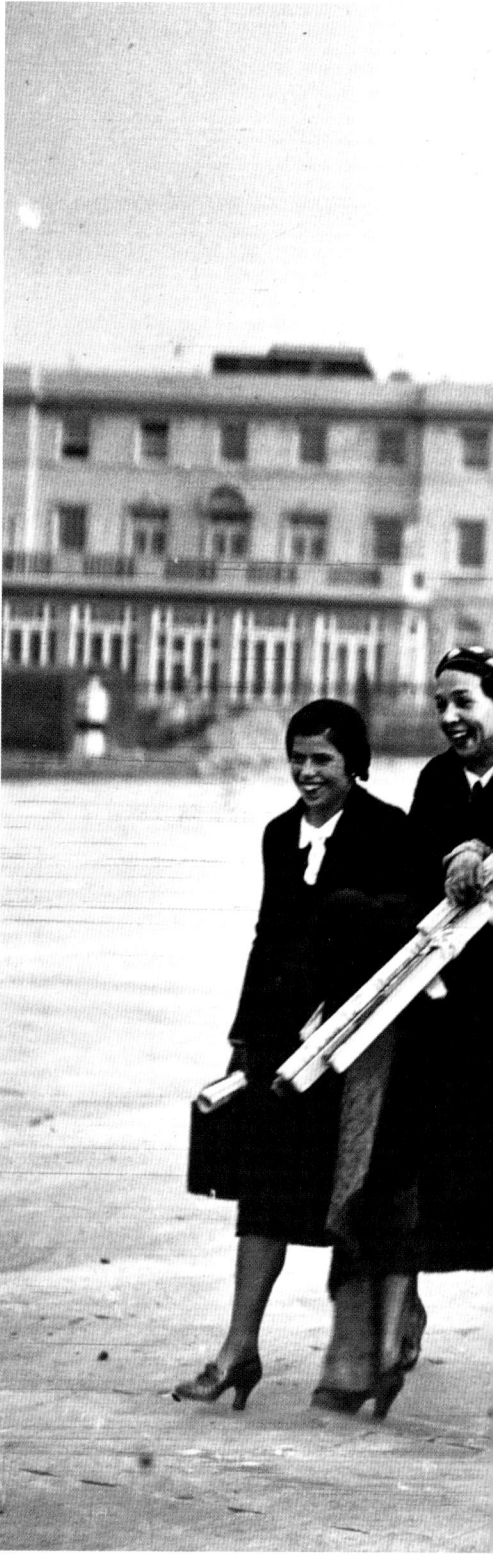

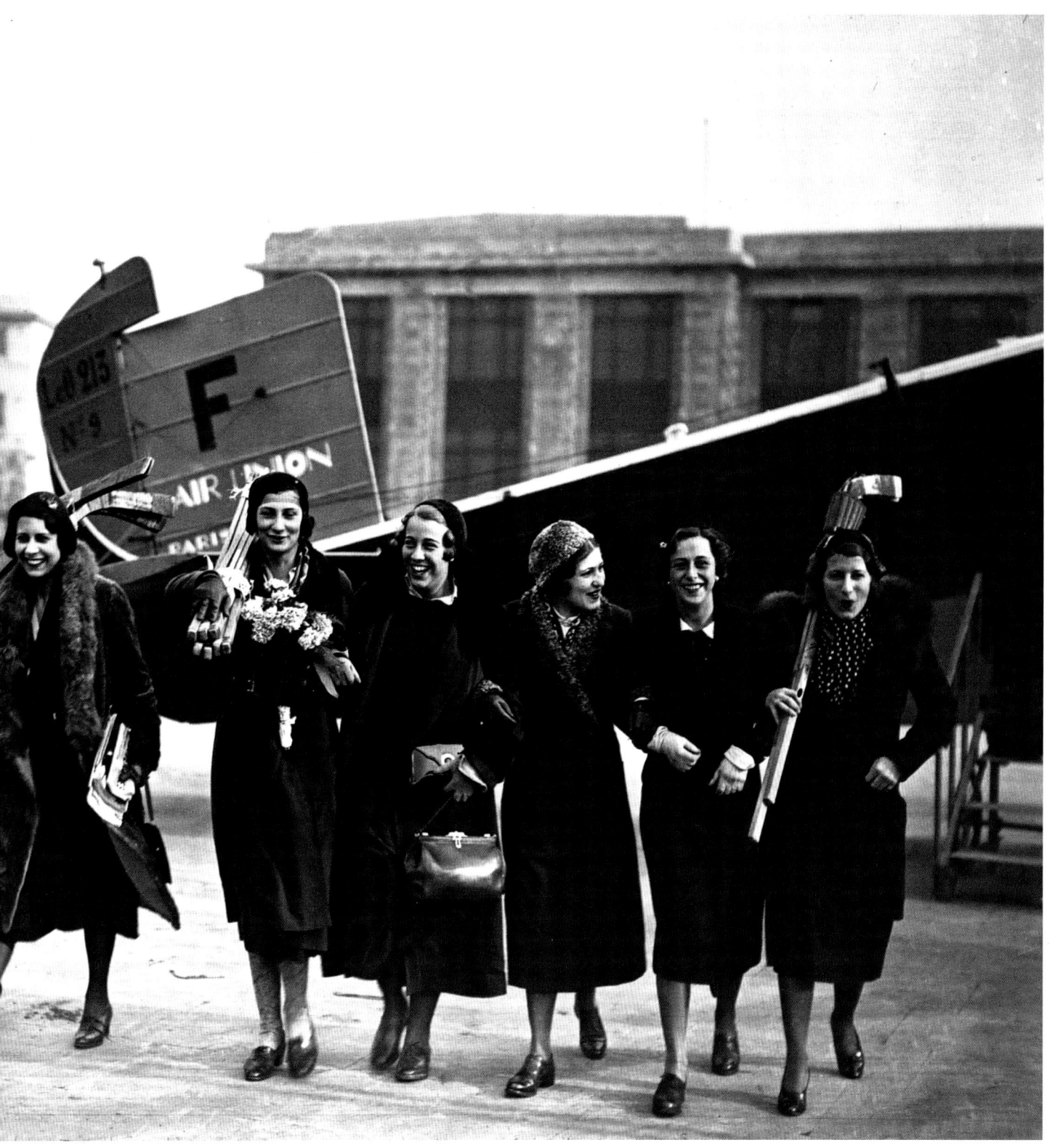

"THE BABE RUTH OF HOCKEY"

December 1, 1934

THERE HAD BEEN stars before him, players like Hod Stuart and Cyclone Taylor and Newsy Lalonde. None could match Howie Morenz. He was a comet with "mercury-dipped skates," to quote the Canadian papers. American sportswriters gave him the biggest accolade possible: "the Babe Ruth of Hockey."

As a boy Morenz wanted to be a goalie, but he let in 21 goals in his first game. He showed greater promise as a forward, becoming known as "the Stratford Streak" at rinks around his Ontario hometown. He scored in his debut for the Montreal Canadiens in 1923, the first of his 271 goals. Ottawa defenseman King Clancy took exception to the 5'9", 165-pound rookie speeding past and knocking him on his rear. "I told him if he tried it again, I would cut his head off," recalled Clancy. "He laughed and said he planned to do it again. Know what? He did."

Morenz was often laughing. The stern expression in this photo doesn't suit him. On the ice, he had an "amiable, earnest, sometimes puzzled face," wrote hockey historian Michael McKinley. "He looked like somebody's uncle who had stumbled into the rink by mistake." He was a joyful player on the ice. In the locker room, he was always singing.

The Chicago Black Hawks sweater in the photo also doesn't suit him. He wept when the Canadiens traded their fading star. From Chicago, he sent newspaper columns back to Montreal, writing with humor and flair about life in the NHL. "Father Time easily overhauls the fastest mortals," he wrote in one piece.

In 1936–37, Morenz appeared to give Father Time a last run for his money. Back in Montreal, the 34-year-old tallied 20 points in the Habs' first 30 games, leading the team to first place. Then on a January night, he went down. Smashed against the boards, Morenz's left leg was broken in four places. The injury drained his joy. Morenz had a nervous breakdown in the hospital. On March 8, 1937, he tripped and suffered a coronary embolism. His casket was placed at center ice in the Montreal Forum. More than 50,000 people filed past, paying their respects to the man who had been hockey's brightest star.

Photograph by BETTMANN

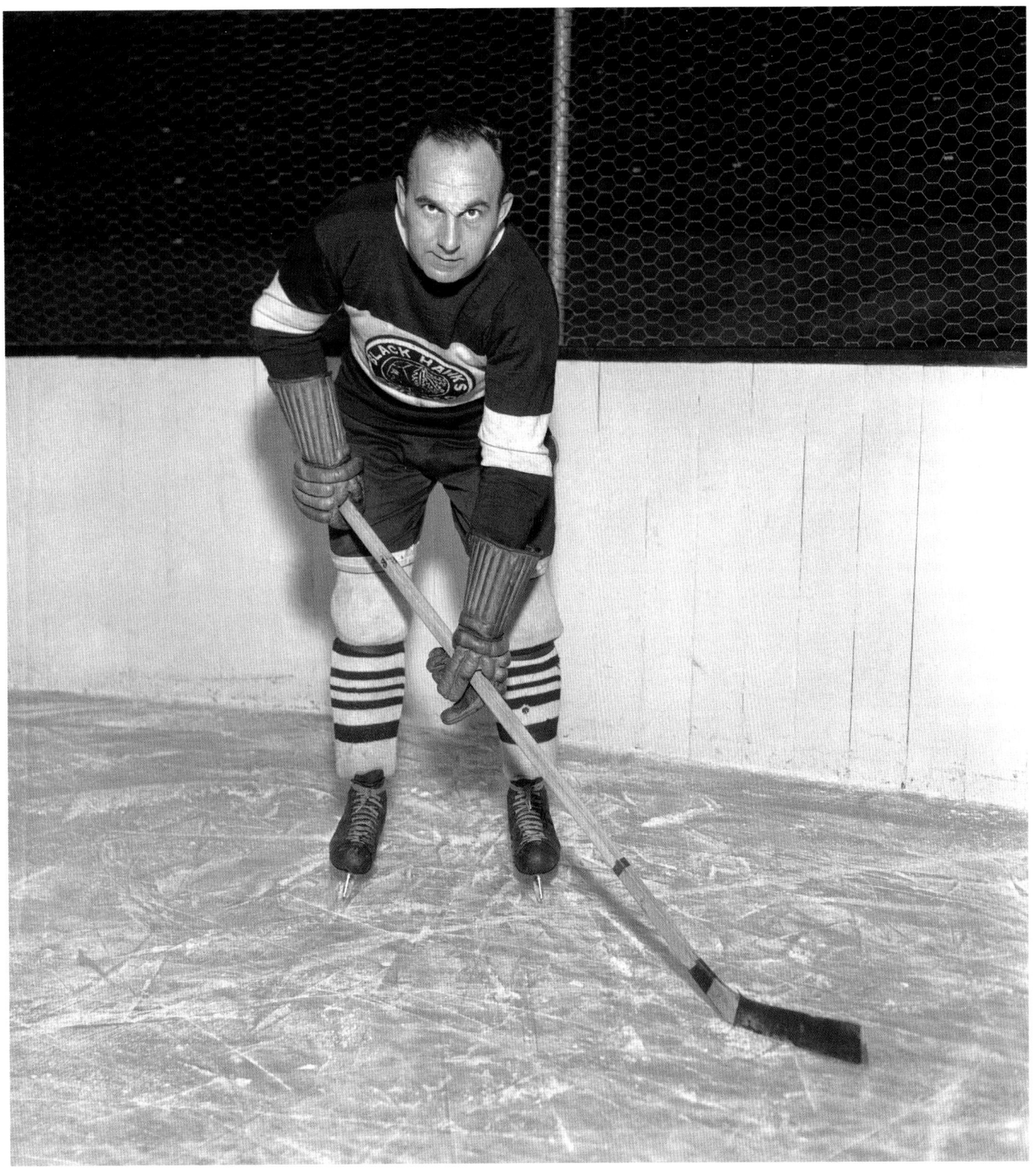

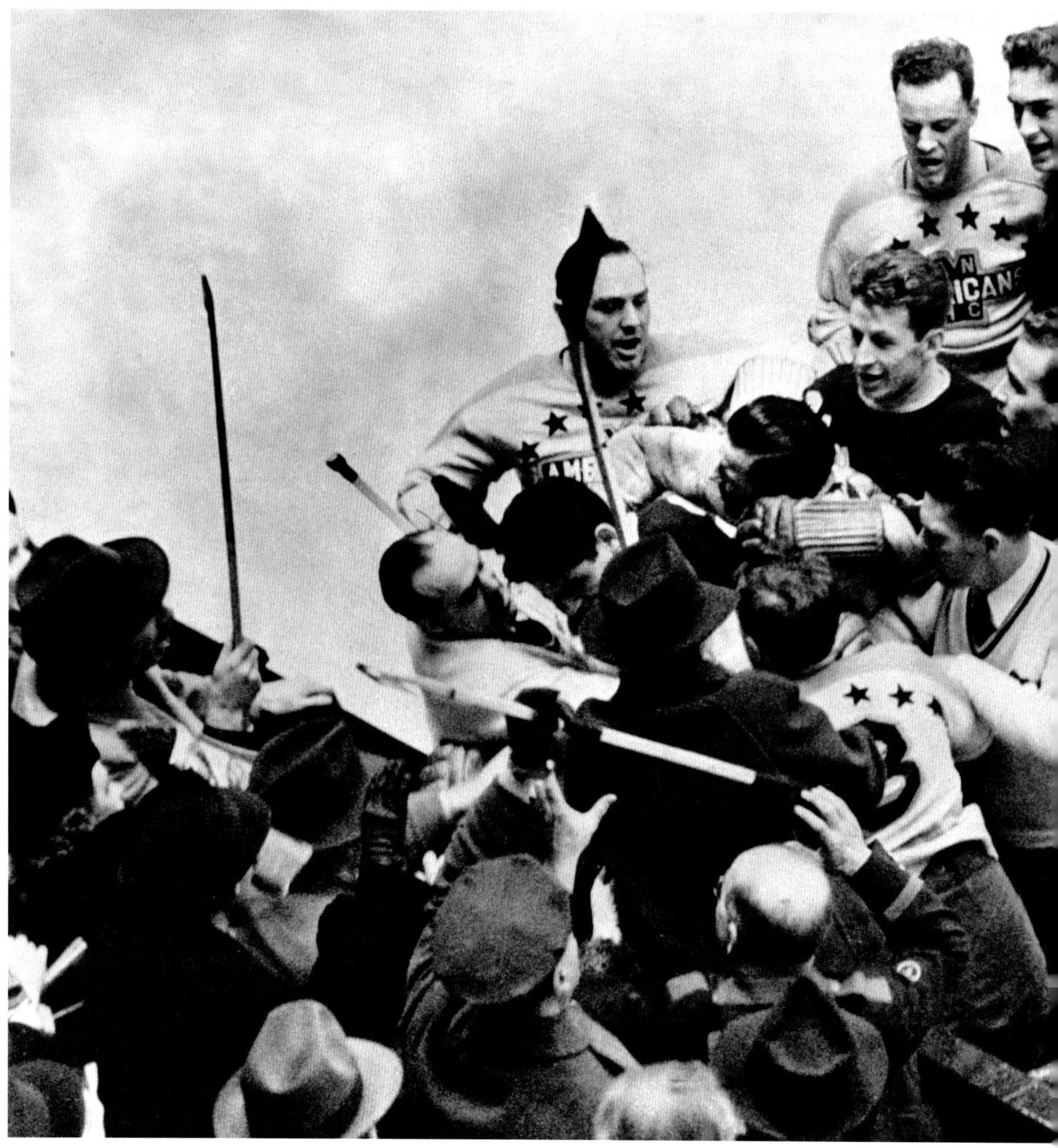

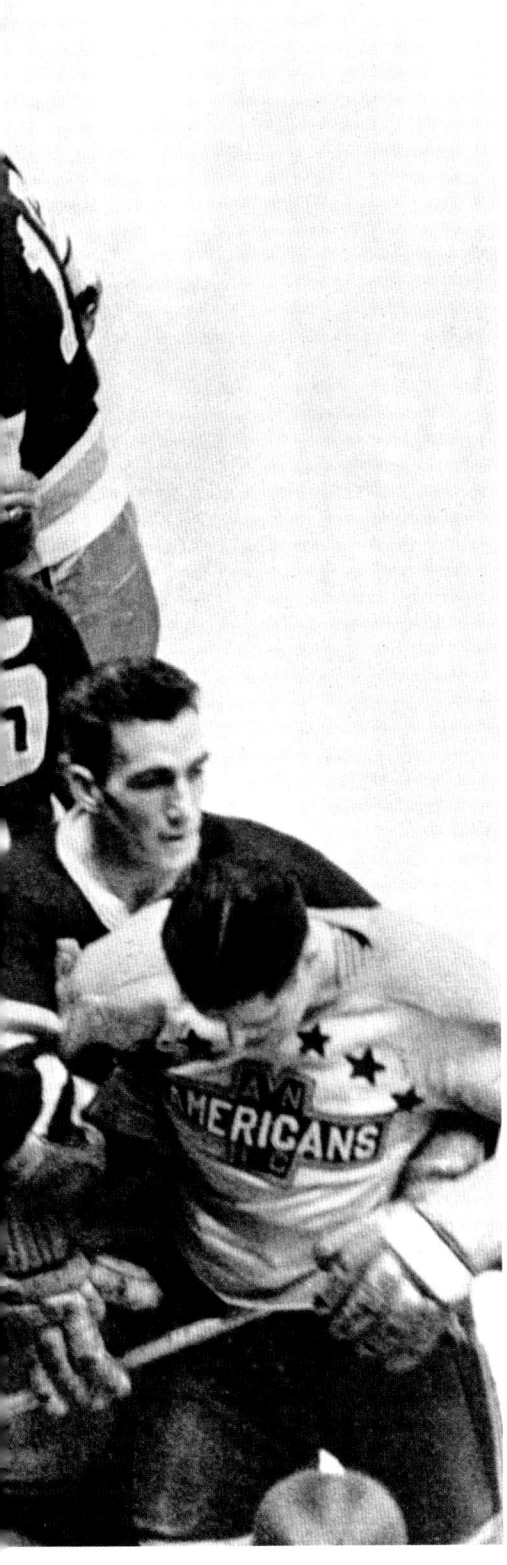

THE AMERKS

MADISON SQUARE GARDEN, NEW YORK CITY | *January 23, 1940*

THE ORIGINAL SIX were not as original as advertised. When the NHL began in the winter of 1917–18, four teams took the ice: the Ottawa Senators, Toronto Arenas and Montreal Wanderers and Canadiens. By 1926 the league had expanded to 10 teams. The Great Depression pared that number down to nine, then eight, then seven. Times were so tough that even the Canadiens thought about moving to greener pastures—in Cleveland.

Among the NHL's early franchises, a special place belongs to the New York Americans. The Americans were not the league's first American team (this honor belongs to the Boston Bruins), but they did bring pro hockey to the Big Apple. In doing that, they transformed the game.

In 1925, promoter Tex Rickard saw pro hockey's potential to fill dates at his new arena, Madison Square Garden, when there weren't bigger events like boxing, wrestling or the circus. Rickard didn't purchase a franchise himself; instead, he convinced bootlegger Big Bill Dwyer to buy into the league and then buy out one of the NHL's top clubs, the Hamilton Tigers. The whole roster moved to Manhattan. The mayor was on hand at the Garden for hockey's opening night, along with 17,000 other people. The year before, the former Tigers had drawn 5,000 to their arena in Hamilton.

Madison Square Garden re-wrote the economic rules of hockey. In their first season, the Amerks drew twice as many fans as the next biggest-drawing team, the Canadiens. Other owners quickly saw they also needed spacious gardens. In the next six years, the Bruins, Chicago Black Hawks, Detroit Red Wings and Toronto Maple Leafs all moved into larger facilities, the storied arenas that would host Stanley Cup battles, political conventions and Beatles concerts in decades to come.

Meanwhile, Tex Rickard was so impressed with hockey that he bought his own franchise. Tex's Rangers became the more popular New York team, in large part because they won. The Rangers lifted the Stanley Cup in their second year, while the Amerks managed only three winning seasons in their 17-year existence. After a last-place finish in 1942, the Americans suspended operations. The Original Seven were downsized to Six.

Photograph by UPI/BETTMANN

PEEWEES AND BANTAMS

MADISON SQUARE GARDEN, NEW YORK CITY | *March 1, 1949*

JUST LIKE LITTLE League Baseball, youth hockey took off in the United States in the years after World War II. The structure was adopted from Canada, where youth leagues had existed for decades. Older teenagers were bantams; younger boys played in peewees. Canadians involved with pro hockey promoted youth teams in cities with NHL teams. The kids tightening their skates at Madison Square Garden played for a team launched by Rangers coach Lynn Patrick. The Red Wings' publicist started a parks league in Detroit. NHL franchises didn't expect to develop future pros. Instead, as the publicist explained, there was a greater chance in young players "becoming hockey fans and remaining fans in their adult years."

Beyond the big cities, youth programs spread in the Northeast and Great Lakes states, the same areas that had been strongholds of American hockey since the early 20th century. Indoor rinks were rare at the time, so youth hockey was largely an outdoor game. During the Depression, the Works Progress Administration had built warming houses at hundreds of community parks in northern states. These served as bases for house teams.

The Baby Boom drove youth hockey's growth in the 1950s. By the early 1960s, there were more than 24,000 players registered with the United States Amateur Hockey Association, mostly in Michigan, Minnesota and Massachusetts. From the beginning, all-star teams and travel tournaments were a regular part of the sport. There were also arguments about ice time between parents and coaches. The Boston area association tried to cool down tempers by mandating equal shifts for all players.

Like today, expense was another concern in the 1950s. The total cost of outfitting a young player was about $70–$100, a considerable sum at the time. Civic organizations or local businesses helped cover costs. Teams in Detroit's parks league were sponsored by auto dealerships and manufacturing companies. In towns on Minnesota's Iron Range, labor unions paid for equipment, much of it shared from kid to kid. Players would take helmets from a big cardboard box on their way to the ice. After the game, they threw the helmets back in the box.

Photograph by BETTMANN

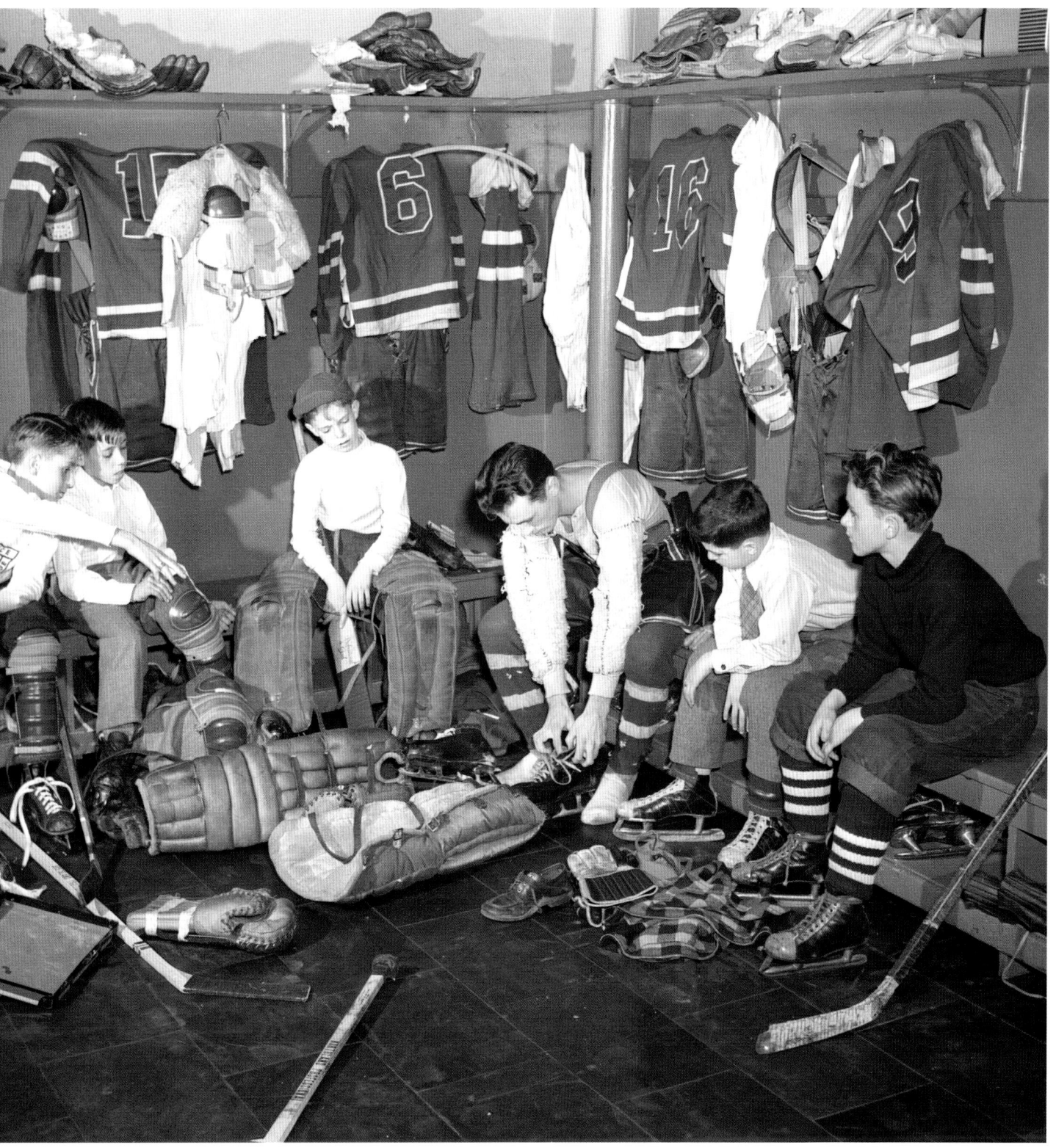

1955 to 1966

The
Original Six

THE ROCKETS

MONTREAL | *November 20, 1955*

IT WAS THE dream of every French Canadian boy, to wear the iconic *bleu, blanc et rouge* sweater and skate alongside the Rocket. The Montreal Canadiens were a defining institution of Quebec, and Maurice Richard (pictured, right) was a hero without equal. "Before he came along, our people had no one we could look up to with admiration," wrote Quebec author Roch Carrier.

Rocket Richard burst into the NHL during the war years, when the league's fortunes were dim. At the end of his first full season, he notched 12 goals and 17 points in nine playoff games, leading Montreal to the Stanley Cup. The following year, he set an unimaginable record of 50 goals in 50 games. He went on to score 544 in his 18-season career, becoming the first player to reach the 500-goal mark, and won the Stanley Cup eight times.

The boy who got his wish to play alongside the Rocket was Henri Richard (pictured, left), Maurice's younger brother. Only six years old when Maurice started with the Canadiens, Henri idolized his big brother like any other boy in his Montreal neighborhood. "I would have signed for anything to play with Maurice and the Canadiens," Henri told an interviewer. "That was my dream, and it came true."

The brothers were linemates for five years: the Rocket at right wing, the Pocket Rocket at center. Of course, there were comparisons, but usually positive. Whereas the Rocket was known for his brute strength, carrying defensemen to the net, Henri was quicker and more cunning. "Henri helped Maurice more than the other way around," a Canadiens official told *Sports Illustrated* in 1961. "He has fantastic speed. He made Maurice dig hard to keep up. Nobody can get the puck like he can. He has incredible stamina and moves as fast in the third period as in the first."

While the Rocket's scoring records were eventually broken, his younger brother has a mark that will never be surpassed. In his 20-year career, Henri Richard won the Stanley Cup 11 times. Only the Boston Celtics' Bill Russell of the NBA can match him. If any record is unbreakable in this age of sports parity, it is a player wearing 11 championship rings.

Photograph by HY PESKIN

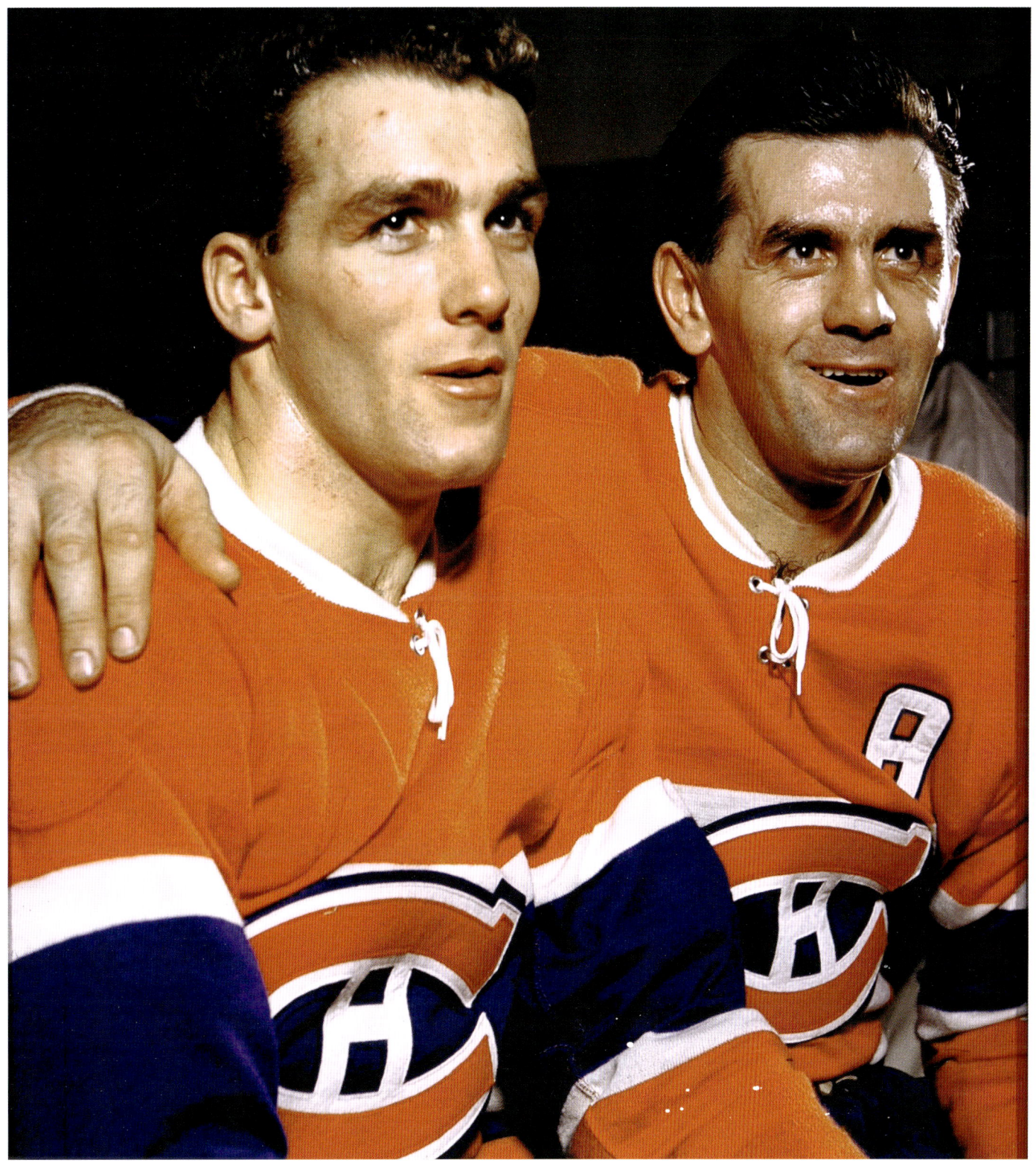

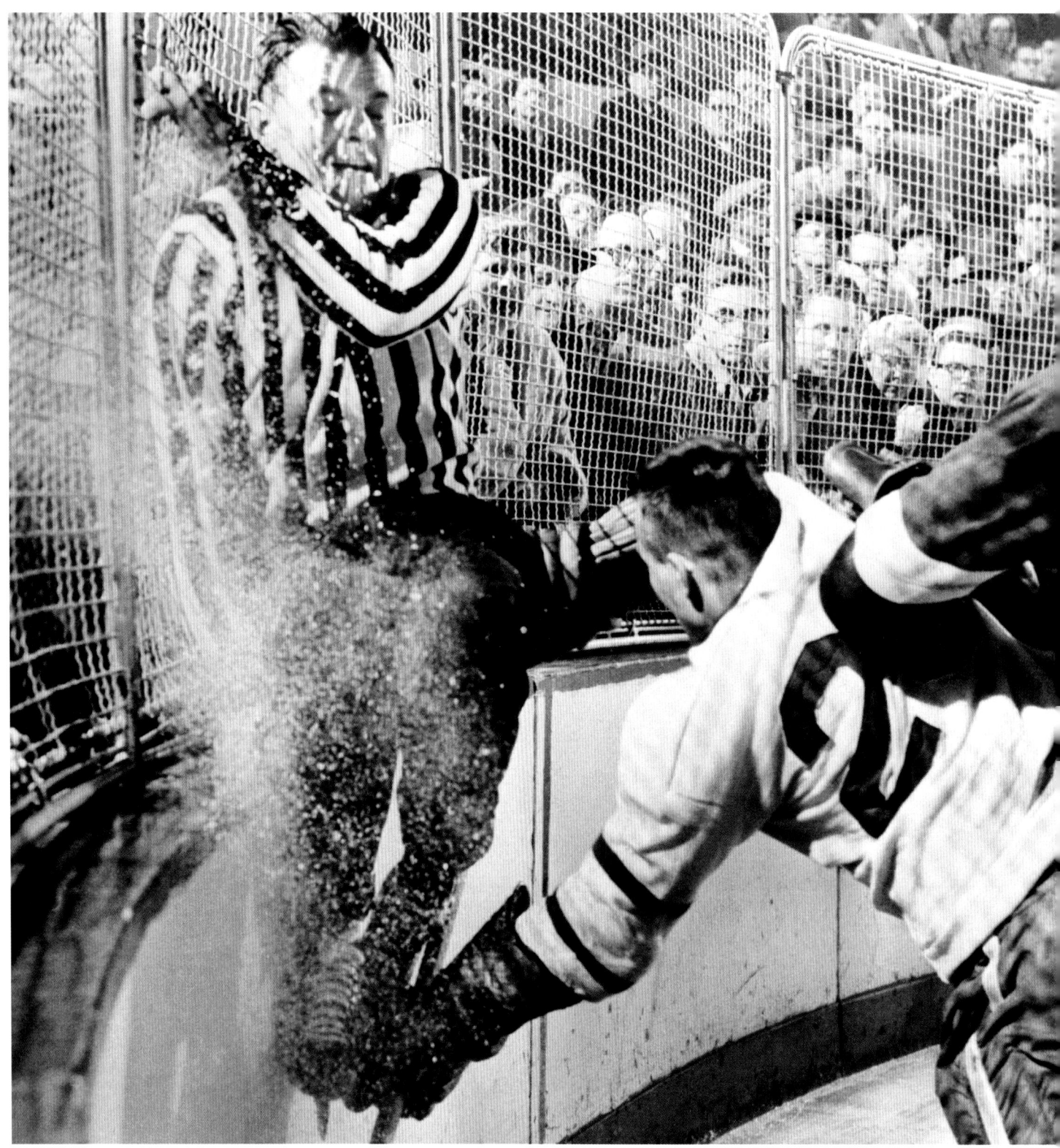

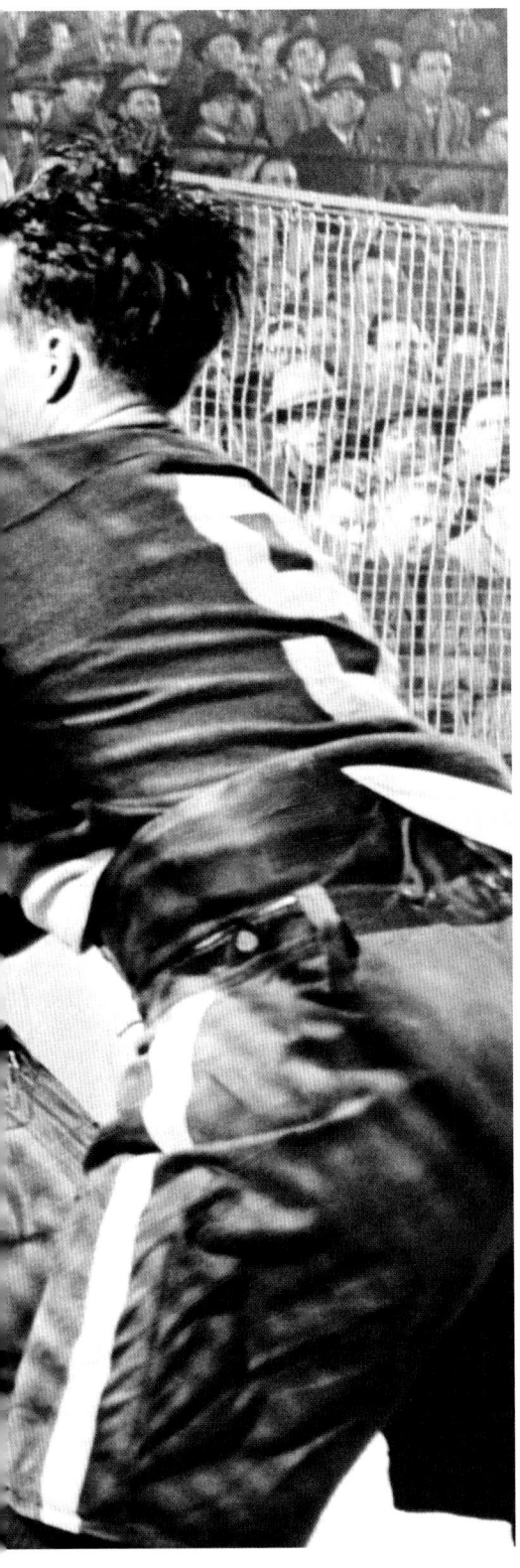

THE HARDEST JOB IN HOCKEY

DETROIT OLYMPIA, DETROIT | *March 18, 1956*

OF ALL THE perils facing hockey referees, booing is the least of their worries.

"The fans who boo NHL referees seldom seem to know what they are booing about," said referee Frank Udvari.

Udvari's career in stripes began by accident. He was coaching a youth team in Ontario when the scheduled referee didn't show up, so Udvari took the whistle. Three years later, he was in the NHL. He spent 15 seasons reffing games, then served 17 years supervising the league's officials.

It is appropriate that we see Udvari in one of the greatest photos from the Original Six era. He had a ref's-eye view of many of the legendary events in those years. On March 13, 1955, Udvari watched Maurice Richard punch out his officiating crewmate, linesman Cliff Thompson, at Boston. Udvari gave the Rocket a match penalty, and then spoke at the league hearing three days later, when NHL president Clarence Campbell suspended Richard for the rest of the season. A former referee himself, Campbell stood by his own call by showing up at the Canadiens' next home game. When the president took his seat in the Forum, a riot broke out and spilled into the streets of Montreal.

Udvari was also there for the most notorious fight of the Original Six years, when New York Rangers defensemen Lou Fontinato decided to take on Gordie Howe at the Garden.

"I want him," Fontinato said to Udvari as he skated past. Howe had lost his balance behind the net, and Fontinato saw his chance to strike.

"Leave him alone," Udvari said. As the photo shows, he had up-close experience with Howe. "Use your head."

"I want him," the defenseman repeated, dropping his stick.

"Be my guest," the referee answered.

Fontinato charged, but Howe's right fist was ready. Udvari described the carnage: "Never in my life had I heard anything like it, except maybe the sound of somebody chopping wood. *Thwack!* And all of a sudden Louie's breathing out of his cheekbone."

Howe gave Fontinato a fractured cheekbone, a crooked nose and a blood-stained jersey. Udvari gave both players a five-minute major.

Photograph by BETTMANN

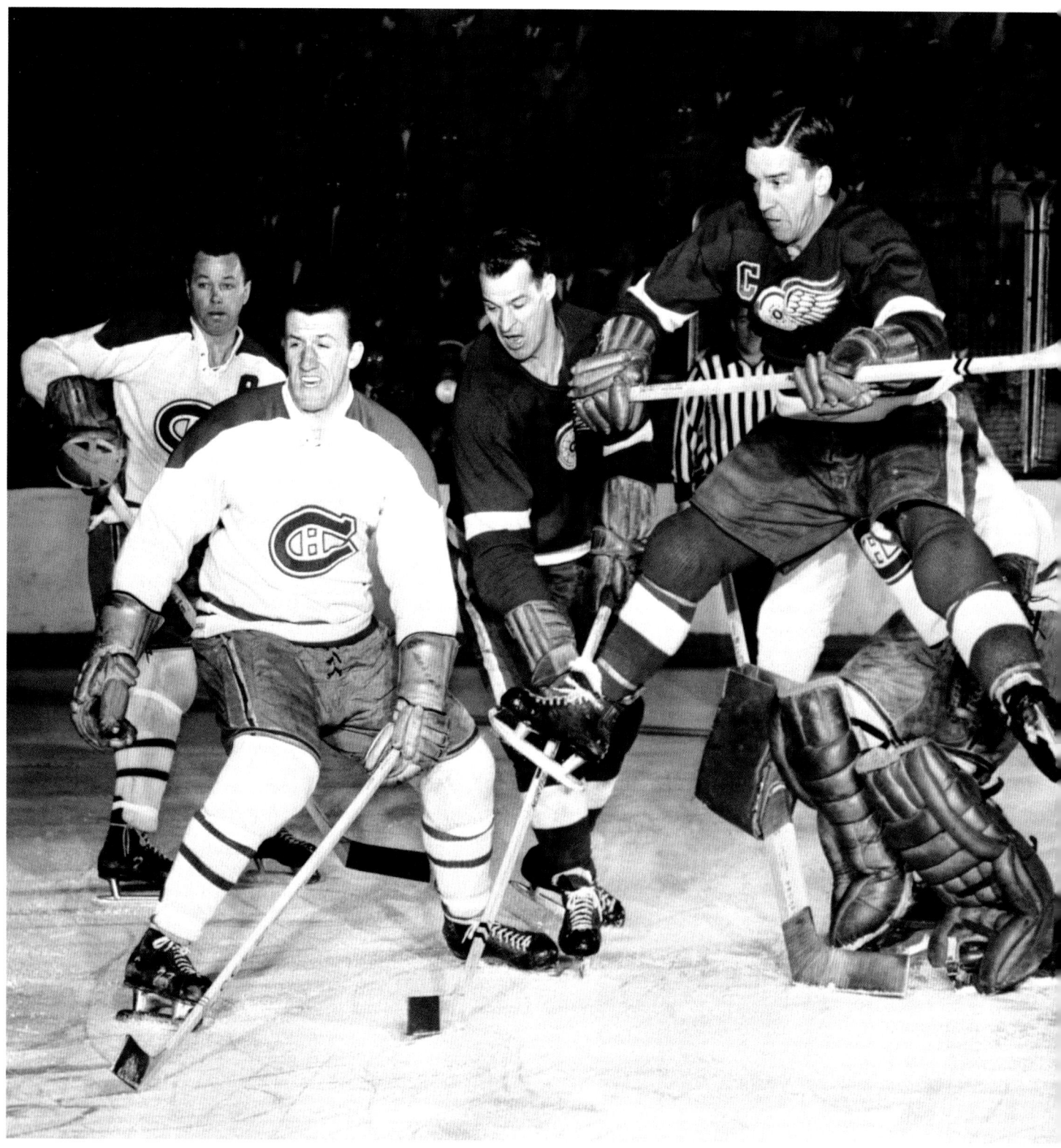

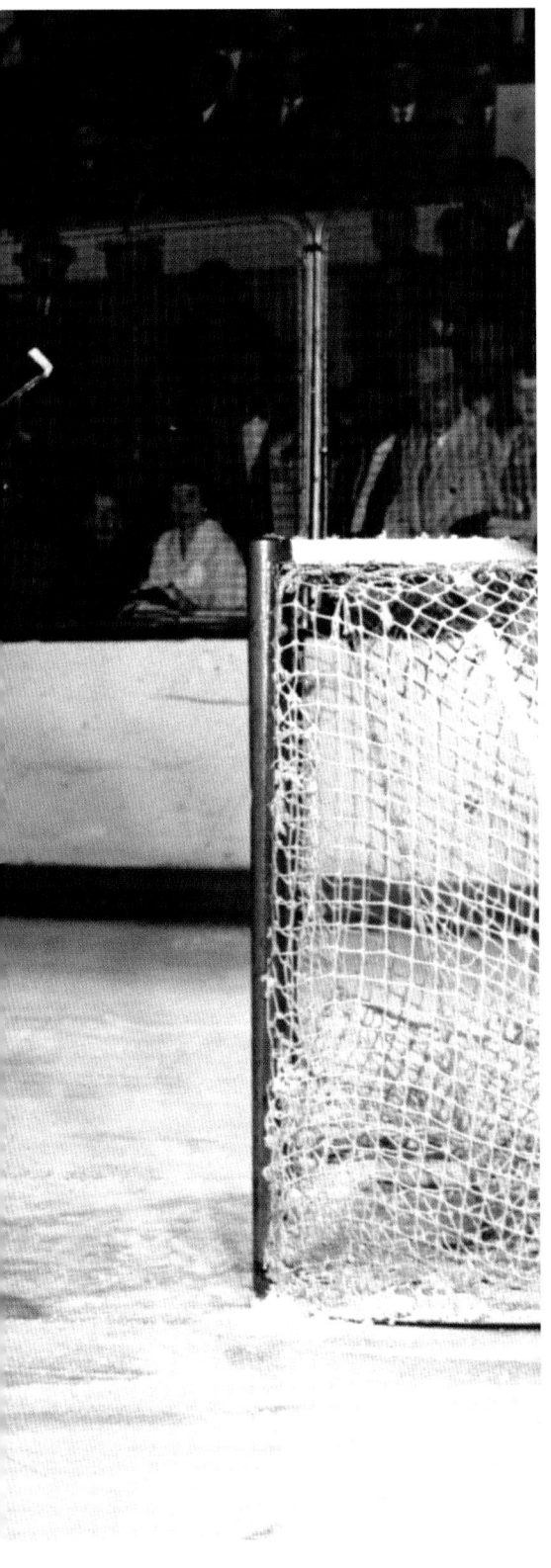

TERRIBLE TED

DETROIT OLYMPIA, DETROIT | *April 8, 1956*

"I'M JUST NOT the type to walk away."

This was how the Detroit Red Wings' Ted Lindsay explained his hard-nosed style of play to *Sports Illustrated*. Unlike linemate Gordie Howe, a six-foot slab of granite, "Terrible Ted" measured only 5'8" and barely broke 160 pounds. "I'm a little guy," Lindsay admitted to *SI*'s Marshall Dann in the March 18, 1957, issue. "A little guy has to have plenty of self-confidence, and I was ready to prove it."

"I've had my ears pinned back plenty of times," Lindsay continued. "I've been slashed, speared, elbowed, board-checked, butt-ended and hit on the head as much as anyone. I just like to keep that ledger balanced. Truthfully, I didn't start 50% of the trouble I've been in."

No matter who started it, Lindsay got in plenty of trouble. In each of the 12 seasons they played together, Lindsay spent more time in the penalty box than Howe.

With Terrible Ted on the left wing and Mr. Hockey on the right, Detroit's first line was one of the most fearsome units in NHL history—and the most potent. With center Sid Abel, they formed the famous Production Line, the only offensive unit to have all three forwards finish an NHL season 1-2-3 in scoring. In 1956, Howe became the third NHL player ever to score 300 career goals. Lindsay became the fourth a year later.

When *SI* published its cover story on the Wings' wingers in 1957, the team had the league's best record and Lindsay was on his way to the most points of his career. Four months later he was traded. Shipping Lindsay to cellar-dwelling Chicago was punishment. He had dared organize a players' association and then sued the league over pensions. Owners stifled Lindsay's efforts to form a union, but they conceded to the demand for better pensions.

Ted Lindsay walked away only once in his hockey life. When he was elected to the Hall of Fame in 1966, he skipped the induction ceremony. Women and children were barred from the men-only event. Terrible Ted refused to attend without his family.

Photograph by BETTMANN

THE BARRIER BREAKER

MONTREAL FORUM, MONTREAL | *January 18, 1958*

IN 1895 BLACK church leaders in Nova Scotia wanted an enriching activity for the young men of their community. They started a hockey league. Excluded by white teams and leagues, the ministers created their own association, the Colored Hockey League.

In the following decades, Black players—like Indigenous and Asian players—were a consistent yet marginal presence in hockey's lower ranks. In the 1950s, community leaders in Cleveland launched a peewee league for Black children. The newspaper of the city's Black community encouraged readers to check out the sport. "Some day we may read about these youngsters performing in big time hockey," mused the reporter.

In fact, it would be nearly impossible for these Black youngsters to navigate the development pipelines for pro hockey. Canadian junior hockey was a tightly controlled system. NHL teams had territorial rights over young players in different parts of the country. With this closed feeder network providing a reliable supply of players, NHL owners did not look to make bold experiments by promoting hockey for all.

This makes Willie O'Ree's climb to the NHL all the more remarkable. A swift winger from Fredericton, New Brunswick, O'Ree made his debut for the Boston Bruins against the Montreal Canadiens on January 18, 1958. Sportswriters largely ignored the fact that the NHL's color line had been broken. O'Ree also missed the moment's significance. "It really didn't dawn on me [then]," he told *Sports Illustrated* decades later.

This doesn't mean O'Ree's path to the pros was smooth. In an interview with journalist Cecil Harris, he recalled his years in junior hockey: "I heard 'n----r' so much on the ice, I thought it was my name."

Decades later, the NHL recognized that it needed to broaden the game's appeal. In 1998 the league hired O'Ree to be director of youth development for its diversity task force. He spent as many as three days a week on the ice, holding clinics for children from diverse ethnic backgrounds. "Breaking into the NHL was great," O'Ree told *SI* in 2008, "but the work that I'm doing now has to be the most rewarding job I've ever had."

Photograph by BETTMANN

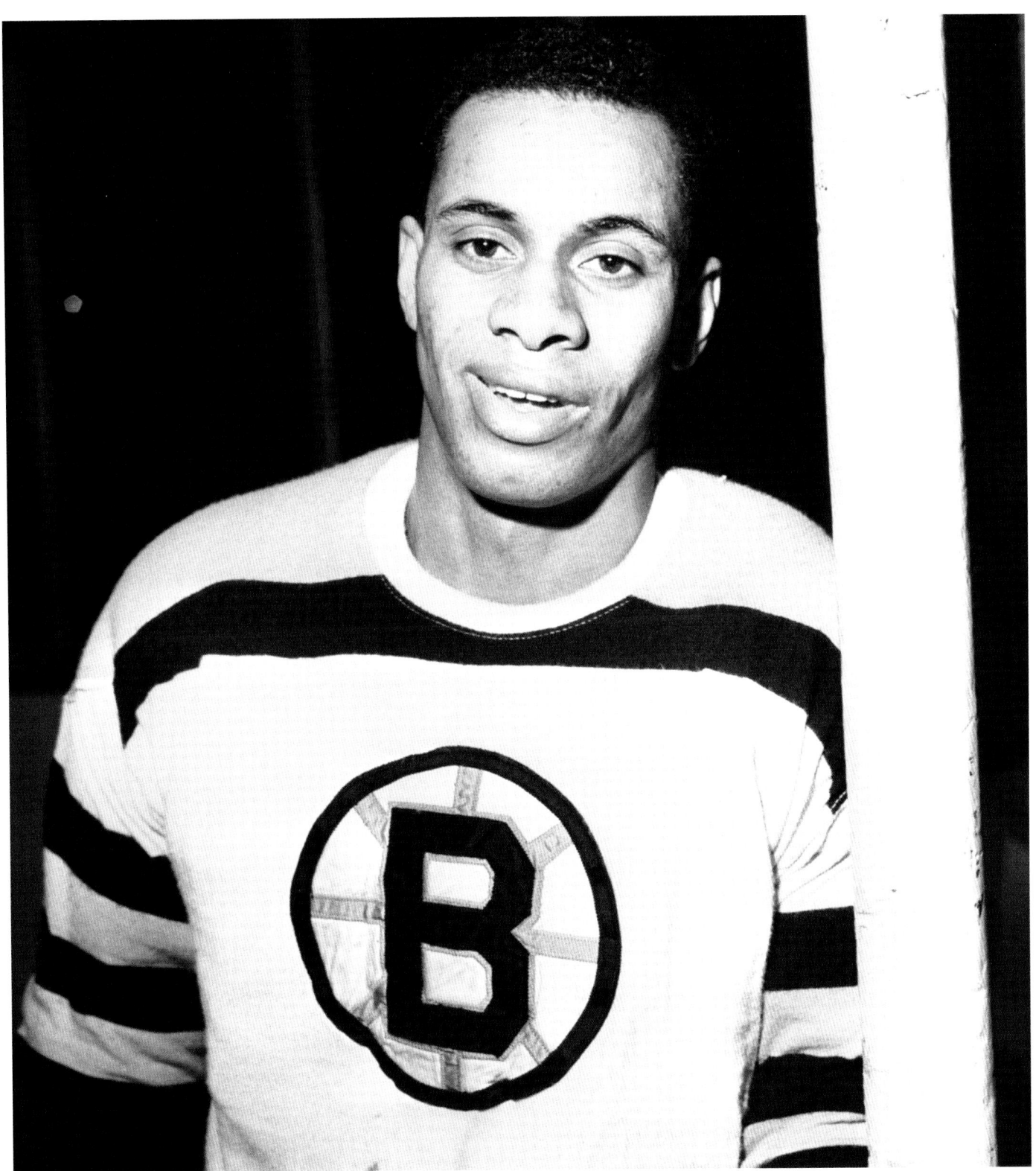

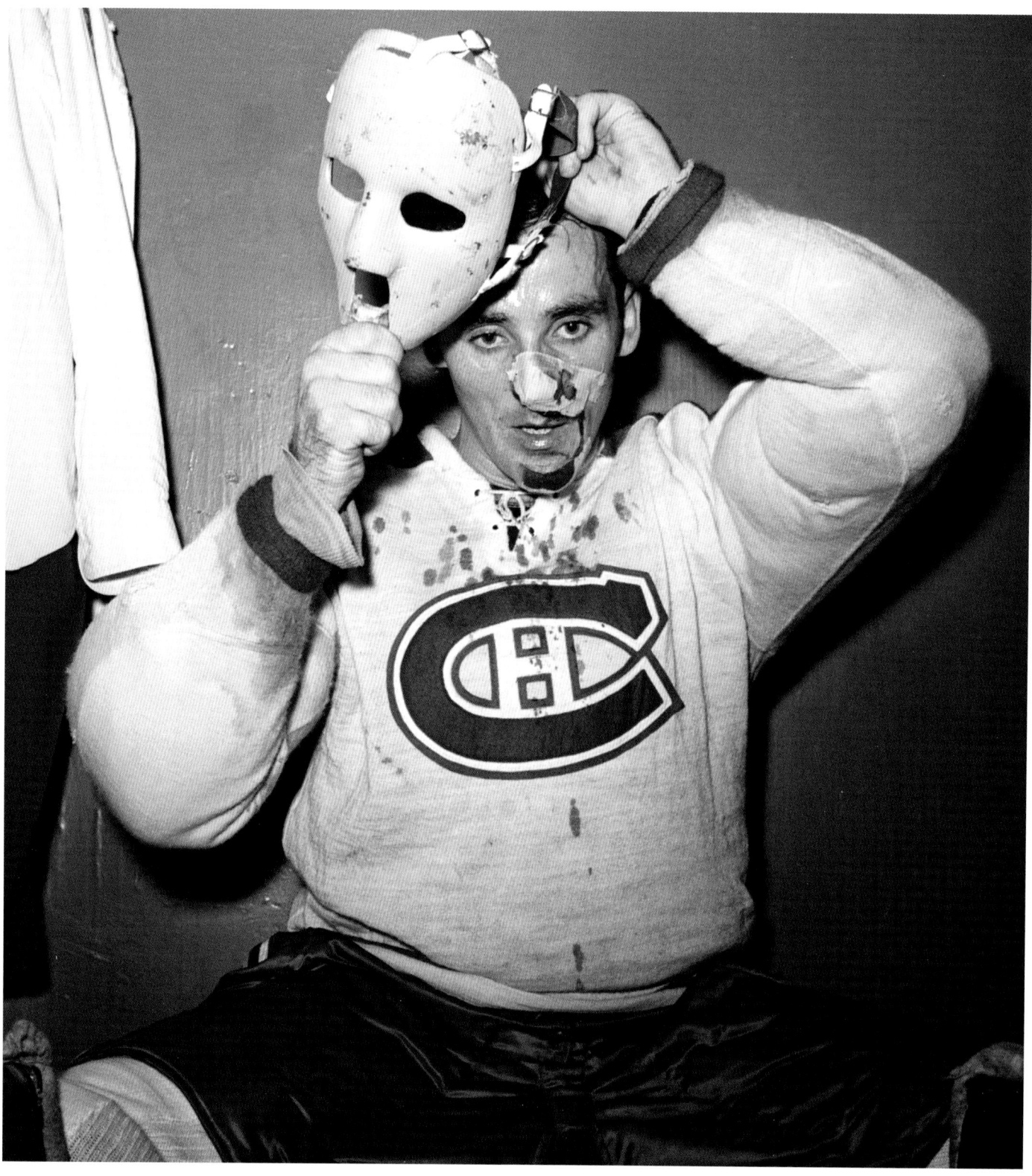

MASKING AGENT

MADISON SQUARE GARDEN, NEW YORK CITY | *November 1, 1959*

JACQUES PLANTE PLAYED goalie like no one had ever seen. He yelled instructions to his defensemen, sent long passes to his forwards and skated far out of the crease to drop on pucks. After games, he gave brilliant interviews in French and English. On the road, he would take out needles and yarn to knit himself sweaters, hats and even underwear.

But the one thing Plante is most remembered for was truly revolutionary. On November 1, 1959, he skated from the Montreal Canadiens bench to the net wearing a mask.

Prior to Plante, goalies had not worn masks for two reasons: First, it was believed that a mask would block the goalie's view of the rink. Indeed, the crude early attempts at masks often left their wearers struggling to follow the puck. Second, hockey wisdom posited that a masked goalie would play timidly. Wearing a mask was an admission of fear, and opposing players would use that to their advantage.

Plante's coach with the Canadiens, Toe Blake, subscribed fully to these hockey principles. After missing five weeks with a shattered cheekbone in 1955, Plante started investigating mask designs. He worked with the sales manager of a fiberglass company to develop a mask molded to his face. Plante wore the mask in practice, but Blake refused to allow it in games.

The coach backed down on the November night in Madison Square Garden. In the first period against the New York Rangers, Plante took an Andy Bathgate slap shot to the face. The gash was stitched up, but Plante refused to go back in the game without his mask. At the time, teams didn't carry a second goalie, so the replacement would have been an arena technician. Blake relented, Plante went to the net and the Canadiens went undefeated in their next 11 games. When the goalie's nose healed, his coach ordered him to take off the mask. The Habs lost.

"Do what you want," Blake finally said. With his mask back on, Plante won his fifth straight Vezina Trophy as the league's best goalie, and the Canadiens took the Stanley Cup.

Photograph by BETTMANN

FALLEN LEAFS

CHICAGO STADIUM, CHICAGO | *April 22, 1962*

IT WAS CANADA'S birthday—100 years since Britain's colonies were united as a self-governing dominion. For the centennial, Canadian hockey fans got the best birthday present they could imagine. In 1967 the country's two NHL teams, the Toronto Maple Leafs and Montreal Canadiens, met in the Stanley Cup Final.

Since the start of the '60s, Toronto and Montreal had each won the Cup three times. Chicago's 1961 win was the only time in the decade the trophy had gone south of the border, and Toronto reclaimed the Cup in 1962, pictured here. By 1967, however, the stars for both the Habs and the Leafs were getting long in the tooth. Jean Béliveau was 35, while Toronto's core of George Armstrong, Red Kelly and Tim Horton were sliding toward 40. (Allan Stanley was already there.) When the Canadiens won the first game of the '67 Final 6–2, it appeared that the Leafs' geriatric squad would take their bows.

Then 42-year-old goalie Johnny Bower took over in Games 2 and 3. The Habs pulled even in Game 4, but Toronto took a decisive win in Montreal to gain a 3–2 series lead. The Final returned to Maple Leaf Gardens with the Buds on the cusp of a title. Toronto's younger goalie, 36-year-old Terry Sawchuk, stopped 40 shots in holding the Habs to a single goal, and Armstrong's empty-netter sealed the 3–1 win. In Canada's centennial year, the country's largest city claimed the country's prized trophy.

Toronto's 1967 win capped a dynastic decade: four championships in six seasons. At the time, Canada's two NHL teams were neck-and-neck in Stanley Cup triumphs: 14 banners hung inside the Montreal Forum, 13 in Maple Leaf Gardens. After 1967, their paths diverged. The Canadiens won the Cup eight more times in the next 12 seasons, and then twice more after that. Toronto hasn't returned to the Final since.

As Toronto's Stanley Cup drought approaches six decades, the banners inside Scotiabank Arena are reminders of distant glory. They are also reminders of years of mismanagement. Longtime owner Harold Ballard used the original banners as paint tarps before selling them. If the hockey deities have indeed cursed the Leafs, it might be payment for this insult to the game.

Photograph by AP PHOTO

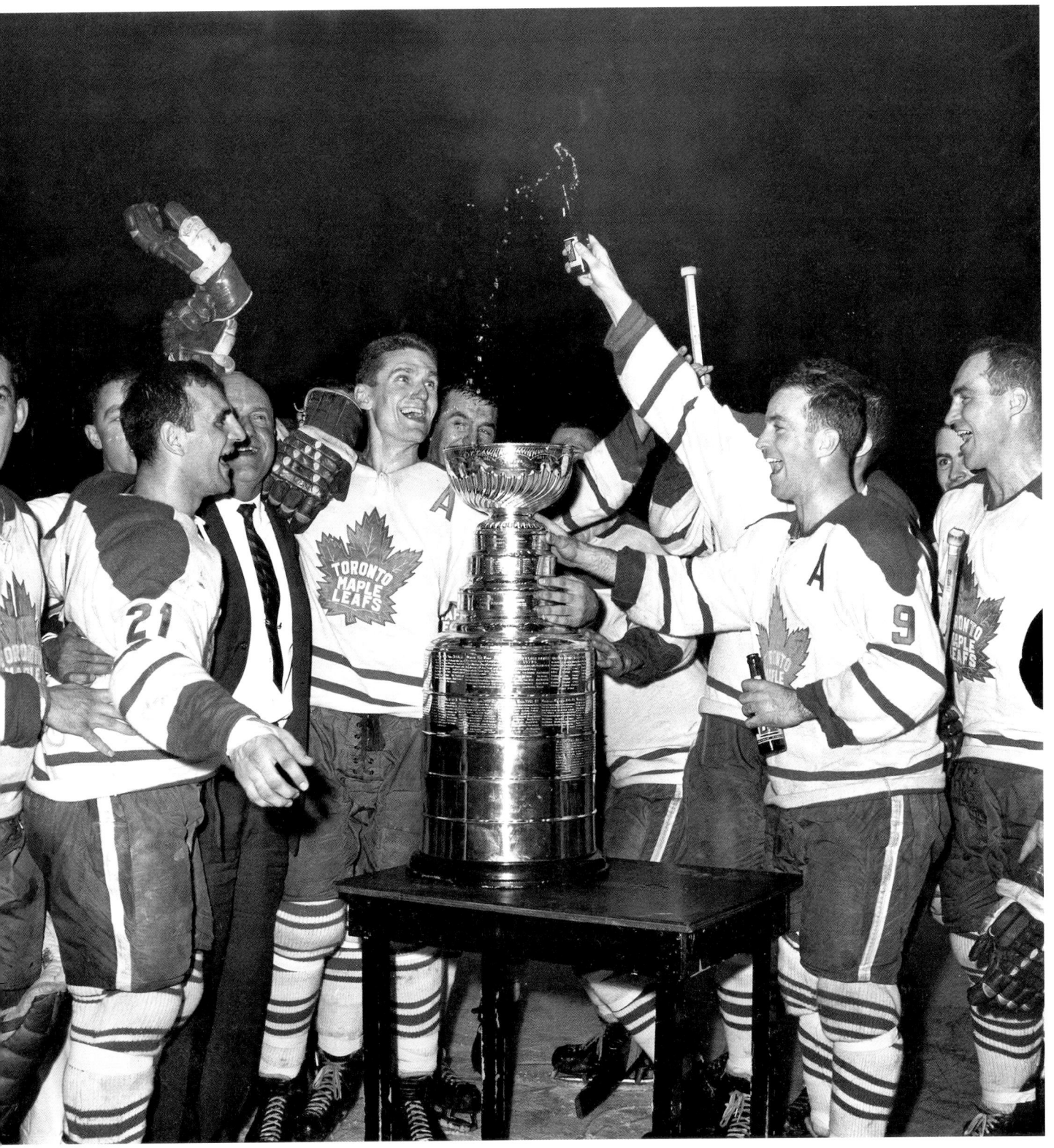

A MAN OF MYSTERY

MAPLE LEAF GARDENS, TORONTO | *February 23, 1963*

JOHNNY KISZKAN LIED about his age to enlist with the Canadian army in 1940. By the time he started playing junior hockey four years later, his birth certificate had gone missing. His true age would remain a mystery throughout his career.

When he signed a contract with the American Hockey League's Cleveland Barons, Johnny changed his last name to Bower. Three league championships earned him a spot with the New York Rangers in 1953–54. A fifth-place finish sent Bower back to the AHL.

Bower got his second shot at the NHL four years later, but he didn't really want it. He declined the offer when Toronto called. The Maple Leafs didn't take "no" for an answer. Three seasons later, he won the Vezina Trophy. Then came three straight Stanley Cup championships. In 1964–65, Bower shared duties with Terry Sawchuk and earned a second Vezina.

Bower also earned 280 stitches in his career. He was acrobatic in goal, known as the master of the poke check, when he would lunge at a forward with his stick and body to knock the puck away. It was a risky move, especially since Bower played most of his career without a mask.

The Leafs goalie was well into his forties when he rescued Toronto in the 1967 Final against Montreal. In Game 2, after the Buds had suffered a first-game drubbing, Bower held the Canadiens scoreless. He then stopped 61 shots in a double-overtime win in Game 3, outdueling 21-year-old Rogie Vachon. Sawchuk stepped in after Bower pulled a muscle before Game 4 and stayed in a goal for the rest of the series.

Late in his career Bower finally got a replacement birth certificate. He needed proof that he was over age 45 to start receiving his NHL pension. He officially reached retirement age on November 8, 1969. A month later he played his final game.

Photograph by BRUCE BENNETT STUDIOS

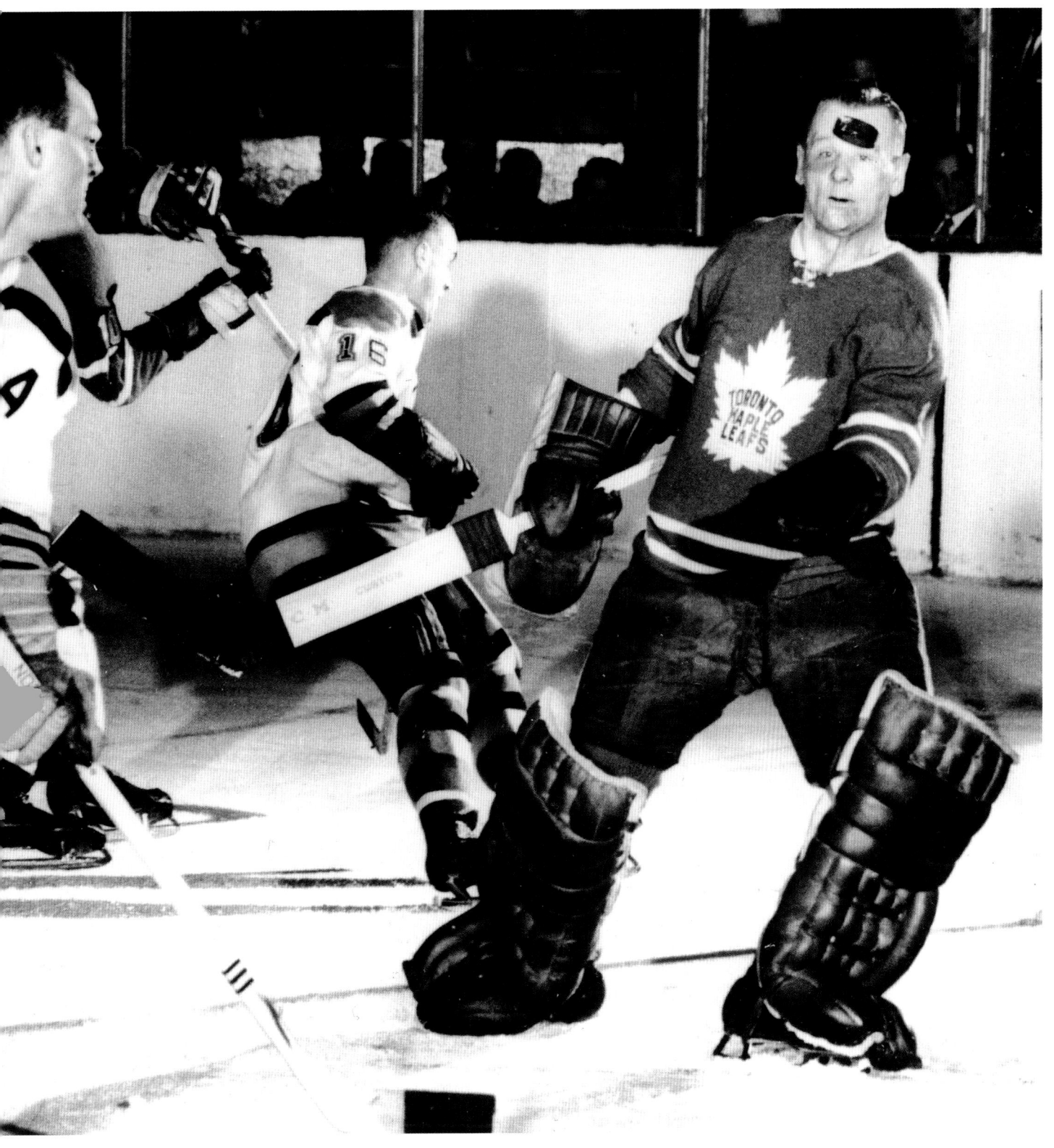

LE GROS BILL

MONTREAL FORUM, MONTREAL | *May 1, 1965*

AT 6'3", JEAN Béliveau stood above the players of his day. His nickname was "Le Gros Bill," for his resemblance to a heroic character in a French Canadian folk song. Béliveau was indeed heroic. Handsome and gracious off the ice, elegant and focused on the rink, he was a nobleman in the lunchpail world of pro hockey.

Béliveau was famous across Quebec already as a teenager, when he tallied 124 points in 46 games for Quebec City's junior team, the Citadels. He stayed to play for the Quebec Aces, in the provincial amateur league. When the Montreal Canadiens tried to sign him, he politely declined. He was making more with the Aces in gifts and his employment contract with the team sponsor. The Canadiens owner responded by buying the entire Quebec league and telling his general manager to sign Béliveau no matter the cost.

That general manager, Frank Selke, told *Sports Illustrated* in January 1956 that Béliveau was the classiest player he had ever seen. "He has a flair for giving you his hockey as a master showman," Selke added. "He is a perfect coach's hockey player because he studies and learns." As for Béliveau's older linemate, Maurice Richard, the Habs GM offered this comparison: "Béliveau is a perfectionist, Richard is an opportunist."

The 24-year-old Béliveau emerged that season, leading the league in scoring and winning the Hart Trophy. He also won the Stanley Cup for the first time in his career. He would sip from the silver chalice nine more times in his career. When he retired in 1971, he had more playoff points than anyone in league history.

In Béliveau's final season, the Canadiens proposed a special night to honor his career. Jean agreed on the condition that he would receive no gifts. Any money involved would be given to charity. In a little more a month over $155,000 was raised. This was the start of the Jean Béliveau Foundation, which would raise nearly $1.5 million for disabled children over the next two decades. The Canadiens' gentle giant stands alone in NHL history: a prince among men.

Photograph by BRUCE BENNETT STUDIOS

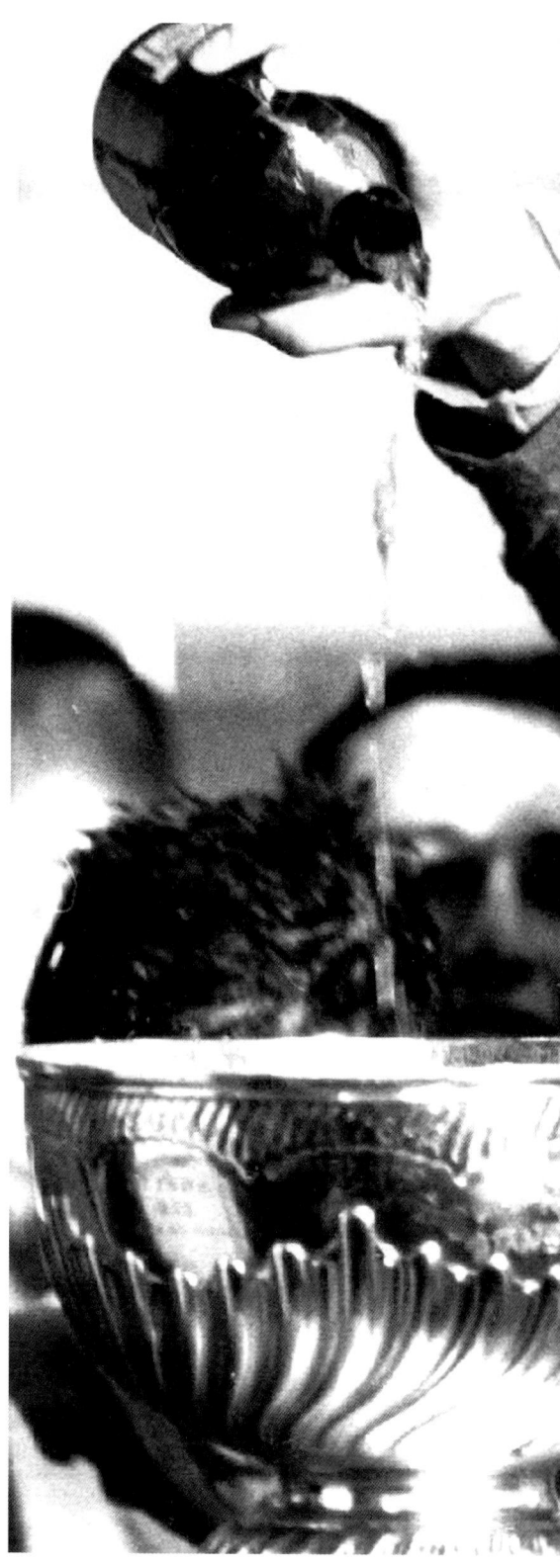

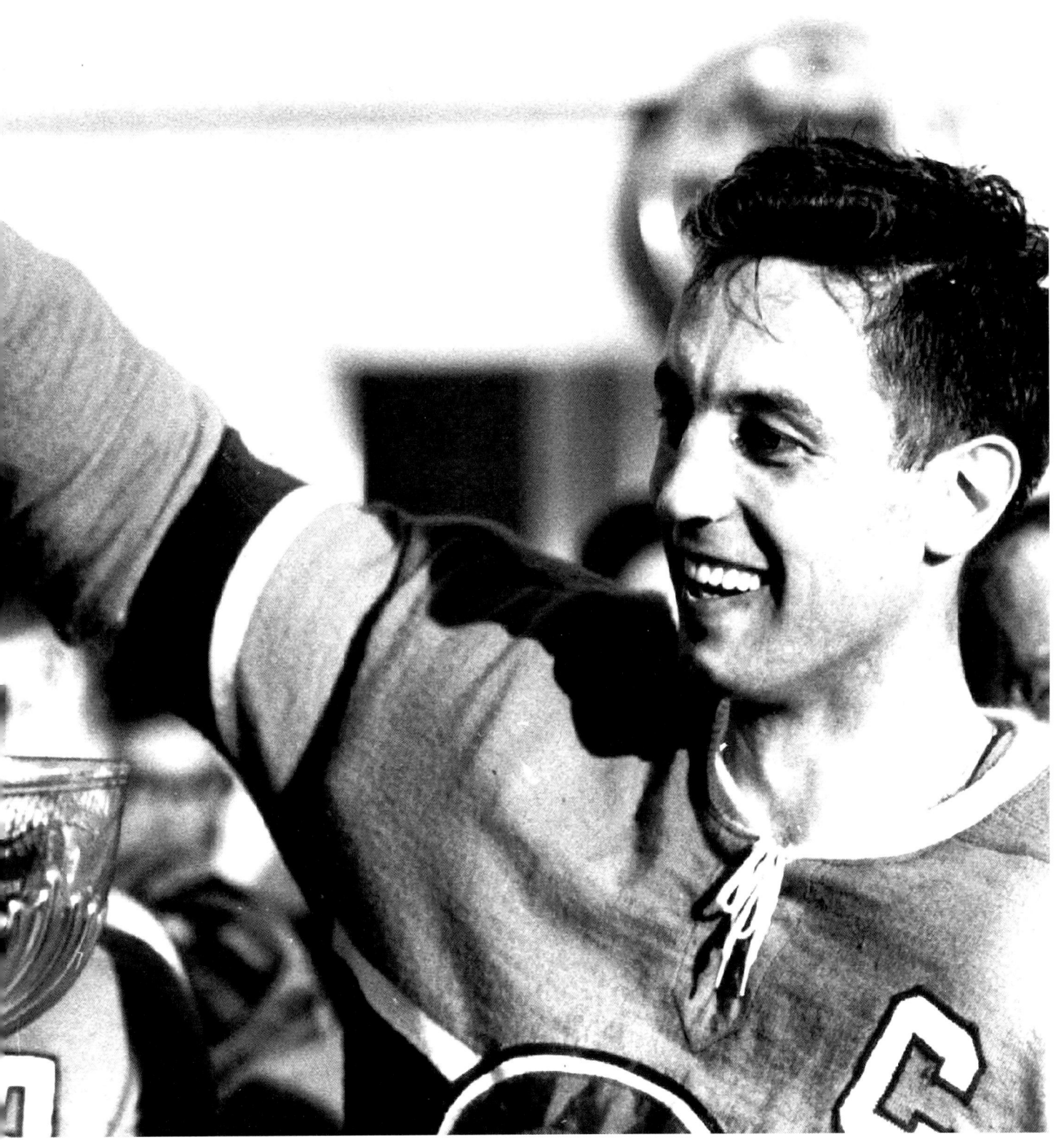

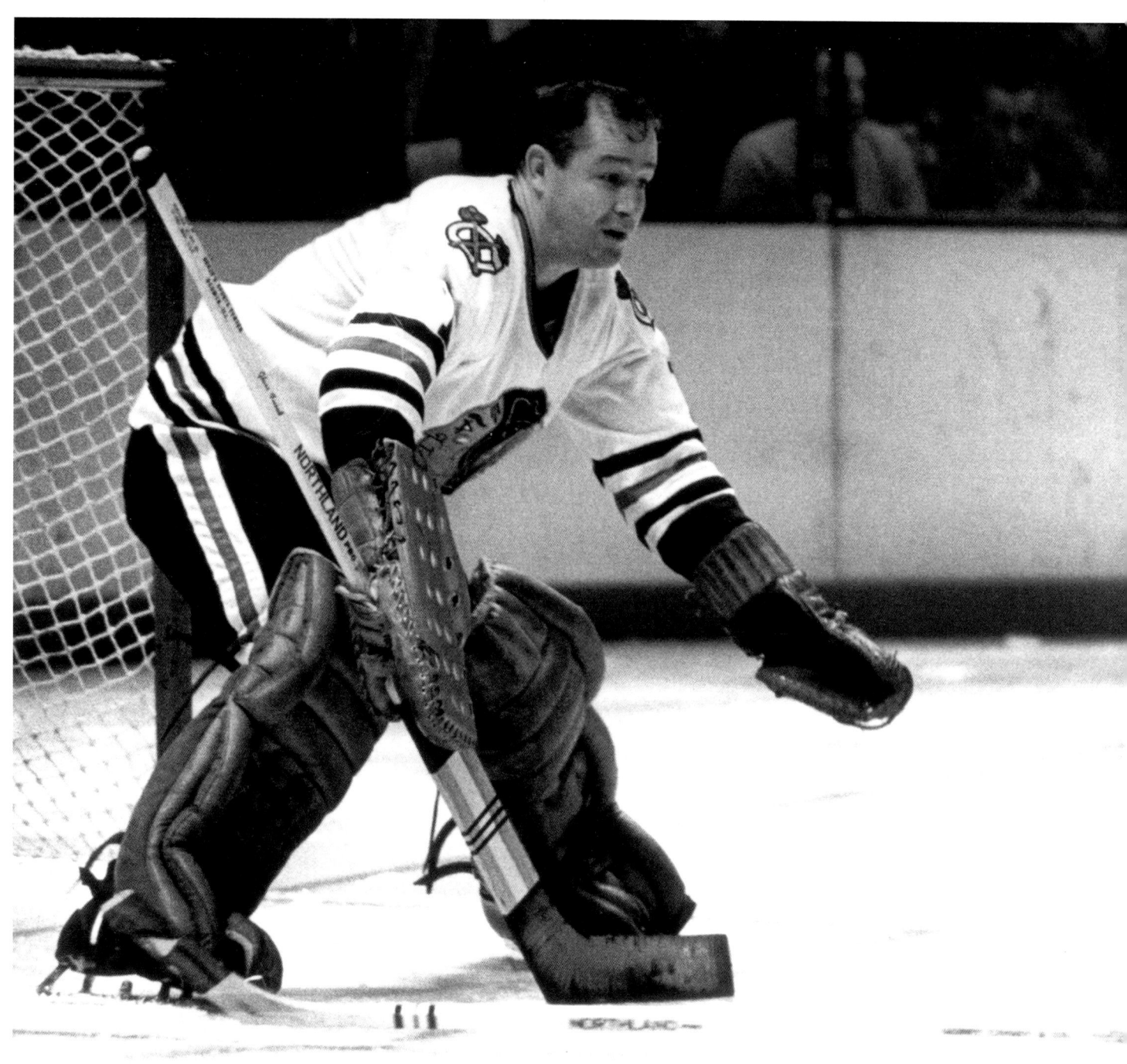

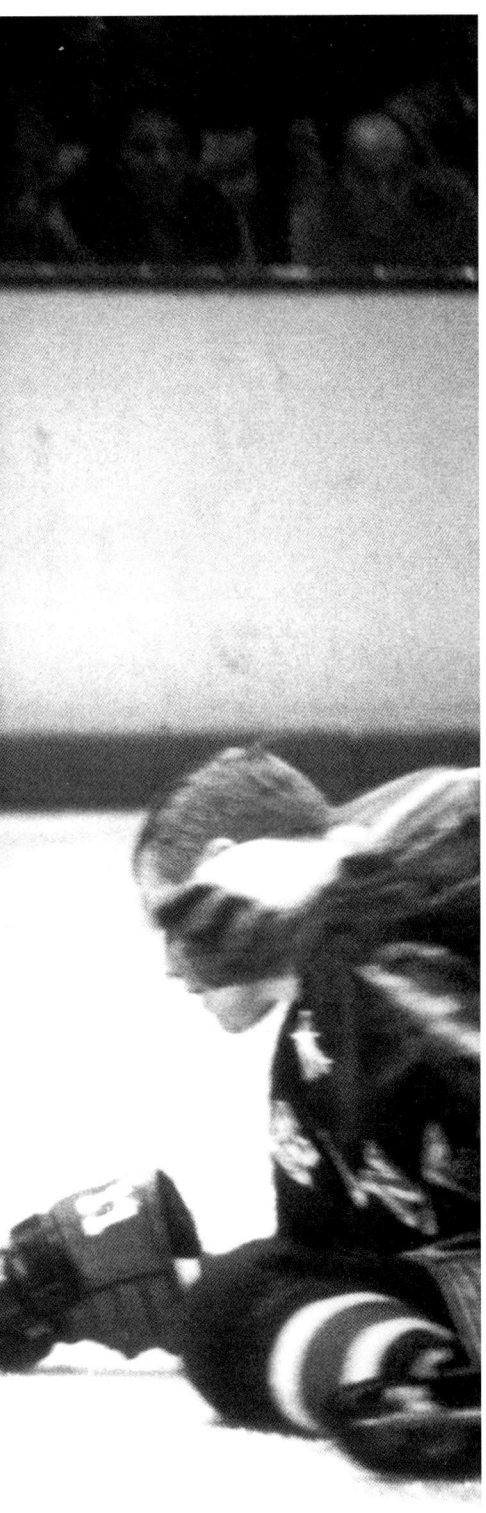

MR. GOALIE

MADISON SQUARE GARDEN, NEW YORK CITY | *November 17, 1965*

HENRI RICHARD'S 11 rings. Teemu Selänne's 76 rookie goals. Wayne Gretzky's 2,857 points.

Among the NHL's unbreakable records we can include the league's greatest iron-man streak. From 1955 to 1962, goalie Glenn Hall started 502 consecutive regular-season games for the Detroit Red Wings and Chicago Black Hawks, amounting to more than half his total of 906 career games. Adding in the playoffs, the streak stretches to 551 games—a feat of endurance that is impossible in today's NHL.

In the March 12, 1962, issue of *Sports Illustrated*, William Barry Furlong profiled the man known as "Mr. Goalie":

"You wouldn't think after all this time," says the goalie, who is now in his seventh full season with the NHL, "that I'd still be so afraid of a bad game I'd get sick about it." Yet in about three out of every four games, either before the first face-off, during the rest periods or after it's over, Glenn Hall quietly and unobtrusively throws up. "I used to be able to fight off the nausea," he says, "but this year, it's worse than ever...."

On the ice Hall follows the puck with the concentration of a gem cutter. (He has 20/15 vision, which means that he can see at 20 feet what the normal eye can see at 15 feet.) "Sometimes I have to talk to myself to sell me on concentrating a little more," he says.

To keep his eyes sharp during the offseason Hall plays ping-pong—as many as 20 games in a row. "I don't really play too well," he says. "I play up close to the table where I'm going to need the same characteristics I need for goalkeeping—reflexes and coordination...."

For years he's experimented with stomach-settling preparations—"but they only come up with everything else." Today, as one of the two best goalies in hockey (Jacques Plante is the other), he accepts nausea without complaint as the burden of trying to straddle two worlds with a single nervous system. "I guess," he once said of goalkeepers, "we're all a little bit sick."

Photograph by BRUCE BENNETT STUDIOS

STAN THE MAN

CHICAGO STADIUM, CHICAGO | *December 15, 1965*

"HE IS NOT as spectacular as Bobby Hull," wrote William Leggett in his *Sports Illustrated* profile of Stan Mikita, "nor is he equipped with Hull's brute strength. Hull's marvelous combination of speed, build, strength and looks forces Stan to play Gehrig to Bobby's Ruth, but Gehrig was a pretty fair ballplayer."

SI put Mikita on the cover of the January 31, 1966, issue. At the time, the Chicago Black Hawks were at the top of the league standings, looking to follow their 1961 Stanley Cup championship with another title. Hull was on his way to setting records for goals and points. But as Leggett made clear, the Hawks' first-line center ranked among the best all-around players in the NHL:

> When Mikita takes over at center ice, he digs into the corners to free the puck and then skates effortlessly over the enemy's blue line with the puck out in front, drawing the defense toward him. Once the defense is committed to Stan's center position, a wingman on the right or left is wide open and Stan's lightning pass often sets up a shot

on the net. Sometimes Mikita's turn lasts only a minute, but last year he assisted on 59 goals, a league record.

The following season, 1966–67, Mikita would match Hull's 1966 record of 97 points. He would also earn the first of two consecutive MVP awards. Mikita won the Art Ross Trophy as the league's top scorer four times, once more than Hull. Yet Mikita was always cast as second fiddle to his more famous teammate.

"We are different types of players," Mikita told Leggett, "and I see what Bobby can do as well as anyone. Bobby has the type of personality that allows him to stand and sign autographs after losing a game, but I am not built that way."

Leggett asked the question directly: "How does it feel to be considered No. 2?"

"Show me the man who ever considers himself No. 2 in anything," Mikita answered.

Photograph by NEIL LEIFER

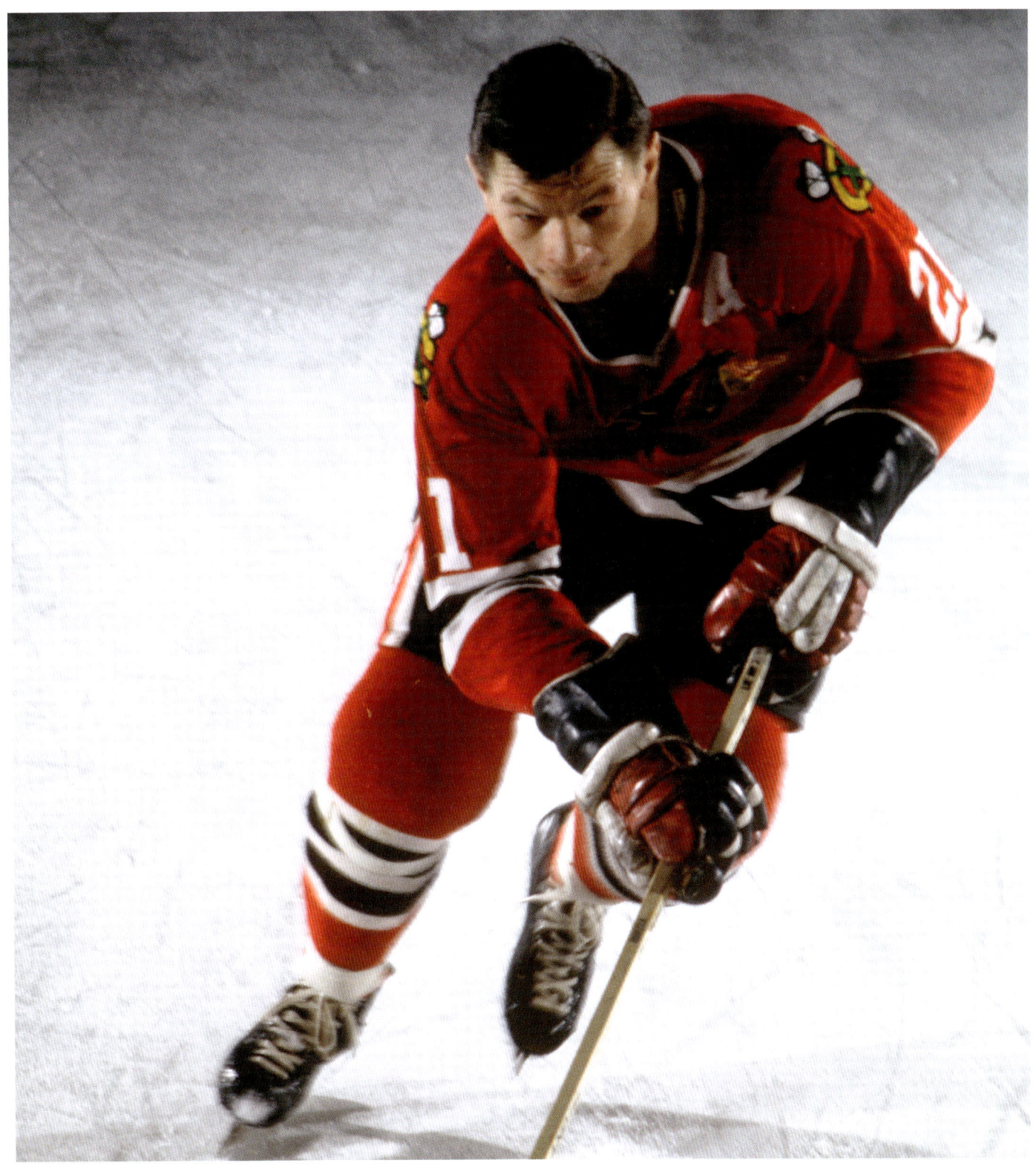

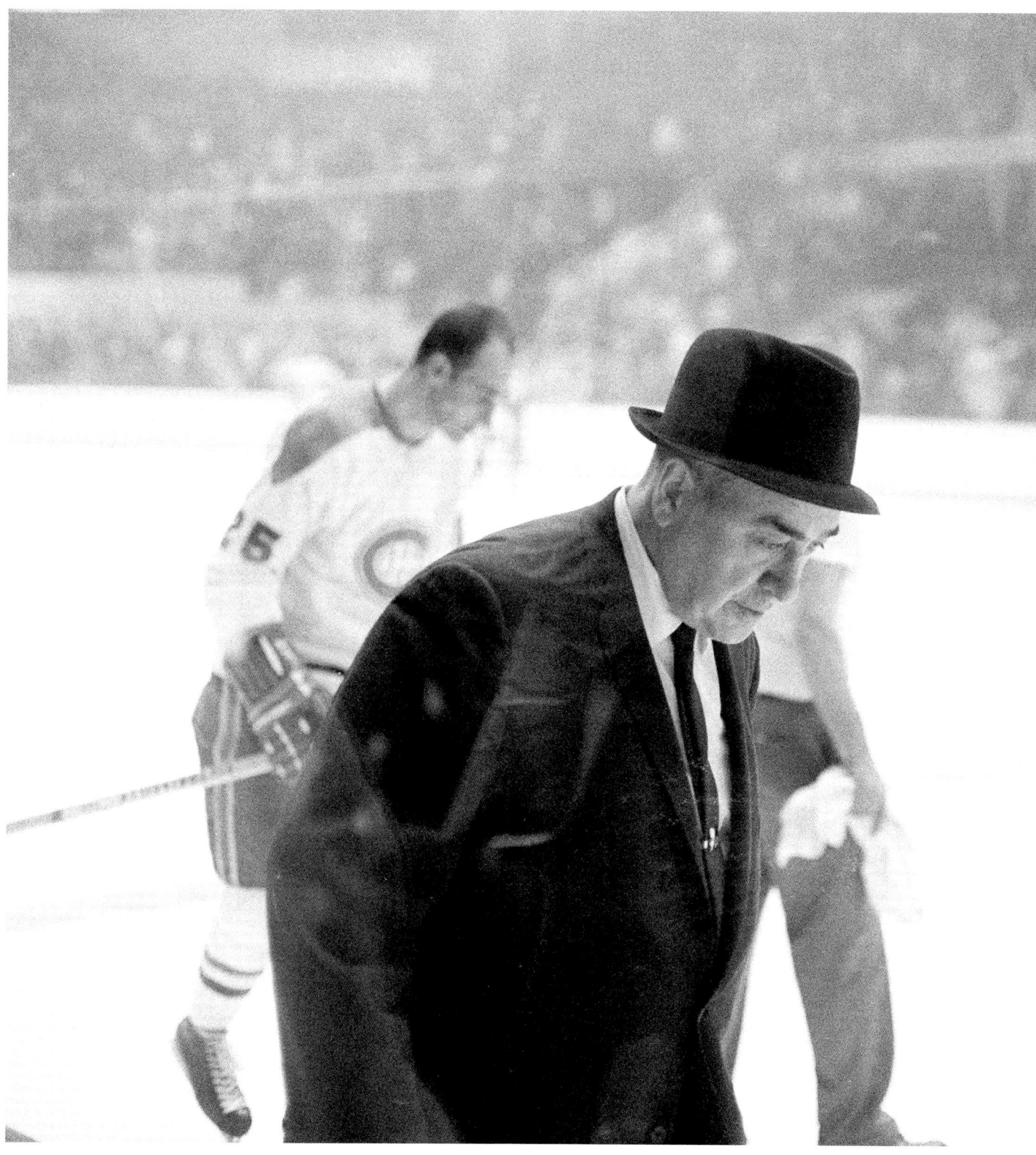

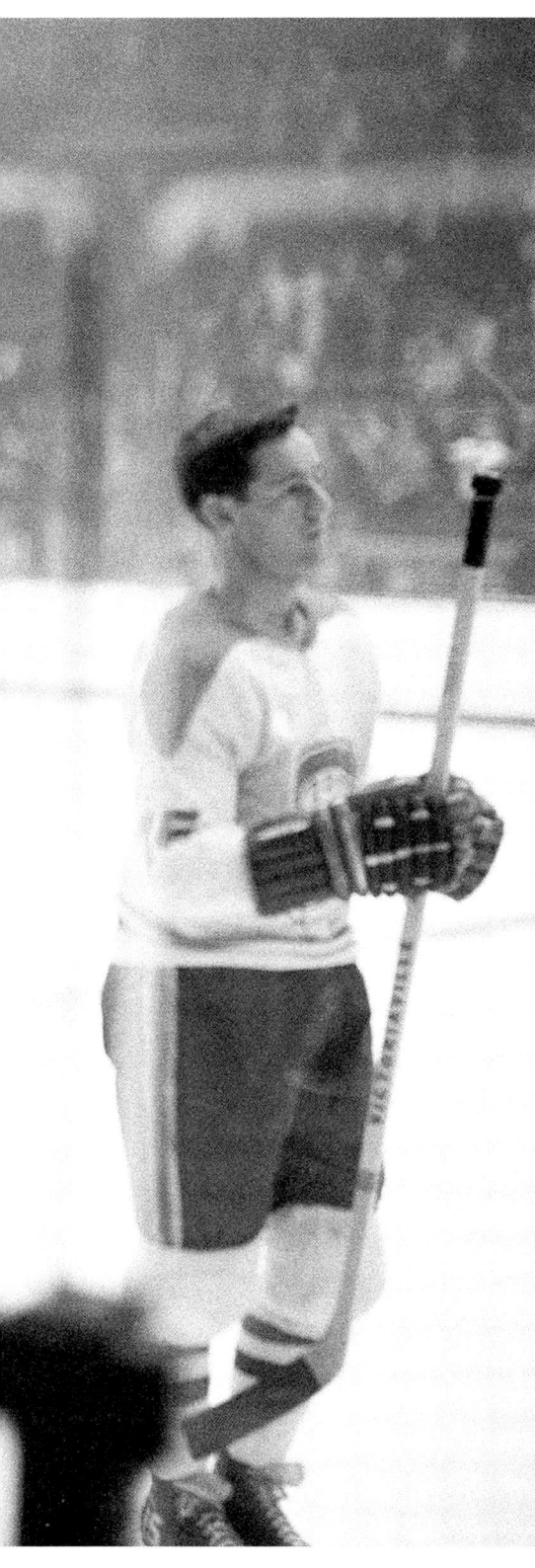

THE OLD LAMPLIGHTER

DETROIT OLYMPIA, DETROIT | *April 28, 1966*

SPORTS DYNASTIES ARE built in different ways.

First, there are the transcendent dynasties. Think of Jordan and the Bulls, the Yankees of Babe Ruth, Gretzky's Oilers. Surrounded by talented teammates, perhaps one just a step below in the pantheon (Gehrig with Ruth, Messier with Gretzky), these transcendent players not only led their teams to multiple championships, they brought the game to new levels.

Second, and most common, are the complete teams. They have their stars, perhaps a once-in-a-generation player, but these teams win thanks to a breadth of talent. In this category we find the Pittsburgh Steelers of the 1970s and Los Angeles Lakers of the '80s. In hockey, the best example—perhaps the greatest complete team in any sport—are the Montreal Canadiens of the 1970s. Stocked deep at every position, the Canadiens had a winning percentage of .786 in the four seasons they won the Stanley Cup. No other dynasty comes close.

By contrast, the Canadiens of the '50s and '60s were a different kind of dynasty. In Toe Blake's first five seasons as coach, the Habs won the Stanley Cup five times—the only NHL team to five-peat. Blake's team won three more times in the '60s and then a fourth title in 1969, the season after he retired. Like the Canadiens of the '70s, these were complete teams with multiple Hall of Famers: the Richard brothers, Jean Béliveau and Jacques Plante, to name a few.

Yet despite the talent on the ice and Blake's savvy behind the bench, the Canadiens' real advantage was away from the rink. No, Montreal did not have unfair rights to French-speaking players, as critics long believed. What they did have was money. The Canadiens filled the largest arena in the league, and they used the ticket revenue to sponsor hundreds of junior and minor-league teams. Before the NHL instituted an open draft in 1967, this pool of prospects was larger than the other five teams combined. The Canadiens were simply the richest team in a small league. In this age of open drafts and salary caps, we won't see their like again.

Photograph by AP PHOTO/ALVAN QUINN

1966 to 1982

The
Expansion Era

SEEING DOUBLE

August 30, 1966

OWNERS OF THE Original Six dug in their heels. When bids for new franchises came from Cleveland in 1952 and Los Angeles and San Francisco in the early 1960s, the owners said no. "You monkey with a good operation and you can mess it up pretty fast," said NHL president Clarence Campbell.

By the mid-'60s, however, it was clear expansion of the league was necessary. American television money was difficult to resist, and West Coast investors wanted to get into pro hockey. NHL owners decided to double the size of the league, with six new teams forming an entirely separate division. The logic was that if the expansion teams played each other, fans wouldn't see how bad they were. The old owners kept a tight hold on their players, leaving only scraps for the new teams.

The expansion franchises started play in 1967, based in Philadelphia, Pittsburgh, Minneapolis–St. Paul, St. Louis, Los Angeles and San Francisco–Oakland. St. Louis had been a controversial choice. No one from the city even submitted a bid, but Chicago Black Hawks owners James D. Norris and Arthur Wirtz insisted that St. Louis

get a team. Norris and Wirtz owned the city's arena, so they stood to make a bundle.

The Salomon family stepped in right away to buy the St. Louis franchise—and the arena. Lynn Patrick (pictured, left) didn't last long as coach, but team owner Sid Salomon III (pictured, right) made an inspired choice for his replacement: 34-year-old Scotty Bowman. The first-time head coach guided the Blues to three straight Stanley Cup finals.

While the Blues were swept each year in the finals, the roster of castoffs and old-timers became favorites in St. Louis. "Blues fans would jump off the Gateway Arch for their team and vice versa," reported *Sports Illustrated*'s issue of April 7, 1969; "there isn't another crowd in the NHL quite like this one." The team created in a backroom deal was the real deal. Meanwhile, NHL owners took a liking to expansion. In 1970, they added two cities snubbed in 1967: Buffalo and Vancouver. By the end of the decade, the old six-team operation had grown to 21.

Photograph by BRUCE BENNETT STUDIOS

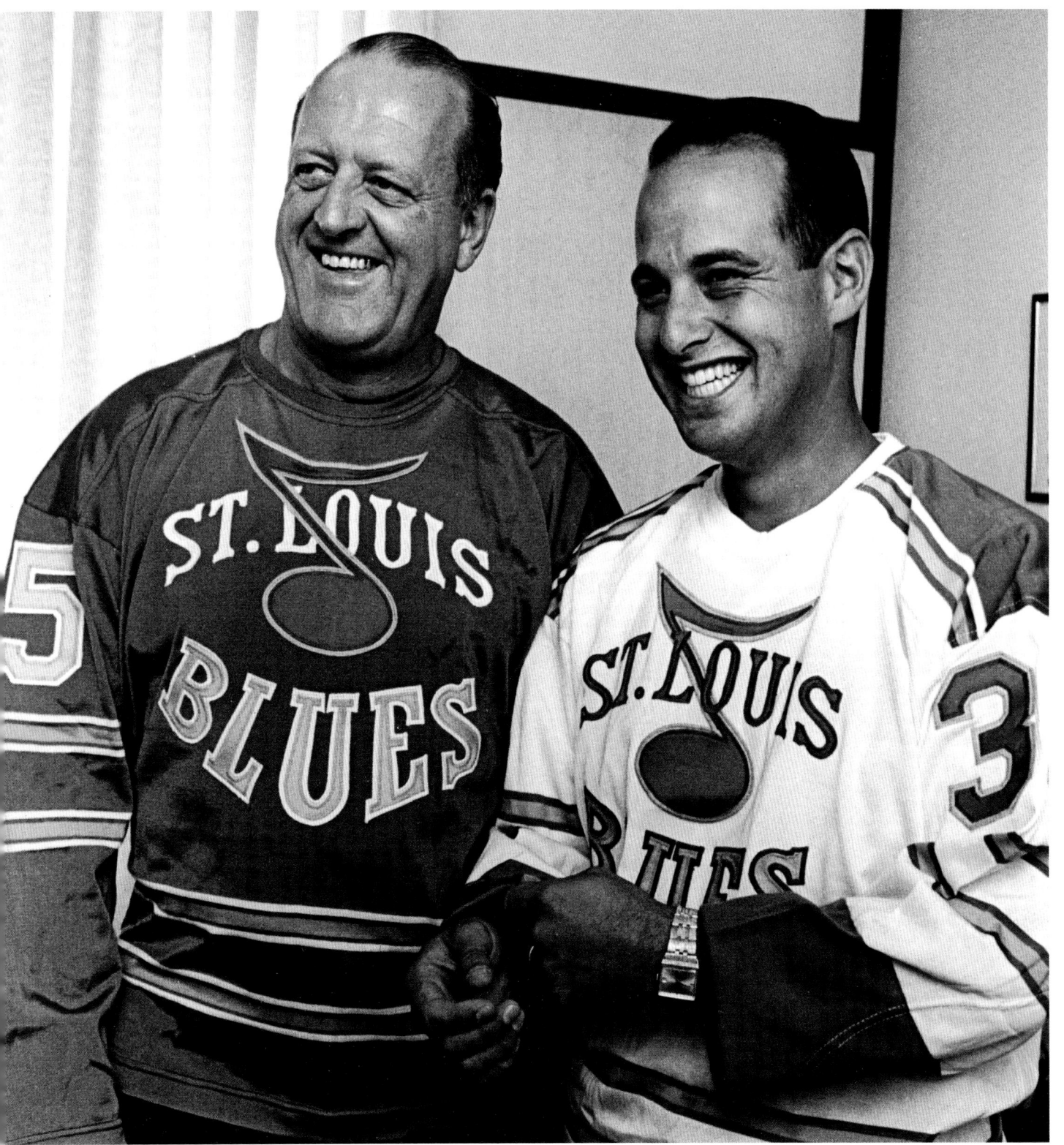

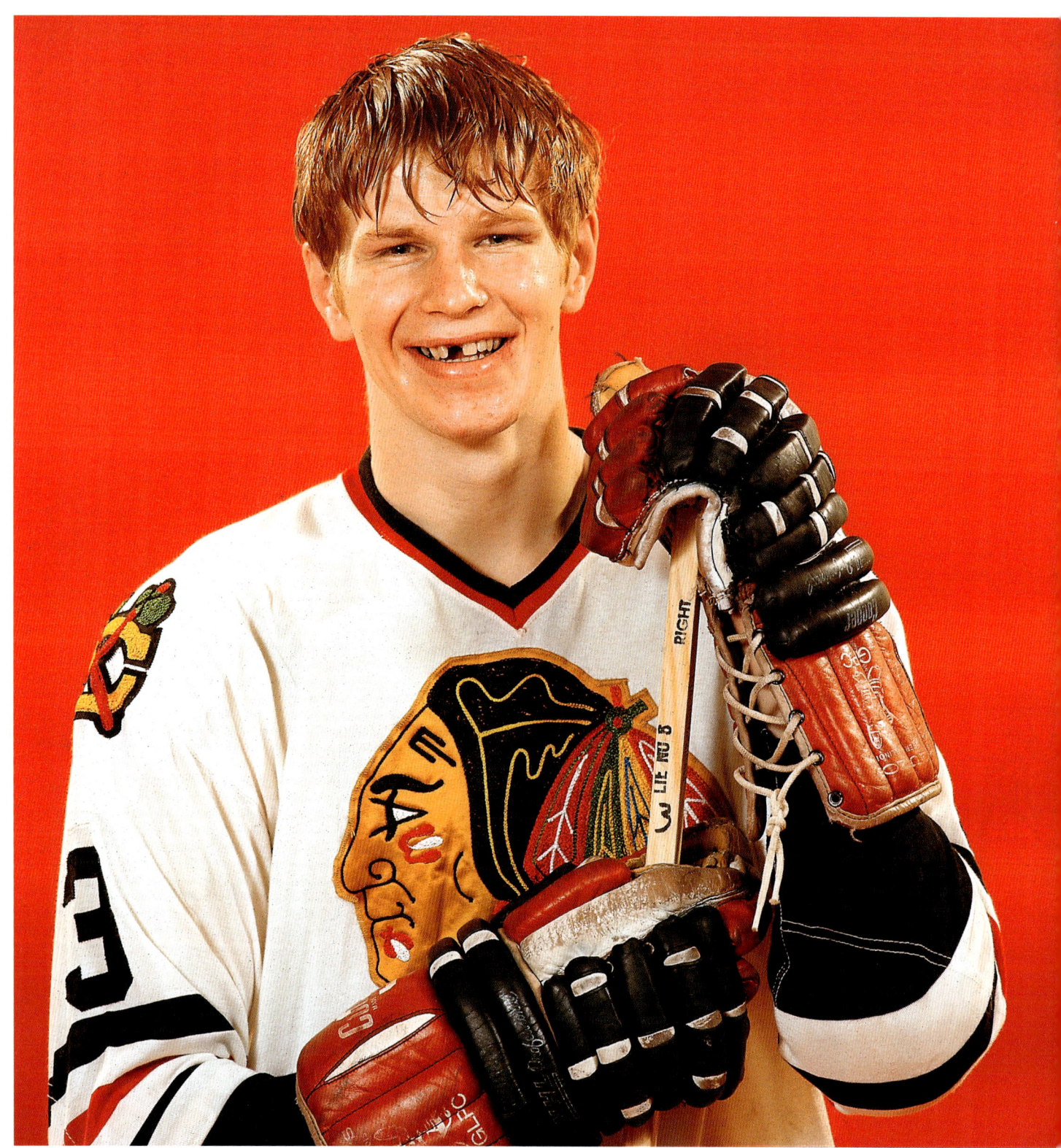

MAGGIE

CHICAGO | *March 27, 1970*

KEITH MAGNUSON WAS a 23-year-old rookie in April 1970, when *Sports Illustrated* put him on the cover. A two-time All-American at the University of Denver, where he led the Pioneers to two straight NCAA titles, Magnuson was at the start of an 11-year career with the Chicago Black Hawks. With the team at the top of the standings, writer Mark Mulvoy shared this account of a young player on the road in Detroit in the teeth of the playoff hunt:

Magnuson lost his jitters in a hurry, thanks to Gordie Howe. With a minute or so gone, Howe caught the rookie—and the referee—looking elsewhere and to the delight of the crowd jerked Magnuson's feet out from under him in front of the Chicago net. When he was only 10 Magnuson had sent away for an autographed picture of Howe, who obliged with, "Good luck and best wishes to my friend Keith." Nevertheless, in his first game at Olympia last November, Magnuson dropped his gloves to do battle with the man who never loses. Howe cuffed Magnuson's ears and turned away, muttering to Doug Jarrett, Keith's partner on defense, "He's a tough kid, but he'll learn."

A beloved teammate, Magnuson played all of his 589 games for the Black Hawks, appearing in the Stanley Cup Final in both 1971 and '73, both losing efforts. He became an assistant and then the team's head coach in 1980, and later established the team's alumni association, cementing his connection to the team and the city.

Magnuson's life came to a tragic end in 2003 when, returning from the funeral of former NHL player Keith McCreary, a car being driven by former defenseman Rob Ramage was involved in a three-car collision just south of Toronto. He was survived by his wife, Cindy, and two children.

"His death was the worst thing to happen—not just to me, but everybody who knew this wonderful, funny, unselfish man, husband and parent," said former teammate and friend Cliff Koroll. "I spent 15 hours at Cindy's house with her, son Kevin and daughter Molly after the accident. Not an hour goes by that I don't think of him."

Photograph by NEIL LEIFER

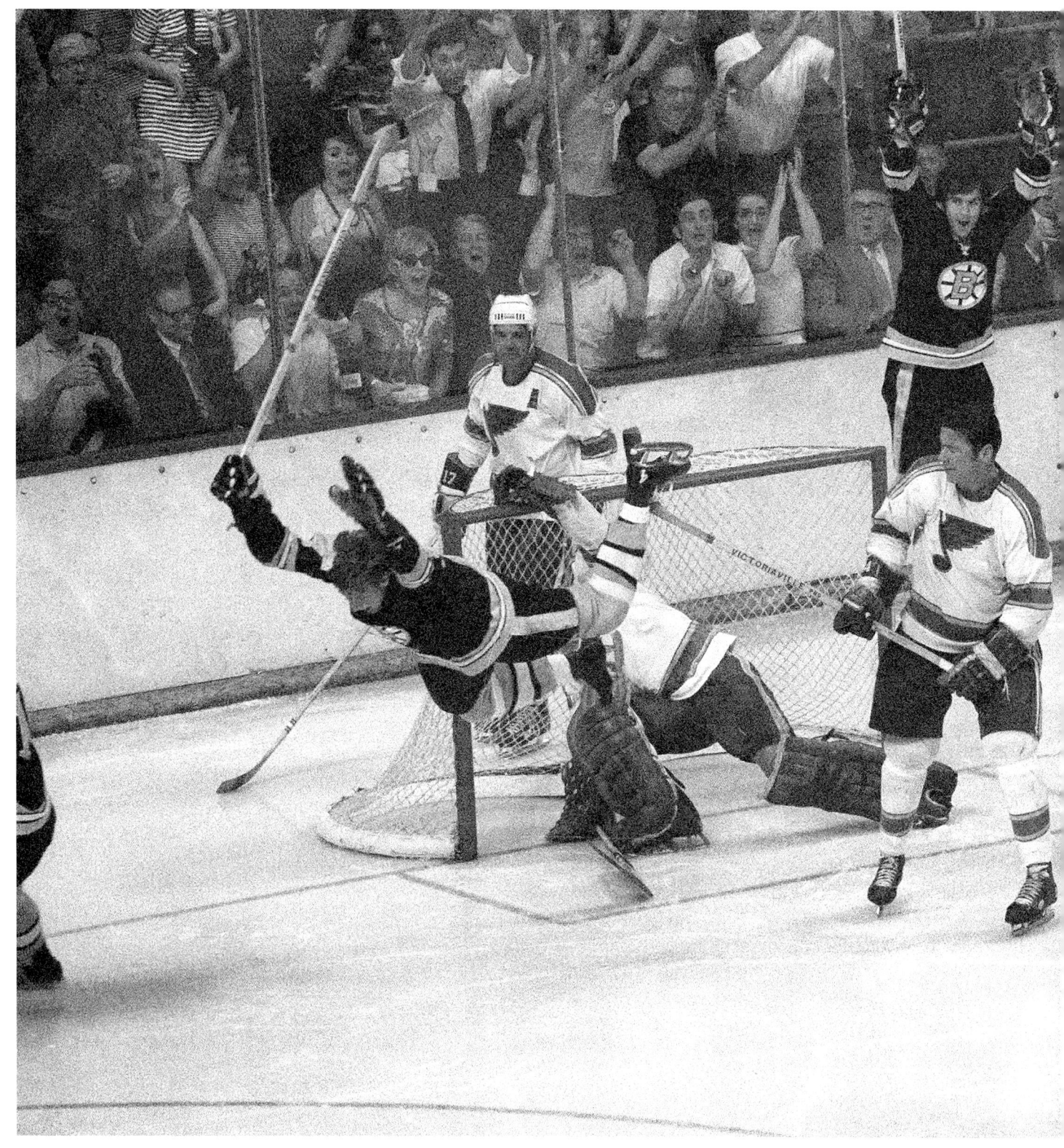

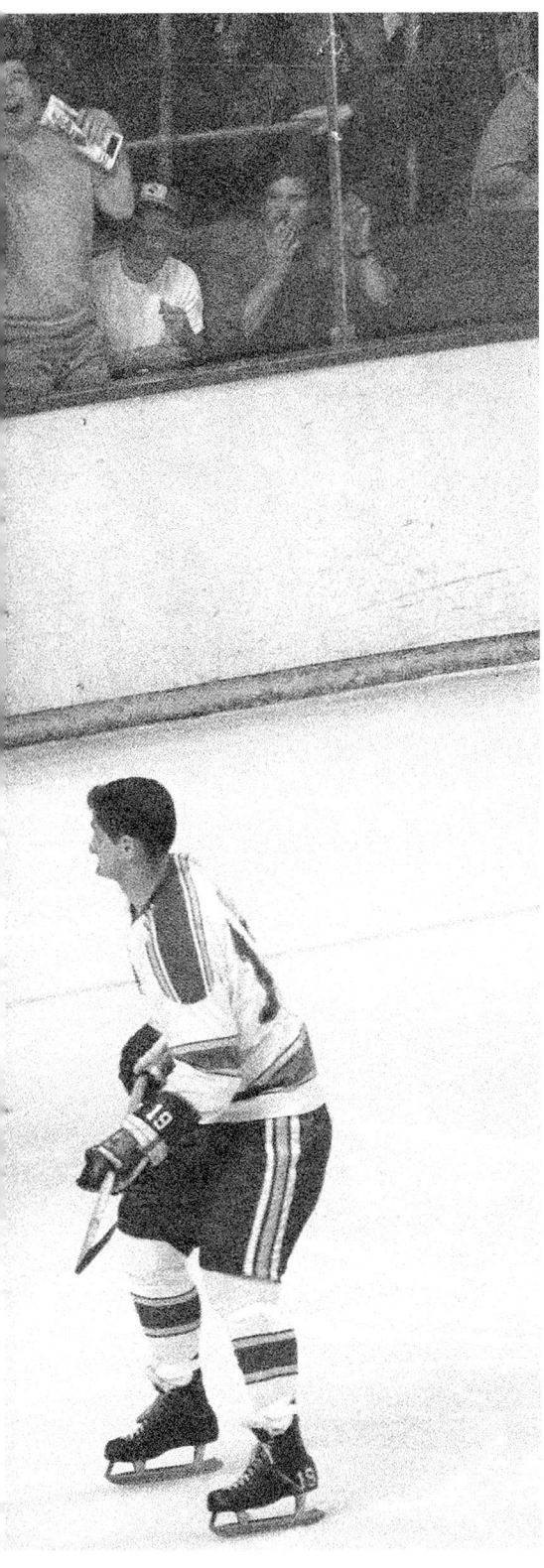

NUMBER 4

BOSTON GARDEN, BOSTON | *May 10, 1970*

THE BOSTON BRUINS had last won the Stanley Cup in 1941. Their last appearance in the Final had been in 1958. In the last eight years of the Original Six era (1960–67), Boston finished at the bottom of the league six times. The other two years the Bruins were second-to-last.

But there was hope. In 1962, the Bruins signed a 14-year-old prospect from Parry Sound, Ontario: Robert Gordon Orr. In each of his three full seasons of major junior hockey, the thin, speedy prospect set new records for goals by a defenseman. By the time he was 17, he was on the cover of Canada's weekly news magazine, *Maclean's*. Boston papers heralded his imminent arrival.

Of all the once-in-a-generation talents who have come out of Canadian junior hockey, Bobby Orr still stands apart. Neither Gretzky nor Lemieux, neither Crosby nor McDavid conveyed the same mystique, the same genius, the same poetry.

It is fitting that the image most associated with Bobby Orr shows him flying. He has just scored the overtime goal in Game 4 of the 1970 Final, sealing a sweep of the St. Louis Blues. The Stanley Cup has returned to Boston, and Orr has capped a season for the ages. For the first time, a player won the Hart Trophy, the Art Ross Trophy as top scorer and the Norris Trophy as best defenseman. Shortly after scoring his Cup-winning goal, Orr added the Conn Smythe as well.

Boston took the Cup again two years later. During the early '70s, Orr rewrote the record books. He was the first to get 100 assists. His plus/minus mark of 124 in 1970–71 is still the league record. (The best Gretzky ever accomplished was plus-100.) In 1974–75, he scored 46 goals, the most of his career. He was 26 years old, still in his prime.

And then his left knee gave out. He played only 36 games over the next four seasons before retiring.

We can't imagine any of the other greats in that photo, suspended in joy above the ice. They were all tethered to earth. Only Bobby Orr flew.

Photograph by AP PHOTO/A.E. MALOOF

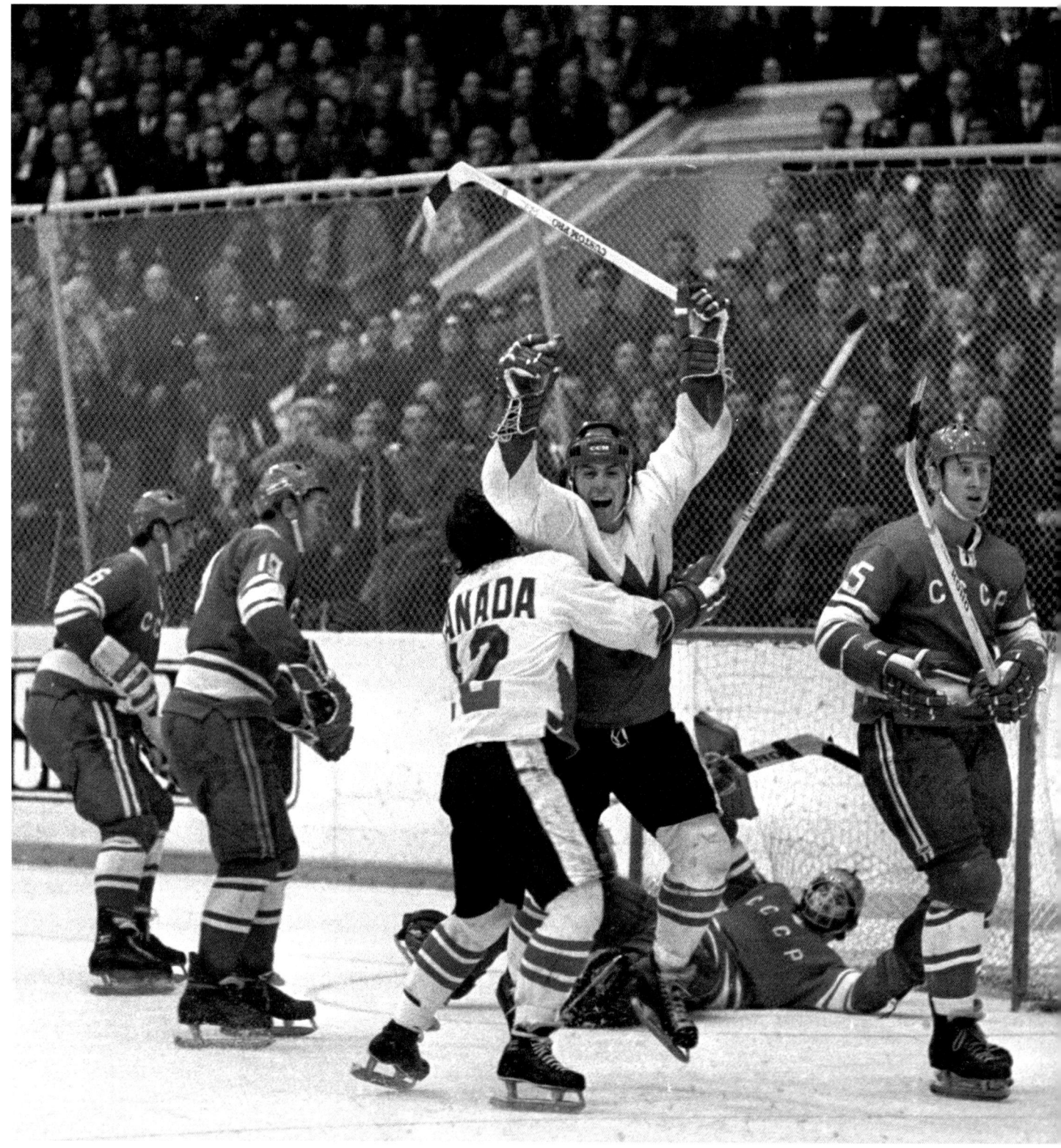

54

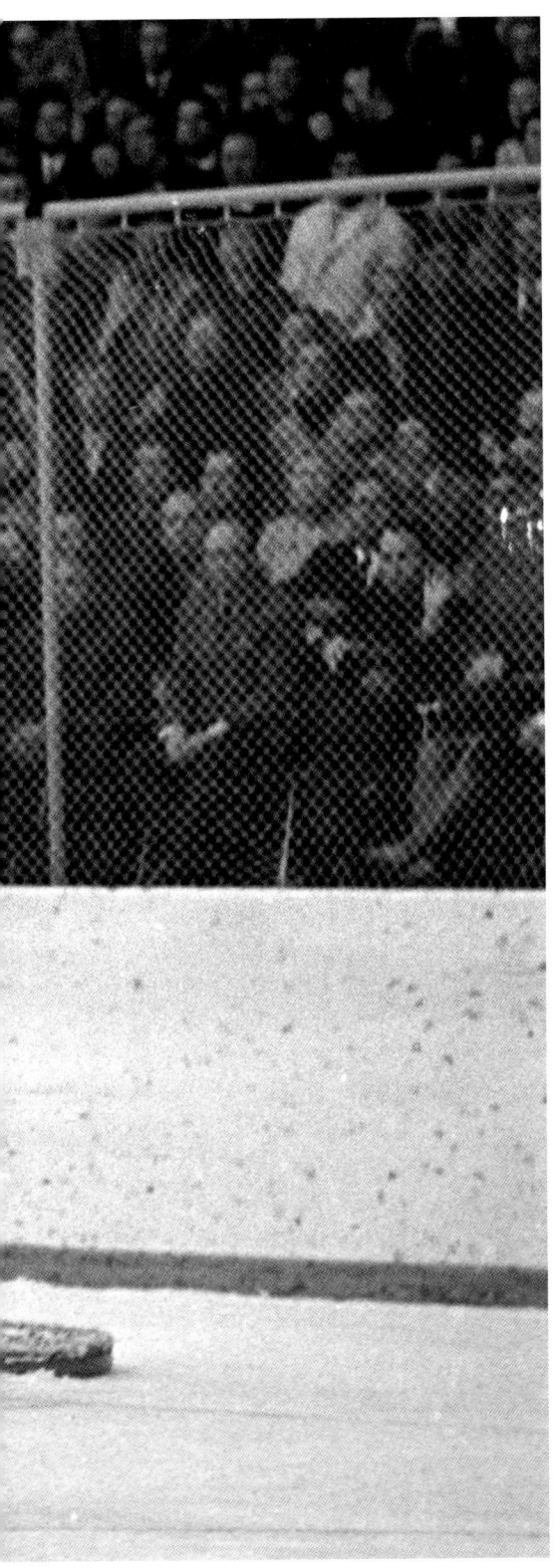

THE GOAL OF THE CENTURY

PALACE OF SPORTS OF THE CENTRAL LENIN STADIUM, MOSCOW | *September 28, 1972*

IT WAS A hockey event unlike any other. The Summit Series in September 1972 brought together the Soviet national team and a squad of NHL players representing Canada. The eight-game series was more than a Cold War showdown between Soviet communism and Western democracy; it was the first matchup ever between top pros and the dominant team in amateur international hockey.

Both sides needed to face each other. Earlier that year, at the 1972 Winter Olympics, the Soviets won their third consecutive gold medal, to go along with 11 titles in the annual world championships. They needed to prove themselves against the world's best. Canada had to show that its NHLers were indeed the best. Amateur teams from hockey's homeland couldn't compete with the Soviets in international matches. It was up to Canadian pros to teach the world how the game was played.

Canadians expected a rout. That's what they got in Game 1. The Soviets trounced the hosts in Montreal, 7–3. Six nights later, in Vancouver, the crowd booed Team Canada off the ice after a 5–3 drubbing in Game 4. Behind two games to one in the series, with one tie, the Canadians set off to Moscow. Another loss in Game 5 put their backs to the wall. Finally, in Game 6, the NHLers stopped playing dump-and-chase and started passing. They still played a rough game—that was clear when Bobby Clarke cracked a bone in Valeri Kharlamov's ankle with a vicious slash—but now they were skating with the Soviets. Two close wins evened the series going into the final game.

Every Canadian who had a pulse on September 28, 1972, remembers the goal. With just 34 seconds left in Game 8, Toronto Maple Leafs forward Paul Henderson completed the comeback and set off celebrations from PEI to BC. Today, the goal is enshrined in Canadian memory, and Henderson is a national hero. Taking the deciding game appeared to confirm that Canadian hockey players were still the world's best. But Canada's footing was not secure. The Soviets proved that NHL hockey was not the only game in the world.

Photograph by FRANK LENNON/ZUMA PRESS/NEWSCOM

THE REBEL LEAGUE

Circa 1973

DURING ITS SEVEN-SEASON lifespan (1972–79), the World Hockey Association looked like a house of cards. Teams popped up, changed names, changed cities and folded—seemingly within the same year. Bernie Parent's Philadelphia Blazers, for example, began their existence in Miami, as the Screaming Eagles. Because the only available arena in South Florida didn't even have air conditioning let alone solid ice, the franchise moved before playing a game. The stop in Philly lasted just one season. The Blazers smoldered in Vancouver for two years, then set off to Calgary. It was there, as the Cowboys, that the franchise finally, mercifully, went to the grave.

For all the empty seats and empty bank accounts, the WHA brought lasting changes to hockey. As Ed Willes writes in his rollicking book *The Rebel League*, the World Hockey Association "revolutionized the game." One of its most important legacies was opening pro hockey to new sources of talent. In less than a decade, the number of major-league franchises grew from the Original Six to 32 (18 in the NHL, 14 in the WHA). Teams needed players, and the traditional Canadian pipeline could not meet the demand. WHA teams in Minnesota and Connecticut signed standouts from local colleges. NHL general managers followed suit and added American players to their rosters.

WHA teams cast their nets even wider. The Jets needed talent to surround the league's marquee star, Bobby Hull. Winnipeg found players in Sweden who could skate with the Golden Jet: two young forwards, Anders Hedberg and Ulf Nilsson, and defenseman Lars-Erik Sjöberg, captain of the national team. Coaches and general managers saw that Europeans could play in North America. Two seasons later, 10 Swedish players and six Finns were on WHA rosters.

With Sjöberg feeding them the puck, Hull, Hedberg and Nilsson played a fast, improvisational brand of hockey. One admirer was Glen Sather, the young coach of the WHA's team in Edmonton. In 1979, Sather's team was admitted to the NHL, along with the Jets, Nordiques and Whalers. The Oilers imported their high-octane offense into the established league, along with talented young players who had their start in the WHA: Wayne Gretzky and Mark Messier. The results were revolutionary.

Photograph by MELCHIOR DiGIACOMO/GETTY IMAGES

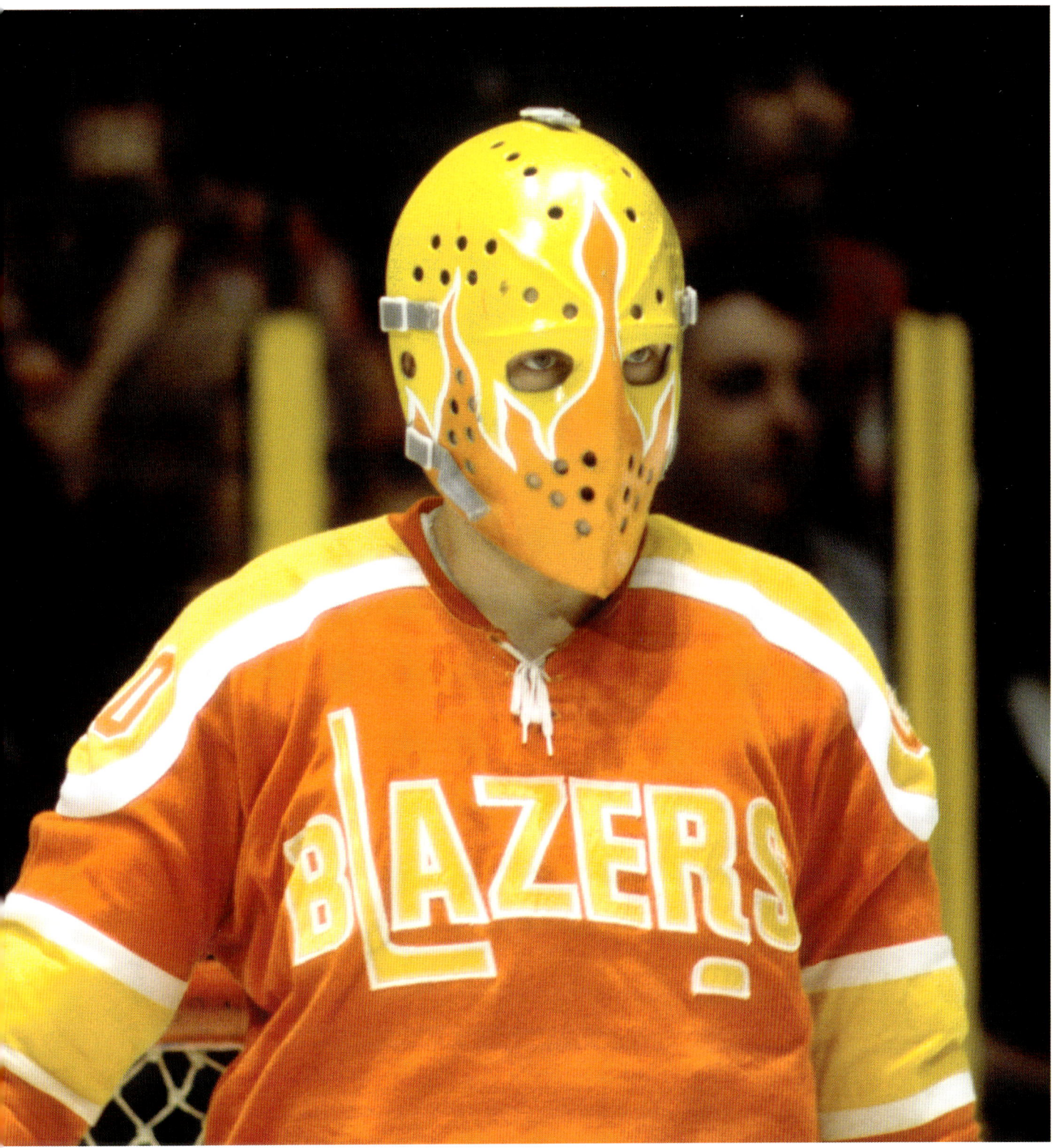

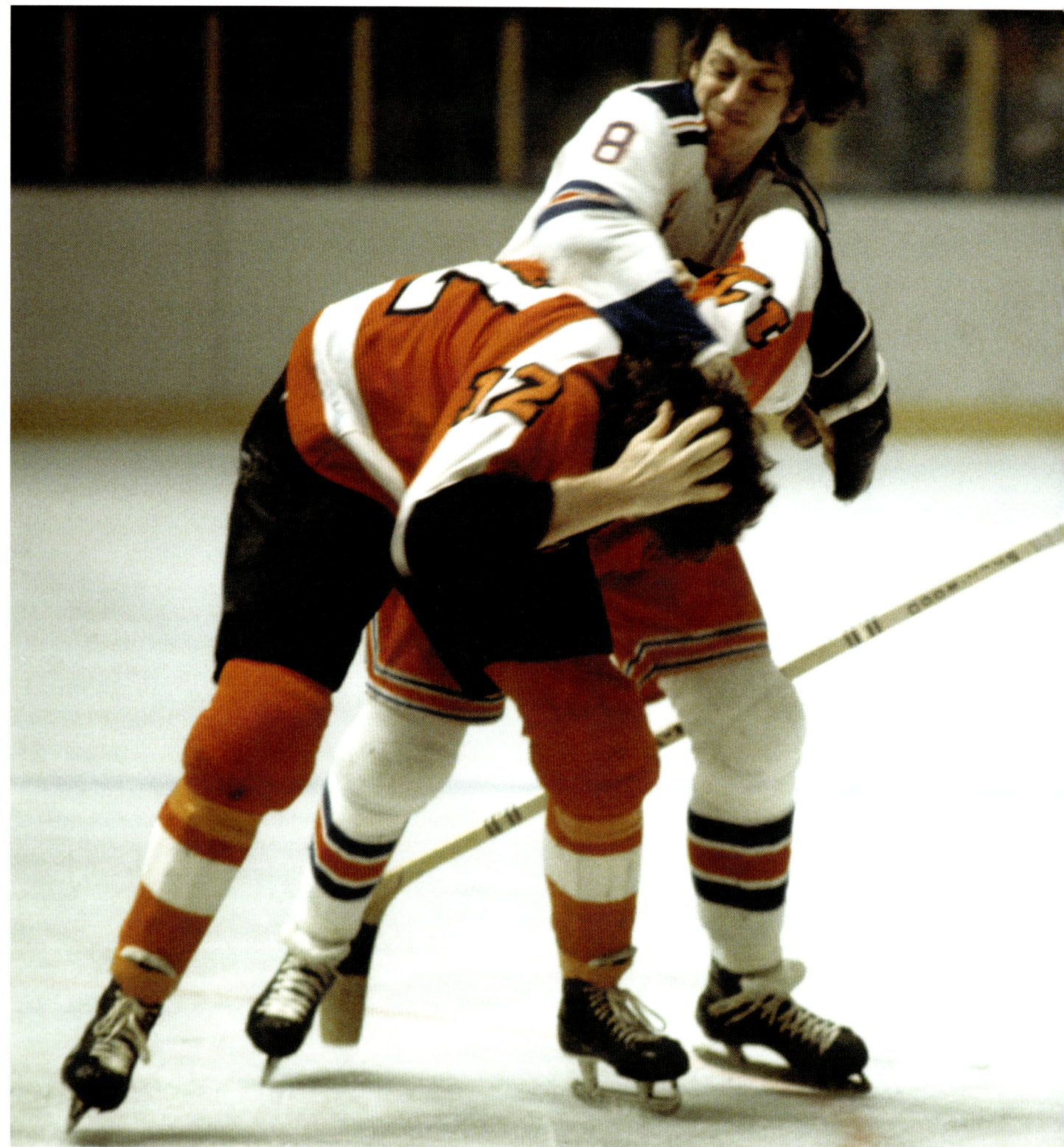

A QUEST FOR VIOLENCE

MADISON SQUARE GARDEN, NEW YORK CITY | *April 25, 1974*

HOCKEY WAS ALWAYS a rough game, but in the 1970s the sport plunged to new depths. Crosschecks and uppercuts became a key part of on-ice strategy. The idea was that if you knocked the other team around, they would play hesitant, defensive hockey. The old dictum of Conn Smythe was enshrined as gospel: "You can't beat 'em on the ice if you can't beat 'em in the alley."

Boston followed this strategy to Stanley Cup wins in 1970 and 1972. Philadelphia won back-to-back titles by ratcheting up the violence. In 1974–75, Flyers players, including Gary Dornhoefer, seen here being bettered by New York's Steve Vickers, spent a total of 1,967 minutes in the penalty box. By comparison, the "Big Bad Bruins" were sweet teddy bears in their second championship season, logging only 1,108 minutes in the sin bin.

Even the threat of legal action didn't keep players from dropping gloves and swinging sticks. In 1975 Dave Forbes of the Bruins was charged with assault after ramming the butt-end of his stick into the eye socket of the Minnesota North Stars' Henry Boucha. The Minneapolis jury did not reach a verdict, but those in the NHL were clear in their judgment: "This trial's a joke," Flyers coach Fred Shero told *Sports Illustrated*.

SI covered the trial in its November 17, 1975, issue. Ray Kennedy quoted Forbes's defense attorney, Ron Meshbesher, who pinned blame for Boucha's injuries not on his client but on the game itself.

Hockey, Meshbesher said, teaches a player "from the age of four on, 'Don't let the other player intimidate you' or otherwise your teammates will think you are chicken or you are yellow." It is hockey, he continued, that tolerated "injuries requiring sutures at least three out of four games" and pursues a "quest for violence."

Researchers in Canada proved Meshbesher correct. According to multiple studies, boys as young as nine were learning that dirty play earned approval from coaches and fathers. The culture of violence was far-reaching and long-lasting. Even in the high-scoring 1980s, fighting increased in the NHL. Only after 1989 did the number of fights begin to decline.

Photograph by JOHN D. HANLON

THE BROAD STREET BULLIES

BUFFALO MEMORIAL AUDITORIUM, BUFFALO | *May 27, 1975*

THE PHILADELPHIA FLYERS were the first expansion team to claim the Stanley Cup. More significantly, the Flyers' 1974 championship certified that intimidation was a winning strategy. The success of the Broad Street Bullies stirred debate around the league: Were the bruising Flyers a sign of where the NHL was going? Mark Mulvoy took the lay of the land in the June 3, 1974, issue of *Sports Illustrated:*

The great debate between admirers and detesters of the Philadelphia style has already begun to produce action as well as words. "Wait and see," predicts one National Hockey League official, "next season there will be six or eight clubs fighting as much as the Flyers fought this year…."

Minnesota president Walter Bush says he could sure use someone to go a few rounds on behalf of his timid North Stars. "We missed the playoffs and we didn't have a single fight all year," Bush says. "Oh, yes, we had one. A lady fan hit a guy over the head with her purse…."

Meanwhile, NHL president Clarence Campbell, aroused over this kind of fight talk, warns that the Flyers have "inaugurated an era of brawling, violence and intimidation" in ice hockey. "Baloney," growls Philadelphia general manager Keith Allen. "We're getting maligned pretty badly now. Sure, we were involved in a lot of fights. Sure, we play a physical game. In the Cup Final Boston challenged us just as much as we challenged them, yet we're the bad guys…."

While Clarence Campbell seems to be aligned with the antifight faction, this is not exactly the case. What really bothers Campbell is the game-delaying sweater pulling and the like, plus the expletives players shout at the officials. "I'm not concerned when two guys fight," Campbell says. "I'm only concerned when they won't stop fighting." Campbell's ire was particularly aroused by the interminable sparring in the fifth game of the Cup Final. There were six main events and a dozen preliminary bouts, not to mention stick swinging, kneeing, butt-ending and spearing, all of which can be far more hazardous than a right cross to the jaw.

Photograph by AP PHOTO

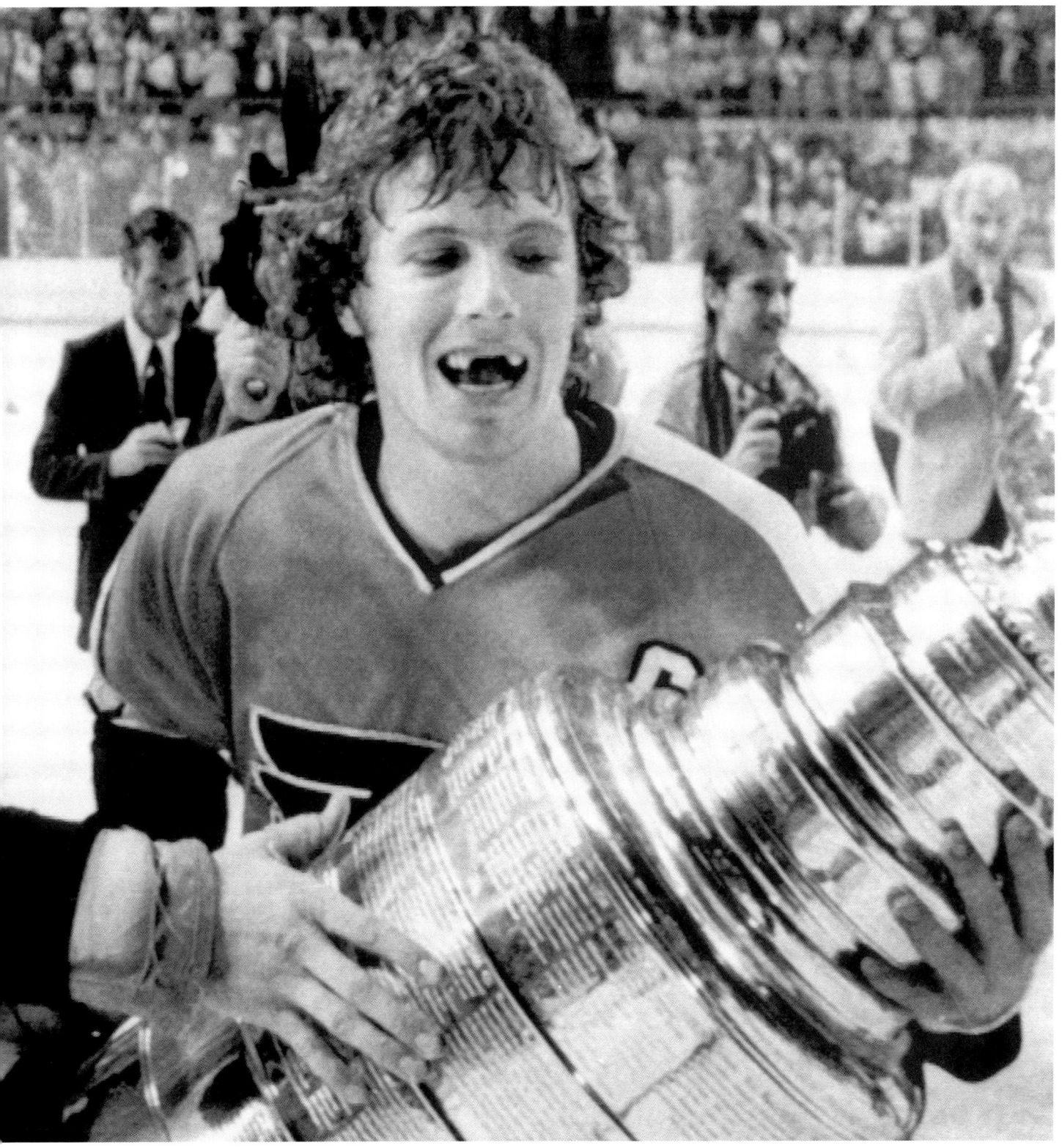

61

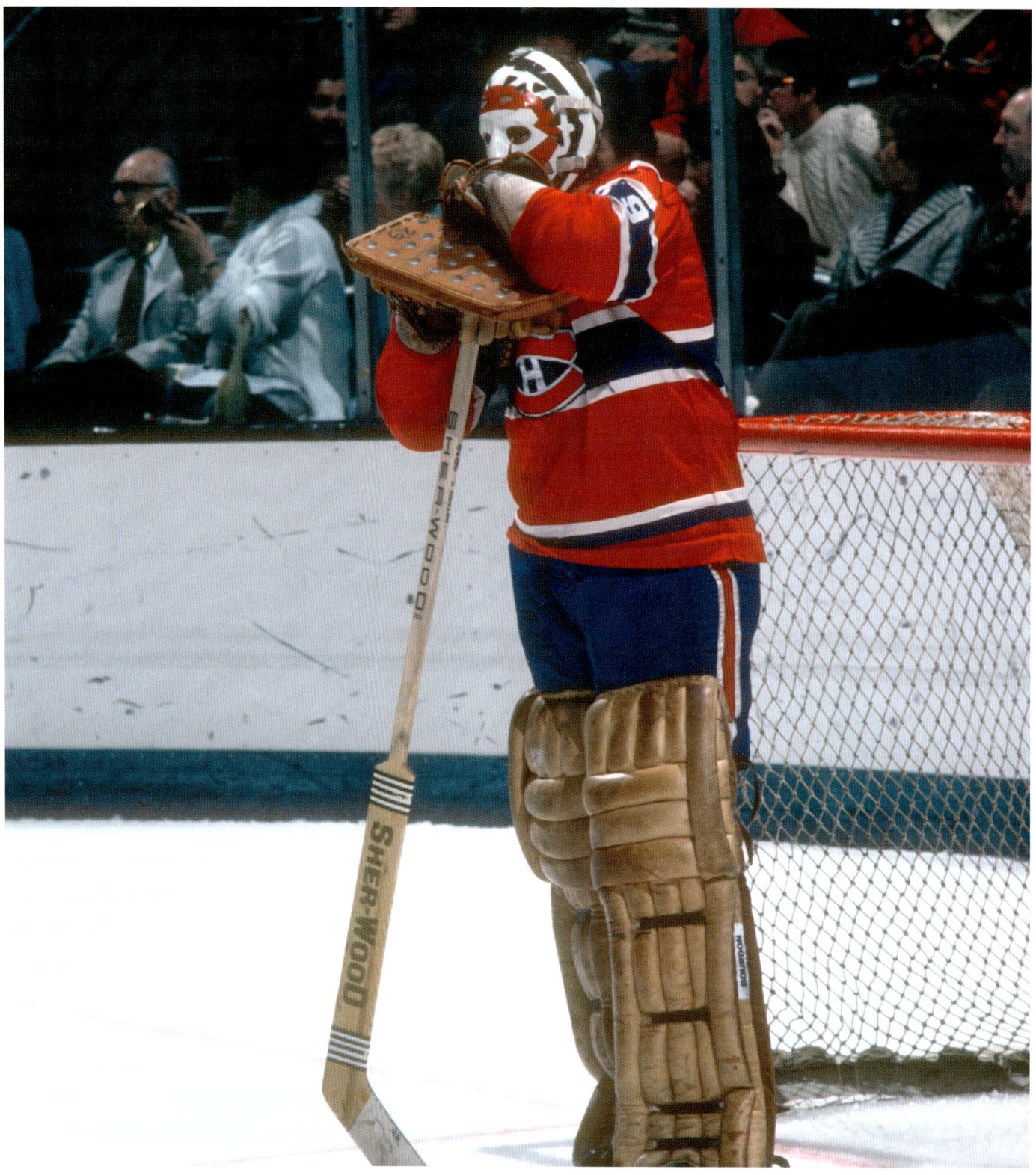

THE GOALIE

OAKLAND COLISEUM, OAKLAND | *Circa 1976*

GOALIES ARE A breed apart. Eccentric. Solitary. They watch the action from a distance, standing, waiting, anticipating.

If you were to make a team of goalies, Ken Dryden would be the goalie. He was an oddity not only in hockey but all of sports. After being acquired by the Montreal Canadiens, he chose to play at Cornell University, not because the Big Red were a powerhouse but because the school had the best history program. In his first three seasons with the Habs, he won the Stanley Cup twice, the Conn Smythe Trophy as playoff MVP, the Calder as Rookie of the Year and his first Vezina Trophy. Then he took an entire year off to finish law school. After returning to the Canadiens, he played only five more seasons before retiring for good at age 31.

The image of Dryden at the goal, resting on his crossed arms as he leans on his stick, is a fitting portrait. Already during his career, he was respected as an observer of the game. A few months after the 1972 Summit Series, he published his diary of the historic matchup. Canadian hockey officials sent him to the USSR, Czechoslovakia and Sweden to study those countries' training methods. After retiring, he reflected on his final NHL season in *The Game*, named by *Sports Illustrated* as one of the 10 best sports books ever published.

Over the decades, Dryden has come to be regarded as the wise sage of hockey. In books and interviews, he has spoken poignantly about the sport. He is also a critic, particularly of the NHL's unwillingness to address the risk of head injuries. It must also be remembered that he is one of the greatest to ever take the ice. He is third all time in career save percentage and eighth in goals-against average. Above all, he won. In eight seasons, he lifted the Stanley Cup six times—a mark that will likely never be matched.

After his extraordinary career ended, Dryden was honored with a bronze sculpture in Montreal. Inspired by the image of him standing in goal, the statue is titled appropriately. It is called simply "The Goalie."

Photograph by BRUCE BENNETT STUDIOS

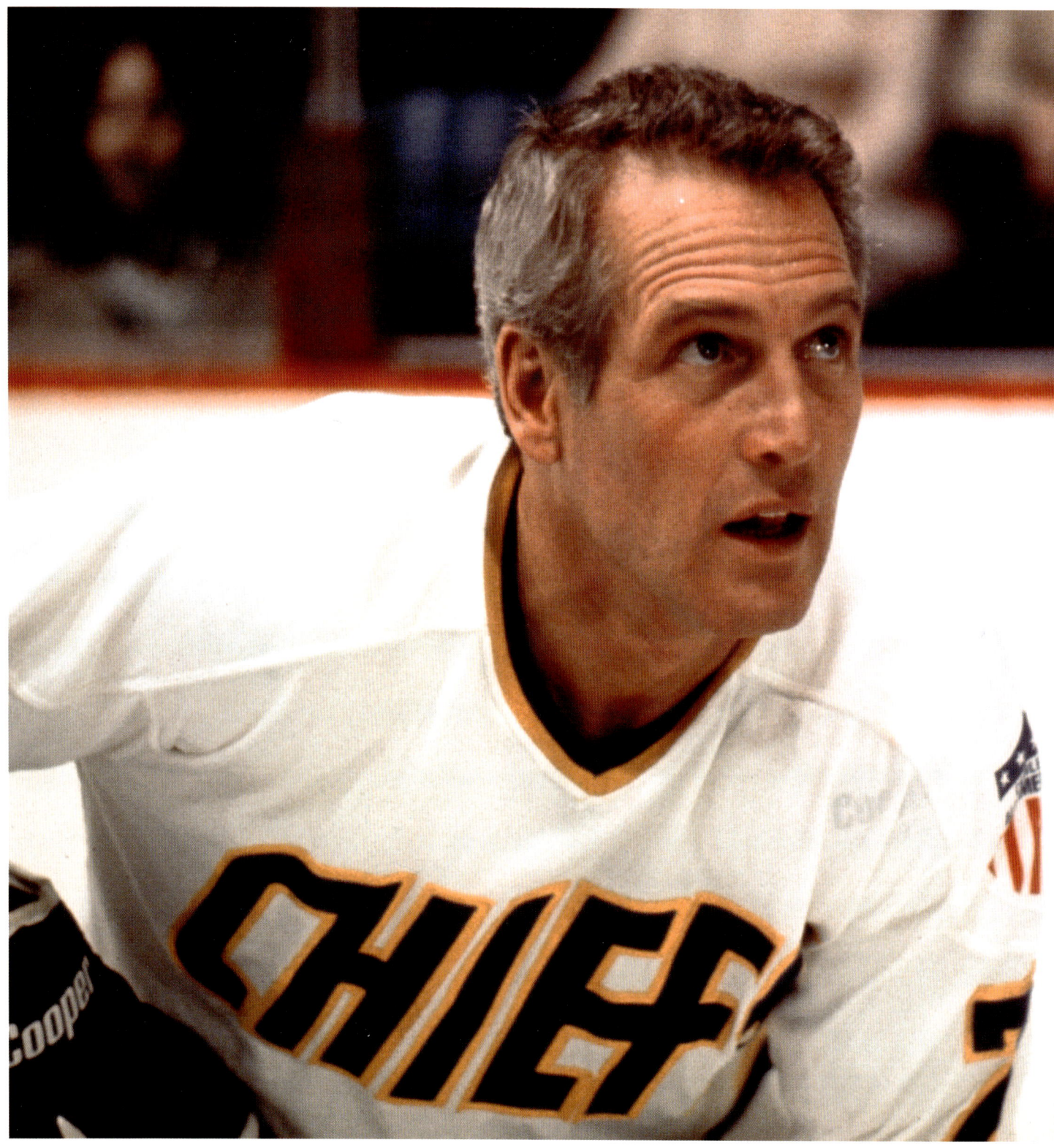

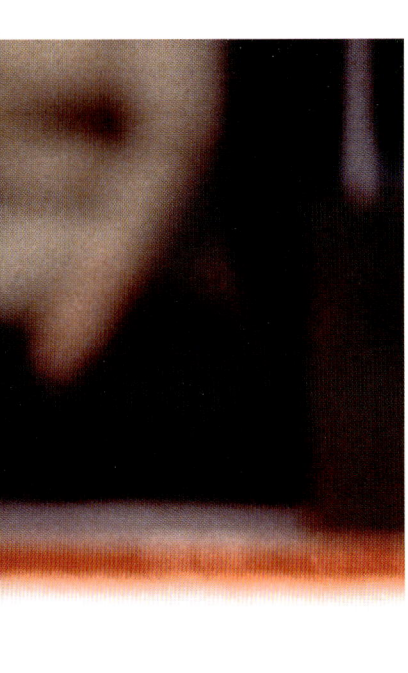

THE CHARLESTOWN CHIEFS

Circa 1977

SPORTS MOVIES ARE among the most acclaimed works Hollywood has ever produced. Think of De Niro at his finest in Scorcese's *Raging Bull*, or Gene Hackman as Coach Dale in *Hoosiers* or Stallone bellowing "Adrian!" at the end of *Rocky*.

These films appeared at the top of *Sports Illustrated*'s ranking of the 50 greatest sports movies of all time, published in the August 4, 2003, issue. Among these cinema classics, one film stood out. It was ranked at No. 5, above Oscar winners like *Chariots of Fire* and cultural touchstones like *A League of Their Own*: a bargain film with a bargain cast, except for its star, who actually suited up to play in the action scenes.

The film was *Slap Shot*, the 1977 comedy starring Paul Newman as the over-the-hill player/coach of the Charlestown Chiefs, a floundering minor-league team in a declining factory city.

SI's first take on the film was not positive. Frank Deford grumbled in his review about the film's violence and profanity. "The dialogue by Nancy Dowd is as puerile as it is unnecessarily vulgar," Deford harrumphed. But the dialogue was accurate. Dowd based the screenplay on her brother's experiences playing minor-league hockey. In fact, she initially thought of telling the story as a documentary. For the times, the language was indeed shocking. "It's foul," Newman told director George Roy Hill after reading the script, "but it's got *it*. Let's do it."

Newman never had as much fun making a film as he did with *Slap Shot*. He was especially fond of the three hockey players turned actors who portrayed the rock 'em-sock 'em Hanson brothers: Dave Hanson and real-life brothers Jeff and Steve Carlson. "They were very professional, and they were completely crazy," Newman told *SI*. "We drank a lot of beer."

When SI profiled the men behind the Coke-bottle glasses in 2007, they were appearing at dozens of events per year. To this day, fans and players alike still quote their lines. Actually, the timeless lines belong not to the Hansons but to Nancy Dowd, the writer who brought hockey to the screen, in all its puerile, vulgar beauty.

Photograph by BRUCE BENNETT STUDIOS

THE FLOWER

MONTREAL FORUM, MONTREAL | *February 23, 1978*

ALREADY IN JUNIOR hockey, Guy Lafleur was a star. In his two seasons with the Quebec Remparts, he scored 233 goals in 118 games. The Montreal Canadiens pulled off one of the most notorious trades in league history to nab Lafleur's draft rights the year he was eligible, swindling the woeful California Golden Seals out of their first-round pick. But condemning the Flower to play in the Seals' green-and-yellow uniforms, in front of empty seats in Oakland, would have been an abomination. He was fated to wear the *bleu, blanc et rouge* and skate in the Forum.

At first, however, it appeared the heralded phenom would be an NHL bust. Lafleur put up pedestrian numbers in his first three seasons. When he arrived at his fourth training camp, veteran linemates Yvan Cournoyer and Henri Richard gave him some advice: lose the helmet. With his flowing blond locks set free, Lafleur found his scoring touch. That season, 1974–75, he more than doubled the previous year's output of goals and points. Through the rest of the '70s, Lafleur topped at least 50 goals and 100 points each year, the first player ever to reach those marks in six consecutive seasons.

Lafleur's unmatched scoring prowess fueled another run of four Stanley Cup championships for the Habs. Coached by Scotty Bowman, this iteration of the Canadiens was one of the most complete teams in history. Ten players from the team are now in the Hall of Fame (along with Bowman). Yet it was Lafleur who stood out. The league's top scorer for three consecutive seasons and the MVP in 1977 and 1978, *le Démon Blond* was the attraction. As Ken Dryden told *SI*, "There is only one legitimate superstar on this team, and that's Lafleur."

He was a superstar, but a hard-working one. "He never took a day off in practice," Bowman told the *Montreal Gazette* in 2022, after Lafleur's death from cancer. "He loved to get on the ice before the rest of the team. He used to go on about 20 minutes earlier. I never had to do much with Guy. I just let him play."

Photograph by TONY TRIOLO

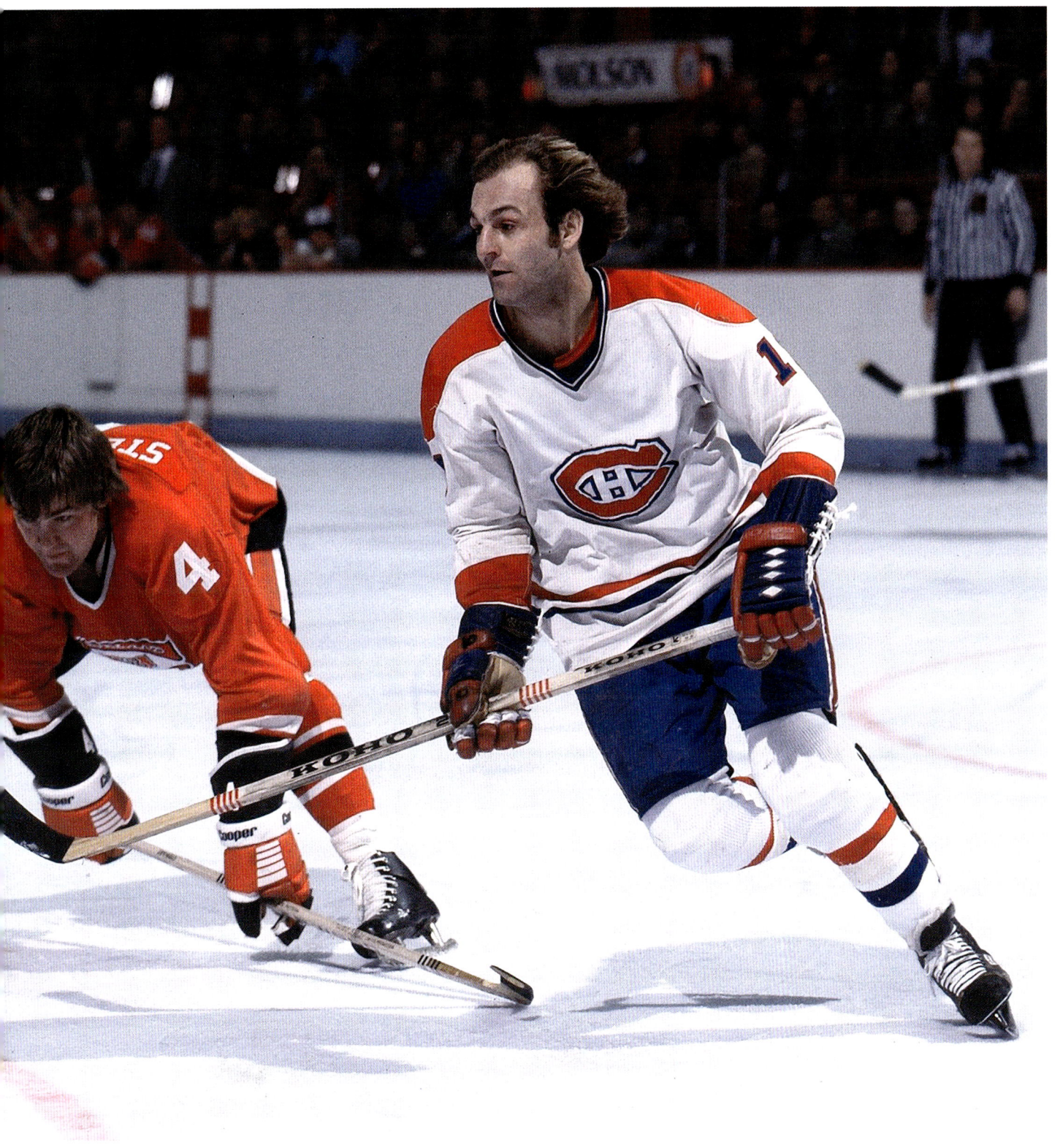

FIGHT NIGHT

MADISON SQUARE GARDEN, NEW YORK CITY |
December 23, 1979

IT HAD BEEN a penalty-filled Sunday night at Madison Square
Garden. When the buzzer sounded on the Boston Bruins' 4–3
win, both teams met near the boards to sort things out. At first,
players just chirped at each other. Then things escalated quickly.

A scrum had started in the corner when New York Rangers fan
John Kaptain reached over the low glass and smacked the Bruins'
Stan Jonathan in the face with a rolled-up program. Jonathan
put his stick up to protect himself, but Kaptain pulled it out of
his hands. Terry O'Reilly immediately came to his teammate's
defense. "There was no way he was going to strike one of my
teammates and steal his stick," O'Reilly told *The New York Times.*

He later insisted that he leaped over the glass only to "detain"
Kaptain.

Other Bruins were soon at his side. Even Peter McNab, who
had only four penalty minutes the whole season, went into the
stands. "Peter was usually the guy who'd pick up our gloves for us
after a fight," observed Stan Jonathan.

The most notorious combatant was defenseman Mike Milbury,
who had already reached the locker room when the fracas broke
out. "I went from happy and content, and ready to go home for
Christmas, to full combat mode in about 20 seconds," he recalled.

Milbury and McNab grabbed hold of Kaptain and pinned
him to his seat. Milbury pulled off the fan's shoe and whacked
him with it. Then, to add insult to Kaptain's injury, he threw the
makeshift weapon back on the ice.

NHL president John Ziegler fined all 18 Bruins who went
into the stands. and handed suspensions to O'Reilly, Milbury and
McNab. "I think I'd jump over the glass and grab the guy again,"
said O'Reilly.

Milbury admitted the mayhem reinforced the negative view
many Americans had of hockey. New England fans, however, were
proud to see their Bruins swinging haymakers in the New York
stands. In the words of Massachusetts native E.M. Swift: "The fact
that it was the Rangers and New Yorkers getting beaten with a
shoe, those guys are folk heroes up here."

Photograph by RAY STUBBLEBINE

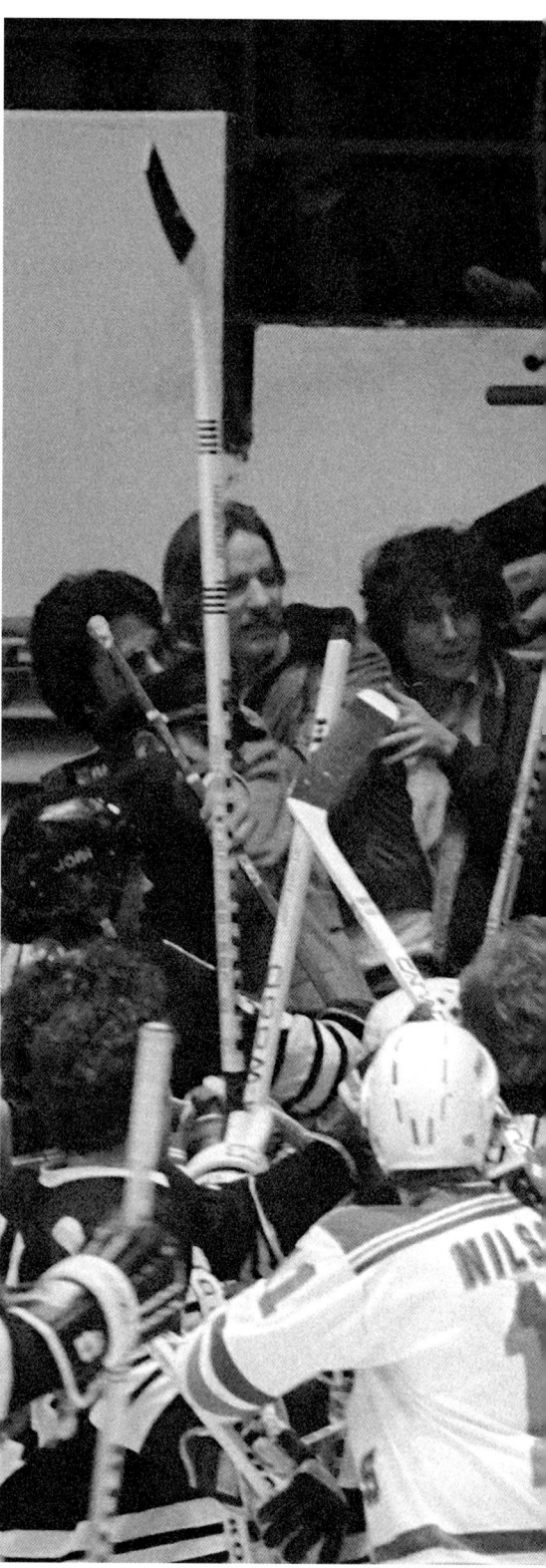

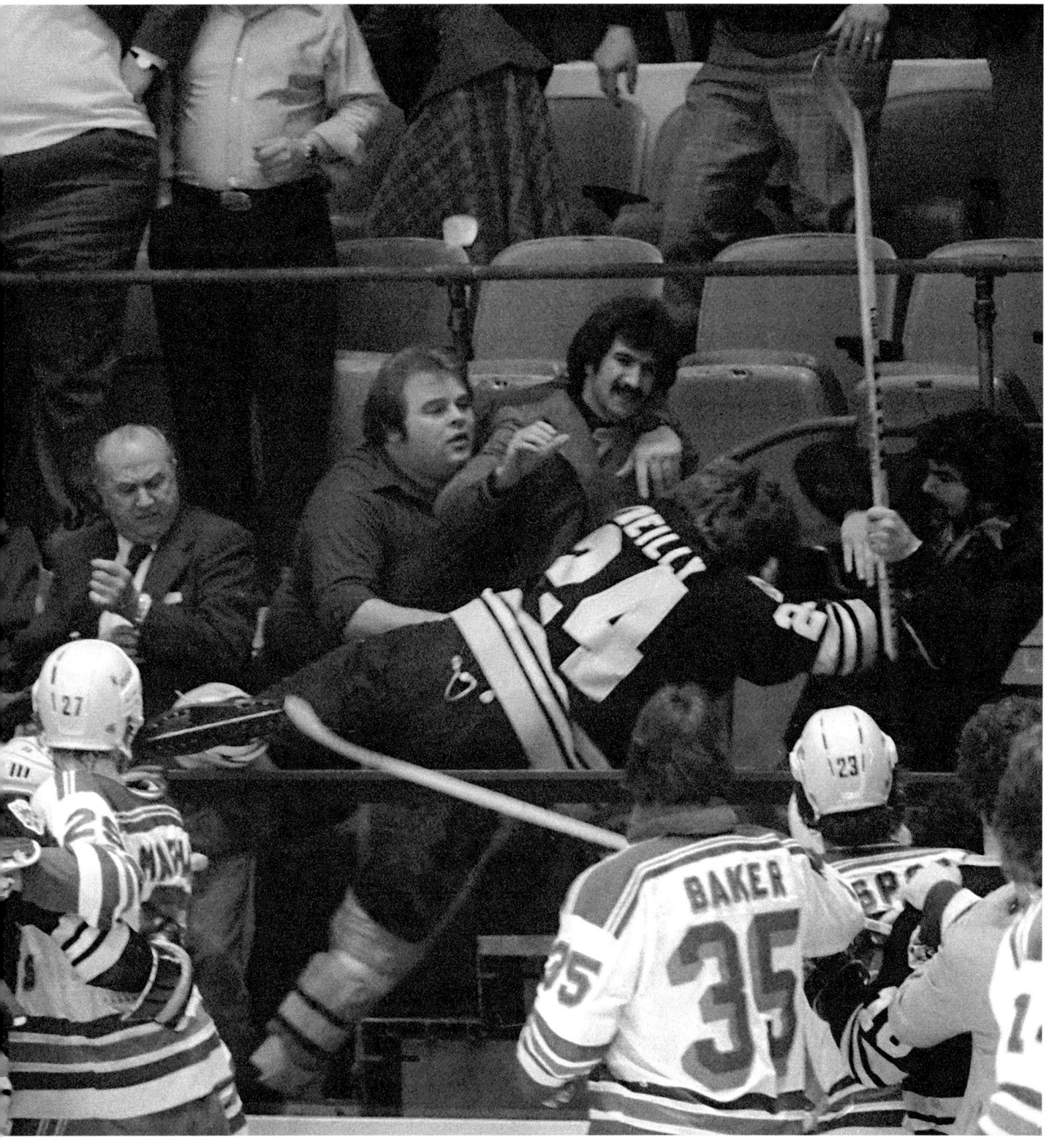

BOSS

NASSAU COLISEUM, UNIONDALE, NEW YORK | *January 8, 1980*

"THE PURE SCORER is a breed apart," wrote E.M. Swift in the January 22, 1979, issue of *Sports Illustrated,* "and Bossy is the best of that breed."

At the time, Mike Bossy was in his second NHL season. The year before, he had smashed the record for most goals by a rookie, with 53. When Swift profiled the New York Islanders' right wing, he was on pace to score 70. (He finished with 69.)

Bossy was always a pure scorer. He still holds the record for all of Canadian major junior hockey, with 309 goals in four seasons with Laval in the Quebec league. Scouts didn't think he was tough enough for the NHL, and 12 teams passed on him in the 1977 draft. "All he did was score goals," said Islanders GM Bill Torrey. "That's what we were looking for; we weren't looking for defense or toughness. If we'd had first choice, we'd have taken Bossy."

Bossy fit perfectly on a line centered by Bryan Trottier, with Clark Gillies on the left wing. Trottier and Gillies could also score. More importantly, they could dig, often battling two defenders in the corners. When the puck came out, Bossy was open.

"Boss'll get the odd goal from far out," coach Al Arbour told Swift, "but his main strength is that he's exceptionally quick and accurate. He's the quickest I've ever seen at getting a shot off."

Bossy also had a drive for scoring. "I like to score goals," he told Swift. "The team comes first, and if the team wins, I'm happy. But I'm still disappointed if I don't score a goal. There's just something in me that's that way."

Mike Bossy scored goals better than anyone. In a 10-year career cut short by injuries, he scored over 50 goals in nine consecutive seasons: the only NHL player to accomplish that. He also stands alone as hockey's most consistent scorer, with a goals-per-game percentage of .762—ahead of Lemieux, Gretzky, Ovechkin, everyone.

Photograph by WALTER IOOSS JR.

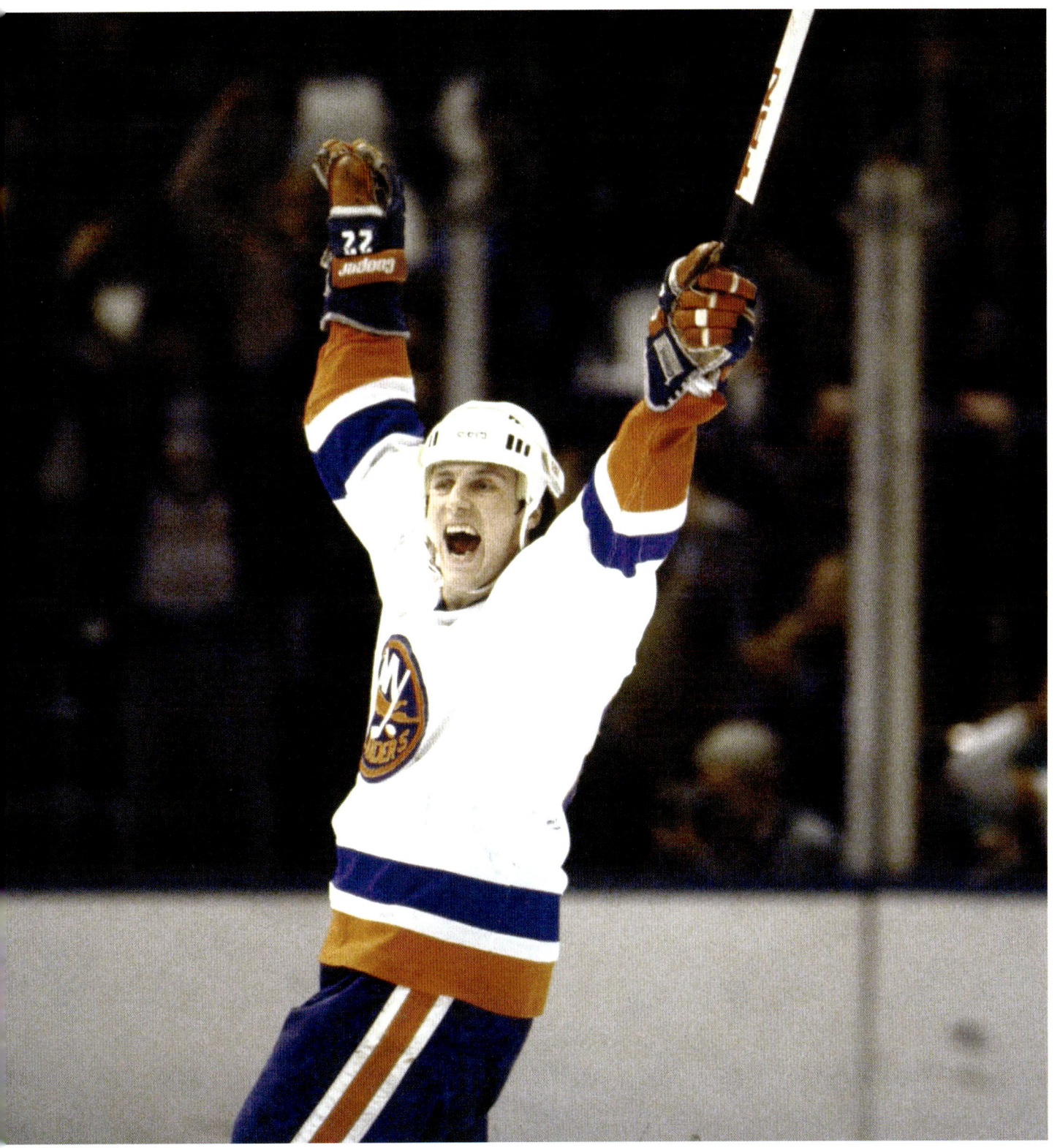

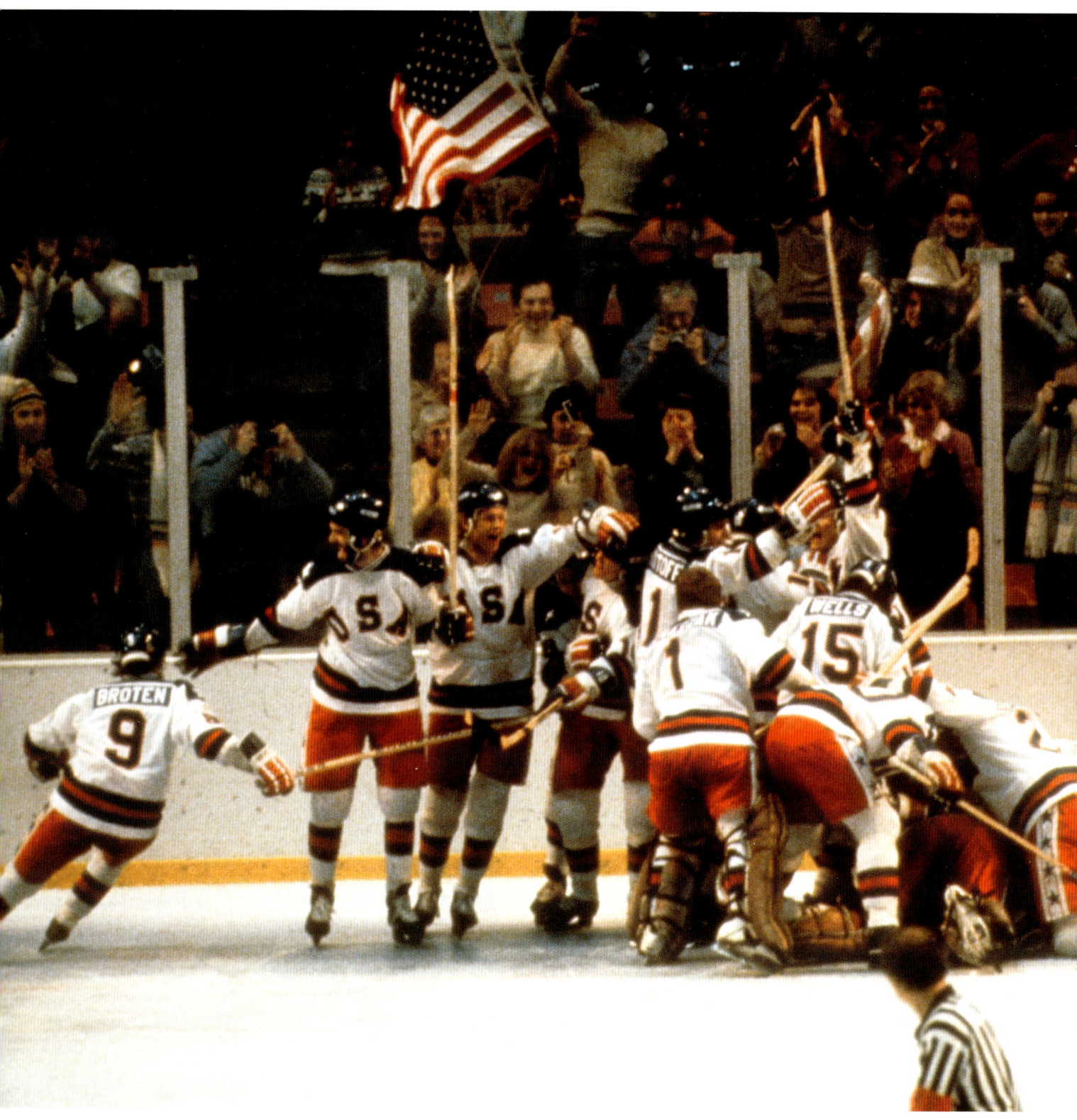

DO YOU BELIEVE IN MIRACLES?

OLYMPIC CENTER, LAKE PLACID, NEW YORK | *February 22, 1980*

"IT WAS AN Olympian moment, the kind the creators of the Games must have had in mind, one that said: Here is something that is bigger than any of you. It was bizarre, it was beautiful."

This was how *Sports Illustrated*'s E.M Swift described the celebration after the U.S. Olympic team's 4–3 win over the Soviets at the 1980 Winter Olympics. Nearly a half-century later, the upset at Lake Placid remains an unforgettable moment, one that resonates in American culture like few other sporting events.

Why is this the case? Why does a hockey game have such deep meaning? On that Friday night, February 22, 1980, an estimated 35 million Americans watched the broadcast on ABC, a taped replay of the afternoon game. A sizeable chunk of those 35 million probably never watched hockey again. Yet the memory of that game, that win, has persisted.

In the 1980 year-end issue honoring the team as *SI*'s Sportsmen of the Year, Swift took stock of what the 20 players had accomplished:

Some will have excellent pro hockey careers. Others will bust. But collectively, they were a transcendent lot. For seven months they pushed each other on and pulled each other along, from rung to rung, until for two weeks in February they—a bunch of unheralded amateurs—became the best hockey team in the world. The best team. The whole was greater than the sum of its parts by a mile.

The players were indeed unheralded amateurs. Nearly all had come directly from college teams. Most hailed from working-class families. Their parents included a teacher, truck driver, carpenter, electrician and auto worker. And Swift's prediction was correct: only some had excellent pro careers.

But they were a team. And above all, they were underdogs. Then as now, Americans identify with figures like Rocky Balboa or the kids from *The Sandlot*—no-names from hard-scrabble backgrounds who rise to the top. The U.S. Olympic team were those underdogs, in real life. E.M. Swift summed it up: "They were a perfect reflection of how Americans wanted to perceive themselves." It's still the case today.

Photograph by BRUCE BENNETT STUDIOS

A WHALE OF A LOGO

MONTREAL FORUM, MONTREAL | *Circa 1980*

THERE IS UNMATCHED hockey greatness in this photograph. Yes, we see two of the game's legendary players, 41-year-old Bobby Hull and 51-year-old Gordie Howe, in the twilight of their long careers. Yet what is striking here are not the graying stars (gray that was, in Hull's case, hidden beneath a notoriously lush toupee). Rather, it's what they are wearing on their chests: the most elegant, harmonious and stylistically perfect logo in all of sports.

In the January 30, 2017, issue of *Sports Illustrated*, Steve Rushin profiled the creator of the Hartford Whalers logo, designer Peter Good:

> When the Whalers commissioned Good, he was a hockey agnostic who withdrew to his Connecticut studio and sketched a W and a trident that revealed, in the negative space, an H for Hartford. This was the save-the-whales 1970s, and Good quickly abandoned the deadly harpoon for a whale's tail, a design made possible by the blind luck of those symmetrical letters, H and W. The result is more famous to more Americans than nearly anything in the Metropolitan Museum of Art.

The transcendent logo has long outlived the team it was created for. The Whalers played 18 seasons in the NHL, with little success on the ice. When Peter Karmanos purchased the team in 1994, he immediately looked to relocate. Meanwhile, the Michigan software entrepreneur baited Whalers fans with promises that the team would stay if they bought 11,000 season tickets and Connecticut built a new home. Fans bought the tickets and the state offered a $150 million arena, but Karmanos still moved the team to North Carolina in 1997.

For the deserted faithful in New England, the Carolina Hurricanes add insult to injury by organizing special Whalers theme nights. Carolina's revenue gets a boost with each appearance of the former team's classic logo. Yet the Whalers don't need scheduling gimmicks to stay in the popular consciousness. Thanks to Peter Good's design, Whalers gear ranks among the NHL's most popular merch. The classic logo even appears far away from NHL arenas. As Good told Rushin, "I get emails that say, 'I saw a Whalers hat in Kathmandu!'"

Photograph by DENIS BRODEUR/NHLI

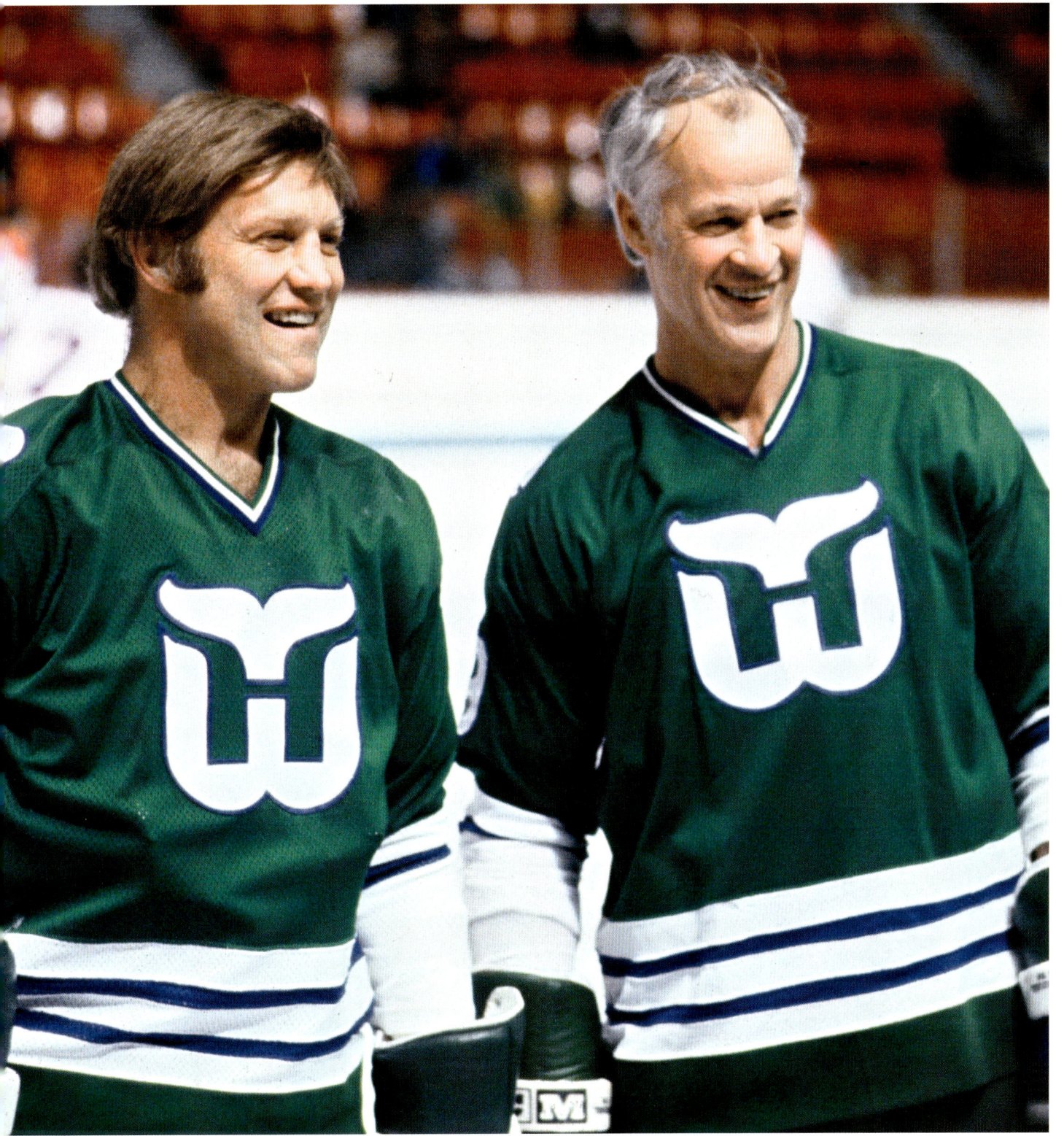

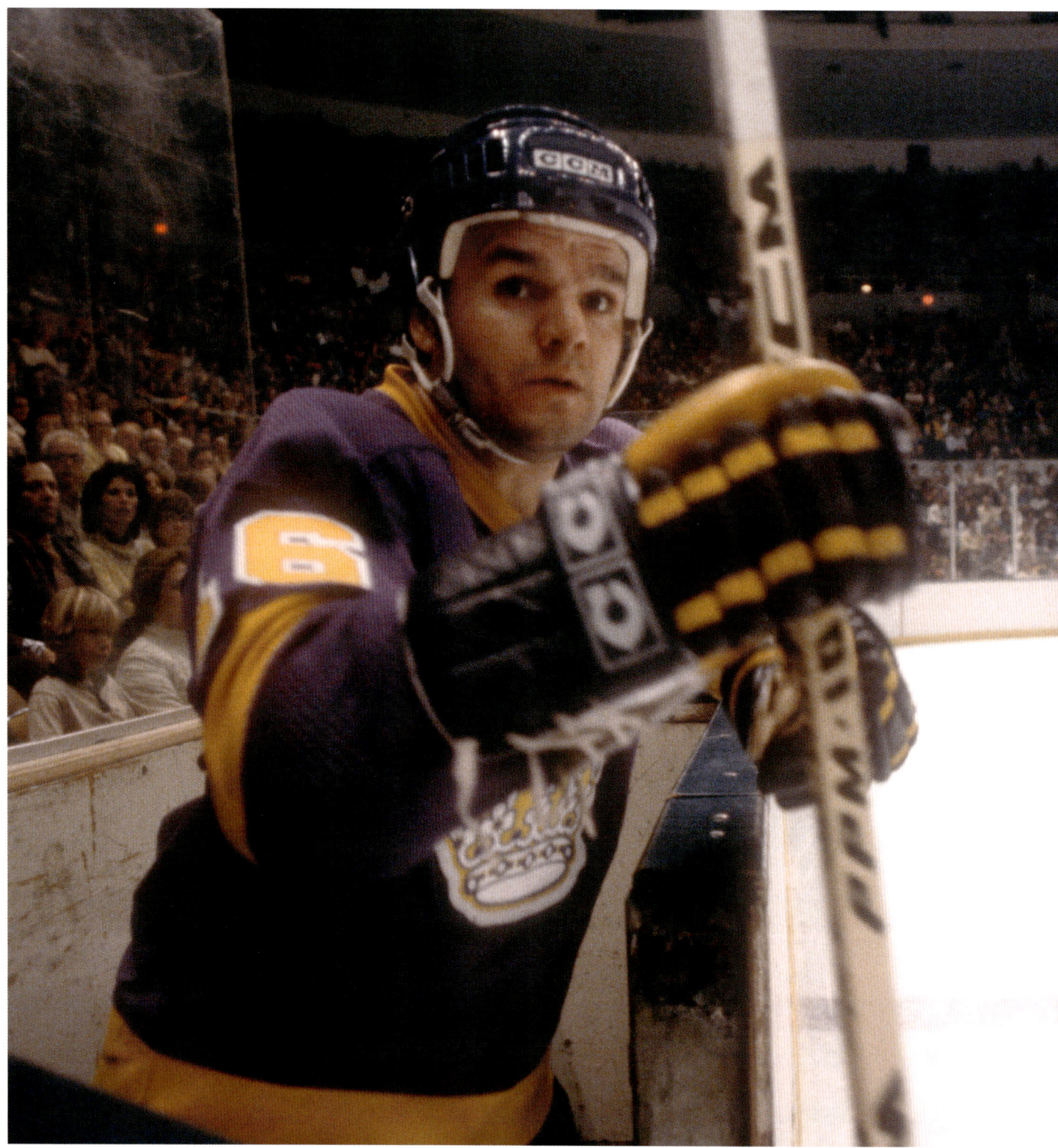

BROKEN DREAMS

NASSAU COLISEUM, UNIONDALE, NEW YORK | *Circa 1980*

EIGHT-TIME ALL-STAR, TWO-TIME winner of both the Lady Byng Trophy and the Lester Pearson Award, top scorer in 1979–80, member of the Hall of Fame. Marcel Dionne accumulated nearly every possible honor in his 18-year career in the NHL. The Quebec native was even immortalized on a Canadian postage stamp. But there is one prize Dionne never claimed: the Stanley Cup. He never got close. Playing with the Detroit Red Wings, Los Angeles Kings and New York Rangers, the furthest Marcel Dionne ever made it in the playoffs was the second round.

Dionne is one of many NHL greats who never lifted the Cup. So here we pay tribute, to All-Stars and award winners, to feared scorers and unbeatable stoppers, to winners of Olympic gold and Hall of Fame inductees, to players who never lifted hockey's most revered trophy.

Joe Thornton: The only player ever to win the Art Ross and Hart trophies for a season during which he played for multiple teams, Thornton played 24 seasons in the NHL. Nineteen times he skated in the playoffs, reaching the Final with the San Jose Sharks in 2016. He won Olympic gold in 2010 and entered the Hall of Fame in 2025.

Ryan Miller and Roberto Luongo: The goalies who faced each other in the thrilling gold-medal game of the 2010 Winter Olympics, Miller and Luongo were two of the top netminders of the early 2000s. Luongo and the Vancouver Canucks played in the 2011 Finals, losing in seven games to the Boston Bruins.

Mats Sundin: The first Swedish player to amass 500 goals and 1,000 points, the Hall of Famer is one of 18 players to have his number retired by the Toronto Maple Leafs. But like many greats who wore the blue and white in the last half-century, he never won the Cup.

Jarome Iginla: Twice the NHL's top goal scorer, Iginla captained the Calgary Flames to the Stanley Cup Final in 2003–04. In Game 3, he got a Gordie Howe hat trick: a goal, an assist and a crowd-rousing fight against Vincent Lecavalier. But the Flames lost a nail-biter in Game 7. Iginla entered the Hall of Fame in 2020.

Photograph by BRUCE BENNETT STUDIOS

ALL IN THE FAMILY

QUEBEC CITY, QUEBEC | *October 1, 1981*

THEIR ESCAPE WAS right out of a spy movie: covert meetings, near-misses with enemy agents, a car chase through Vienna, even a nameless driver known only as 007.

The Šťastný brothers—(left to right) Peter, Marián and Anton—had been linemates for Czechoslovakia's national team as well as their hometown club, Slovan, in the Slovak capital of Bratislava. The Quebec Nordiques front office had its eyes on the brothers and drafted Anton in 1979. Team officials tried to make contact at the 1980 Olympics in Lake Placid, but they couldn't sneak past team security.

In August 1980, the brothers saw their chance. Slovan was playing in the European club championship in Innsbruck. After the final game, Anton, Peter and Peter's pregnant wife slipped away from the team hotel to a red Mercedes driven by 007. Marián was in on the plan, but his wife and children were still in Bratislava. He said goodbye to his brothers, thinking they would not see each other for a long time. The two younger Šťastnýs slipped away off for the white-knuckle race to the Canadian embassy in Vienna, with Czechoslovak secret police close behind.

Transitioning to life in Quebec was difficult, as was transitioning to NHL hockey. The first months were a struggle. At the end of January, the Nordiques were at the bottom of their conference. Then came a breakthrough. Both Anton and Peter got hat tricks in a blowout of the Vancouver Canucks. In the next game against the Washington Capitals, each brother tallied eight points. Quebec climbed into a playoff spot, while Peter finished the season with the record for most points as a rookie.

The following season, Peter and Anton were joined by Marián, who had escaped with his family. Playing together over four seasons, the Šťastný brothers became one of the NHL's most potent lines. The playmaker was Peter, who amassed more points in the 1980s than anyone other than Wayne Gretzky. In 1994, he returned to the Olympics in the jersey of his home country, the independent nation of Slovakia. At age 37, he was named to the all-tournament team.

Photograph by BRUCE BENNETT STUDIOS

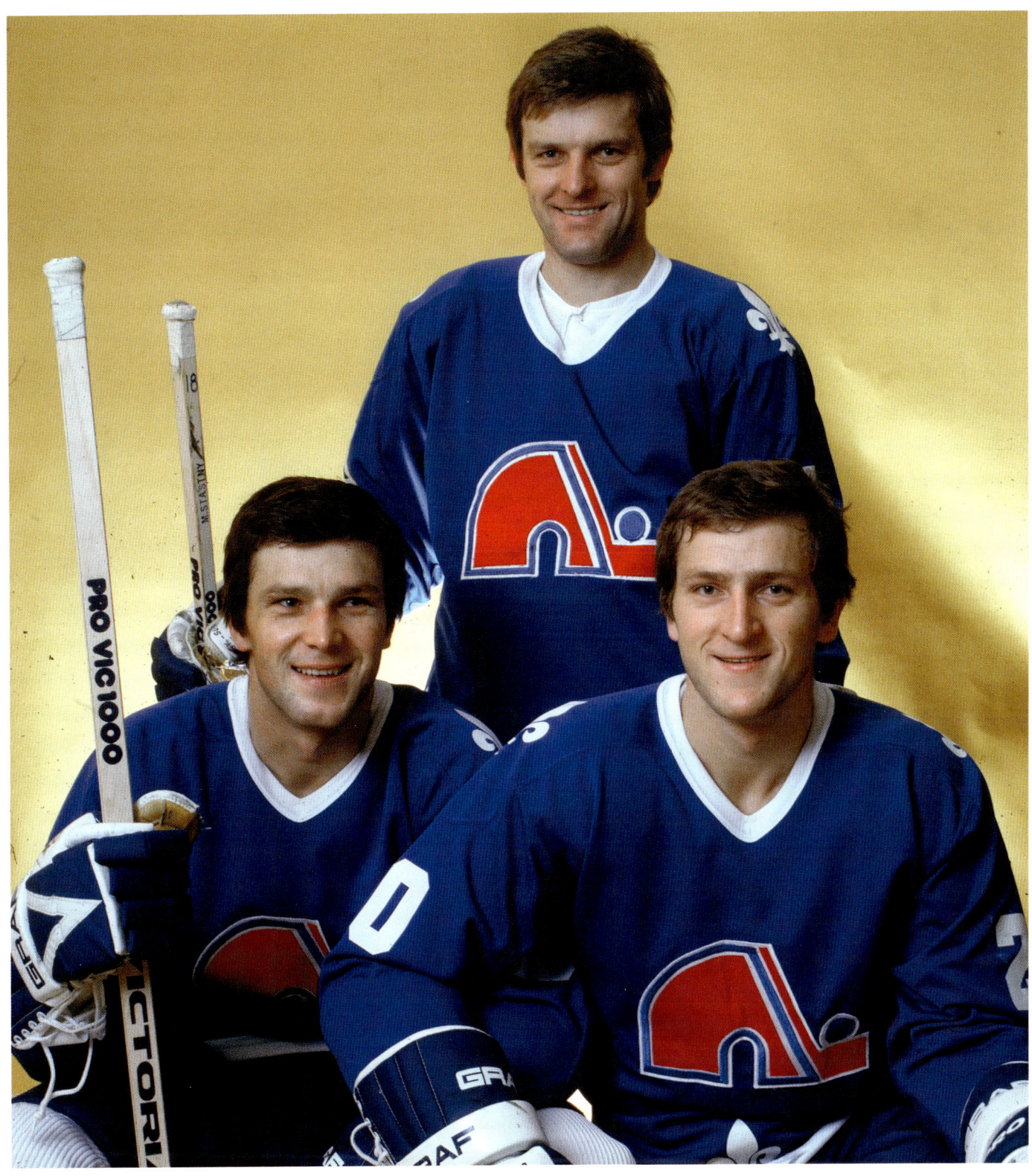

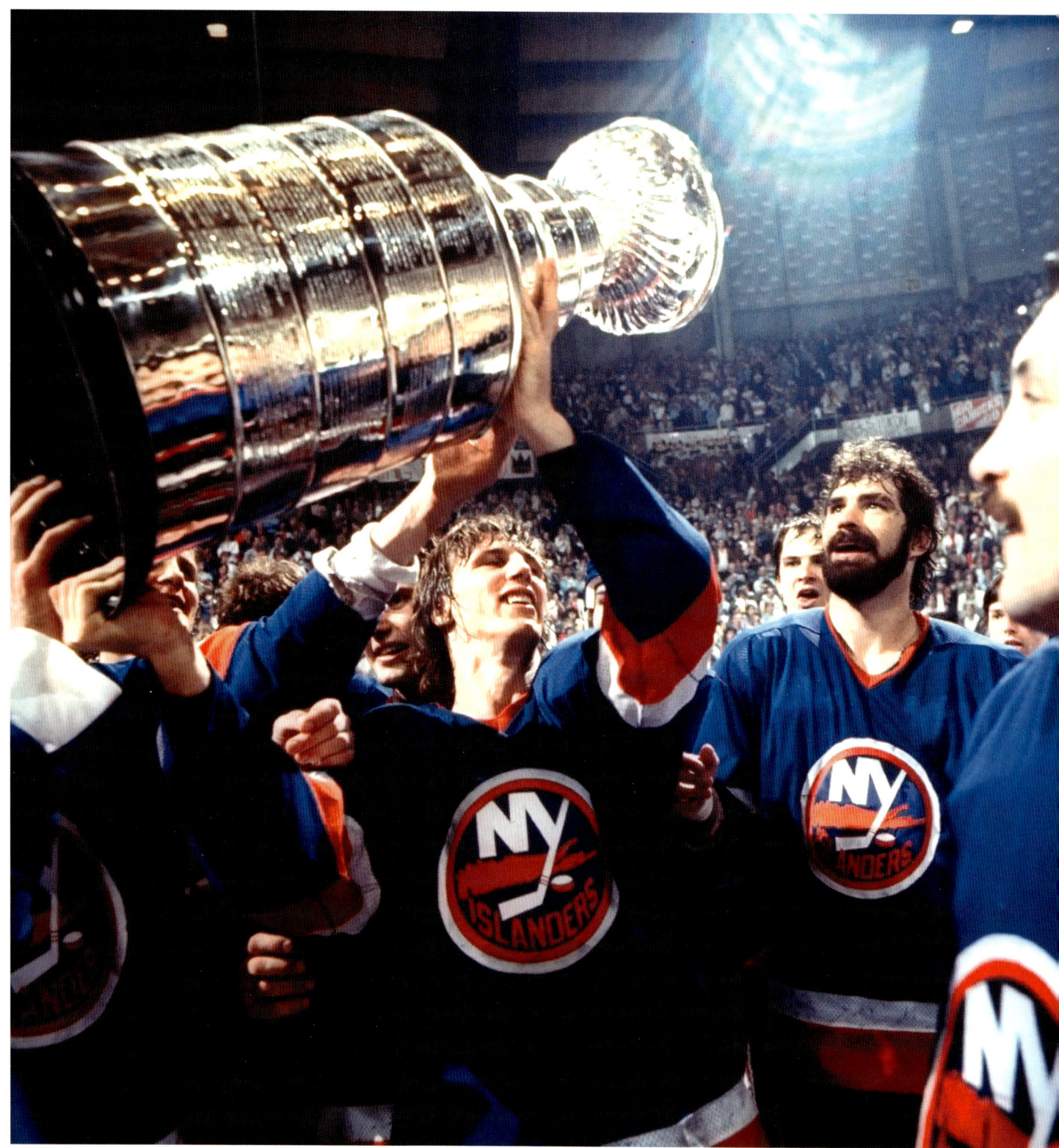

FROM WORST TO FIRST

PACIFIC COLISEUM, VANCOUVER | *May 16, 1982*

IN THEIR INAUGURAL season, the New York Islanders stumbled to one of the worst records in NHL history, managing a winning percentage of just .192. These early Isles gave up more than twice as many goals as they scored in 1972–73.

A decade later, in 1983, the Islanders celebrated their fourth straight Stanley Cup championship. From the sorriest of expansion franchises to dynasty in less than 10 years, New York's rise provided a textbook in how to build a championship team from scratch.

The architect was general manager Bill Torrey, who had learned how *not* to build a team as GM of the California Golden Seals. He found goalie Billy Smith in the expansion draft. Then he resisted pressure to trade his picks in the amateur draft, using them to select future Hall of Famers Denis Potvin in 1973, Clark Gillies and Bryan Trottier in 1974 and Mike Bossy in 1977. *SI*'s E.M. Swift wrote, "Torrey had his team now. First, goaltending, then defense, then goal-scoring. He had built from the bottom up, as if he were putting up a house. All that was missing was character."

Torrey got that at the 1980 trade deadline, when he dealt for Los Angeles Kings center Butch Goring. With 19 points in the playoffs, Goring was the last piece the Islanders needed on the way to their first Cup win.

The Islanders have the misfortune of being bookended by two of the most brilliant dynasties in NHL history. Compared to the 1970s Montreal Canadians and Wayne Gretzky's Edmonton Oilers, the Isles can appear more like a lunchpail crew of role players. But no team has even won three in a row since they won four straight in the early '80s.

Fittingly, the Islanders have an important place in hockey annals. Heading into the 1980 playoffs, the idea emerged in the locker room that the players should stop shaving. Some say it was Goring's idea; others say it was Gillies's. Whoever was the inspiration, the Islanders stopped shaving and kept winning. The playoff beard was born: the legacy of one of the NHL's truly great dynasties.

Photograph by JOHN IACONO

1984 to 2002

The
Great Age

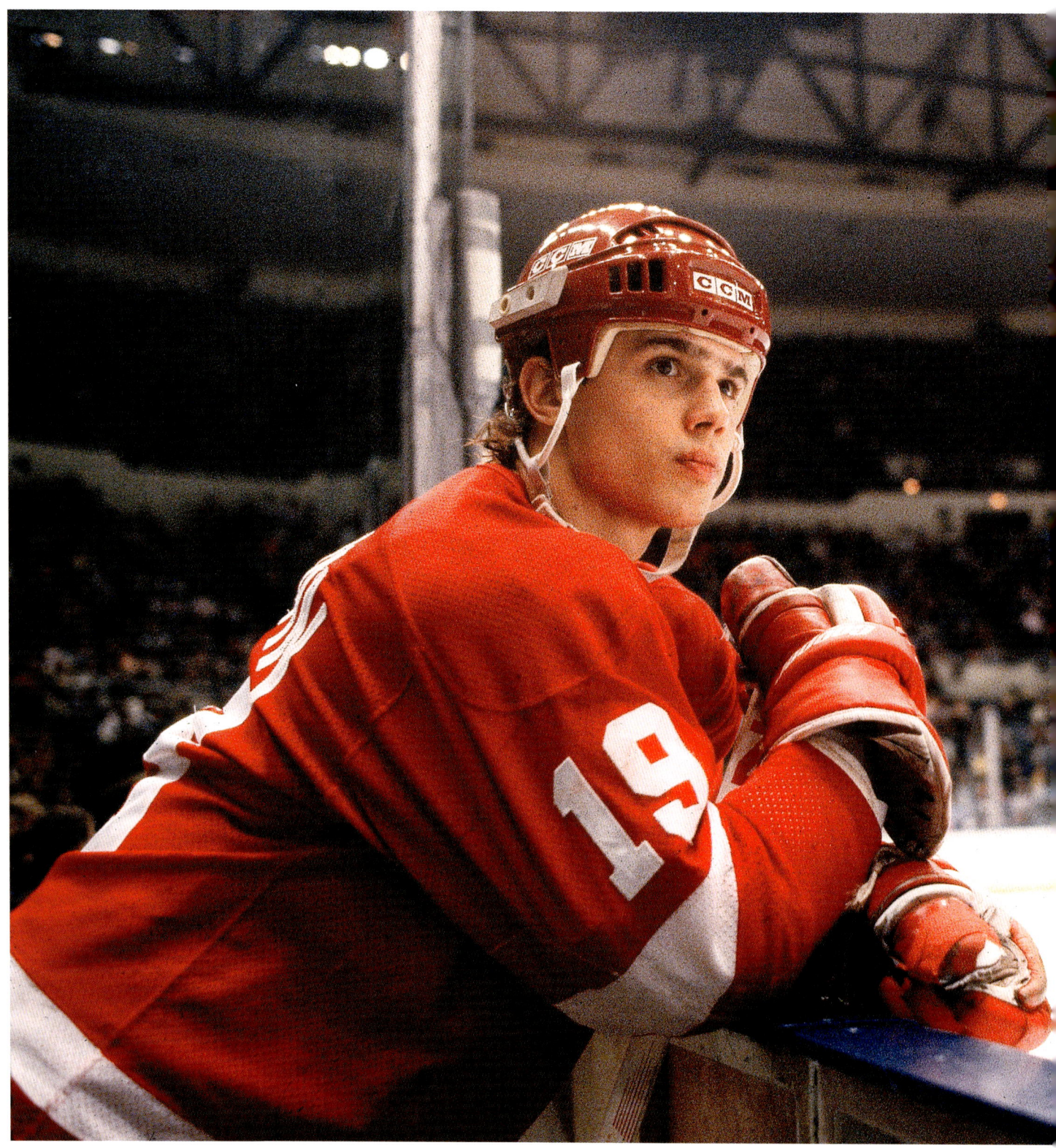

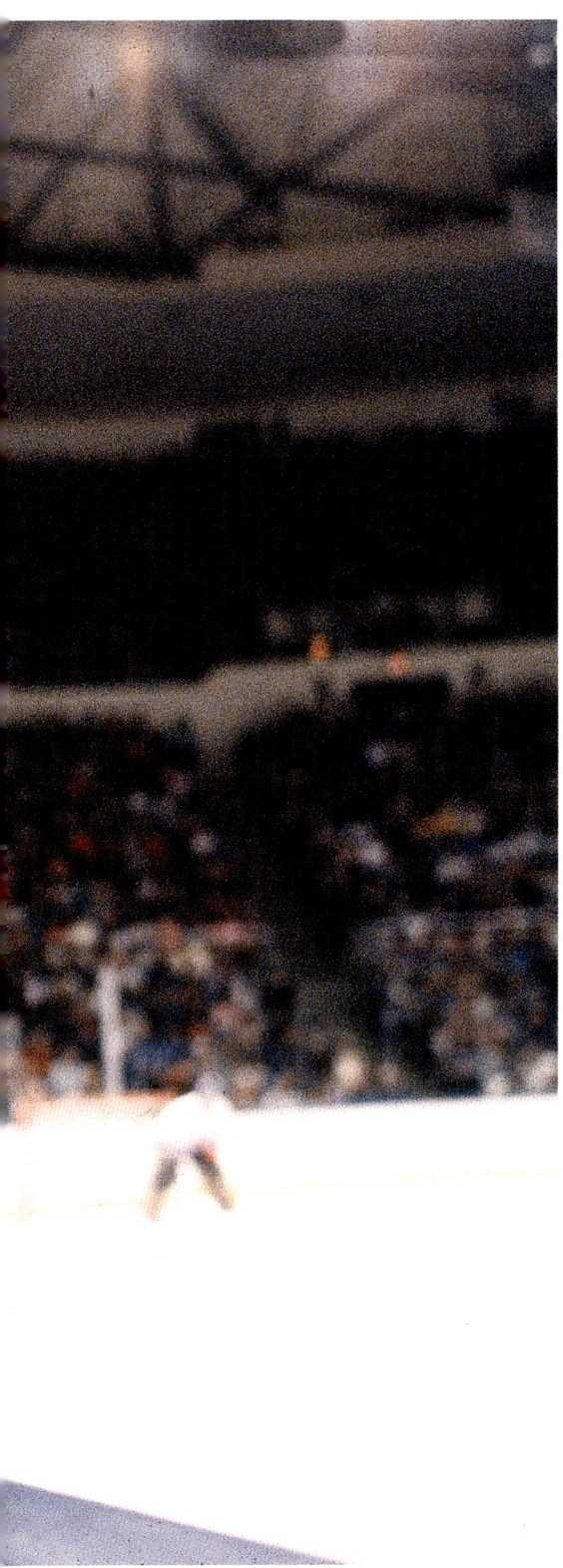

STEVIE Y

NASSAU COLISEUM, UNIONDALE, NEW YORK | *Circa 1984*

IT HAD BEEN a decade since their last winning season when the Detroit Red Wings drafted Steve Yzerman in 1983. Detroit wanted hometown talent Pat LaFontaine, who had already been profiled in *Sports Illustrated* as a juniors player, but he was drafted by the New York Islanders with the third pick. Detroit GM Jim Devellano was quoted as saying the Red Wings had to "settle" on Yzerman with the fourth selection. LaFontaine became a Hall of Famer. Yzerman became a legend.

Before the start of his fourth season, when he was just 21 years old, Yzerman was named team captain. He served in this role for the next 20 seasons, making him the longest-serving captain in any North American sport. During those two decades, Yzerman shared the Wings locker room with a legion of greats, but he remained the team's undisputed leader.

By all accounts, Yzerman was not the kind of captain to lead with fiery speeches. "When he does talk, he really knows how to grab your attention," teammate Harold Snepsts told *Sports Illustrated*. Yzerman also showed a willingness to adapt his game for the needs of the team. After six straight seasons with over 100 points, he became a two-way player once Scotty Bowman arrived as coach. "I didn't have to do much convincing," Bowman said.

The new Yzerman went into corners and blocked shots. The high-scoring star was transformed into the suffocating defender. "He is the most changed hockey player I've ever seen in my life," scout Mark Howe told *SI* in 1997. Yzerman lifted the Stanley Cup for the first time that year. After being called forward by Gary Bettman, he had to ask the commissioner what to do next. He would get accustomed to handling the silverware: the Red Wings won two more Cups before Yzerman retired.

At the end, when he was a 40-year-old with failing knees, Stevie Y was showered with tributes. The Dead Wings who had drafted him were no more. Detroit was again Hockeytown. "No player of his era was more selfless, more respected and more complete," wrote *SI*'s E.M. Swift.

Photograph by BRUCE BENNETT STUDIOS

THE GREAT ONE

NORTHLANDS COLISEUM, EDMONTON | *Circa 1984*

WAYNE GRETZKY MADE his *Sports Illustrated* debut in the February 20, 1978, issue, when he was 16 years old. Playing for the Sault Ste. Marie Greyhounds, the gangly teenager was drawing sellout after sellout in Ontario's Junior A league. E.M. Swift described the scene in Hamilton:

> First sellout of the year for a Junior A game, and in a blizzard to boot, everyone out getting stuck in the snow to see some kid called The Great Gretzky, whom every paper in Ontario has hailed as the next Bobby Orr since he was eight years old.

Six years later, Gretzky was on *SI*'s cover, passing Orr for most cover appearances ever by a hockey player. He was also breaking records on the ice: Orr's tally for most assists in a season, Phil Esposito's record for most goals, the legendary run of 50 goals in 50 games, first set by Rocket Richard and matched by Mike Bossy. In his first years in the NHL, the Great Gretzky was not only surpassing these marks; he was obliterating them.

In 1981–82, the Edmonton Oilers center was the first NHL player to amass 200 points (92 goals, 120 assists, for a total of 212 points). When he hit *SI*'s cover on the January 23, 1984, issue, Gretzky was on pace for 200 again. Since the start of the season, he had notched a goal or assist in every game. In his interview with Jack Falla, Gretzky dismissed comparisons to Joe DiMaggio's 56-game hitting streak. DiMaggio had only four or five at-bats per game, Gretzky observed, whereas he had five or six shifts per period. "I get more chances," he said.

Humble, polite and with an actor's good looks—as Falla wrote, it was hard to express just how unique Gretzky was. For crying out loud, he was even friends with Andy Warhol, who had just painted the hockey player's portrait. "As an artist, what I see in Wayne is great joy and energy," said the icon of Pop Art. Searching for words to convey the Great One's greatness, Falla turned to pop music: "He is the genius of his sport and, like DiMaggio, a hero to turn one's lonely eyes to."

Photograph by NEIL LEIFER

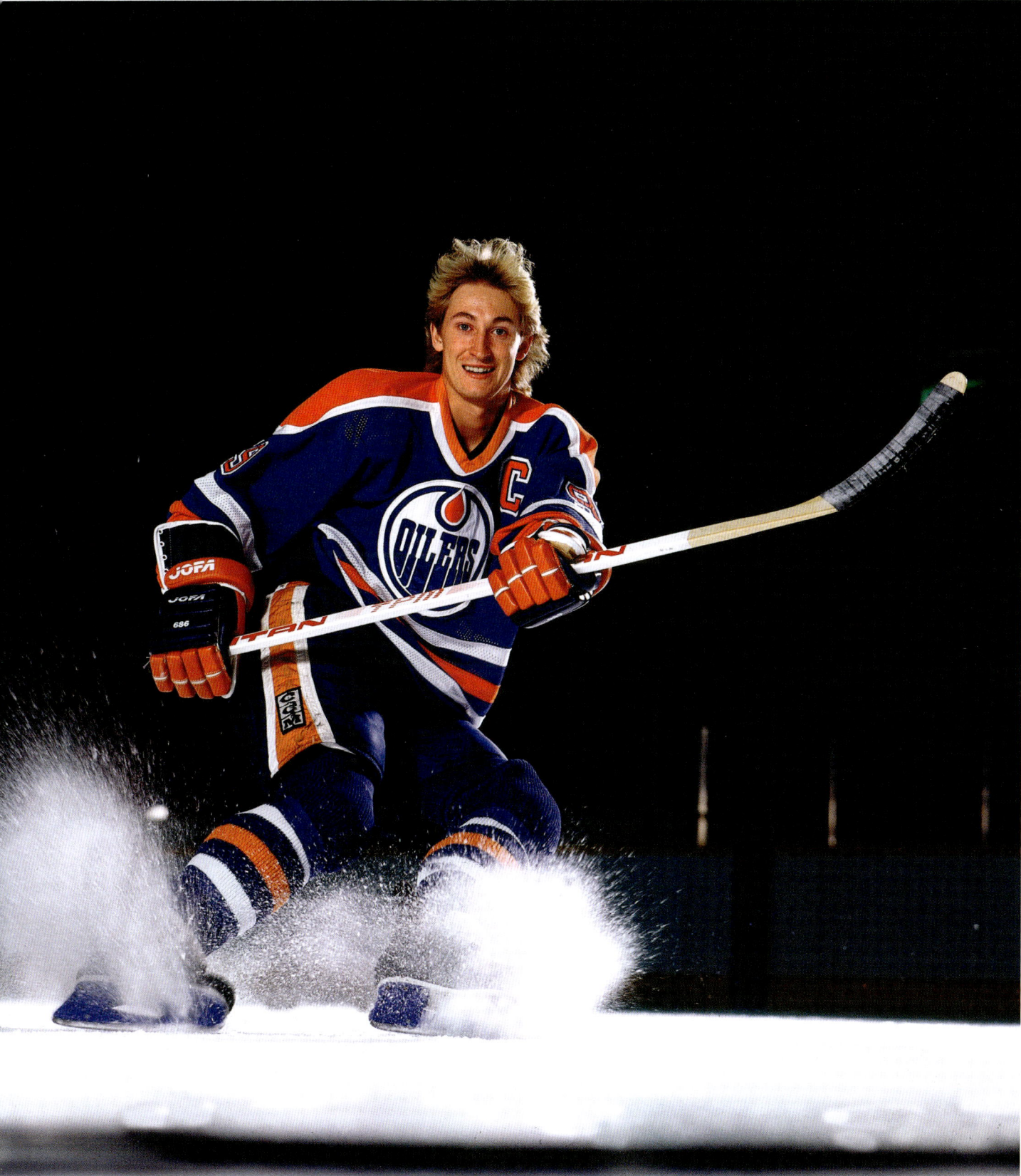

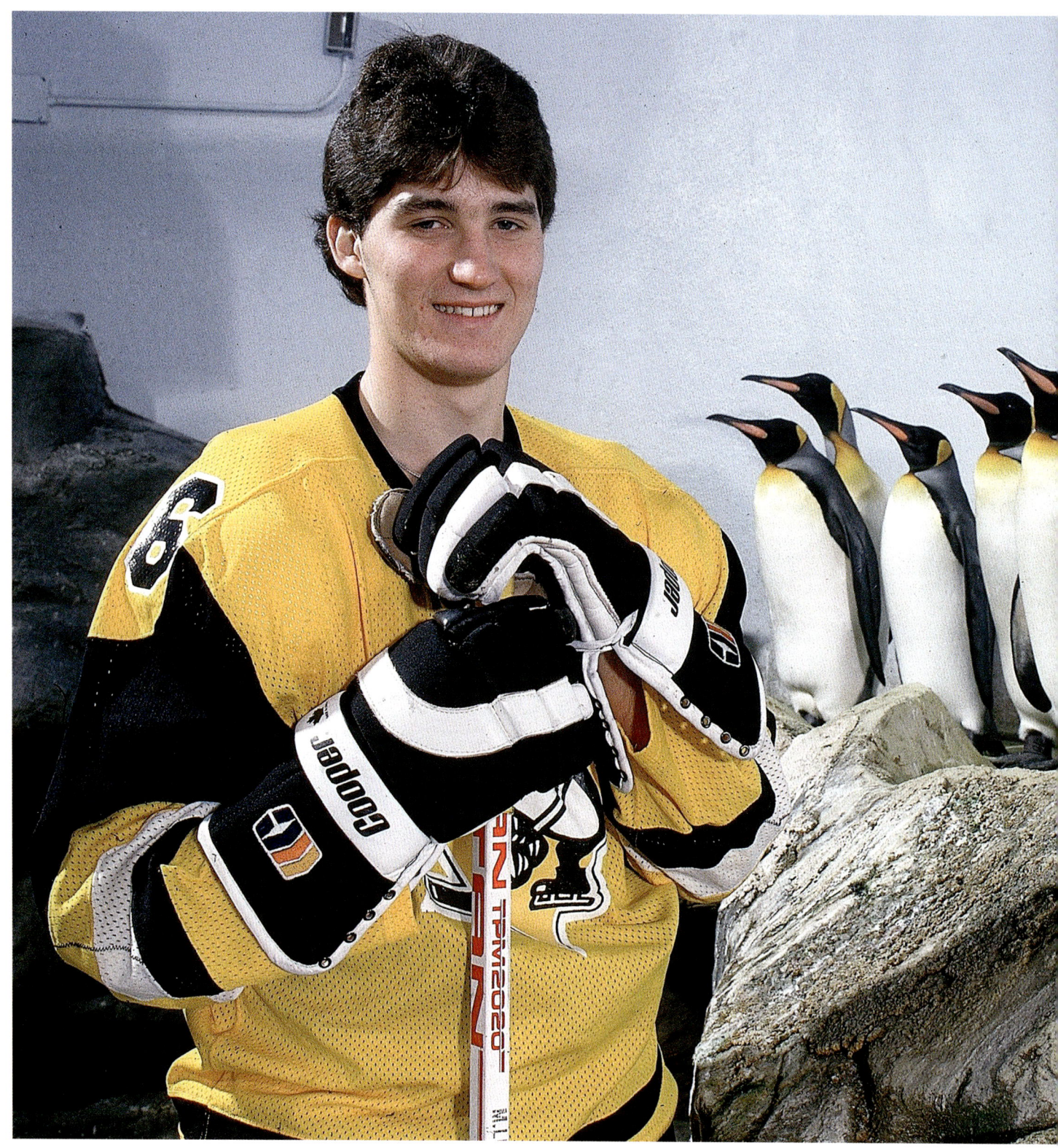

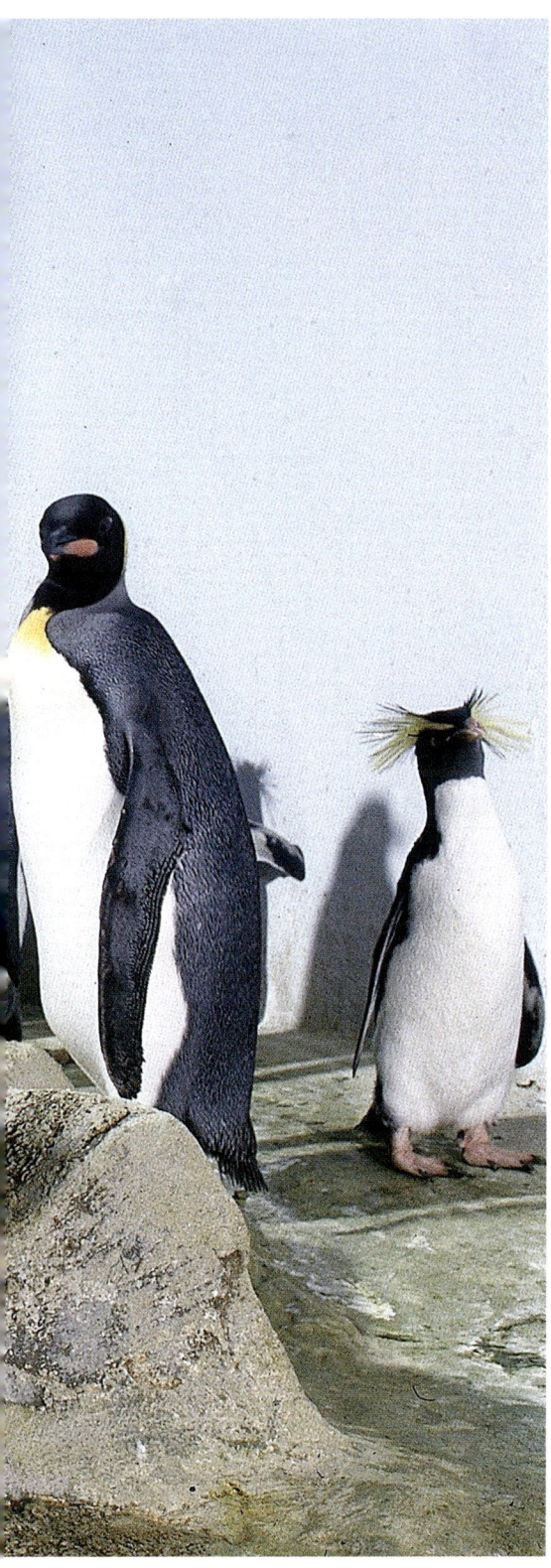

SUPER MARIO

PITTSBURGH ZOO, PITTSBURGH | *October 1, 1984*

THE LEAGUE'S ALSO-RANS traded accusations. "I think the Penguins' talent is better than they've shown," said a New Jersey Devils executive after Pittsburgh dropped their 48th game of the season. "What he said about our team is a disgrace," responded Pens coach Lou Angotti. "We do everything we can to win every game we can."

Sure, everyone wants to win. But in the 1983–84 season, losing had its benefits. The top draft pick was on the line, and this meant a chance to draft 18-year-old Mario Lemieux. The 6'4", 200-pound center finished his season in the Quebec Junior League with 113 goals and 282 points in 70 games. Never before in NHL history had a prospect so big, so skilled, so magnificent been available in the open amateur pool. (Previous phenoms from Bobby Orr to Wayne Gretzky had been snapped up before reaching the draft.) Even if the Penguins had done a little less than everything to win, they could be forgiven.

Lemieux arrived in Pittsburgh in the nick of time. Attendance for the perennially putrid Pens was down to 6,800 fans per game, and there were rumors of a move. Lemieux made his debut in Boston, on October 11, 1984. On his first shift, he stole the puck from future Hall of Famer Ray Bourque and scored a goal with his first shot. Lemieux went on to record 100 points (43 goals, 57 assists) and earn the Calder Trophy as top rookie.

In his fourth season, Lemieux wrested the Hart and Ross trophies from Gretzky. The Penguins also had their first winning season in a decade. The team's first championship came in 1991. Lemieux's breathtaking one-on-one goal in Game 2 against the Minnesota North Stars is in the annals of all-time greatest goals. But it was his dominant performance in Game 6 that took the Cup: a shorthanded goal and three assists in an 8–0 rout.

Whether or not the '83–84 Penguins laid down for Lemieux, the payoff was worth it. As goalie Tom Barrasso told *SI*, "There wasn't going to be hockey in Pittsburgh anymore if not for Mario."

Photograph by LANE STEWART

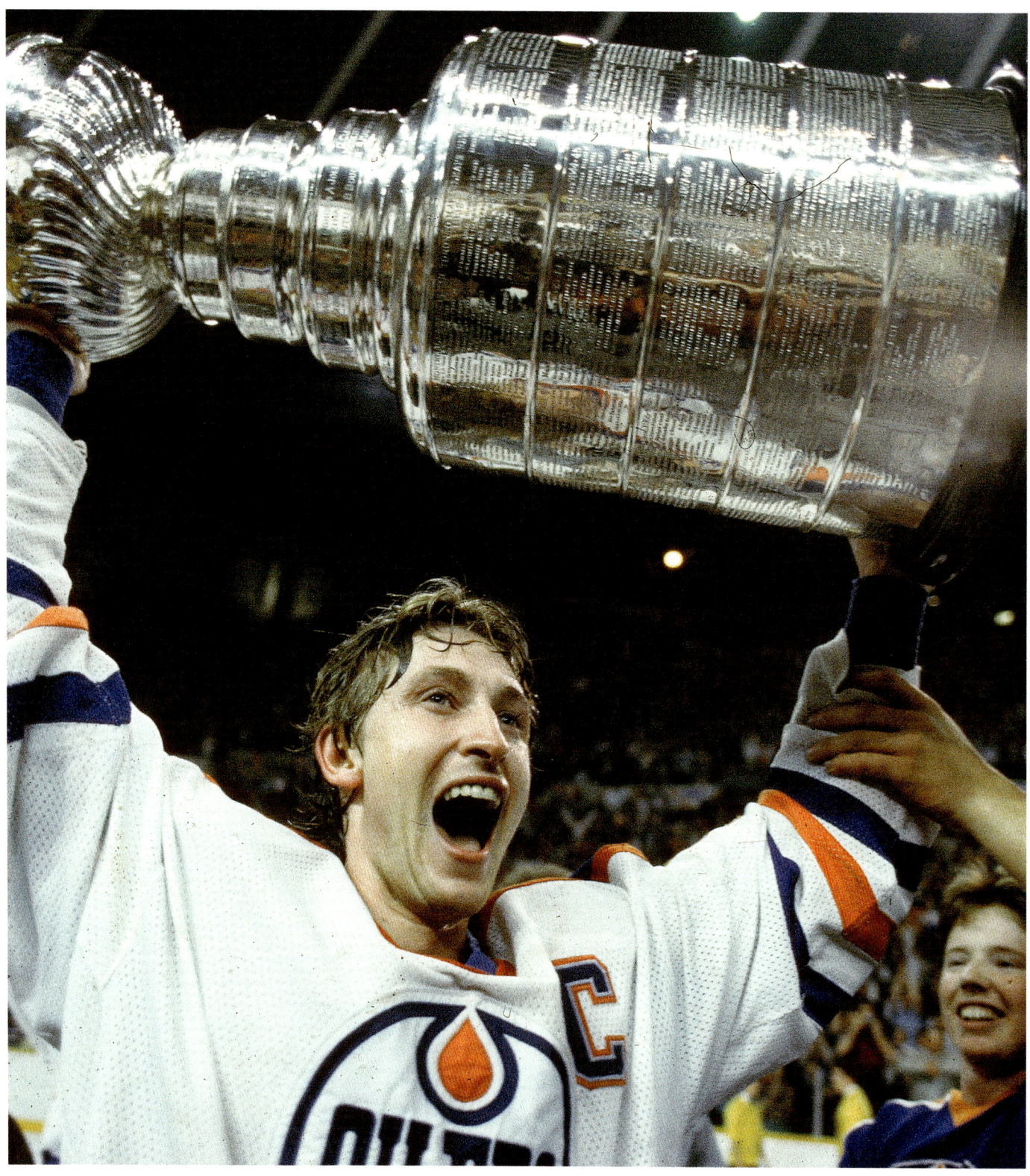

A WELL-OILED MACHINE

NORTHLANDS COLISEUM, EDMONTON | *May 19, 1984*

NO TEAM IN NHL history had a more potent attack. Along with the Boston Bruins of Bobby Orr and Phil Esposito, the 1980s Edmonton Oilers were the only team to average more than five goals per game. The Bruins did it once, in 1970–71. The Oilers did it *five seasons in a row*. During each of those five seasons, from 1981–82 to 1985–86, the team amassed more than 400 goals—the only teams ever to reach that mark. As a point of comparison, the highest-scoring team in 2024–25, the Tampa Bay Lightning, collected 294 goals in 82 games.

Of course there was Wayne Gretzky. These were the years of the Great One's most staggering production, when he set single-season records for goals (92 in 1981–82), assists (163 in 1985–86) and points (215 in 1985–86). Yet others could score as well, starting with linemate Jari Kurri. In 1985–86 the Finnish right wing matched Gretzky with 54 even-strength goals. The second line had Mark Messier and Glenn Anderson, who both notched 100 points in multiple seasons. And then there was defenseman Paul Coffey, whose single-

season marks for goals, assists and points put him in the company of Orr.

These five scorers are in the Hall of Fame, as are the two Oilers responsible for stopping opponents: defensemen Kevin Lowe and goalie Grant Fuhr. The dynasty's mastermind, coach and general manager Glen Sather, is also enshrined. Indeed, Sather was hailed during the '80s for devising the Oilers' revolutionary playing style, a combination of the physical North American game with the speed and creativity of European hockey.

This was the lasting legacy of the 1980s Oilers. "They radically changed hockey from the way North Americans had been playing it for the last 30 years," Ken Dryden told *Sports Illustrated* after Edmonton first won the Stanley Cup. None have equaled the Oilers' output, nor has any team matched their run of five titles in seven years. But throughout today's NHL, the Oilers' hybrid attack has plenty of imitators.

Photograph by BRUCE BENNETT STUDIOS

THE KING

MAPLE LEAF GARDENS, TORONTO | *October 26, 1985*

"WE ARE NOT chicken Swedes," declared Börje Salming to *Sports Illustrated* in the October 29, 1973, issue.

For years, "chicken Swede" was the taunt NHL players and fans directed at imports from Scandinavia. In North American eyes, Swedish players lacked the toughness to play the game the way it should be played. When Boston offered a tryout to Sven Tumba in the 1950s, Sweden's best forward got scornful looks even as he suited up in the locker room, especially when he put on a helmet. On the ice, the Bruins let him have it. "They never dared treat the players on the other team the same way they treated me in the practices," Tumba told *SI*.

By the early 1970s, expansion and the start of the WHA had drained Canadian sources of hockey talent. *SI*'s Mark Mulvoy reported that the NHL gave Sweden another look after Team Canada stopped to play the Swedish national squad in 1972, on their way to Moscow. In a 4–4 tie, the Swedes skated, slashed and speared with the Canadian pros. "It was obvious that some Swedes could play in the NHL as well as, if not better than, many of the Canadian-born professionals," Mulvoy wrote. The following year, Toronto signed two players from that Tre Kronor team, defenseman Salming and forward Inge Hammarström.

Hammarström never lived down the "chicken Swede" label. Leafs owner Harold Ballard scoffed that he "could go into the corner with a half a dozen eggs in his pocket and not break one of them." Salming was another matter. In his first game, the rookie defenseman was named first star. Even in the last 10 seconds of the game, with Toronto up 7–4, he was dropping to the ice to block shots. "This is the kind of player the Leafs need," declared the *Toronto Star*.

Salming played 16 seasons with the Leafs, gaining renown as one of the league's best defensemen. His lasting legacy was opening a path for his countrymen. Swedish players are no longer seen as chicken, but rather as the model for what an NHL player should be.

Photograph by GRAIG ABEL/GETTY IMAGES

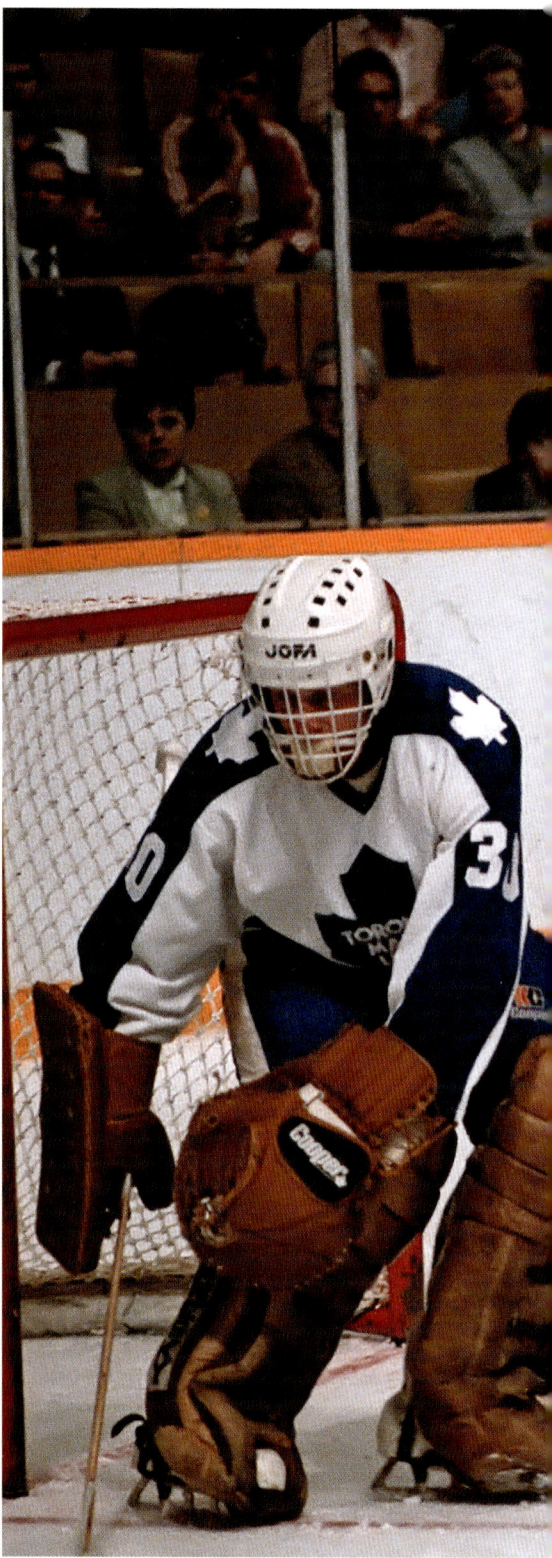

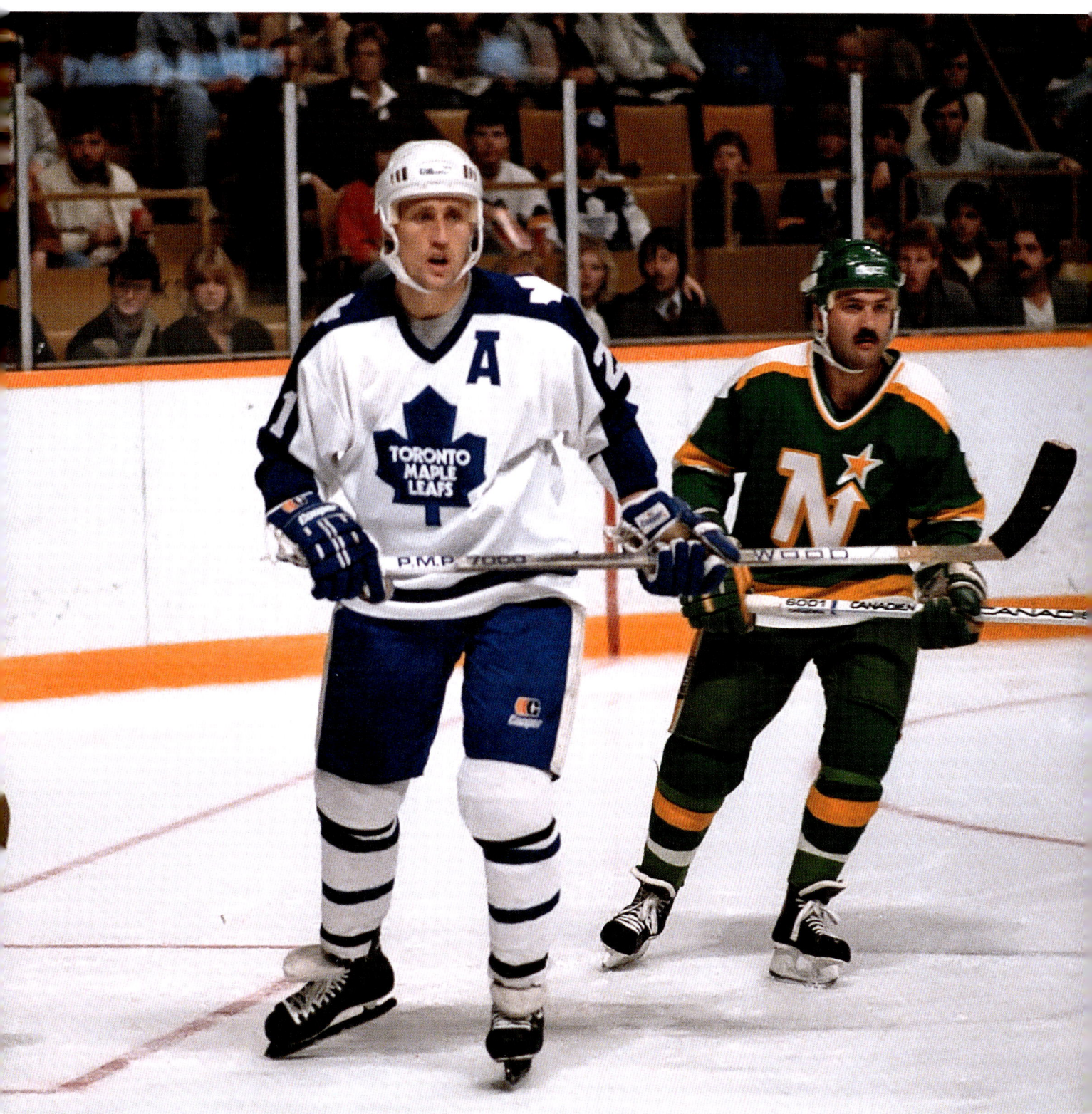

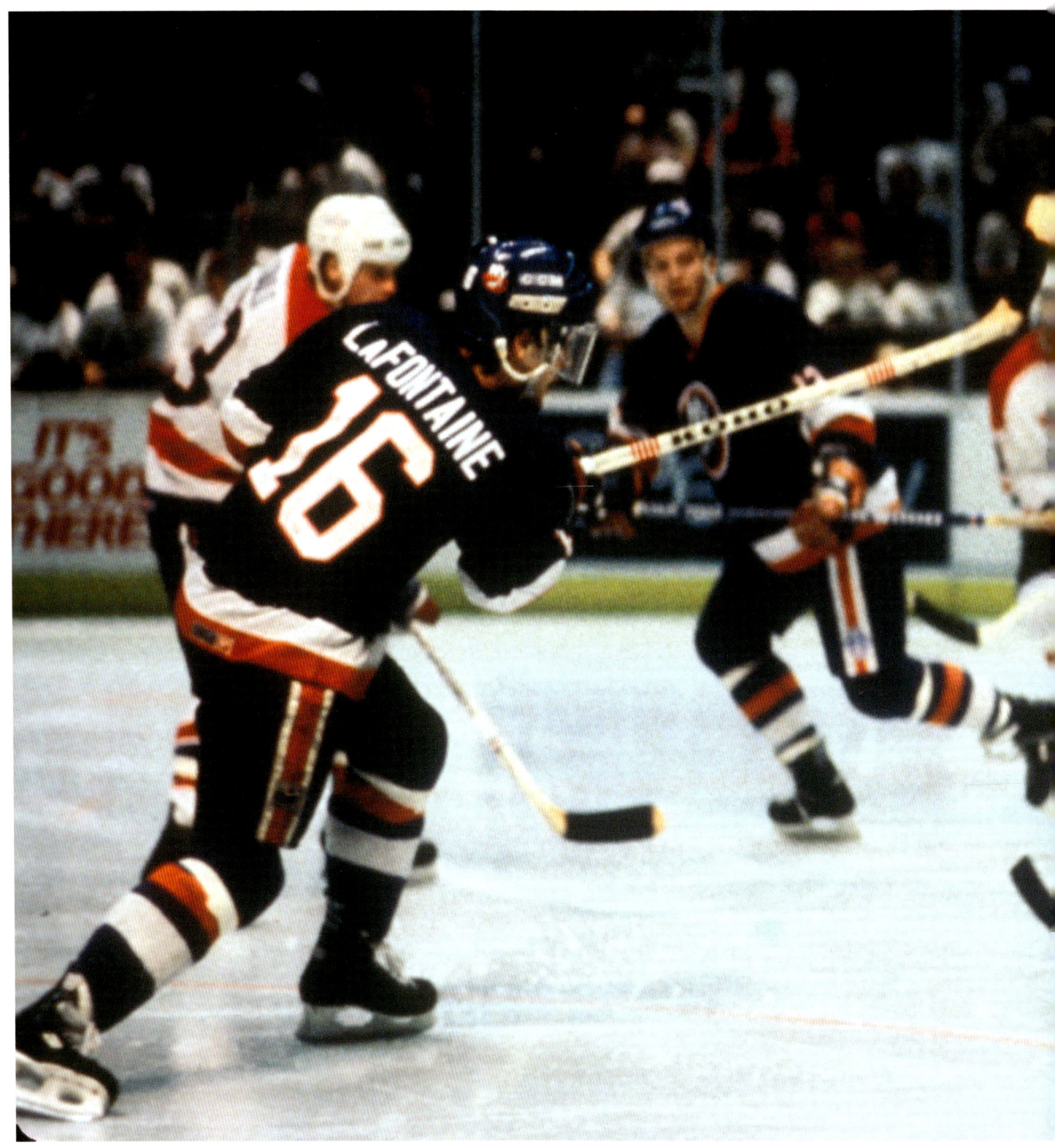

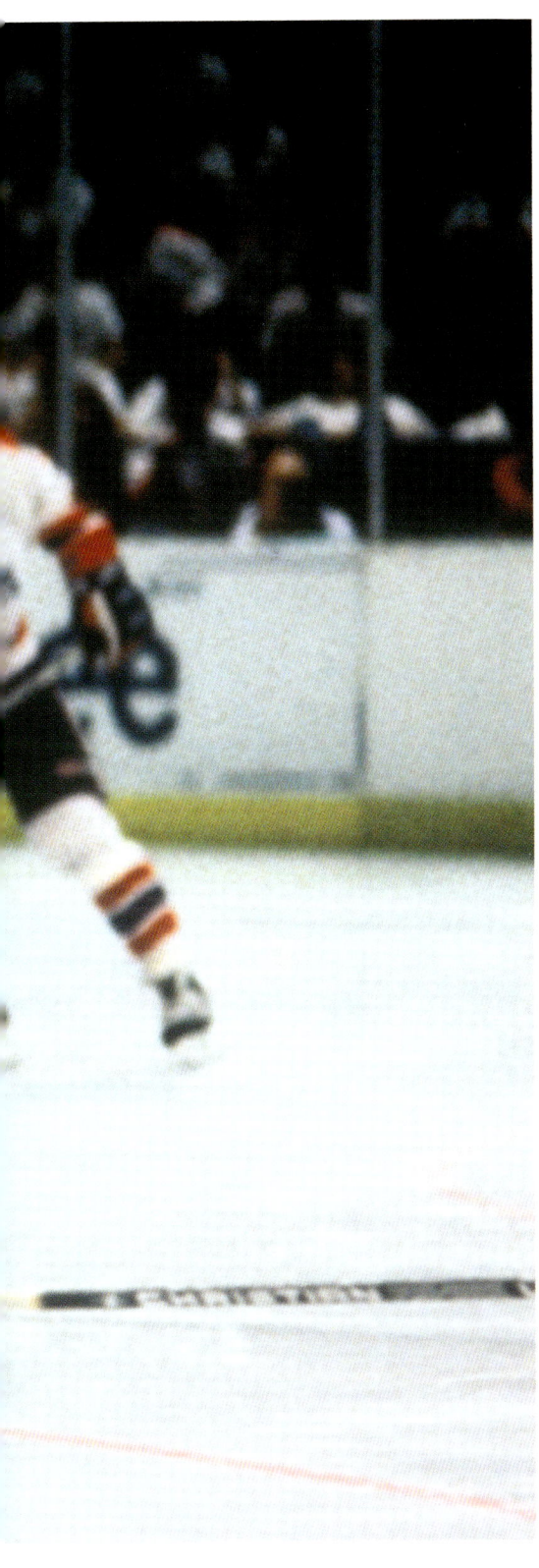

THE EASTER EPIC

CAPITAL CENTRE, LANDOVER, MARYLAND | *April 19, 1987*

WITH THE THIRD pick in the 1983 NHL Draft, the New York Islanders selected Pat LaFontaine. The Michigan native, who had racked up scoring records in Quebec's major junior league, was a solid third-line center for the Isles in his first seasons. His breakout came in 1986–87, most notably in the playoffs. Facing elimination in Game 6 against the Washington Capitals, LaFontaine led New York with two goals and an assist. Game 7 was scheduled for Saturday, April 18, in Capital Centre. Austin Murphy reported what happened in the next week's issue of *Sports Illustrated*:

> They began play at 7:40 on Saturday night, more than six hours ago. Right now the score is 2–2, and they have just begun their fourth 20-minute, sudden-death overtime period. Goaltender Kelly Hrudey of the Islanders, who has turned away 72 shots and will stop one more, has lost all track of time. The other players have long since stopped jumping over the boards to go out on their shifts, opting instead to shuffle through the door. Zamboni driver John Millsback has already groomed the ice seven times and still has no idea when he will be able to go home. "I'm down to a quarter tank," he says with concern.
>
> At 1:58 a.m., the fifth-longest game in NHL history—and the longest since 1943—ended abruptly when Islander center Pat LaFontaine beat goaltender Bob Mason with a 35-foot slap shot. LaFontaine's shot, the 57th that Mason had faced, came at 8:47 of the fourth OT, after the weary teams had played 68:47 of sudden death and 128:47 in all. The game was longer than two games….
>
> Because of exhaustion, the Islanders' exultation at their victory was tame. Few of the joyous, surprised, panting players could muster the strength to execute even a medium-high five. Besides, it was time to start thinking about Philadelphia . The Islanders would face the Flyers on Monday night, which had now become tomorrow.

LaFontaine's career led ultimately to the Hall of Fame. But he is remembered most for his goal early on Easter morning, with fans sleeping in their seats.

Photograph by BRUCE BENNETT STUDIOS

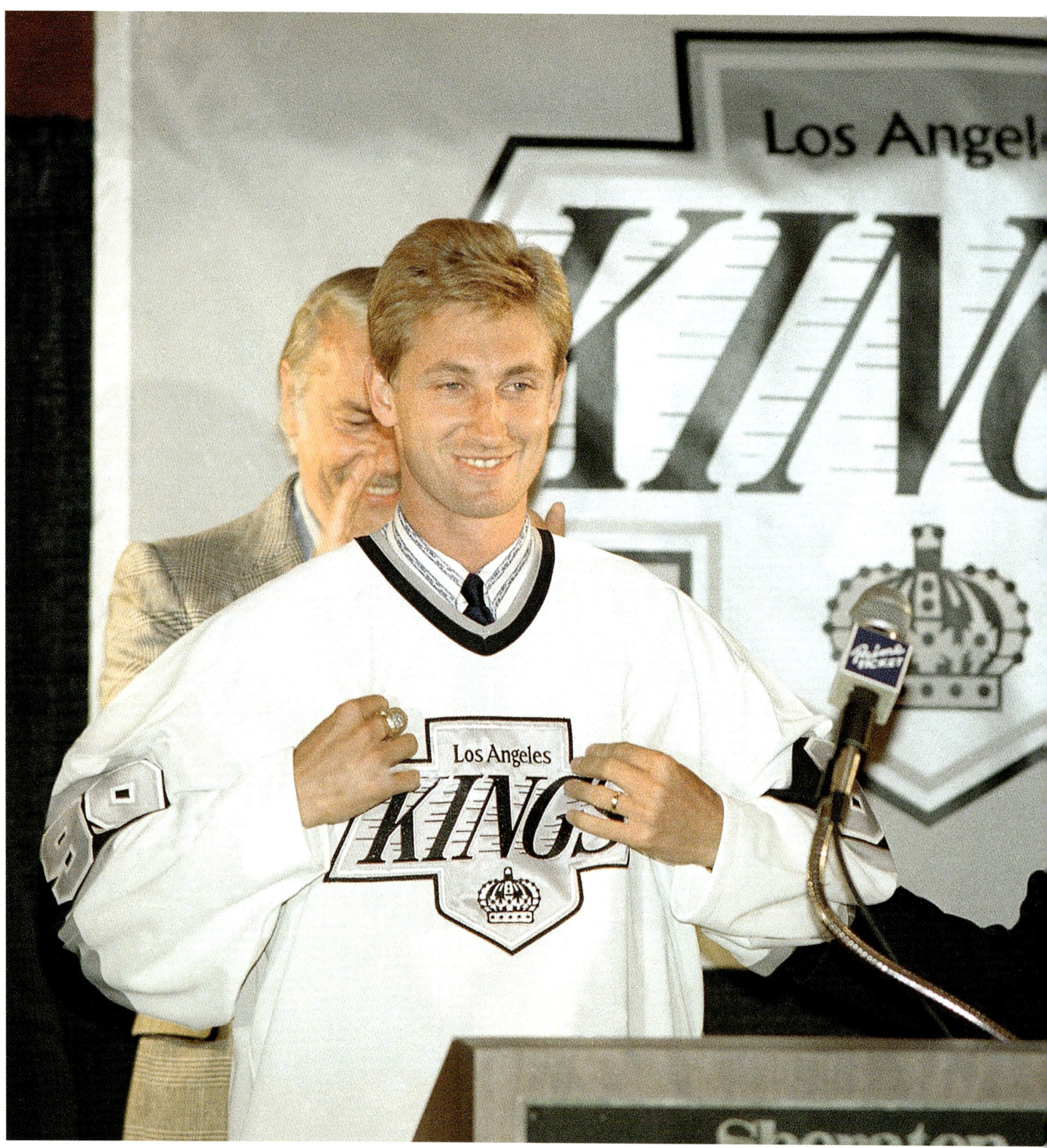

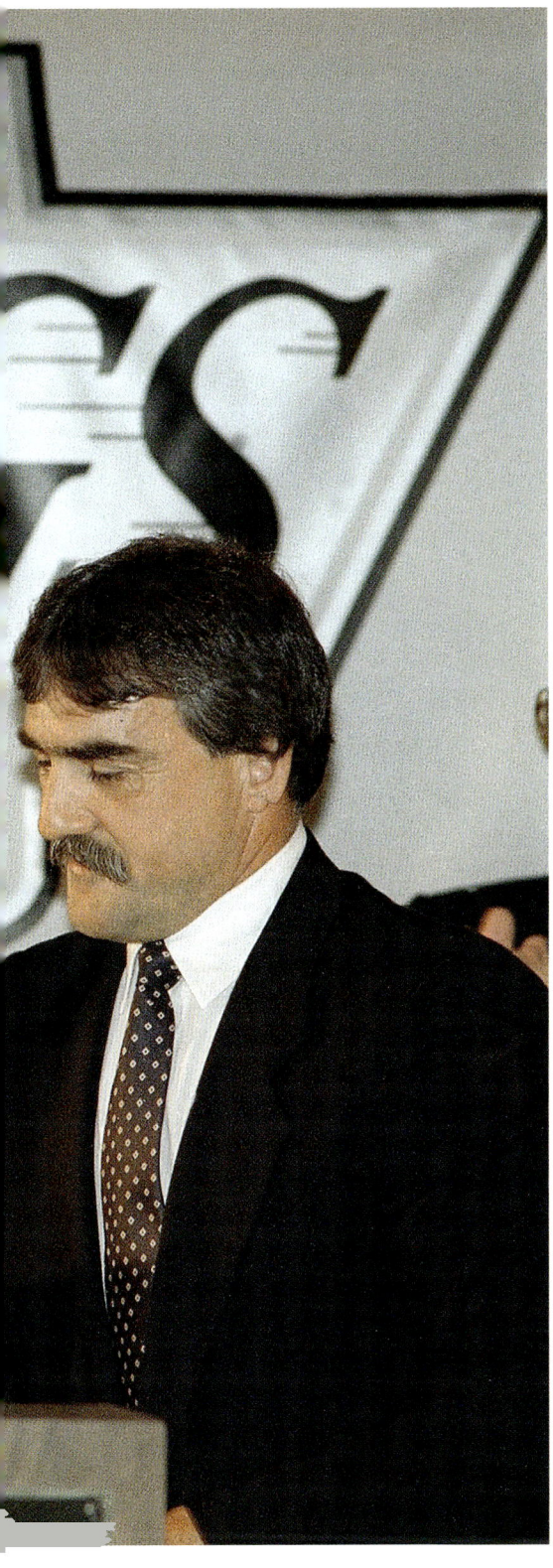

THE TRADE

SHERATON PLAZA LA REINA, LOS ANGELES | *August 10, 1988*

IN THE HEAT of August 1988, the winter game captured the sports world's attention. Hockey's biggest star was on his way from Edmonton to Los Angeles.

At age 27, Wayne Gretzky was still in his record-setting prime. Just a few months earlier, he had led the Oilers to their fourth Stanley Cup win in five years. Trading the Great One was a move for the history books, like the Red Sox sending Babe Ruth to the Yankees in 1920. Just as Sox owner Harry Frazee had sold his young star to boost investments outside baseball, the Trade was all about money. "All my companies are very healthy financially," Oilers owner Peter Pocklington told *Sports Illustrated*. He wasn't entirely truthful. Pocklington's bottom line had been rocked by collapsing oil and real estate markets. Along with players and draft picks, he got a much-need dose of cash from Kings owner Bruce McNall: $15 million ($41 million in 2025).

The Trade hit Canada like a seismic blast. Gretzky's departure was seen as further proof of the country's economic dependence on the United States. Worst of all was that their national treasure was going to California. "They might as well send Wayne to the moon as to L.A.," said a member of parliament. "Everybody knows that Los Angeles isn't a hockey town—they wouldn't know a hockey puck from a beach ball."

L.A. may not have been a hockey town, but it was a city of stars—and it knew a star when it saw one. Before the Great One arrived, the Kings were perennially near the bottom in attendance. Losses were in the millions. After the Trade, ticket orders poured in. The team's new black-and-silver jerseys flew off the racks. In the next two seasons, ticket revenue tripled; television rights nearly quadrupled.

The Trade transformed a franchise, and it transformed the NHL. The Kings' revival showed that hockey could thrive in places where snowflakes rarely fall. In the next decade, teams took root in San Jose, Dallas, Tampa Bay, Anaheim, Miami and Nashville. Even more than his records, this was the Great One's greatest legacy, that hockey could win fans in the Sun Belt.

Photograph by AP PHOTO/REED SAXON

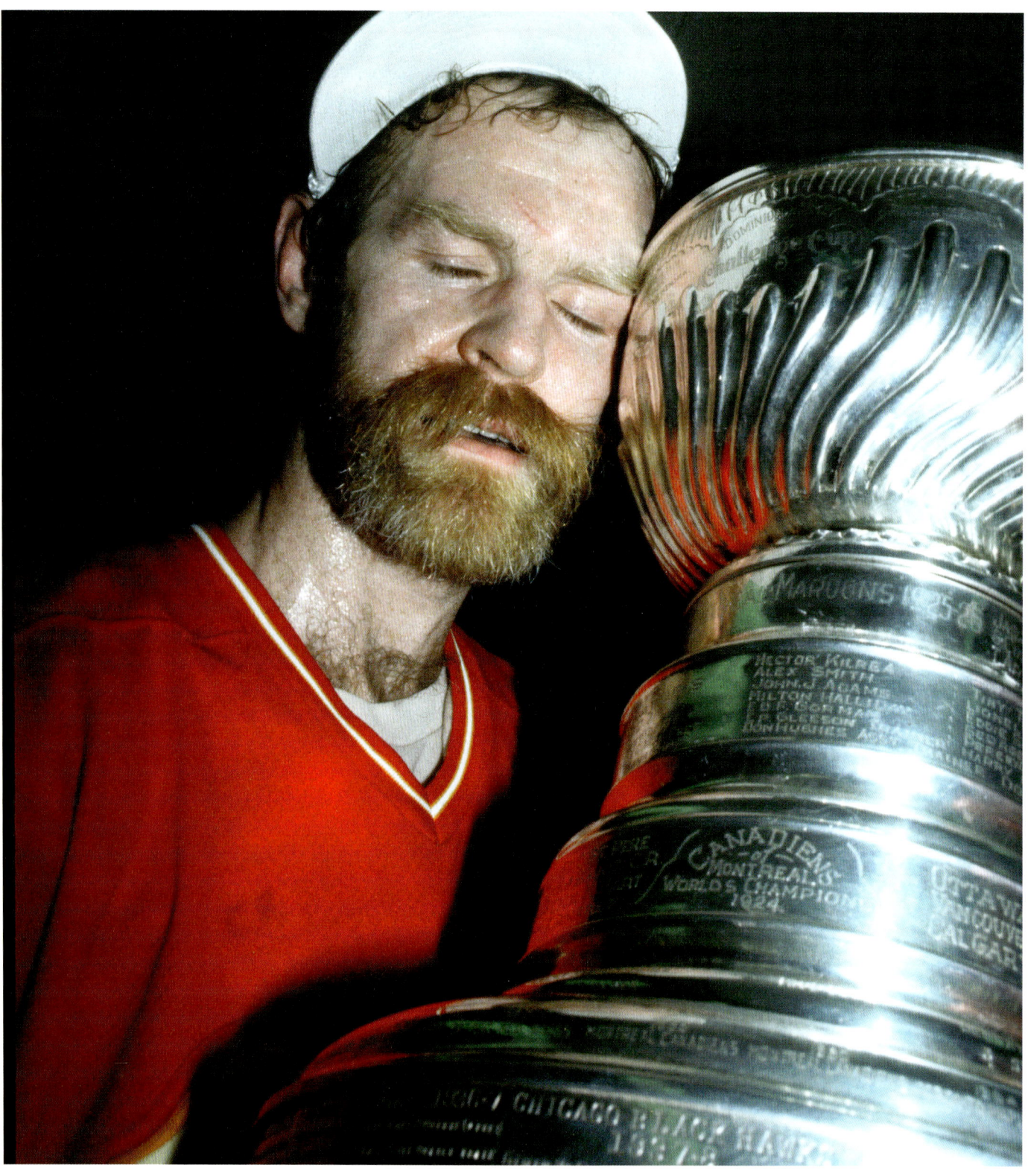

OLD 'STACHE

MONTREAL FORUM, MONTREAL | *May 25, 1989*

LANNY McDONALD KNEW how to finish a career. His last regular-season goal was number 500. His last playoff goal helped Calgary win the Stanley Cup. The Flames' captain was the first player in franchise history to have his number retired and the first to be inducted in the Hall of Fame.

But what he's remembered for is the moustache. Gloriously bushy and boldly red like the Flames' jerseys, McDonald's facial hair inspired Calgary fans to wear fake 'staches to games. Twenty years after retiring, McDonald's upper lip was still bristly when *Sports Illustrated* profiled him for the 2009 "Where are they now?" issue:

> The familiar moustache is faded from its old ginger to a bouquet of gold and gray, but it is still untamed in its glory and as dense as a James Joyce novel. Lanny McDonald has carried this tangle above his upper lip for 35 years, having spurned offers from razor companies to shave it. But like McDonald himself, the 'stache has never been for sale. There are things more important than money to this Hall of Fame winger, who believes in life, liberty and the hirsute of happiness.

According to the dictates of playoff hockey, McDonald's moustache flourished into a luxuriant beard in 1989. The Flames' two-month odyssey had carried them to a 3–2 lead over the Canadiens in the Stanley Cup Final, but McDonald mostly had been along for the ride…. He had no idea if he would be playing in the potentially decisive Game 6 in Montreal until 10 minutes before puck drop….

With the score 1–1 in the second period, McDonald came out of the penalty box after a hooking minor—"As a good Catholic boy, I said 200 Hail Marys in the box hoping they wouldn't score"—took a feathered pass from Joe Nieuwendyk and roofed a shot over goalie Patrick Roy. Calgary won 4–2.

Lanny McDonald now owns a microbrewery in Montana. If you stop in, you can order a barrel-aged porter appropriately named Old 'Stache.

Photograph by BRUCE BENNETT STUDIOS

A CHERRY ON TOP

Circa 1991

IN 1980, DON Cherry was out of work after steering the Colorado Rockies to the NHL's worst record. The former coach took a test run as color man on game broadcasts, but he tended to root for—and against—certain teams. Producers at CBC decided to try something new. Starting in 1982, they sat Cherry next to an announcer after the first period of the weekly *Hockey Night in Canada* game. Cherry had a couple of minutes to share his opinions about the week in the NHL. The segment, called "Coach's Corner," was a hit.

A decade later, in the March 29, 1993, issue of *Sports Illustrated*, Leigh Montville took stock of Cherry's standing in Canada:

> Polls have shown that he is the most recognizable figure in the country, more recognizable than any pop star, any politician, even any of the hockey players he discusses. He is so big that he cannot walk on any street in Canada without drawing a crowd. He is so big that he doesn't do banquets anymore, can't, because the demand is so great. He is so big that there have been petitions to put him on the ballot to replace the retiring Brian Mulroney as prime minister. Prime minister? How did this happen?

Cherry had indeed reached a level of renown matched by few Canadians. A 2004 poll named him the seventh greatest person in Canada's history, topping even the Great One himself. Unlike Wayne Gretzky, Cherry saw his influence as extending far beyond hockey. "Coach's Corner" was his platform to extol the virtues of community and patriotism—and, of course, hard-nosed hockey. He ranted against Europeans ruining the Canadian game, as well as foreigners ruining the Canadian nation.

Cherry was a master showman, but the routine wasn't an act. "I'm trying to keep this country together," he told a Canadian interviewer, "I'm the f------ glue that holds it together." Producers put his commentary on a delay, yet offensive remarks still hit the airwaves. An on-air rant against immigrants led to his firing in 2019. When Cherry left "Coach's Corner," he was the most popular man in Canadian sports media, and the most hated.

Photograph by BRUCE BENNETT STUDIOS

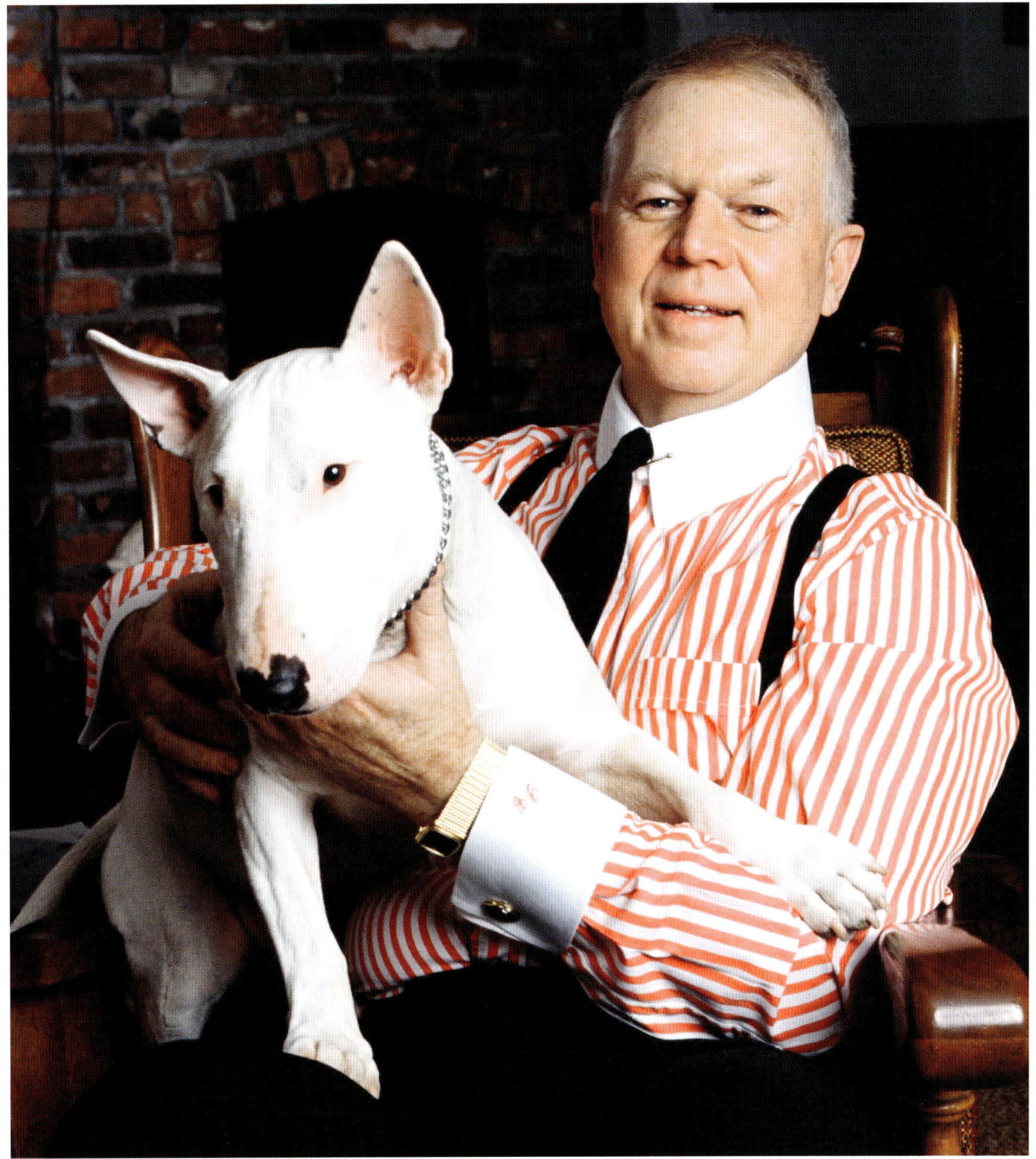

SAINT PATRICK

Circa 1991

THE CALGARY FLAMES sending rookie Brett Hull to the St. Louis Blues. The Detroit Red Wings shipping Marcel Dionne to L.A. Edmonton unloading the Great One, and then trading Mark Messier three years later.

Near the top of any list of the worst trades in NHL history is the midseason deal swung on December 6, 1995, by Montreal Canadiens GM Rejean Houle. Just six weeks on the job, Houle looked to resolve a standoff between goalie Patrick Roy and first-year coach Mario Tremblay. There was already bad blood from their days as teammates, and tensions boiled over in a blowout loss to the Red Wings. Even though it was clear his All-Star goalie was having a bad night, Tremblay left Roy in the game. Nine goals later, he finally relieved the battered star.

"It's my last game in Montreal," Roy declared as he stepped off the ice.

Four days later, the GM sided with his rookie coach over one of the best goalies ever. "Nobody's more important than the team," Houle remarked.

Roy was sent to Colorado, along with his three Vezina Trophies and two playoff MVP awards, earned when he twice led the Canadiens to the Stanley Cup. Roy lifted the Cup again six months after the trade. In the deciding game, he stopped all 63 shots he faced, shutting out Florida in three overtimes.

When *Sports Illustrated* saluted Roy on his retirement, in 2003, writer Michael Farber dubbed him the best NHL goalie ever, an influential athlete who redefined how the position was played:

His litany of accomplishments includes 551 regular-season wins, 151 playoff victories, two Stanley Cups each with the Montreal Canadiens and the Colorado Avalanche, and three Conn Smythe Trophies. Roy, 37, was a technical goalie, scientifically precise on his angles as he dropped into his familiar butterfly: pads splayed and stick covering the five hole, leaving only pinpricks of daylight over his shoulders at which shooters could aim.

Farber asked Roy which shooters he had feared most in his 19-season career. "To be honest with you," Roy answered, "there's none." An innovator, a champion and always uncompromising.

Photograph by DENIS BRODEUR/NHLI

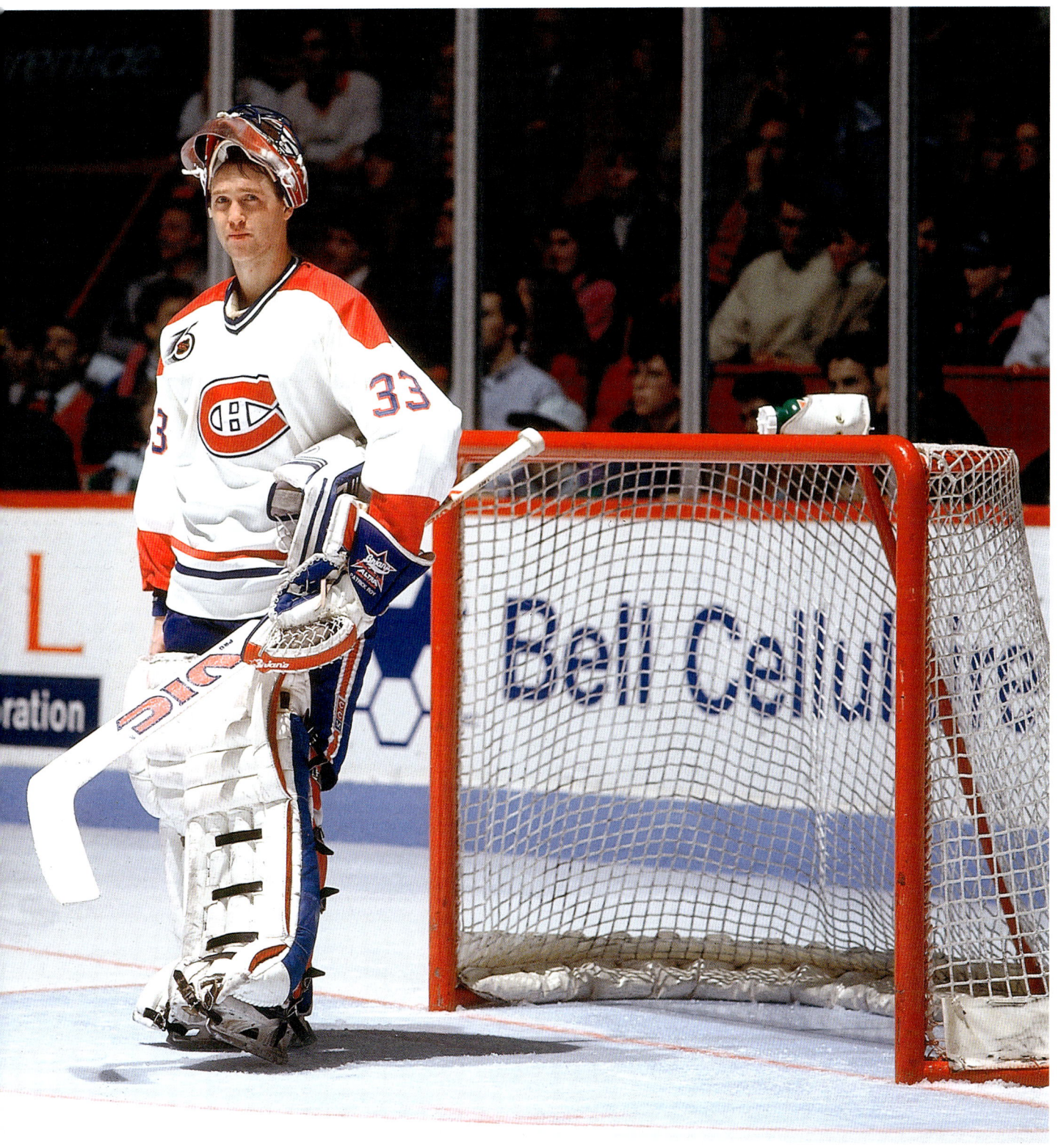

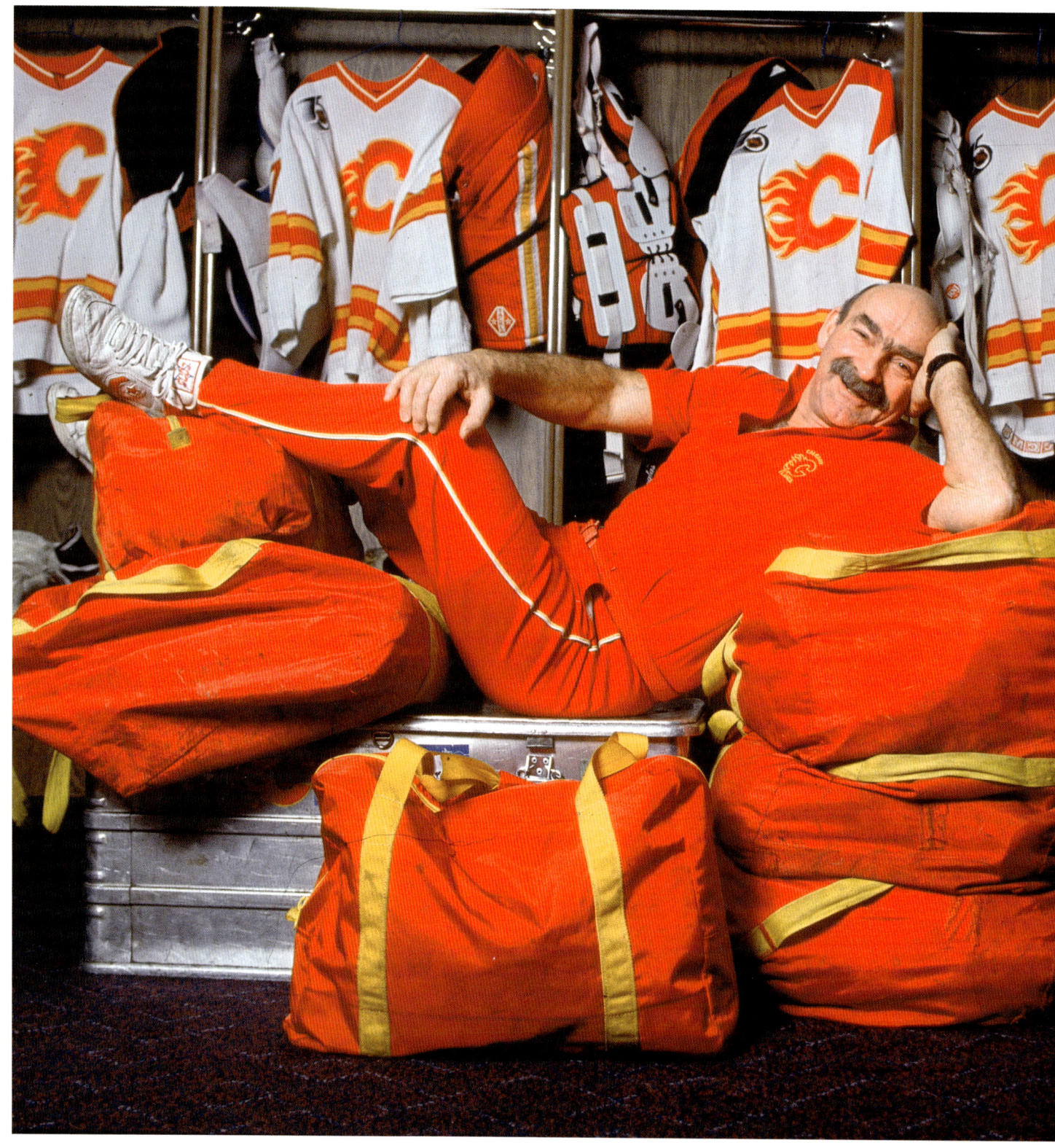

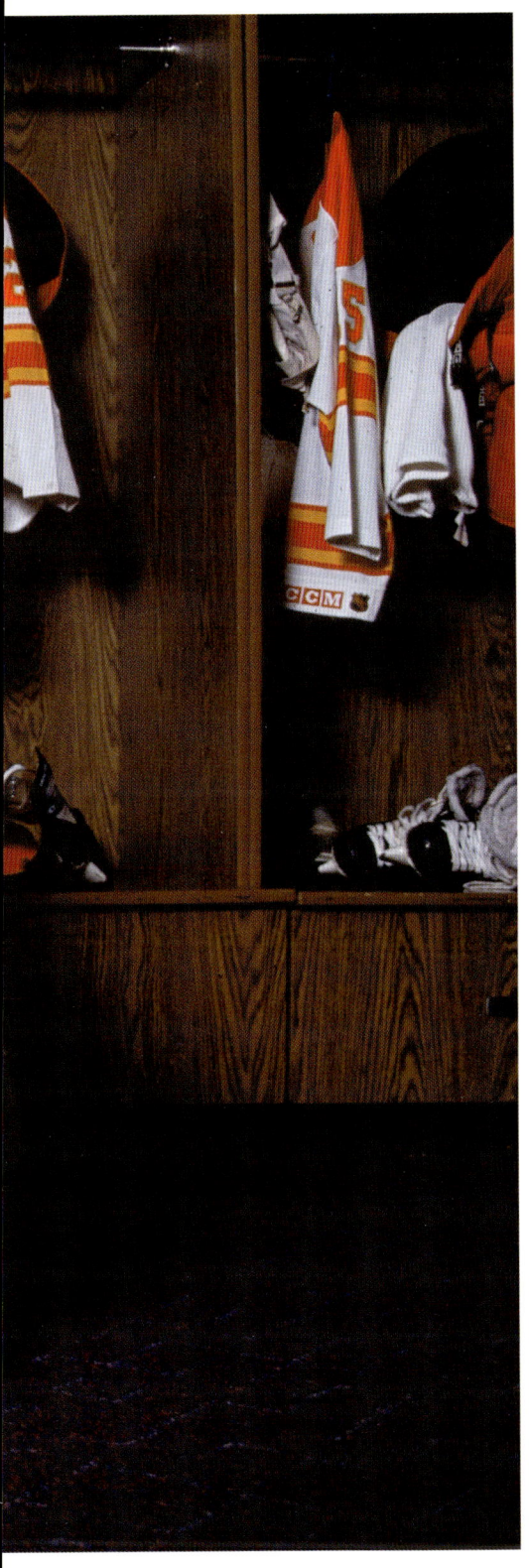

THE UNSUNG HEROES

OLYMPIC SADDLEDOME, CALGARY | *February 1, 1992*

AN NHL ROSTER has 23 players. Four coaches are allowed on the bench, with another two to four watching from above. Beyond that, a team will have upwards of 100 people on the payroll, from the GM to scouts, dieticians to conditioning coaches, data analysts to equipment managers. It is a major undertaking to get a hockey team on the ice, let alone to keep players fed, clothed and stitched up for up to nine months.

Few of the people who do this behind-the-scenes work get their moment in the spotlight. Even when a team wins the Stanley Cup, only 52 names can be engraved on the trophy's base. One of the names carved in silver with the 1989 Calgary Flames is Jim Murray. Space didn't allow for his sobriquet, the name by which he was famous throughout the NHL: Bearcat.

Before the Flames moved to Calgary in 1980, Bearcat Murray was a mainstay in Alberta hockey—coaching kids, sharpening skates, stitching cuts. He learned the craft of being a hockey trainer on the job. "He was always reading, studying, making himself better at his job," said former Flame Perry Berezan. "You felt safe with him."

Nevertheless, Bearcat didn't always follow standard procedure. One of his best-known moments came when he leaped over the boards to check on goalie Mike Vernon, while play was still going on at the opposite end. The Flames scored a goal on the rush, and the Los Angeles Kings went crazy. "[Wayne] Gretzky was going ballistic," Vernon recalled. To top it off, the goalie had faked his injury, in hope of drawing a penalty.

"All of a sudden there's Bearcat kneeling overtop of me," Vernon told the *Calgary Herald.* "'Vernie, Vernie, are you hurt?' I told him: 'No, Bear, I'm fine.'"

Bearcat also ignored protocol when Prince Albert of Monaco visited Calgary and was introduced to one of the city's celebrities. The short, balding hockey trainer with the bushy moustache didn't quite catch the royal visitor's name.

"I've got friends in Prince Albert," Bearcat replied, referring to the metropolis of northern Saskatchewan. "Colder 'n hell up there!"

Photograph by BRUCE BENNETT STUDIOS

THE AGELESS WONDER

PITTSBURGH CIVIC CENTER, PITTSBURGH | *May 26, 1992*

IN THE EARLY 1990s the National Hockey League became a global league. Europeans and Russians amounted to 15 percent of the NHL's total number of players. Future Hall of Famers like Nicklas Lidström, Teemu Selänne, Dominik Hašek and Sergei Fedorov made their debuts.

Another European from this era is a lock for the Hall, if he will ever stop playing. As of 2025, 53-year-old Jaromír Jágr was still taking the ice for his hometown club, the Kladno Knights (which Jágr also owns). The three-year waiting period for induction into the Hall of Fame won't begin until the ageless Czech forward finally hangs up his skates.

In 1990, when Jágr made his debut for the Pittsburgh Penguins, few would have predicted that he would still be taking shifts 35 years later. As a rookie, he was stunned by the length and intensity of an NHL season. He was also hit hard by homesickness. Although he was a fan favorite in Pittsburgh, thanks to his iconic mullet and his radio weather reports delivered in broken English, teammates saw the toll. He spent hours on the ice by himself. Even four seasons later, after winning the Stanley Cup twice with the Pens, Jágr still longed for home. As he explained to Garry Callahan for a 1995 *Sports Illustrated* profile, "Sometimes I wish I could bring Czechoslovakia to America. Then I would be the happiest guy in the world."

When Jágr's NHL career came to an end, in 2018, the withdrawn young man was long in the past. A platoon of fans followed him around the league, wearing jerseys of the nine different teams he played for—along with fake mullets. He was now one of the game's most quotable stars and a master of social media, along with being one of the all-time leaders in career goals, assists and points. (Only Wayne Gretzky has scored more NHL points than Jágr.) The long hours he spent on the ice as a homesick rookie transformed into long hours of conditioning that kept him in the NHL for a quarter-century, and still keep him out of the Hall of Fame.

Photograph by BRUCE BENNETT STUDIOS

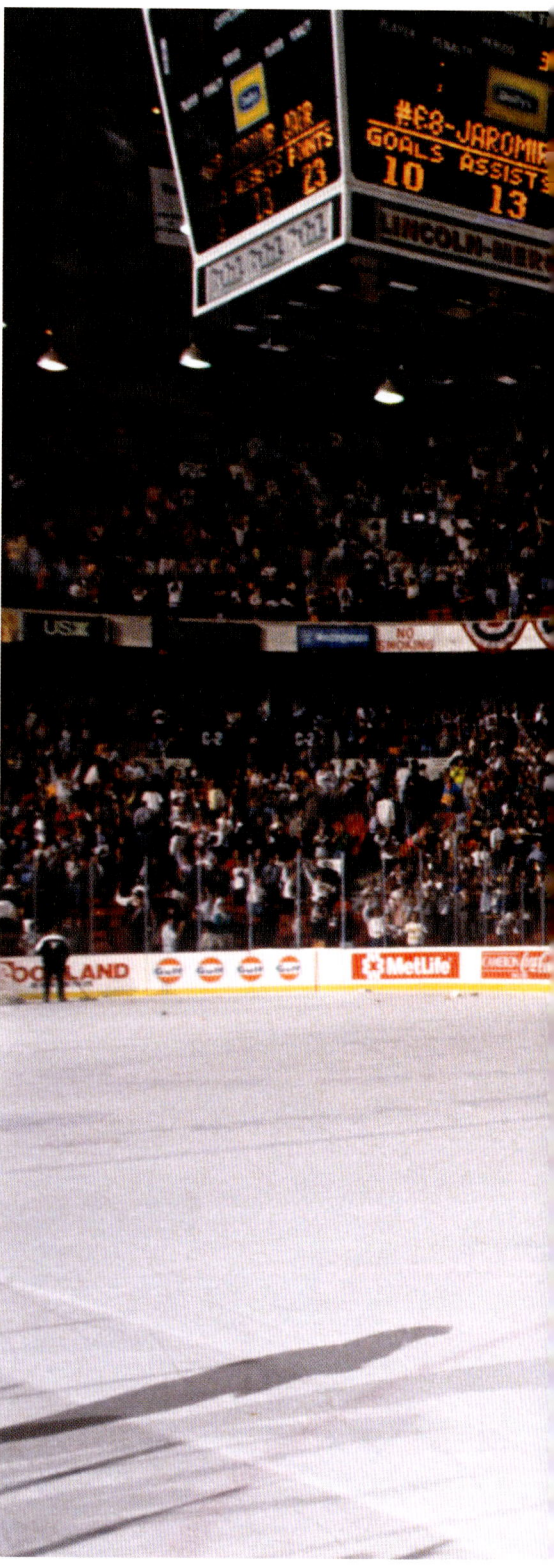

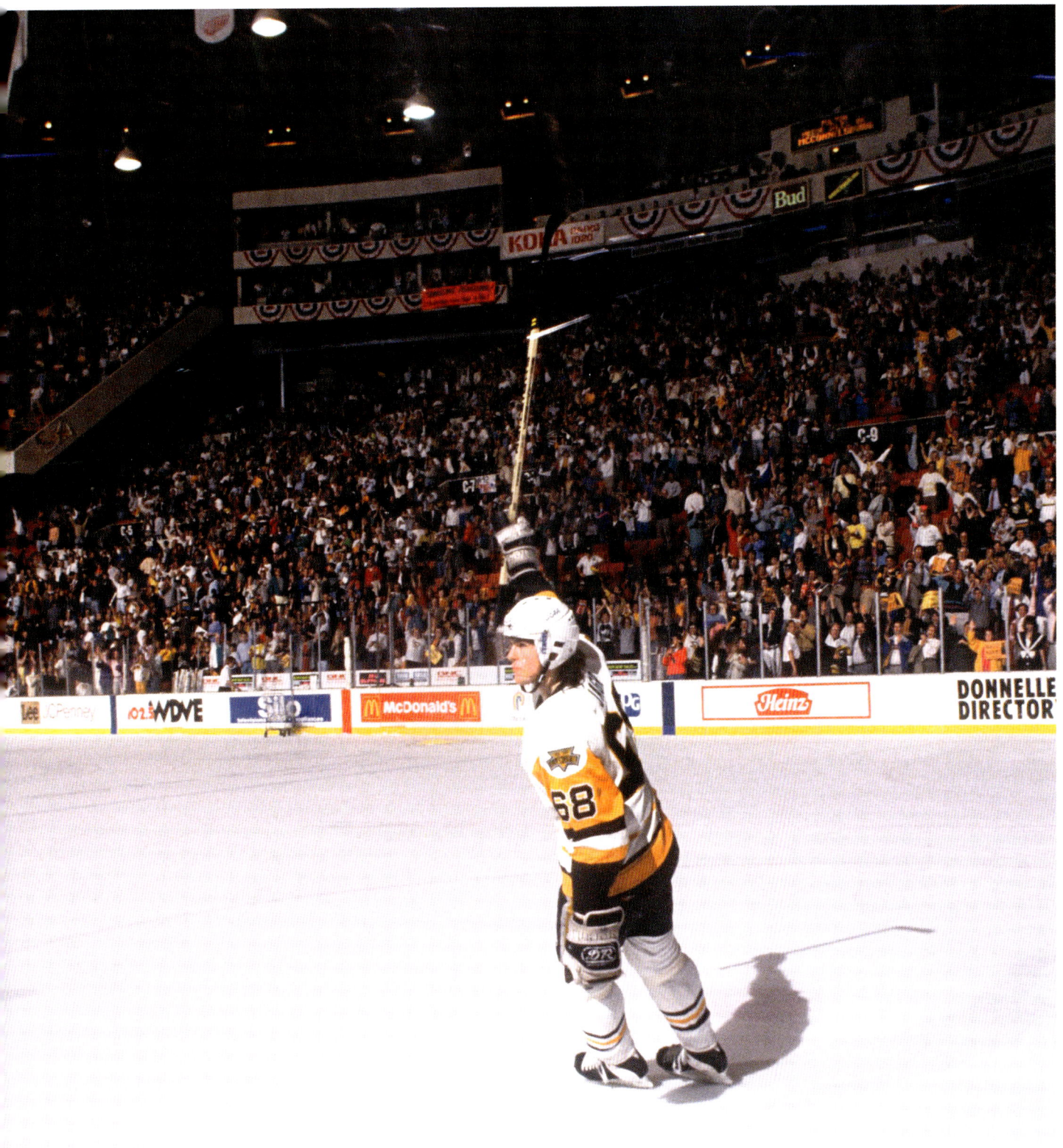

FOWL PLAY

ANAHEIM, CALIFORNIA | *March 1, 1993*

IF THE UNVEILING was any indication, these Ducks were going to be lame. The quack calls, the ugly green jersey, the Frontierland banner—the design team didn't put a lot of time or money into the press conference announcing the NHL's 26th franchise.

First, there was that name. *The Mighty Ducks* was the title of Disney's 1992 comedy film about a rag-tag team of kids playing hockey at a neighborhood park in Minnesota. Even in Southern California, the name brought howls of laughter. In Canada, the Mighty Ducks were an abomination. "The whir you hear is Lord Stanley spinning in his grave," grumbled the *Montreal Gazette*.

Others recognized that Disney's arrival was no laughing matter. Just as Tex Rickard remade pro hockey in the 1920s by bringing the sport to Madison Square Garden, the creation of a Disney-owned franchise in Southern California pushed hockey into a new age. By the time the Mighty Ducks played their first game, in October 1993, marketing had worked out the kinks. On opening night at The Pond, Anaheim's new $123 million arena, fans cleared the racks of merch—redesigned in eggplant-and-jade with a menacing goalie-mask logo. The Mighty Ducks brought in $300,000 that night and went on to sell more gear in 1994 than any other U.S. pro team, in any sport. When sales dropped in subsequent years, Disney designed colorful variations on the home and away jerseys to keep cash registers ringing.

Many of the marketing devices Disney introduced in the early 1990s, such as third and fourth jerseys, are now standard in the NHL. Today's pregame spectacles featuring images projected on the ice are a direct descendent of the Mighty Ducks' openings. Disney stayed in the hockey business only 13 years before selling the franchise, but the sport bears the imprint of their innovations. The Mighty Ducks ushered in an era in which sport, entertainment, media and merchandise were not a clamor of quack calls but a perfect harmony.

Photograph by AP PHOTO/DOUG PIZAC

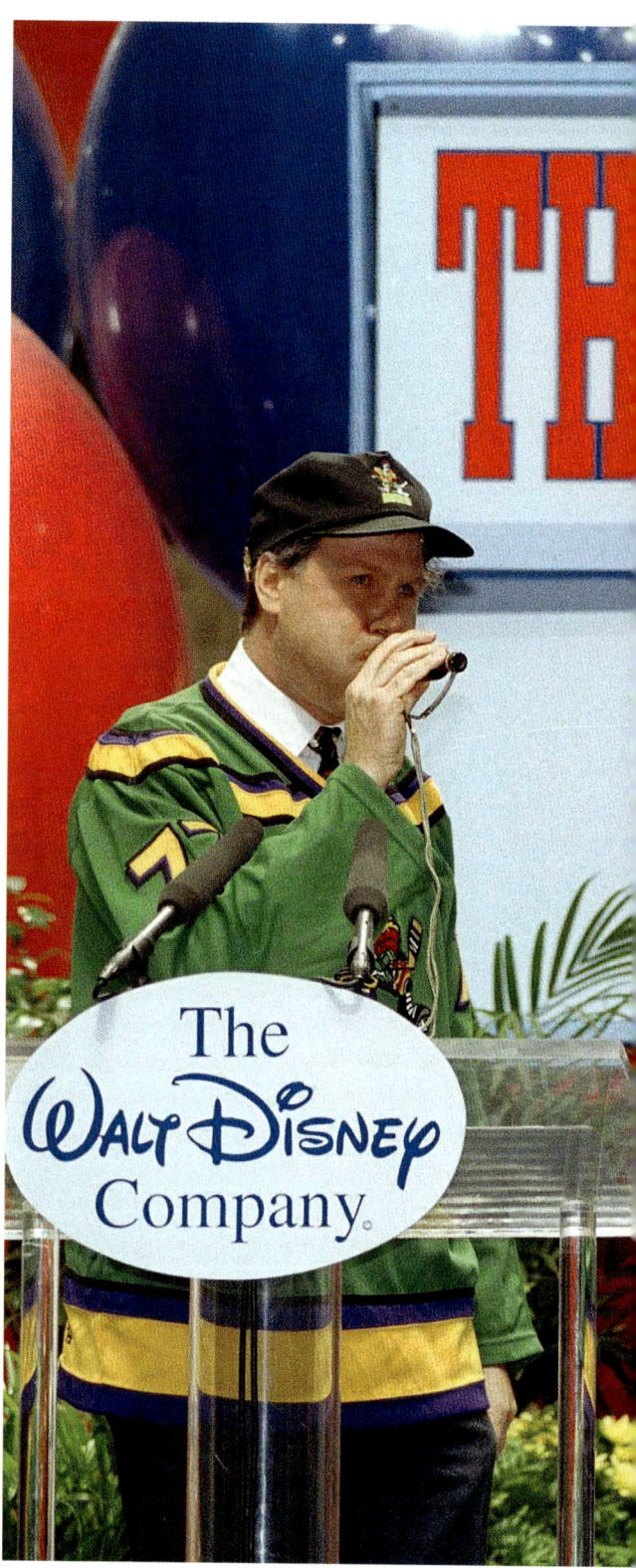

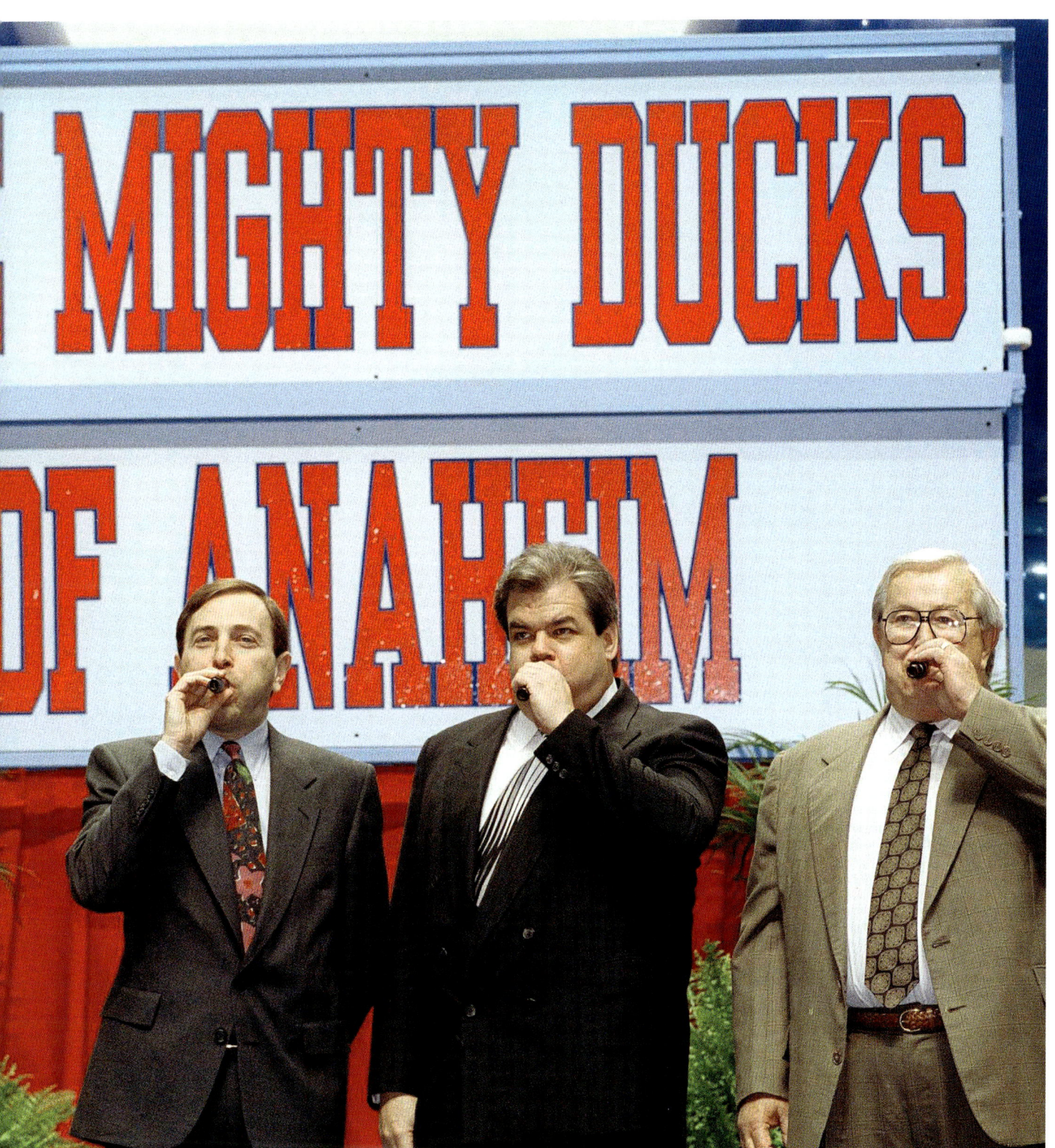

THE NEXT ONE

MIAMI | *Circa 1993*

ERIC LINDROS WAS destined to be the player of his generation, the next phenom who would claim Hart Trophies, Art Ross Trophies and the Stanley Cup. He was dubbed the Next One, the player who would follow the Great One.

"There has never before been a player with his combination of size, strength, power, speed and playmaking ability," wrote Michael Farber in the February 9, 1995, issue of *Sports Illustrated.* In his first two injury-shortened seasons, Lindros averaged 1.4 points per game. "There is little doubt that, if he stays healthy, he will dominate the NHL for years to come," Farber judged.

In the next seasons, it appeared *SI*'s prediction was spot-on. Lindros tallied 115 points in 1995–96. The next season, after missing 30 games due to injuries, he was the top scorer in the playoffs while leading the Philadelphia Flyers to the Final. He notched his 500th career point on February 28, 1998, the fifth-fastest player in NHL history to reach the milestone. Only Wayne Gretzky, Mario Lemieux, Mike Bossy and Peter Šťastný hit the mark earlier.

A week later, he suffered his first concussion. The Flyers sent him to a migraine specialist. In the 1999–2000 season, he suffered five more concussions. His parents feuded openly with the Flyers about his health care, particularly with general manager Bobby Clarke. The Flyers responded by stripping his captaincy. Choosing to leave Philadelphia, Lindros played five more seasons, for the New York Rangers, Toronto Maple Leafs and Dallas Stars. But he was a role player rather than the player of his generation. He retired in 2007.

SI profiled Lindros again in 2017, when he was pushing for greater attention to head injuries in sports. Lindros pointed out that change had already come. When Sidney Crosby fell victim to concussions, Pittsburgh Penguins coaches, execs and fans all recognized his health was more important than his team. "Concussions are part of the Crosby story, just as they were part of Lindros's, but it's a different ending," *SI* observed. "This makes Lindros happy."

"He's got the respect," Lindros said of Crosby. Unfortunately, this respect for injured players came only through Lindros's trials.

Photograph by AP PHOTO/AL MESSERSCHMIDT

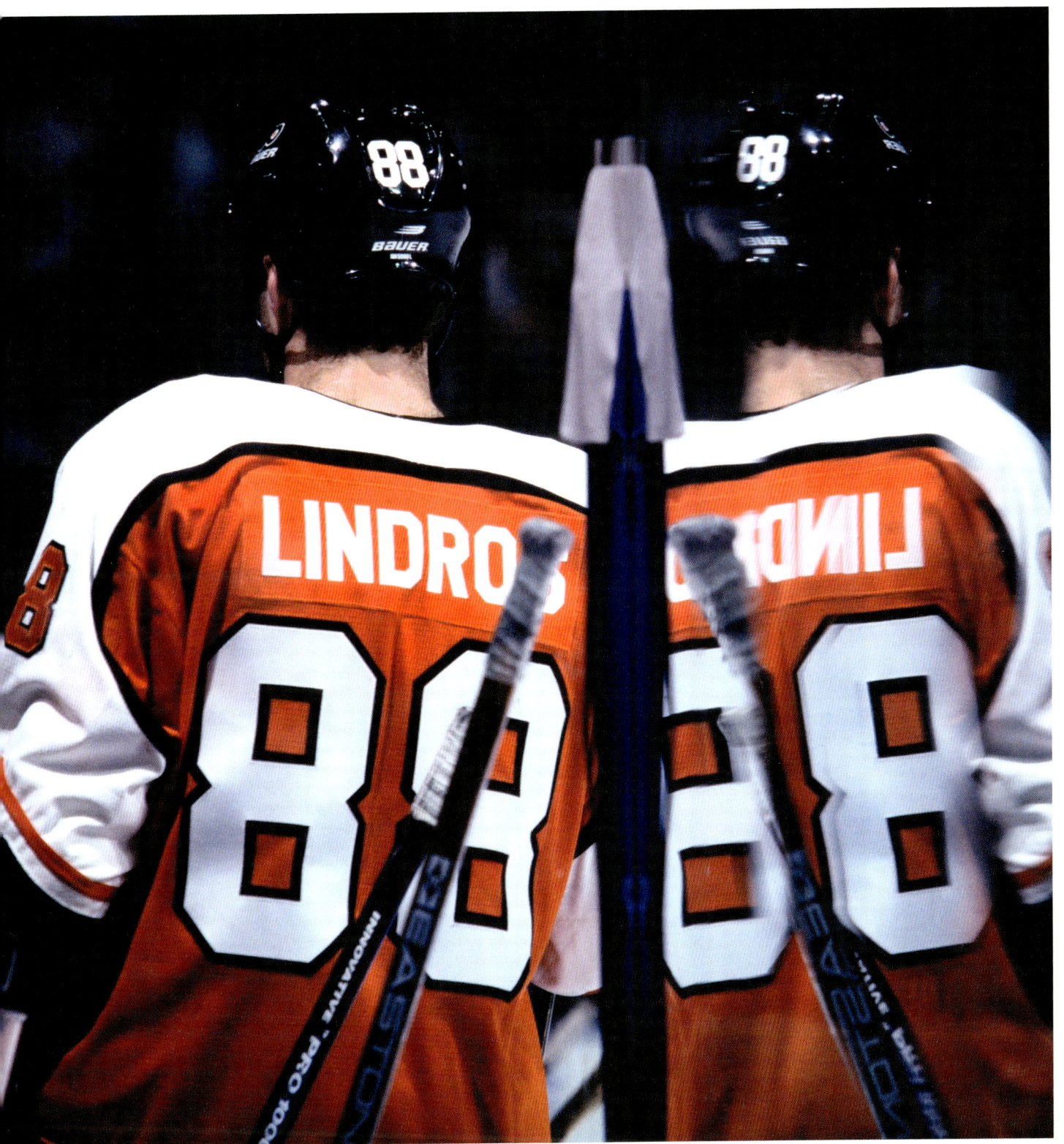

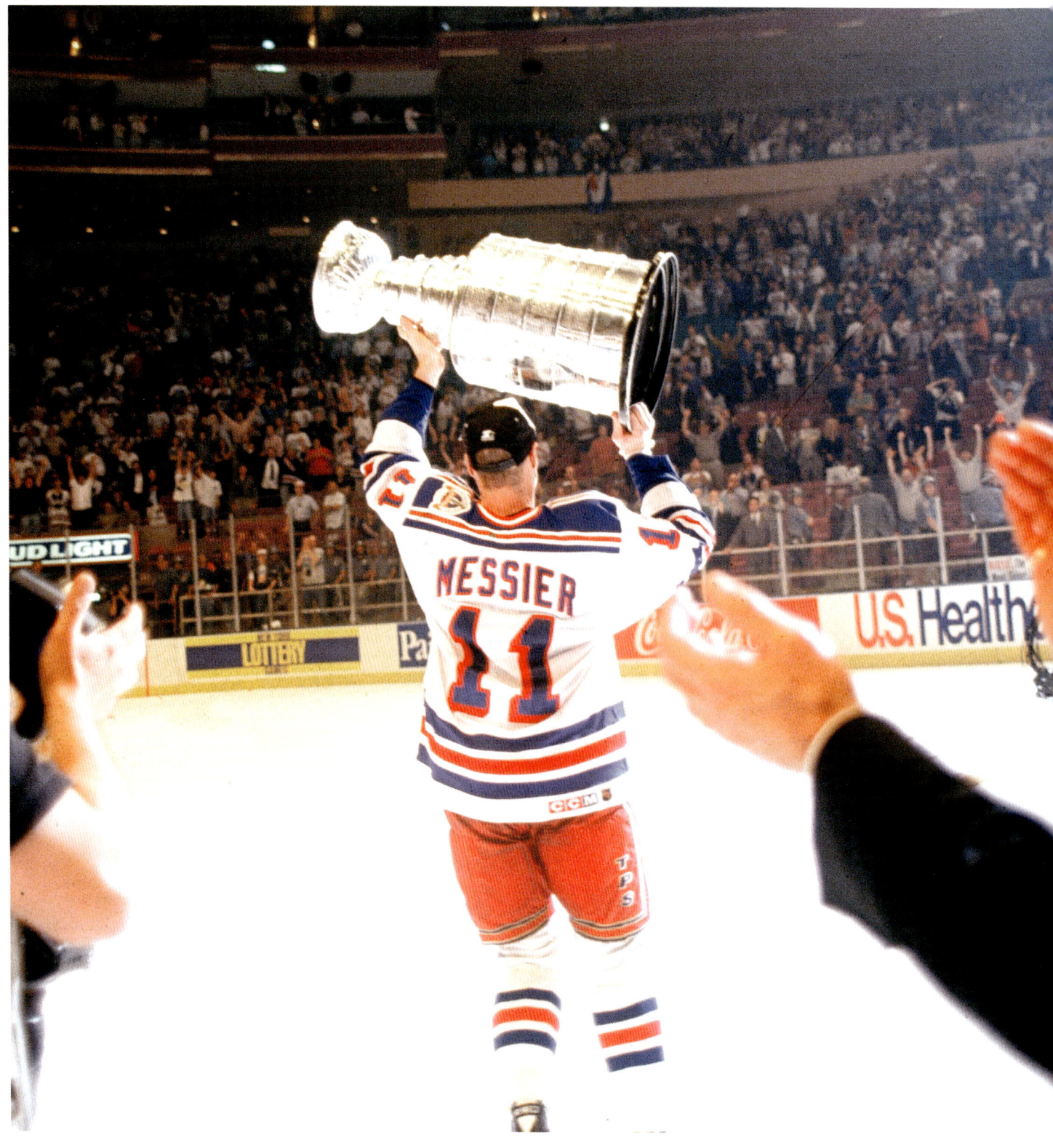

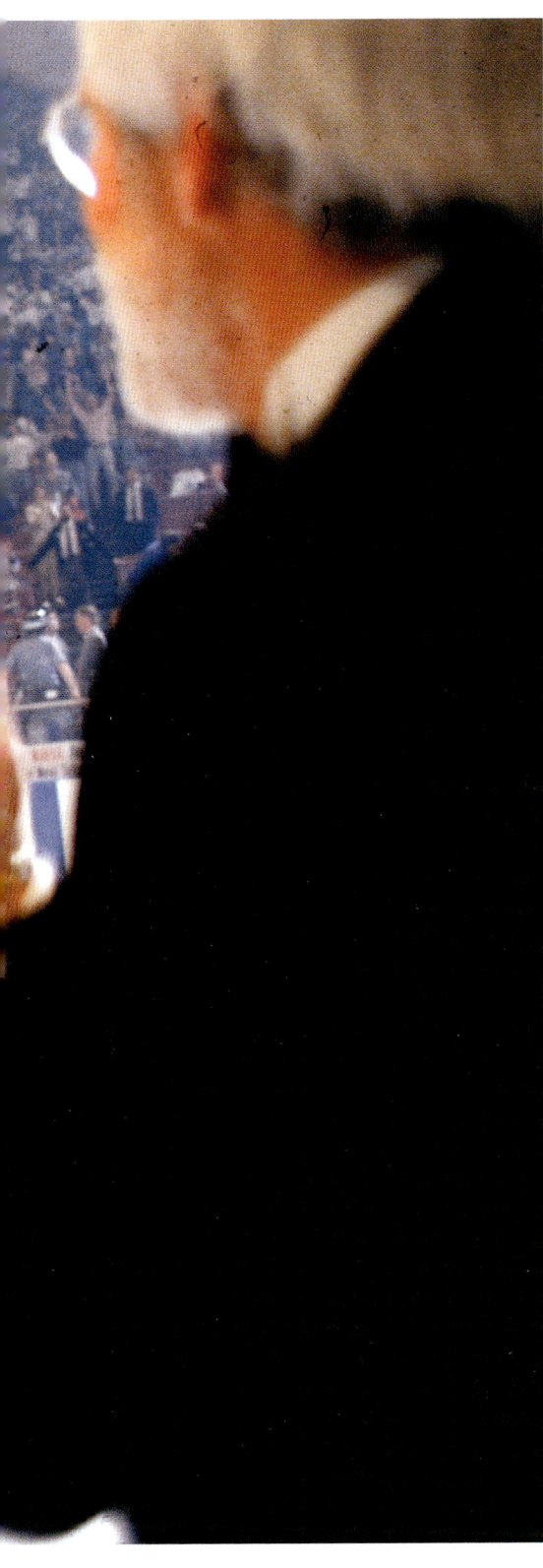

THE GUARANTEE

MADISON SQUARE GARDEN, NEW YORK CITY | *June 14, 1994*

OVER THE DECADES, New York Rangers money had lured many greats to Madison Square Garden: Boom-Boom Geoffrion came from the Montreal Canadiens, Anders Hedberg and Ulf Nilsson signed after lighting up the WHA, Herb Brooks went behind the bench after the Miracle, Marcel Dionne finished his career in New York. None could bring the Cup to Broadway.

The Rangers were champions in 1928, their second season in the league. They went to the Final five more times in the next 12 years. When the Rangers beat Toronto for their third NHL title, in 1940, they had won the Stanley Cup more times than the Bruins, Chicago Black Hawks, or Detroit Red Wings. Then the dry spell began.

The Rangers played for the Cup only one more time in the Original Six era. Their 1950 loss to the Red Wings was one of the best Finals ever, culminating in a double-overtime thriller in Game 7. But that was small consolation for the following years of futility. Before expansion, teams had to win only one series to the reach the Final, something the Blueshirts couldn't manage.

Then in 1991, the Rangers picked up Mark Messier from the Edmonton Oilers. Unlike the team's other big-name acquisitions, the 30-year-old center was still in his prime. In his first season in New York, he led the team to the league's best record and won the Hart Trophy as MVP. Once again, the Rangers disappointed in the playoffs, with a second-round loss to Pittsburgh. After missing the playoffs entirely the next season, the Rangers won another President's Trophy in 1993–94 and looked to end their drought.

But the jinx would not go without a fight. The Rangers were down 3–2 to the New Jersey Devils in the conference final when Messier told reporters his team would win Games 6 and 7. They did. In the Final, another Game 7, against the Vancouver Canucks, went down to the last seconds, but the home team held on for a 3–2 win. Three days later, the Stanley Cup took a trip up Broadway beneath a shower of ticker tape. The Curse was buried.

Photograph by BRUCE BENNETT STUDIOS

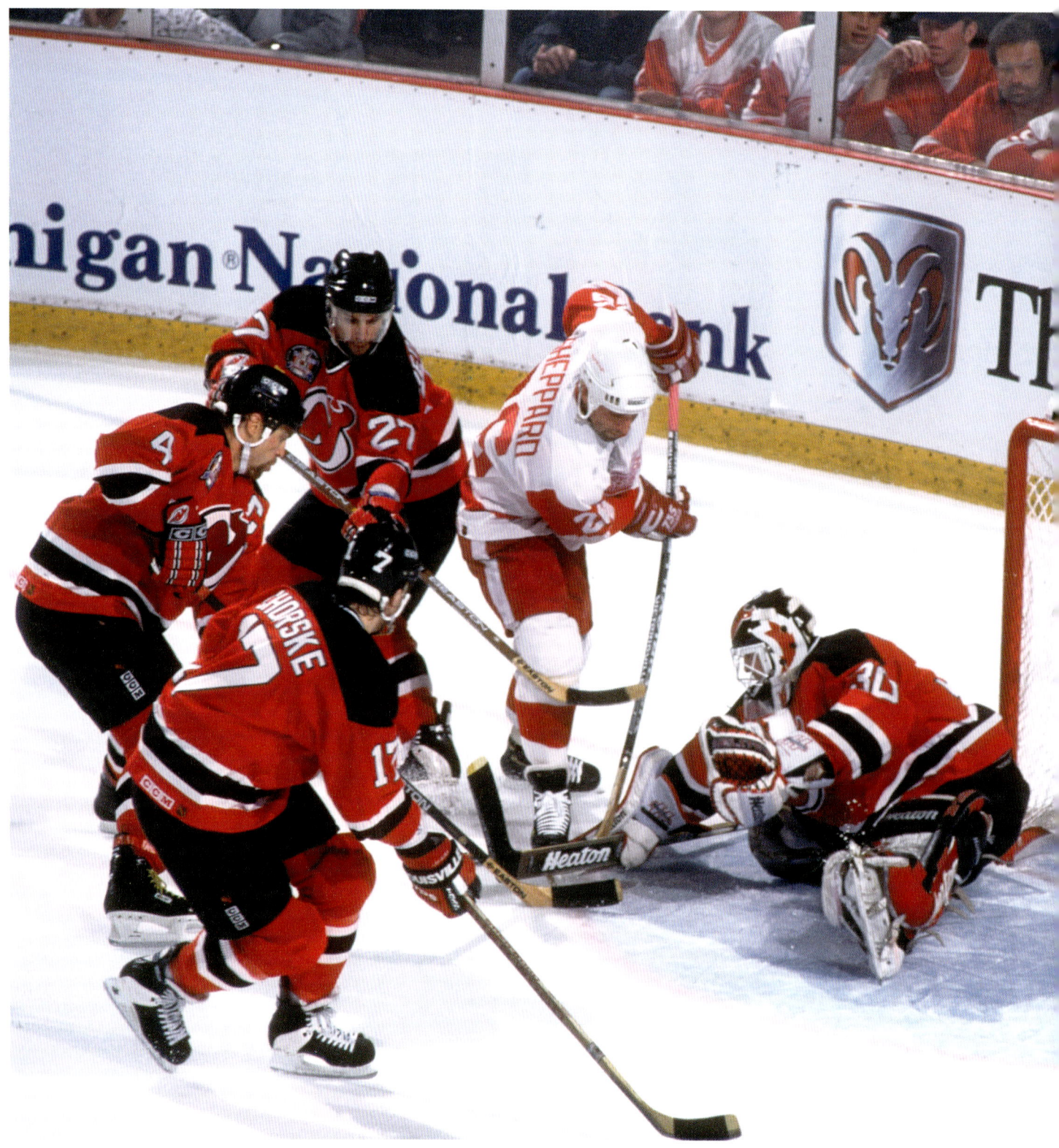

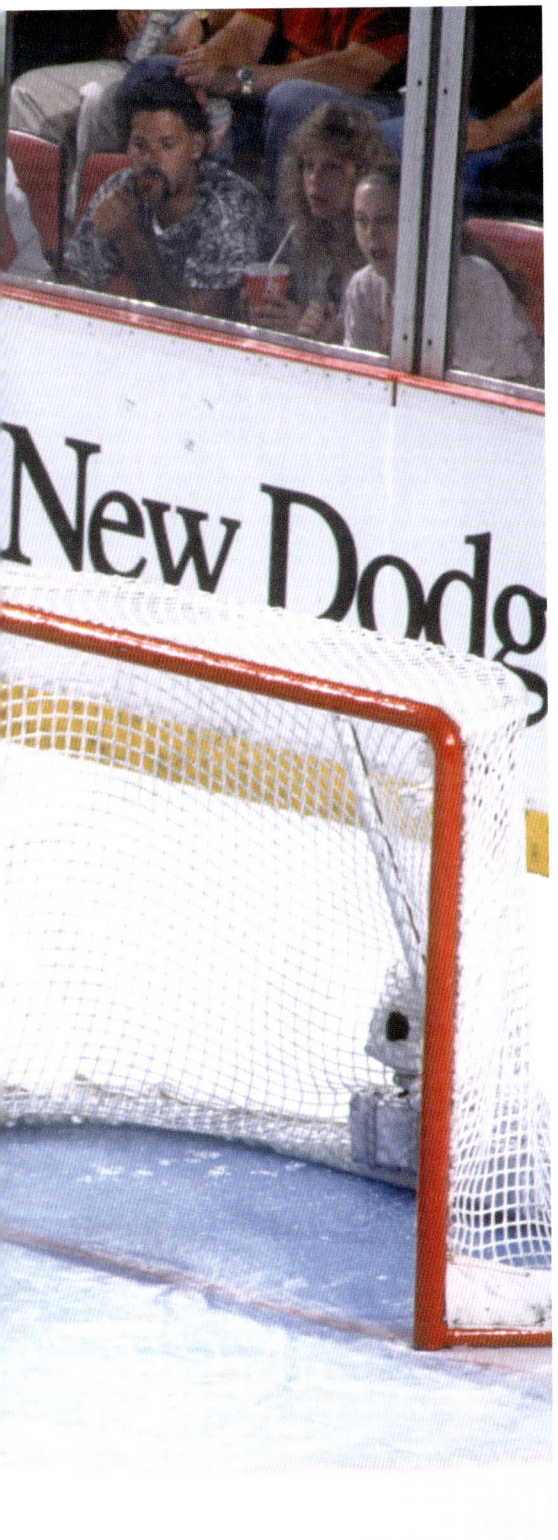

THE NEUTRAL ZONE TRAP

JOE LOUIS ARENA, DETROIT | *June 1995*

ACCORDING TO SOME hockey watchers, the New Jersey Devils of the 1990s ruined hockey just as badly as the Philadelphia Flyers of the 1970s. The Flyers twice won the Stanley Cup by pounding opponents into submission. The Devils won their two championships by trapping.

As New Jersey was on its way to its first Stanley Cup title, *Sports Illustrated* warned that their victory was a threat to "the very soul of the game." In the June 26, 1995, issue, Michael Farber explained the menace of the dreaded neutral-zone trap:

> For nonpuckheads, here is a primer on the Devil version of the trap, hockey's newest four-letter word: The New Jersey forechecker, usually the center, forces the puck carrier toward the boards, where he is intercepted by a Devil winger. The weak-side winger then clogs the middle along with the two defensemen, who cut off the passing lanes. Suddenly the neutral ice looks like a New Jersey mall the Saturday before Christmas….

> The problem isn't New Jersey as much as it is Devil worship. Eighteen of the 26 teams already use the trap, (Leafs scout Pierre) Page says, and he guesses the number will be 21 or 22 if the Devils win the Cup. The NHL is nothing if not imitative…. The trap seems to be the flavor of the decade.

Indeed, plenty of teams borrowed the Devils' recipe. The Red Wings, who lost to New Jersey in the 1995 Final, later used their own version of the trap, called "Left Wing Lock," to win the Cup in 1997 and '98. Of course, Scotty Bowman is hailed as a genius and Detroit's dynasty is celebrated, while the Devils are evil. The Devils' advocates point out that New Jersey was among the top scoring teams of the late '90s; they were not winning games 1–0. Overall, however, fewer goals were being scored, and this bothered the NHL. After the 2004–05 lockout, the league removed the red line and allowed two-line passes in hopes of increasing offense. Scoring still has not returned to pre-trap levels.

Photograph by BRUCE BENNETT STUDIOS

FAN APPRECIATION

MIAMI ARENA, MIAMI | *June 8, 1996*

ACCORDING TO THE Chinese zodiac, the Year of the Rat wasn't set to begin until February 1996. But in South Florida, it started four months early, on the night of the Panthers' home opener.

It all began when Panthers winger Scott Mellanby one-timed a locker-room rodent against the wall before the game, then used the same stick to score twice in Florida's win over Calgary. Goalie John Vanbiesbrouck dubbed Mellanby's feat a "rat trick," and Panthers fans scurried with the quip. For the rest of the season, plastic rats flooded the ice after goals, and the Panthers kept winning. In their third NHL season, the expansion team made the playoffs for the first time. The rat craze reached its peak as Florida made its way to the Stanley Cup Final. Security guards checked hats, pockets and armpits, but contraband rodents still found their way to the ice. On some nights more than 3,000 rats would rain onto the rink.

Detroit Red Wings fans have an older and slimier tradition. At the start of the 1952 playoffs, brothers Pete and Jerry Cusimano hurled a dead octopus onto the ice at Olympia Stadium, its eight arms symbolizing the eight playoff wins needed to hoist the Stanley Cup. That spring, the Wings swept through the playoffs, and the octopus became the team's good-luck charm. Over the decades, tossed octopodes grew in both numbers and size: in one 1995 game, fans threw 36 mollusks, including one weighing 38 pounds. The NHL tried to ban Zamboni driver Al Sobotka from twirling octopuses when he retrieved them, but that simply added an element of rebellion to every toss.

Then there's the oldest and most common ritual: the hat trick. Since the 1940s, when a haberdasher in Guelph, Ontario, offered free fedoras to any three-goal scorer, fans have marked the feat by flinging their hats onto the ice. Today, every NHL arena has its own protocol for hurled headgear. Some teams donate the hats. Columbus started the practice of showcasing hats in a giant transparent bin in the concourse. Fans can see hats they've thrown and look forward to the next celebration.

Photograph by AP PHOTO/HANS DERYK

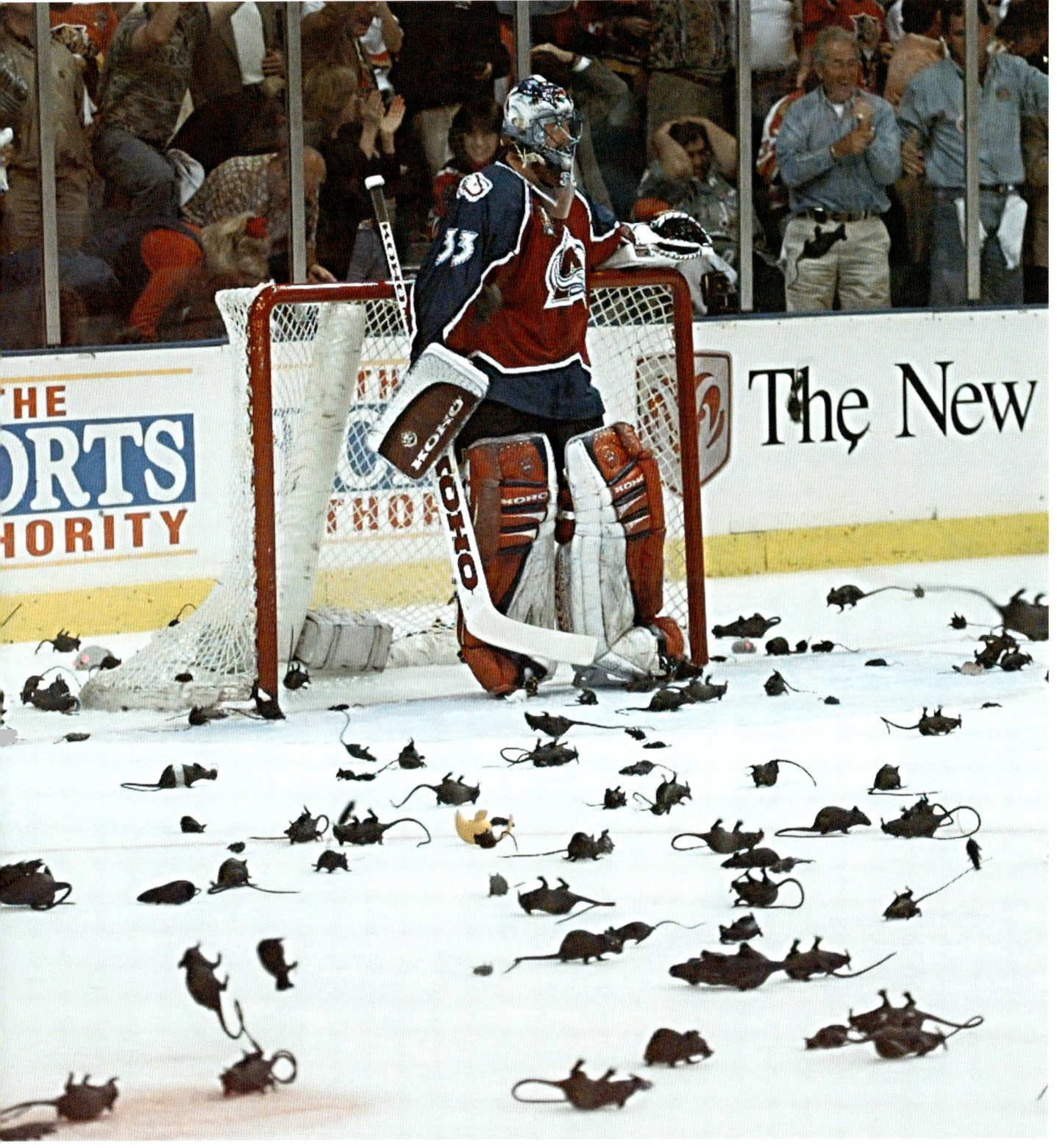

CAPTAIN AMERICA

THE BIG HAT, NAGANO, JAPAN | *February 17, 1998*

CAMMI GRANATO'S MOM bought her a figure-skating costume. She hoped frills and sequins would draw her four-year-old daughter away from hockey. But Cammi wouldn't be swayed. She wanted to play hockey with her three older brothers. They watched the Miracle on Ice together. They played pickup games together on a neighborhood pond. And Cammi went along to their games and practices. When she started playing organized hockey herself, it was with a boys' team in her hometown of Downers Grove, Illinois.

All three Granato brothers played hockey at the University of Wisconsin, but there were no women's teams at Midwestern schools when Cammi started college in the late 1980s. She went out east instead, to Providence College and then Concordia University in Quebec. Tallying three points per game for the Friars brought her a first flash of attention. "It's incredible what she's meant to hockey," Islanders general manager Mike Milbury told *Sports Illustrated*. "She's given it a profile in this country, more than good men players have been able to do."

Her brother Tony agreed. A goal-scoring forward for the Los Angeles Kings at the time, the eldest Granato told *SI* in 1997 that his little sister had become the family's best hockey player. "She has surpassed me," he said. "She's not my sister. I'm her brother."

Cammi Granato was the face of American women's hockey as the sport emerged in the 1990s. She played for Team USA at the first Women's World Championship in 1990. When women's hockey made its Olympic debut at the 1998 Nagano Games, she was team captain—and scored the first U.S. Olympic goal. After losing to Canada in the finals of four straight World Championships, Granato and the Americans finally topped their rivals, taking Olympic gold.

Granato is still the top scorer in the history of USA women's hockey. Over 205 games for the national team, she scored 186 goals and added 157 assists for 343 total points. In 2010, she and Angela James were the first two women inducted into the Hockey Hall of Fame in Toronto.

Photograph by BRUCE BENNETT STUDIOS

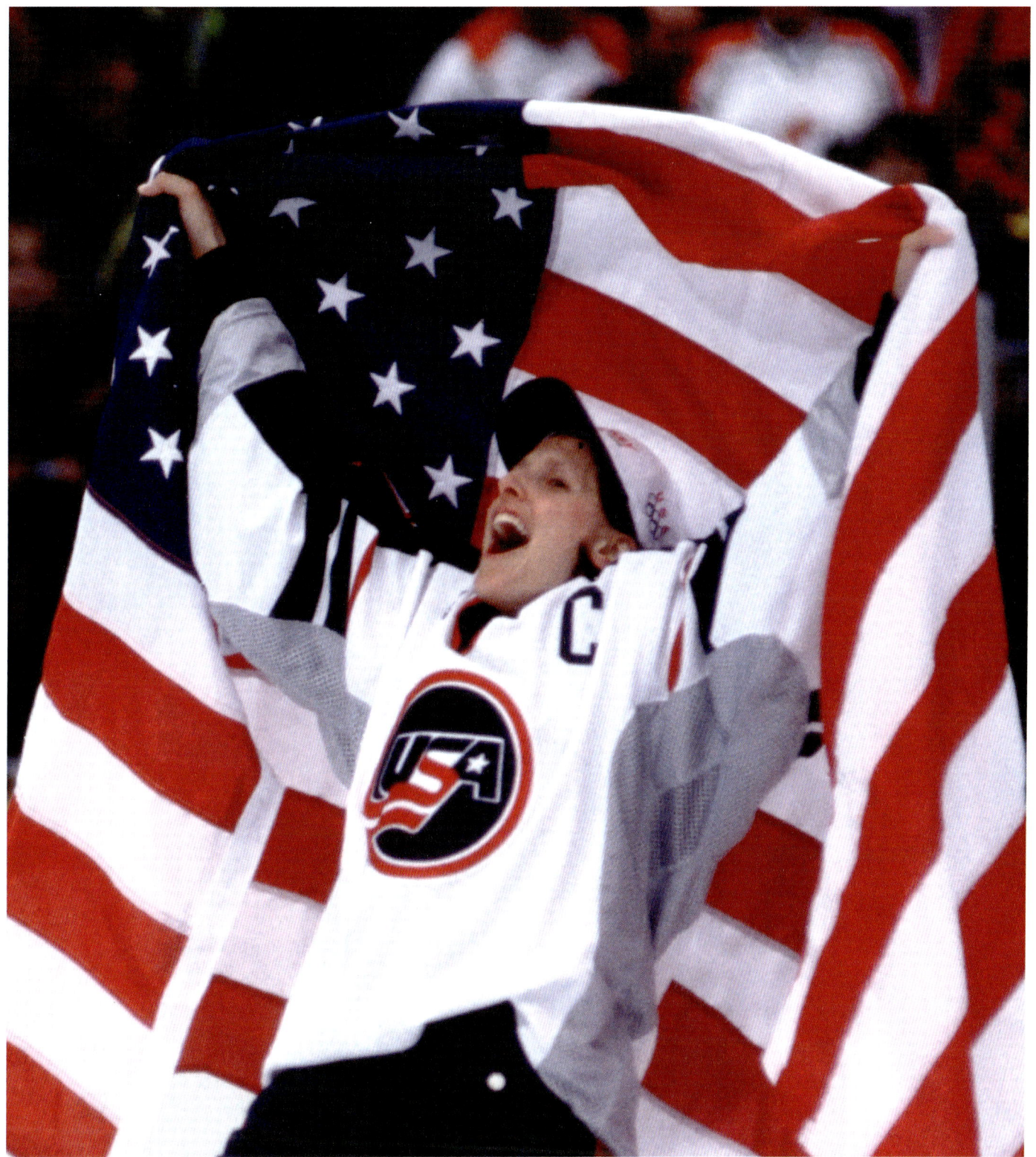

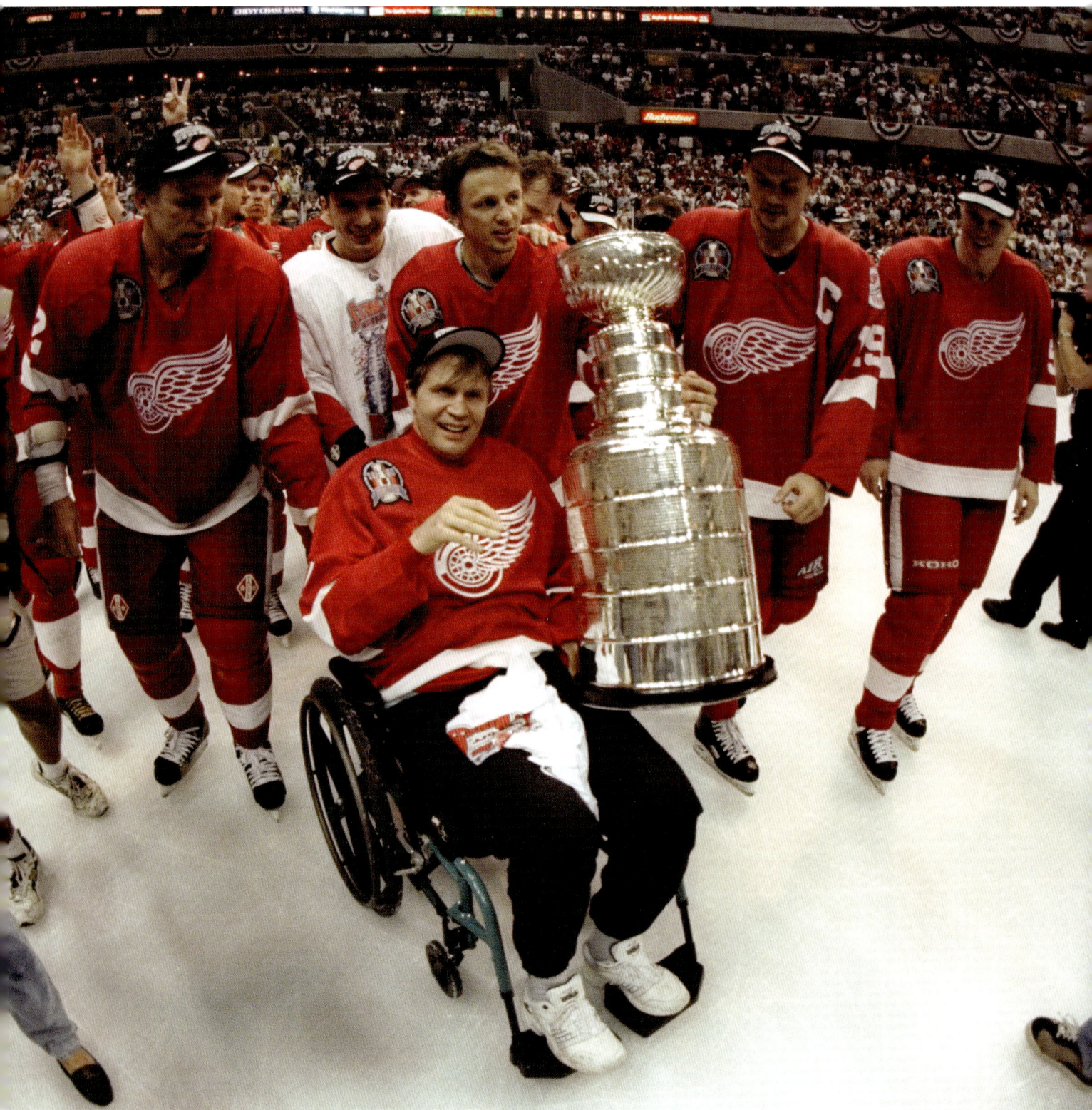

THE RUSSIAN FIVE

MCI CENTER, WASHINGTON, D.C. | *June 16, 1998*

THE PRODUCTION LINE. The Triple Crown Line. The French Connection. The Šťastný Brothers. One line stands apart from these great combinations of NHL history—the Russian Five.

As the name says, the Russian Five were not a line but a full unit: Igor Larionov, Sergei Federov and Slava Kozlov as forwards; Slava Fetisov and Vladimir Konstantinov on defense. Five skaters consistently playing together had been a trademark of Russian hockey, but it wasn't done in the NHL. It was Detroit Red Wings coach Scotty Bowman who recognized that sending a Russian platoon over the boards together could change a game. Michael Farber described the results in the March 18, 1996, issue of *Sports Illustrated:*

> Sometimes they pass to open spaces instead of players. They double back. Larionov can delay and delay and delay some more and then hit a streaking winger, giving Kozlov and Fedorov the puck in position to score goals.

The Russian Five stood out not only for their fluid attack; they were also tough on defense. Konsantinov was especially feared across the league. "If Vladi's mother were standing in the crease, he'd cross-check her," teammate Joey Kocur told *SI.*

Above all, the Russian Five stand out for their meteoric existence. Bowman put the unit together for the first time in October 1995, after the team had acquired Larionov. The following season, they led Detroit to the Stanley Cup Final. The difference-maker against the Philadelphia Flyers was Konstantinov. His Game 3 hit on Dale Hawerchuk led to a Detroit goal and knocked the Philly center out of the series. After completing the sweep, the 1997 Red Wings claimed the Cup for the first time in 42 years.

And then it came to a tragic end. Six days after the series, Konstantinov suffered debilitating head injuries in a car crash. The Red Wings dedicated the 1997–98 season to their teammate, who worked to regain his speech and mobility. When the team repeated as NHL champions in 1998, captain Steve Yzerman brought the trophy directly to Konstantinov. Joined by their teammates, the Russian Five went around the ice one more time, with the Stanley Cup taking a ride in Konstantinov's wheelchair.

Photograph by RICK STEWART/ALLSPORT

THE ARCHITECT

DETROIT | *June 18, 1998*

"SCOTTY BOWMAN MAY be a lot of things," wrote Ken Dryden in *The Game,* "but he is not someone you like."

The Hall of Fame goalie, who played seven full seasons of his career under Bowman, dedicated pages of his memoir to his former coach. Bowman was a mystery to hockey's intellectual, a puzzle Dryden couldn't solve.

"Abrupt, straightforward, without flair or charm, he seems cold and abrasive, sometimes obnoxious, controversial, but never colorful," Dryden wrote. "He is not Vince Lombardi, tough and gruff with a heart of gold. His players don't sit around telling hateful-affectionate stories about him…. He is complex, confusing, misunderstood, unclear in every way but one. He is a brilliant coach, the best of his time."

When Dryden wrote these words, Bowman had won the Stanley Cup five times with the Montreal Canadiens. By the time he retired, in 2002, Bowman had touched the Cup four more times, once with the Pittsburgh Penguins and three times with the Detroit Red Wings. He finished his career with 1,244 regular-season wins. No other NHL coach has 1,000. In 30 seasons behind the bench, his teams only missed the playoffs twice. He also won the Stanley Cup five times as a member of an organization's front office.

More than three decades after first writing about Bowman, Dryden asked his former coach if he could write more. The result was a biography, published in 2020, with a twist: Dryden asked Bowman to pick the eight best NHL teams of all time, during their best seasons, then the coach analyzed what would happen in a playoff series. The historical fantasy was designed to illustrate how Bowman thought like a coach.

"There are philosophies of virtually every other highly successful coach," Dryden explained in an interview for Toronto's *Globe and Mail* newspaper. "It's the Wooden way, the Phil Jackson way, the Lombardi philosophy. You don't hear that about Scotty Bowman."

Indeed, he would have won in any era. As Dryden explained, his former coach had a simple philosophy: "How do we find a way to win? If this doesn't work, you try something else."

Photograph by RALF-FINN HESTOFT/CORBIS

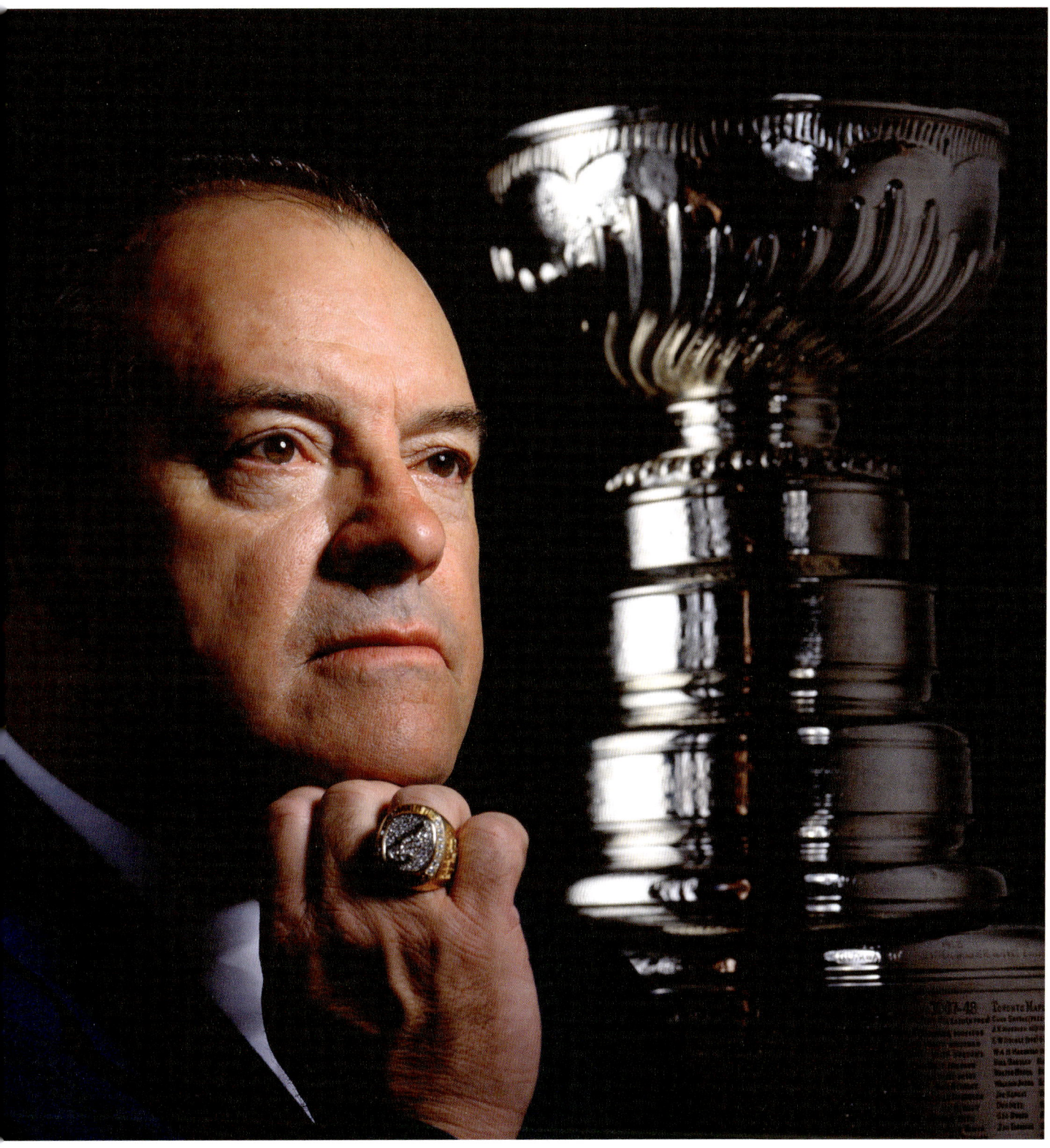

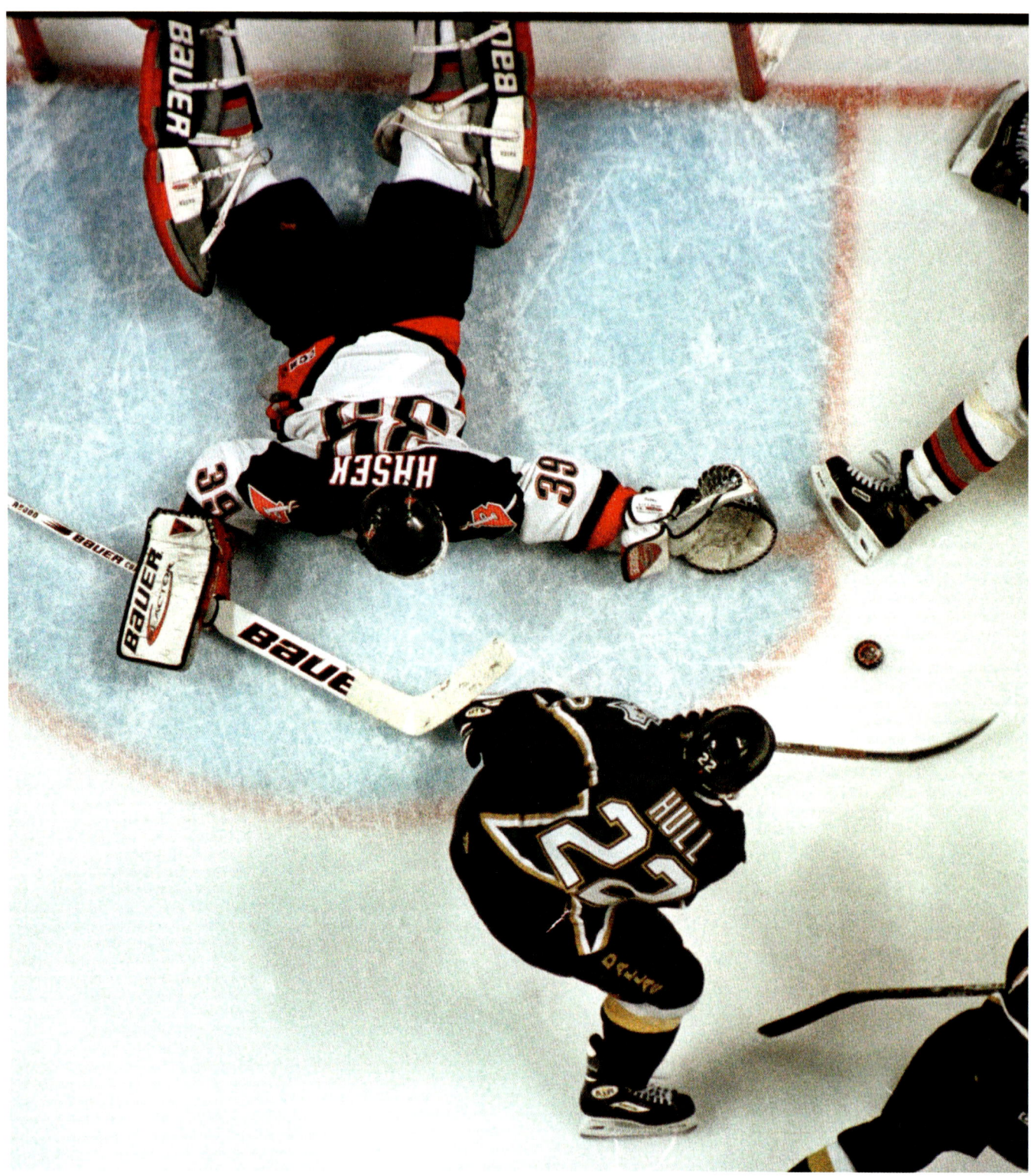

GOAL OR NO GOAL?

MARINE MIDLAND ARENA, BUFFALO | *June 19, 1999*

FEW GOALS IN NHL history are as controversial as Brett Hull's Stanley Cup–winning rebound in Game 6 of the 1999 Final. We'll let Michael Farber tell the story, from the June 28, 1999, issue of *Sports Illustrated:*

For almost six periods Buffalo and Dallas had been entrenched in another taut defensive standoff, a 1–1 match that resonated in the soul if not on the scoreboard. Then Dallas center [Mike] Modano took control of the puck at the half boards. He passed it to the front of the cage, where it reached his right wing, Hull, who took a shot on Dominik Hašek. Hašek made the save, and the puck clearly left the crease for an instant, although Hull's left skate didn't. Hull then corralled the rebound and shoveled the puck past the left arm and leg of the prone Hašek with his forehand, touching off a wild on-ice celebration…. "The play happened so fast, and the next thing you know, there's 500 people on the ice," Buffalo captain Michael Peca said about an hour after the game. "What the heck is the NHL going to do? Open the floodgates by making the right call?"

The league insists it did make the proper call. Director of Officiating Bryan Lewis looked at the replays within seconds of Hull's goal, as did two other replay officials, and ruled that the goal counted because of a March 25 directive issued by NHL senior vice president Colin Campbell regarding the crease rule. The clarification to the rule states that an attacking player can stay in the crease even if the puck leaves the blue-painted area as long as he maintains control of the puck…. Lewis decided that Hull, a righthanded shooter, had simply been kicking the puck to his stick and was thus in control, a liberal interpretation. When Hašek saw the replay in the dressing room, he got ready to tug his sweater back on because he assumed the game would start again. "They told me, 'Dom, it's over,'" Hašek said, "and I said, 'But it's not a goal.'"

Photograph by AP PHOTO/GENE PUSKAR

PAVING THE WAY

CALGARY | *September 16, 1999*

IT HAD HAPPENED before in pro hockey: three Black players on the same team. Starting in 1941, Herb Carnegie centered a line with his brother Ossie and Manny McIntrye that became famous as the "Black Aces." For a decade, the unit hopped among different teams in the semi-pro Quebec league. One of their fans was 13-year-old Jean Béliveau. "I tried to duplicate what Herbie was doing at faceoffs and making passes onto the blade," Béliveau recalled when Carnegie passed away in 2012.

There was no question Herb Carnegie had the skill to play in the NHL. Conn Smythe recognized his talent as an 18-year-old, but the Toronto Maple Leafs owner refused to sign him. "I'll give $10,000 to anyone who can turn Herb Carnegie white," Smythe said.

Decades later, when young Jarome Iginla was playing in the Edmonton area, he was still hearing that a Black player couldn't make the NHL.

"Fortunately, I was able to have some answers for them," he recalled. Iginla followed the league's Black players so he could push back against the doubters. "But to also know what was possible," he said.

Above all, Iginla took inspiration from Grant Fuhr. He was a kid when Fuhr was the Vezina-winning goalie for the Edmonton Oilers. Following his hero, Iginla started out as a goalie in youth hockey. "There wasn't enough action," he recalled. "So I decided to play out."

It was a good decision. In a 20-year career (16 with the Calgary Flames), Iginla was one of the NHL's premier power forwards. He twice won the Rocket Richard Trophy for most goals and finished with a total of 625. He's also near the top of the list with 12 Gordie Howe hat tricks.

Iginla and Fuhr were teammates for only one season, Fuhr's last in the NHL, along with goaltender Fred Brathwaite, pictured here. Fuhr and Iginla joined each other again in the Hall of Fame. Fuhr was the first Black player inducted, in 2003. Iginla followed in 2020.

Herb Carneige was inducted posthumously in 2022.

Photograph by RONALD C. MODRA

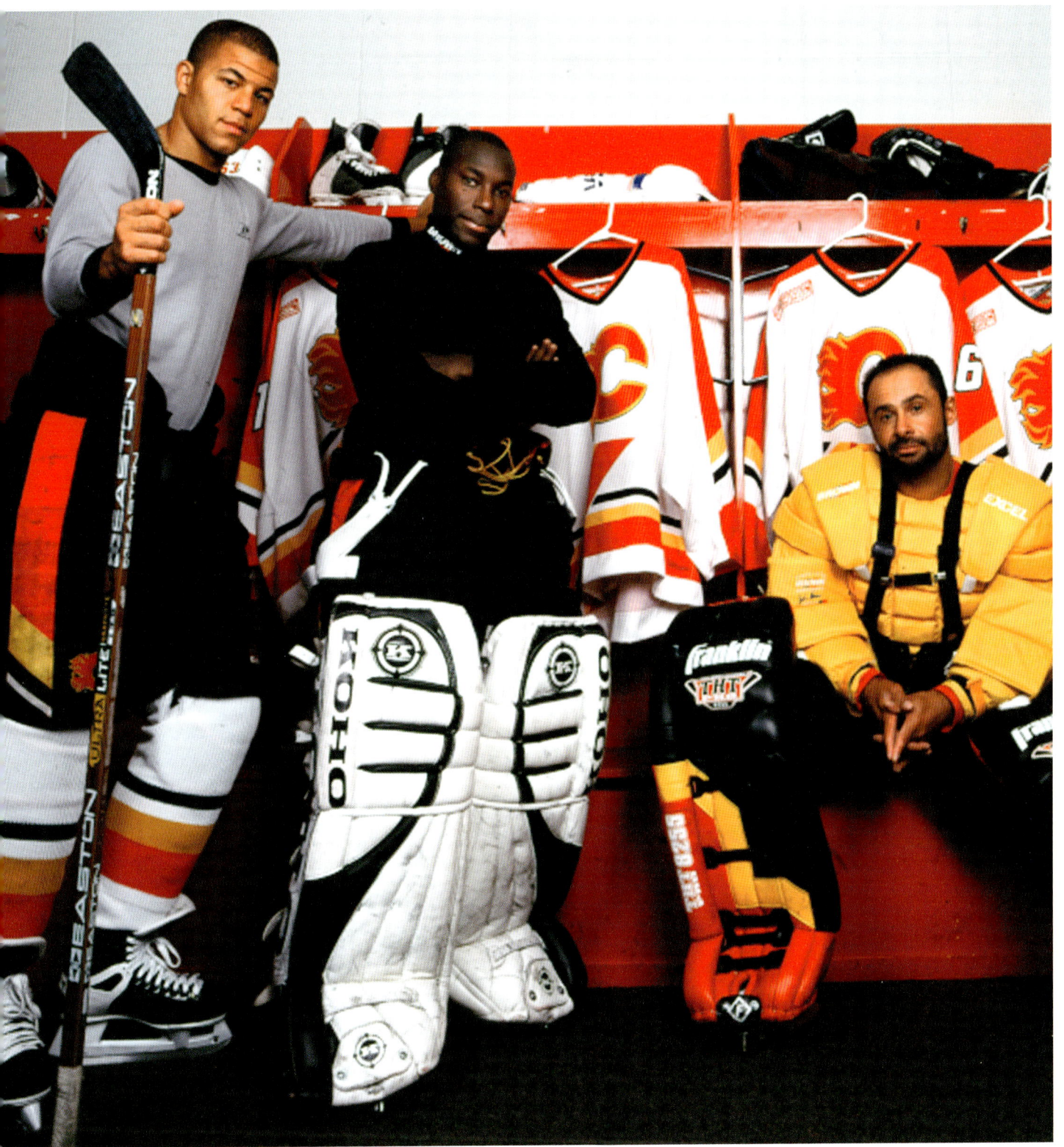

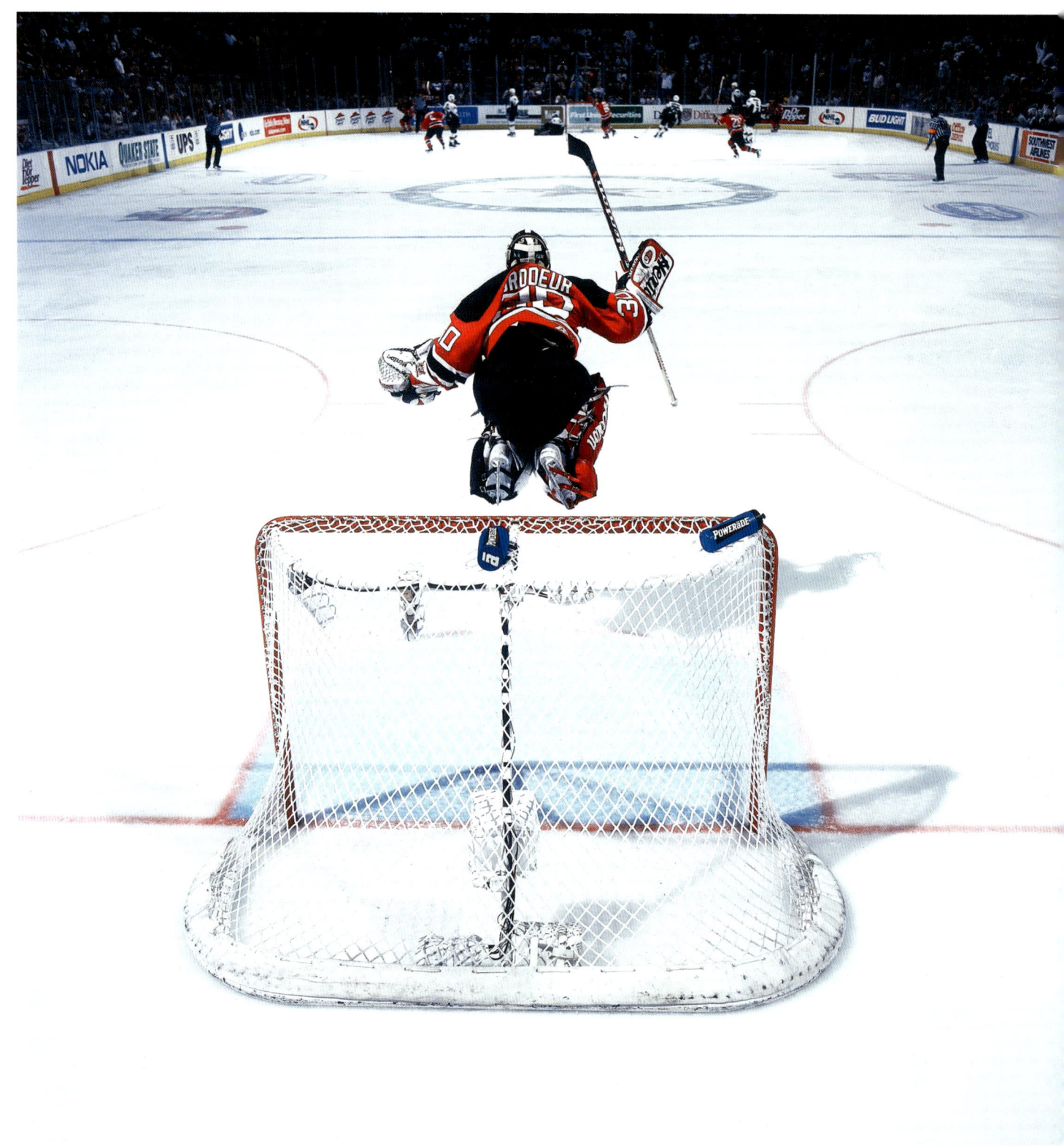

MARTY

MARTIN BRODEUR NEVER needed theatrics to own the crease. Playing a position defined by quirks, volatility and occasional bouts of madness, the New Jersey Devils legend stood out for something rare: composure. Across 22 NHL seasons, Brodeur rewrote the record book. With three Stanley Cup titles, two Olympic gold medals and a staggering 691 regular-season wins, he's universally recognized as one of the greatest to ever pull on the pads.

Brodeur's dominance was built on more than numbers. His hybrid style—equal parts old-school stand-up and modern butterfly—confounded shooters and frustrated forecheckers. His puck-handling was so good the league repainted the lines on the rink to limit his influence beyond the crease. And while other goalies made highlight-reel dives, Brodeur specialized in economy of motion, making hard saves look routine.

Unlike most iconic goalies, Brodeur appeared, well, normal. Former teammate Sheldon Souray remembered the goalie's habit of sipping Sprite and nibbling a bagel between periods. "He's talking and joking with the guys in the room," Souray told *Sports Illustrated*'s Michael Farber. "Then he'll go out and stop 10 shots in the third."

The calm masked a fierce competitive streak, sharpened especially by his rivalry with fellow Quebecois great Patrick Roy. The two traded records for years, their differing styles a study in contrasts: Roy, the butterfly's patron saint; Brodeur, its wry critic.

Brodeur's résumé is unmatched: 12 straight 30-win seasons, eight years of more than 40 wins, a record 125 shutouts (by contrast, Roy finished with 66). And then there was the ironman workload: 10 straight seasons playing over 70 games, a testament to Brodeur's durability in hockey's most punishing position. Even a torn biceps tendon in 2008 couldn't slow him; he returned after 16 weeks with back-to-back shutouts.

When Brodeur retired, in 2015, after a brief final chapter with the St. Louis Blues, he held records that may never be touched. More importantly, he left as the rare goaltender who combined statistical dominance with genuine likability, a competitor whose legacy was as much about his calm persona as it was about the milestones. Among hockey's brotherhood of weirdos, Martin Brodeur was its most normal genius.

Photograph by DAVID E. KLUTHO

SUPER MARIO RETURNS

MELLON ARENA, PITTSBURGH | *December 27, 2000*

MARIO LEMIEUX'S NHL career stretched over 17 seasons. But he actually took the ice in the equivalent of 11 seasons—915 games. Throughout his career, Super Mario was grounded by health problems. In the first months of the 1992–93 season, he was tallying 2.6 points per game, a pace that would have put him in the neighborhood of Wayne Gretzky's single-season record. Then in January, he was diagnosed with Hodgkin lymphoma. Radiation treatment limited him to just 22 games the next year, then kept him out for the entire 1994–95 campaign. When he came back the following season, he was the league's top scorer and MVP.

Even more debilitating than cancer was Lemieux's back. He underwent surgeries for a herniated disc and herniated muscle. The chronic pain was so grueling he needed someone else to tighten his skates. Ultimately, back problems forced him to retire in 1997, at age 31. The Hockey Hall of Fame waived its three-year waiting period and inducted him immediately. The next year, he became co-owner of the Penguins. Lemieux kept his pledges to fully pay the team's debts and keep the Pens in Pittsburgh. His retired number hung from the Igloo's rafters, alongside the two championship banners he helped the team win.

Three years and eight months later, No. 66 was lowered to the ice. On December 27, 2000, Lemieux took off his owner's suit and pulled on his jersey. The pregame ceremony, welcoming the Magnificent One back to the game, stirred goosebumps and tears for fans watching across North America. But then, as soon as the puck was dropped, the comeback turned in a direction even Hollywood couldn't have scripted. Thirty-three seconds into the game, Lemieux assisted on a goal by linemate Jaromir Jagr. In the second period, he scored a goal of his own. Later, Lemieux assisted on another. The Penguins won 5–0.

"Lemieux's nearly 21-minute performance was so impeccable, his accomplishment so pure," wrote David Farber in *Sports Illustrated*'s January 8, 2001, issue, "that it had to be reduced to fit our shrunken frame of reference."

Photograph by DAVID E. KLUTHO

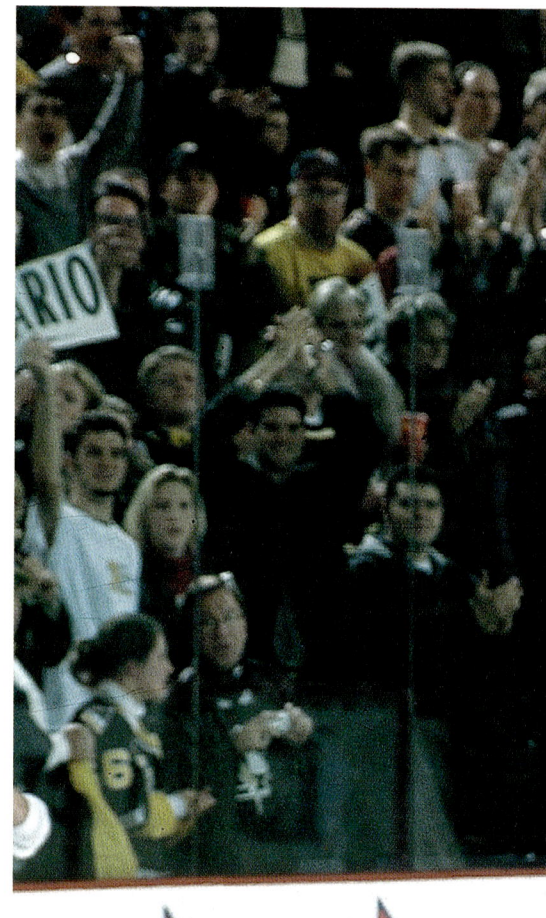

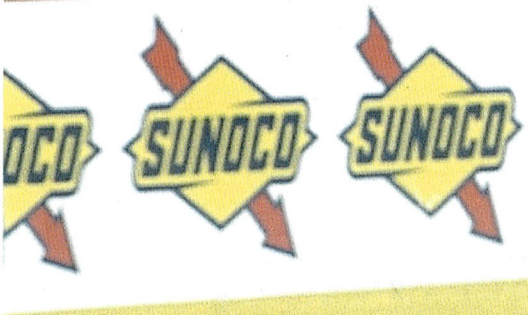

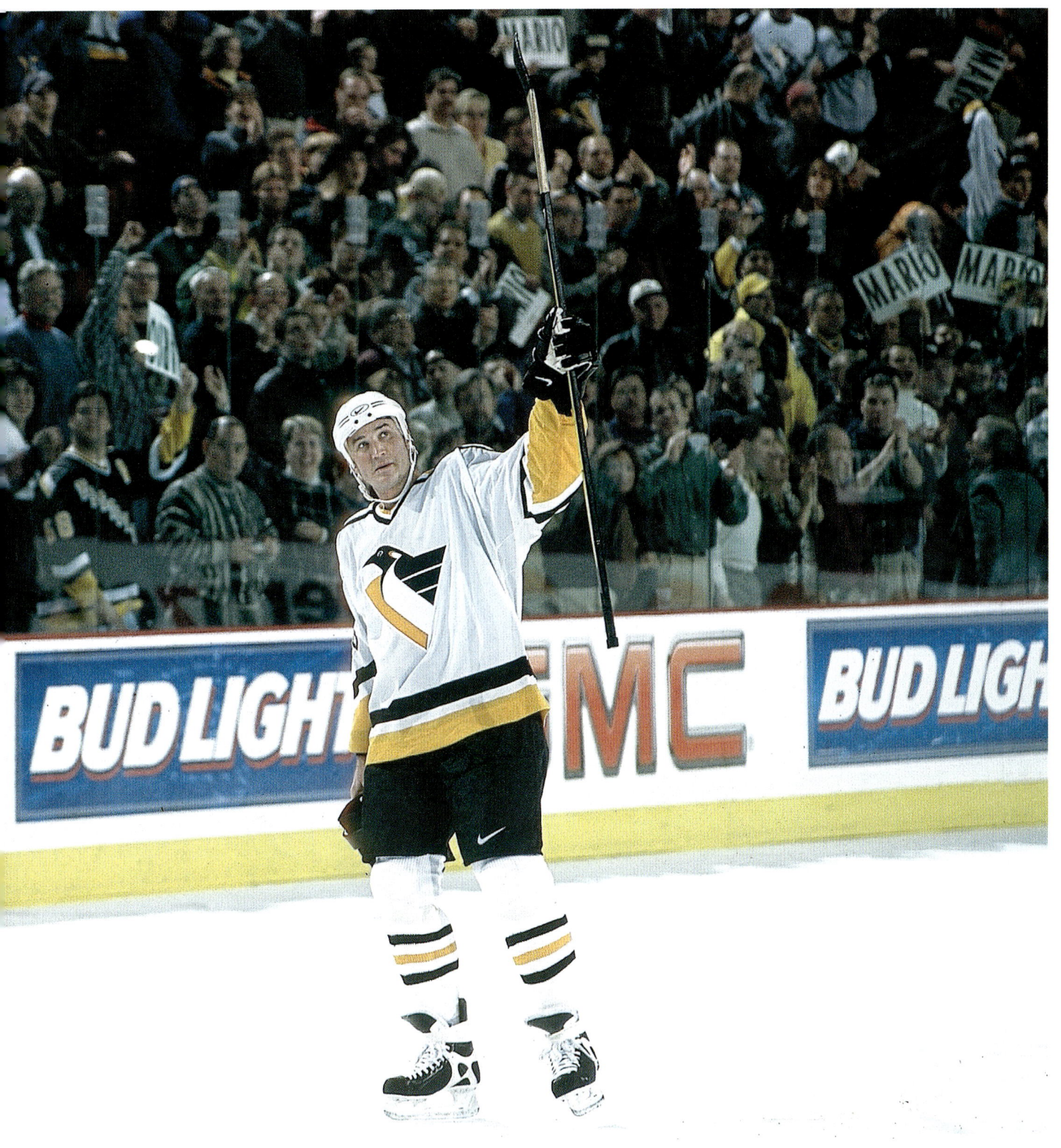

THE FIGHTER

Circa 2000

THEIR DEATHS BROUGHT a sobering realization: hockey can be hazardous to its players' health.

When Bob Probert passed in 2010, there were no clear signs of hockey's influence. Probert died of heart failure at age 45, while boating with his family. The former Detroit Red Wings and Chicago Blackhawks enforcer was remembered as one of the game's most colorful players. He had always lived large, and addictions plagued him throughout his life. Yet he was also involved in charity games and youth clinics. Teammates described him as a teddy bear off the ice. He was always willing to play up his reputation as one of the NHL's toughest fighters, even appearing as a contestant on the figure-skating reality show *Battle of the Blades*.

But eight months after Probert's death came the ominous report. Researchers at Boston University found evidence of chronic traumatic encephalopathy in his brain tissue. Probert's widow, Dani, told *The New York Times* that uncharacteristic memory loss and a tendency to lose his temper had led him to wonder if he had C.T.E. The analysis of his brain tissue, which Probert had decided to donate, confirmed that the sport had taken a heavy toll.

Dani Probert did not believe that fighting caused her husband's brain disease. Yet it was hard to not ask whether 246 fights over a 16-year career had lethal results. In the following months, this question took on greater weight.

In 2011 the deaths of three players—Derek Boogaard, Rick Rypien and Wade Belak—brought attention to the terrible cost of being an NHL enforcer. Rypien and Belak both took their own lives. Family and friends revealed each player had suffered depression for years. Boogaard's death was ruled an accidental overdose. One of the league's most feared enforcers, he had become addicted to painkillers, which numbed the effects of fighting: constant headaches and chronic pain in his hands, shoulder and back.

Researchers also found evidence of C.T.E. in Boogaard's brain tissue. The NHL insisted hockey was not to blame. "It's unfortunate that people use tragedies to jump to conclusions that probably at this stage aren't supported," said league commissioner Gary Bettman.

Photograph by BRUCE BENNETT STUDIOS

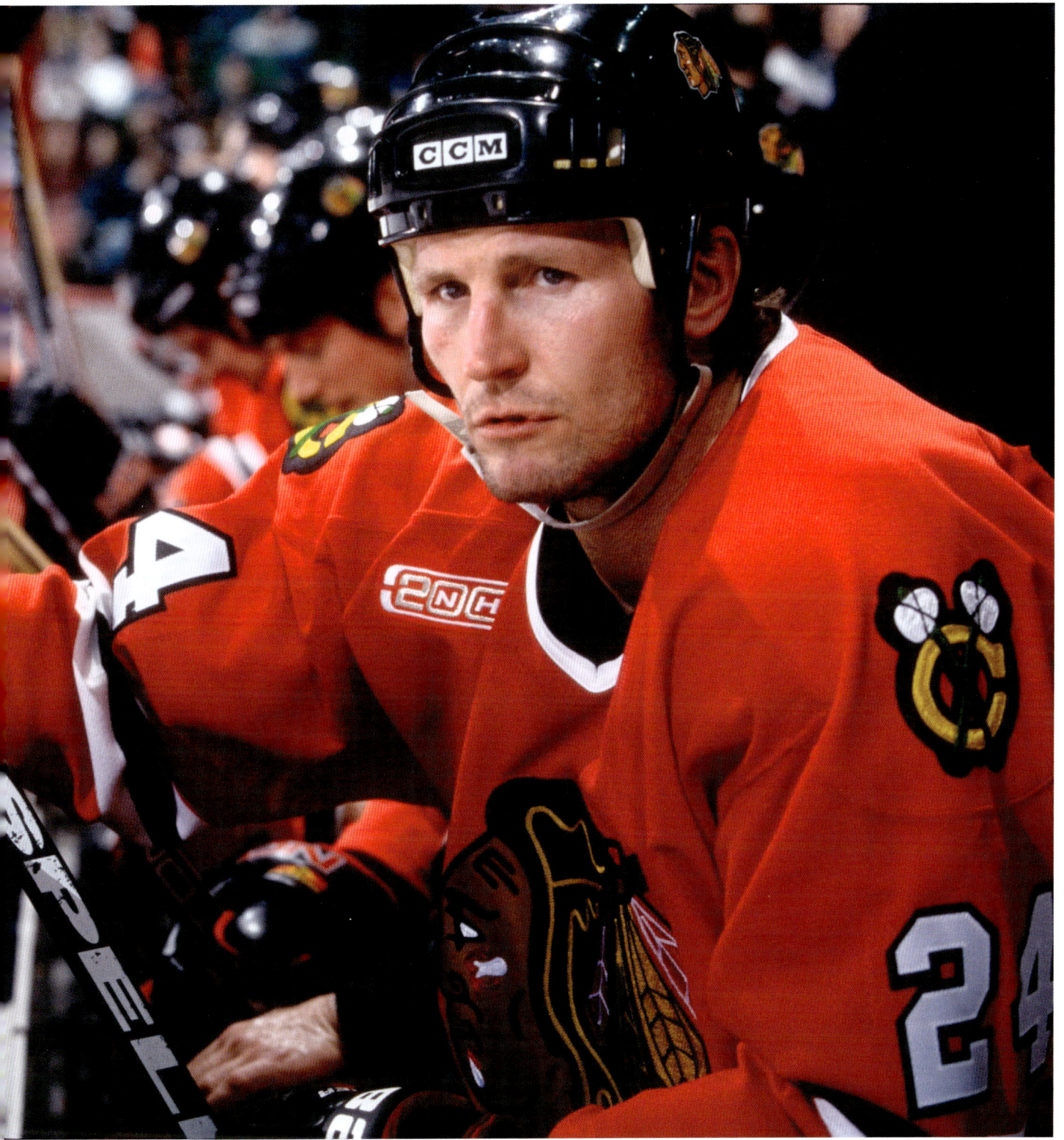

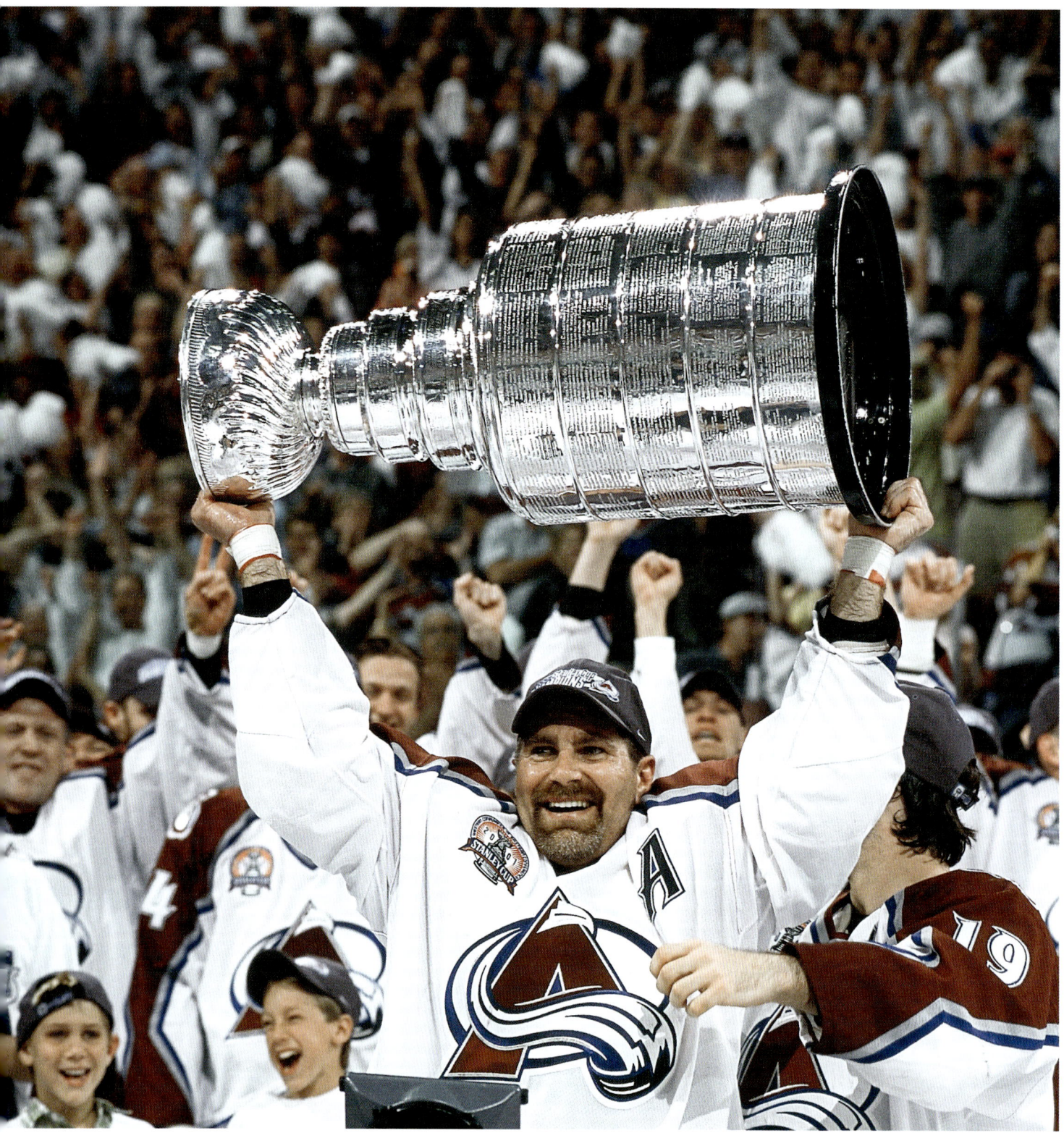

AT LAST

PEPSI CENTER, DENVER | *June 9, 2001*

IN 22 NHL SEASONS, Ray Bourque was named to 19 postseason All-Star teams and earned the Norris Trophy as the league's top defenseman five times. He set records for most goals, assists and points by a defenseman.

Bourque spent two decades in Boston, but as his career neared its end he yearned for the one prize in hockey that eluded him. He had played in the Final twice but left empty-handed. Late in the 1999–2000 season, when it was clear the Bruins were nowhere close, Bourque asked GM Harry Sinden to trade him to a contender. Sinden obliged and sent him to the Colorado Avalanche.

"This was a selfish move in terms of my career," Bourque told *Sports Illustrated*. "I know it's a shocker that I made a move like this."

The future Hall of Famer brought an immediate spark to the underachieving Avs. "It was almost like guys were trying to impress Ray," said defenseman Aaron Miller. "Like, Look at me! See what I can do!" After the trade, Colorado finished the season 12–2–1 and won their division. But they fell short in the 2000 playoffs, losing the conference final in seven games.

Bourque was not disappointed. "We competed for the Stanley Cup, and it rejuvenated my game," he said.

The following season, the Avs had the league's best record, and Bourque led the team in minutes played. Michael Farber described the final game, which was also the final game of Ray Bourque's illustrious career:

> The Stanley Cup, the most coveted piece of silverware in North American sports, celebrates the team over the individual, but perhaps for the first time in its 109-year history, the chalice was about one man, a 40-year-old defenseman with a graying goatee who never had anything handed to him—at least not until [captain Joe] Sakic pressed the object of desire in his hands. Bourque raised the Cup over his head, the weight of careerlong expectations replaced by 34½ pounds of sterling. He was shocked. "Maybe it's because I'm old or I was tired," he said, "but it felt really heavy."

Photograph by DAVID E. KLUTHO

MADE IN AMERICA

LOS ANGELES | *Circa 2002*

CHRIS CHELIOS'S ROAD to immortality didn't start at a hockey rink; it started on a San Diego beach. Cut from his college team and twice rejected by Canadian junior clubs, the 19-year-old transplant from Chicagoland to SoCal was, in his words, "a teenage beach bum delinquent." A friend urged him to call a juniors coach in Moose Jaw to give his hockey career another try. Asked his position, Chelios answered, "I play defense." He didn't, but the bluff paid off: Chelios ended up being a first-team NHL All-Star defenseman five times and won three Norris Trophies.

Chelios shares the record with Gordie Howe for most NHL seasons: 26. His longevity is testament to a legendary work ethic. Early in his career, Chelios pioneered brutal summer regimens, at a time when most NHL players spent the offseason golfing and fishing. At Gold's Gym in Venice Beach, he ground through hour-long, no-rest circuits six days a week. Off the clock, he pushed even harder, with 40-mile bike rides along the Pacific Coast Highway and paddle-surfing with big-wave legend Laird Hamilton.

Even in his forties, Chelios's conditioning bordered on superhuman. Teammates remember him pedaling a stationary bike in the sauna. "He doesn't make mistakes because he's used to being tired," said one NHL coach, "or because he's not tired compared to everybody else."

Chelios's career had three chapters: seven seasons with the Montreal Canadiens, nine with the Chicago Blackhawks, 10 with the Detroit Red Wings. At each stop, he was an All-Star who reached the Stanley Cup Final, winning once in Montreal and twice in Detroit. While he didn't bring the Cup to Chicago, the years in his hometown were the most meaningful. "I was like a lion coming out of a cage," he said of his first game with the Blackhawks in 1990, when he got a Gordie Howe hat trick. Thirty-four years later, the team retired his number. The 62-year-old Hall of Famer looked fantastic—just what you'd expect from Chelios.

Photograph by DONALD MIRALLE/NHLI

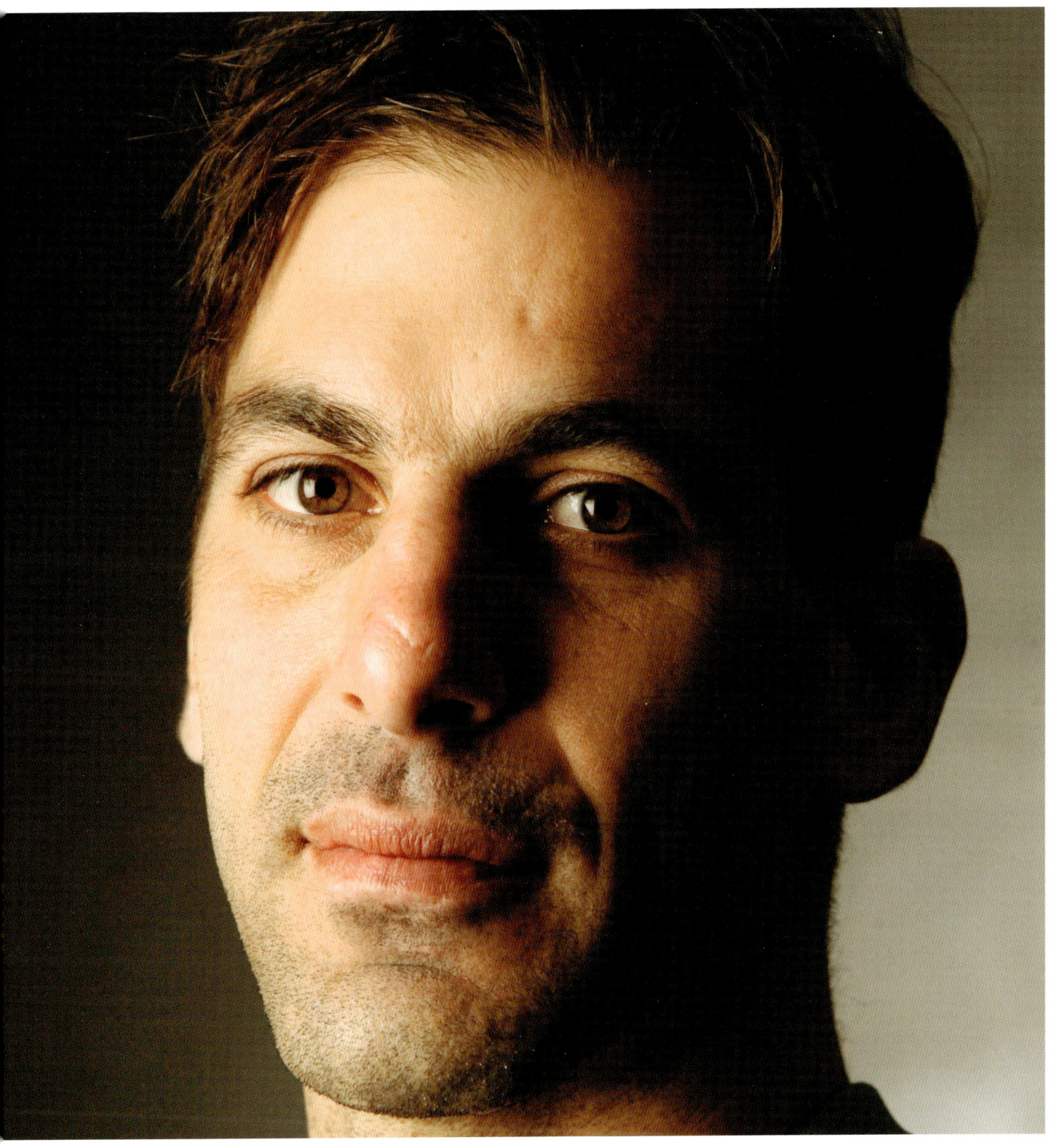

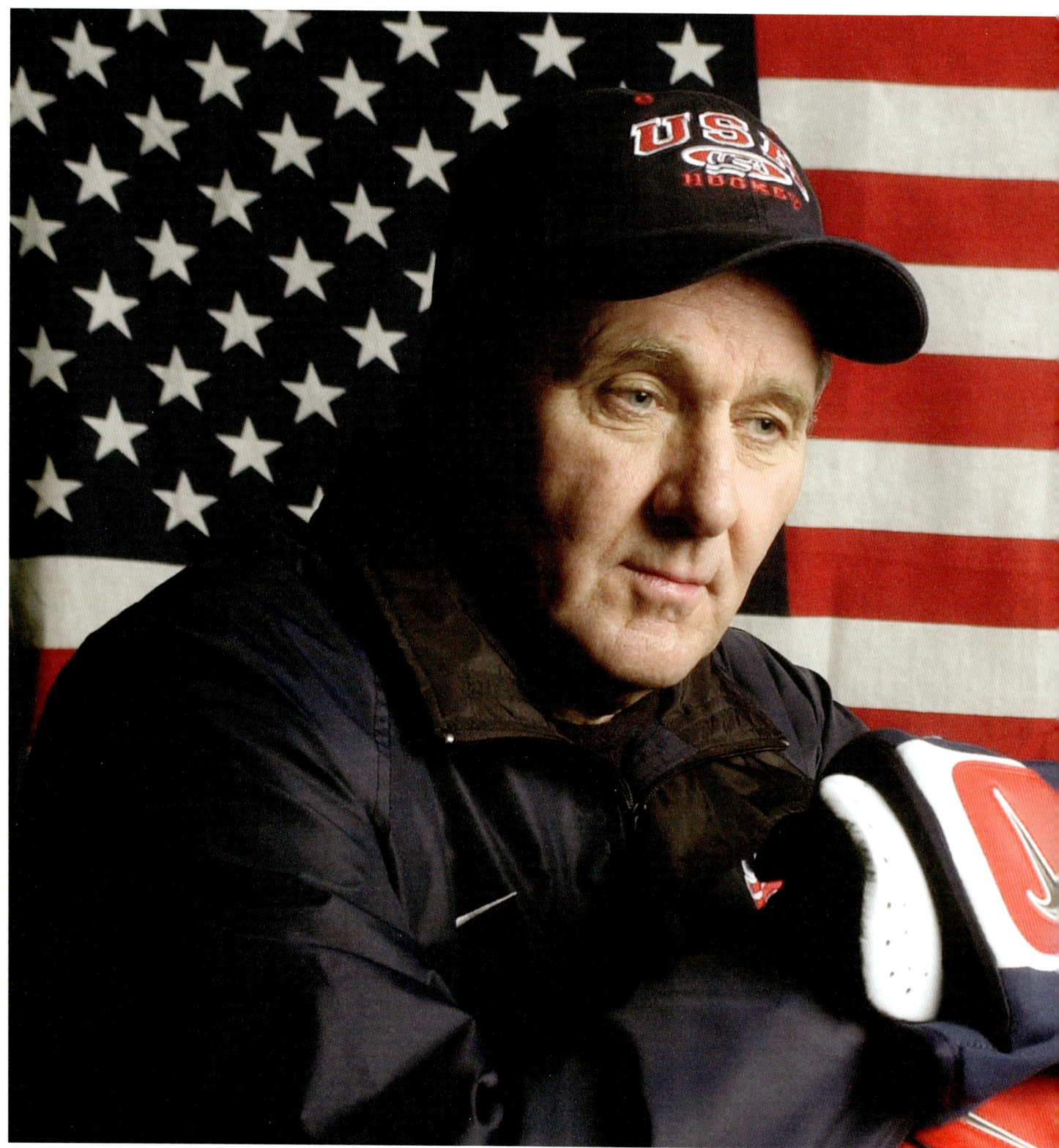

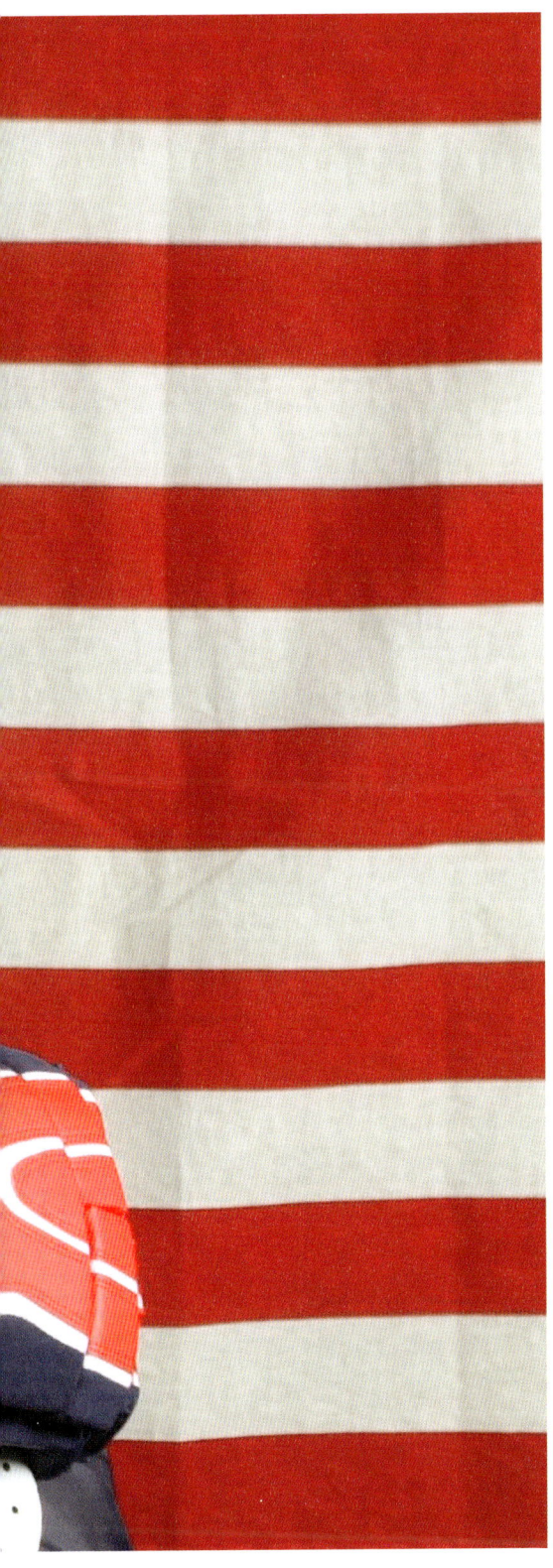

MIRACLE MAKER

Circa 2002

THE SPEECH WAS simple, Herb Brooks insisted. In the press conference after the U.S. Olympic team's win over the Soviets at the 1980 Winter Games, the American coach showed the yellow piece of paper on which he had scrawled his pregame notes. There were reminders about strategy, and some remarks to motivate his young players. The words have become legendary.

"You were born to be a player. You were meant to be here. This moment is yours."

Hollywood fleshed things out for the 2004 film *Miracle.* Screenwriters consulted with former team members, to make sure the movie speech matched what they remembered from the locker room. All agreed Kurt Russell's performance captured their former coach's personality. Brooks "had a bit of statesman in him," Dave Silk said in a National Public Radio interview.

Statesmanlike. Not fiery. And certainly not approachable. Brooks was a master motivator, but he was not easy to play for. Even as a player, his intensity set him apart. When he took over as coach at the University of Minnesota, he ran the team like a business manager, analyzing what was needed to win, then driving his players to implement the plan. With Brooks at the helm, the Gophers won three national titles in six years.

Sports Illustrated offered a glimpse of Brooks's approach in the December 10, 1979, issue, as the Olympic team prepared for Lake Placid. The coach was implementing a new hybrid strategy, a mix of European passing and Canadian toughness. "International hockey is a more subjective game," Brooks explained, "and it requires good skaters and good thinkers. Overall, it accelerates people's skills, makes them better stickhandlers and calls for a much more subtle physical game. I think it combines the best of both worlds."

Olympic gold led to NHL jobs, but Brooks's hybrid strategy and technocratic coaching did not find a place in the pros. At least not in the '80s. Today's NHL is different. North American players have speed and skills. Europeans can hit. The pro hockey we see today is what Brooks envisioned before Lake Placid: the best of both worlds.

Photograph by JOHN DOMAN/KRT

2002 to 2025

The Modern Era

RED WAVE

JOE LOUIS ARENA, DETROIT | *October 2, 2002*

DYNASTIES ARE MEASURED in titles. But championships alone do not do justice to the Detroit Red Wings of the 1990s and 2000s. From 1993, when Scotty Bowman took over as coach, to 2011, the Wings won the Central Division 13 times, claimed six Presidents' Trophies and won four Stanley Cups. Overall, the Red Wings had a .568 winning percentage, an extraordinary run of dominance.

To understand Detroit's success, one must start at the top, with owner Mike Ilitch. After buying the "Dead Wings" in 1982, Ilitch opened his wallet for players and, more importantly, for hockey minds to run the team: along with Bowman, he entrusted the team to Jimmy Devellano, who helped build the New York Islanders dynasty of the 1980s, and GM Ken Holland.

Bowman transformed the team after his arrival, convincing top scorer Steve Yzerman to become a two-way center. Leadership on the ice defined the Wings, first under Yzerman's captaincy and then that of Nicklas Lidström, one of the greatest defensemen ever. Around them, stars like Brendan Shanahan, Pavel Datsyuk and Henrik Zetterberg embodied Detroit's unselfish ethos, blending skill with relentless two-way play.

Before the salary cap, the Wings stockpiled All-Stars such as Chris Chelios, Brett Hull, Mike Vernon and Dominik Hašek. But thanks to scout Håkan Andersson, a former fishing guide, Detroit also netted big catches late in the draft: Datsyuk (171st overall pick), Zetterberg (210th) and Tomas Holmström (257th) all became franchise cornerstones.

The salary cap ultimately accomplished what it was intended to do, limiting Detroit's ability to keep both their talented draftees and established veterans signed as free agents. In 2009, when they made their last trip to the Final, the team could sign either Zetterberg or Marián Hossa to lucrative, long-term contracts, but not both. Hossa went to Chicago, where he won the Cup.

While it lasted, the Red Wings' dominance was a perfect blend of management, coaching and exceptional talent. More than a dynasty, Detroit was the last, great example of a team that could do it all, year after year. In the salary-cap NHL, such a run is almost unimaginable.

Photograph by DAVID E. KLUTHO

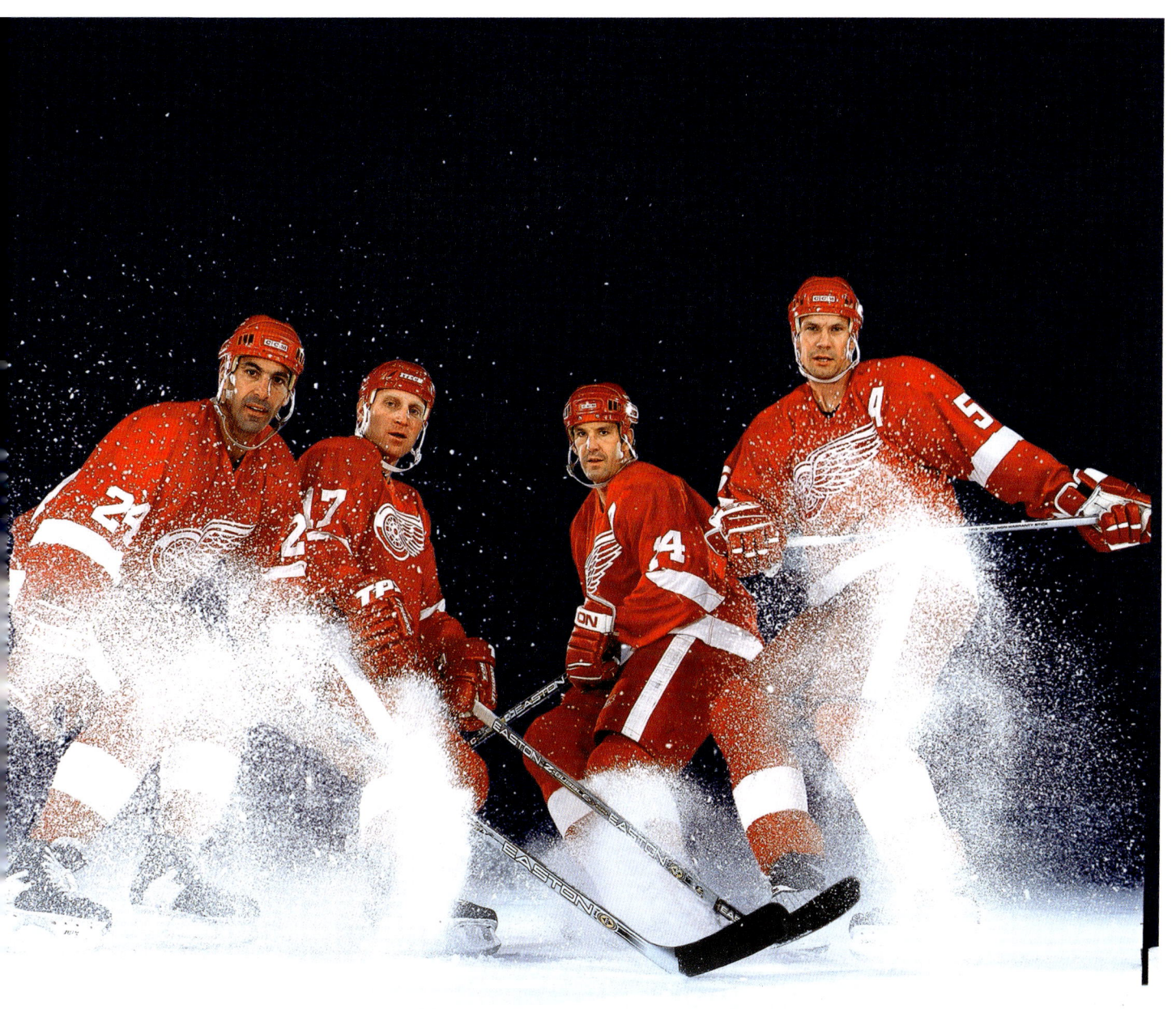

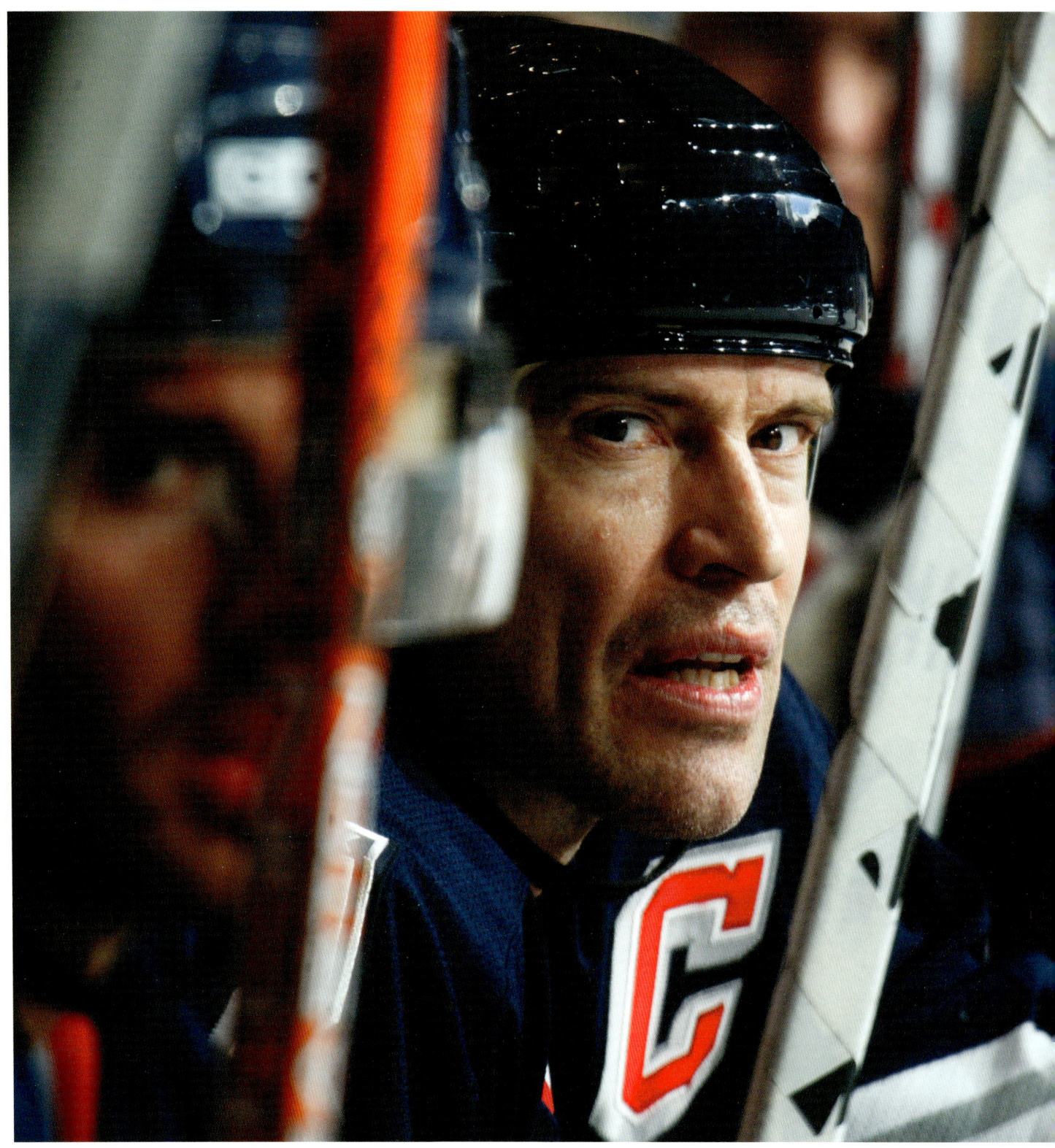

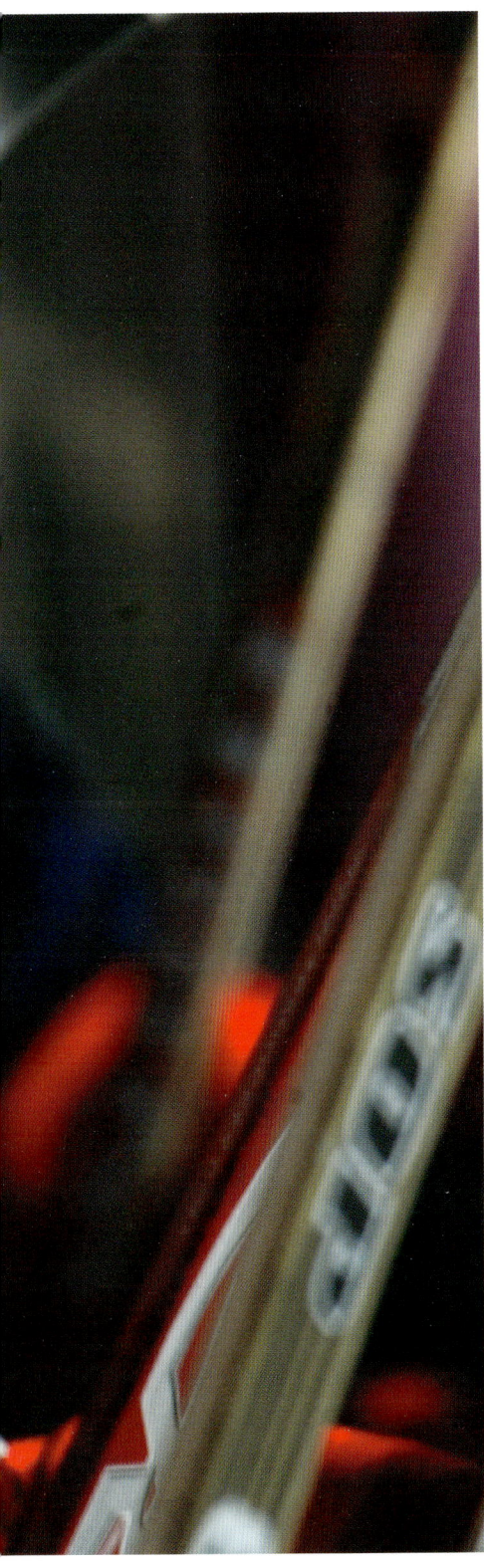

THE MESSIAH

Circa 2004

"WHO IS THIS Mark Messier?" asked Leigh Montville in *Sports Illustrated*. "Is he for real? How can he be doing the things that he is doing?"

When Montville asked his question in March 1992, Messier was finishing his first season with the New York Rangers. He had come to the team in an October trade, after winning five Stanley Cup titles and the Hart Trophy in Edmonton. At the time he arrived, the Rangers had the league's best defenseman (Brian Leetch), a proven scorer (Mike Gartner) and an unmatched goaltending duo (Mike Richter and John Vanbiesbrouck). But there was something missing. As Montville wrote, it was Messier who brought all the pieces together:

> Try to put a finger on the things he has done and sometimes you touch substance, but mostly you touch air. Changed air. A team that has been trailed by a history of postseason failure—that hasn't won the Stanley Cup since 1940—is riding toward its future at the top of the standings, best record in hockey. There is a change in confidence, a change in outlook. There is leadership. Poof. One man. There is a difference.

> "You make a trade, you hope for the best," Rangers general manager Neil Smith says. "In this case, we were looking for Mark to give us as much help off the ice as on the ice. He has done even more than we expected."

There was even more to come. Two years later, with the Rangers facing elimination in the conference final against the New Jersey Devils, Messier uttered the words now engraved in NHL lore: "We'll win tonight."

Leetch read his captain's guarantee in a newspaper left on the team bus. "I guess we're going to win tonight," he told teammate Nick Kypreos.

Sure enough, they did—thanks to Messier's hat trick. The Rangers went on to win the series, and then win the Cup. Leetch earned the Conn Smythe Trophy as playoff MVP, but Messier earned his place in hockey history, his granite face carved on the Mt. Rushmore of the sport's greatest leaders. He remains the only player to captain two different teams to the Stanley Cup.

Photograph by BRUCE BENNETT STUDIOS

THE LOCKOUT

BARRIE, ONTARIO | *September 17, 2004*

IN SEPTEMBER 2004, the National Hockey League turned off the lights. The 2004–05 lockout was more than a labor disagreement; it was one of the most consequential economic events in pro sports history. The 10-month stalemate erased an entire season, alienated fans and reshaped the league's financial structure.

By the early 2000s, payroll disparities were vast. Small-market teams in cities such as Calgary and Edmonton struggled to compete with those in New York and Detroit, whose payrolls exceeded $75 million. According to a league report, teams were spending roughly 76 percent of revenue on salaries, and many franchises were hemorrhaging money. Commissioner Gary Bettman demanded a salary cap. The NHL Players Association, led by Bob Goodenow, countered with suggestions of revenue sharing and a luxury tax.

Neither side blinked. On February 16, 2005, Bettman canceled the season, the first time a North American league had done so because of a labor dispute. Fans were furious, with the majority putting the blame on players. But Bettman bet on hockey's diehards. After the two

sides reached agreement in July 2005, the faithful came back for the start of the new season. Total attendance in 2005–06 was nearly a half-million over the last season before the lockout.

The collective bargaining agreement gave Bettman the salary cap he wanted, but it also included revenue sharing and guaranteed player contracts. The cap's initial $39 million ceiling was tied to league revenues, ensuring a fixed percentage for player salaries. Small-market clubs could now compete with the Detroits and New Yorks of the league. Parity became the NHL's hallmark: any team that made the playoffs had a shot to go deep.

Financially, the gamble paid off. The lockout bruised hockey's image in the short term, but it remade the NHL's business model, creating a new era of competitive teams and valuable franchises. By 2025, team values had climbed from a pre-lockout average of $163 million to $1.9 billion. In sacrificing a season, the league secured its long-term stability: a costly, but transformative, victory for the game.

Photograph by AP PHOTO/ADRIAN WYLD

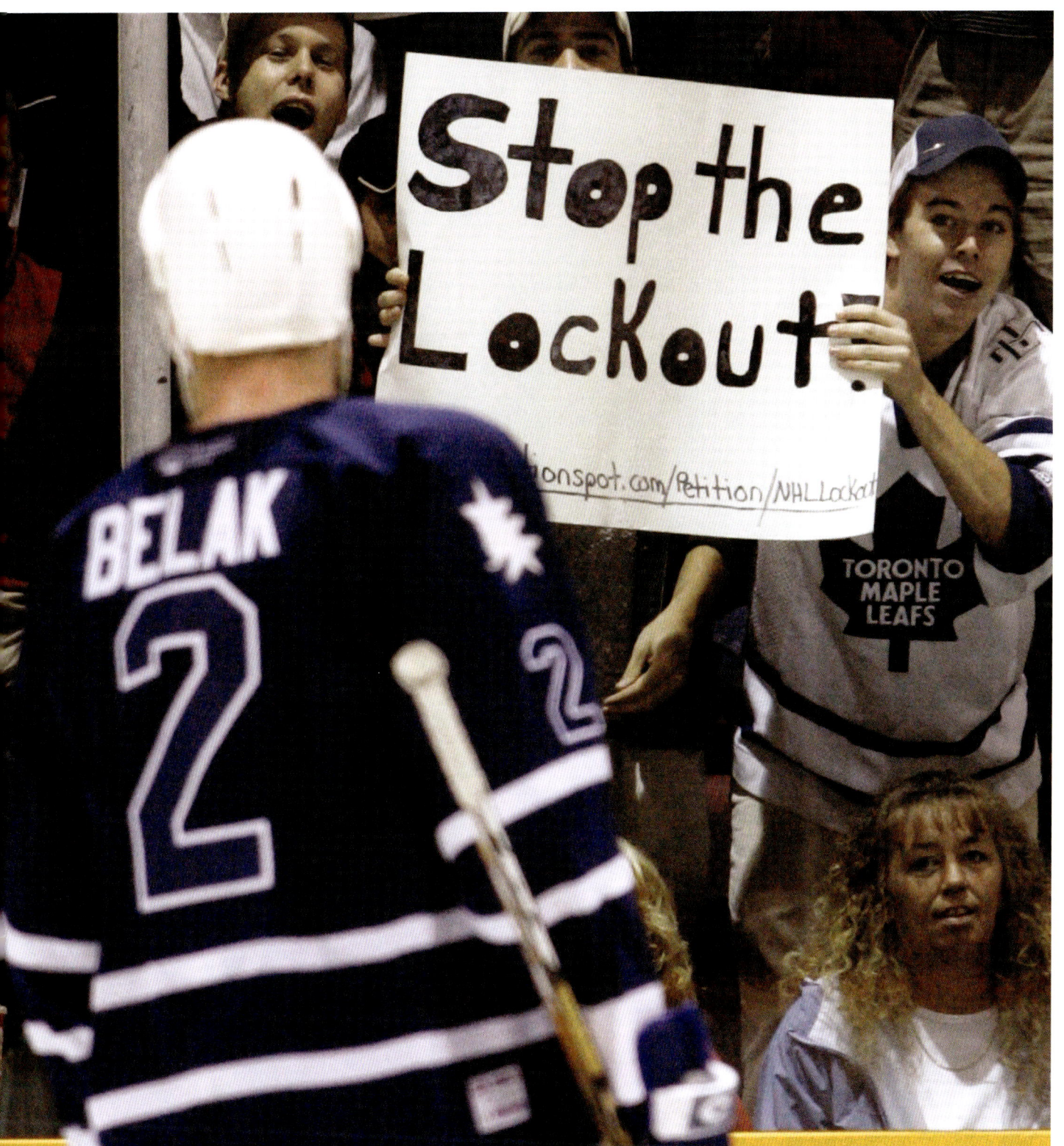

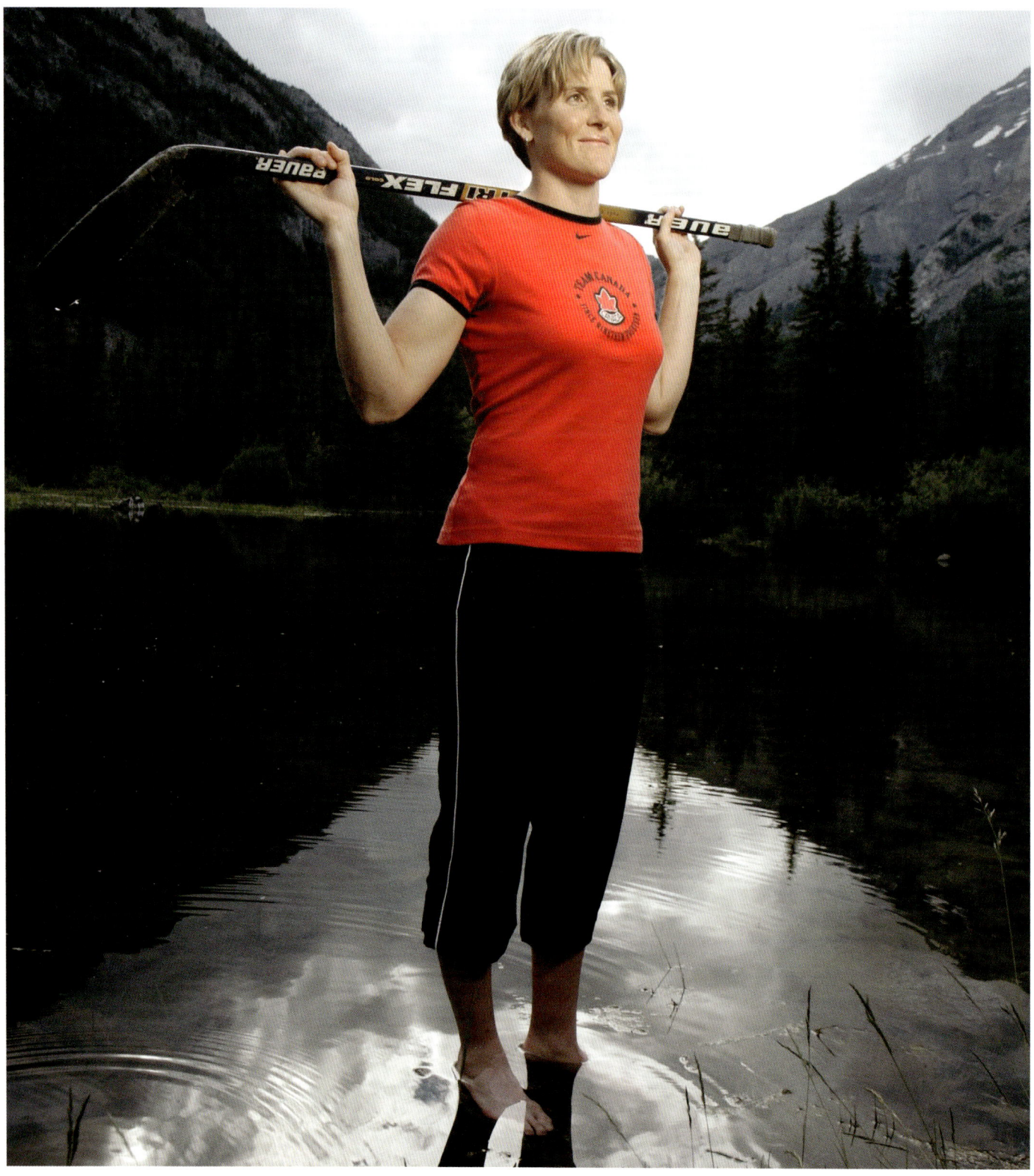

THE GAME CHANGER

CALGARY | *July 8, 2007*

WHEN HAYLEY WICKENHEISER retired from hockey in 2017, Wayne Gretzky was there to pay tribute. "You played with heart, desire, finesse, speed and skill," he said.

Leigh Montville described where it all began for Wickenheiser in the February 9, 1998, issue of *Sports Illustrated*, shortly before the first Olympics to include women's hockey:

> There never was a lot going on in Shaunavon, Saskatchewan, a farming town 75 miles from the big-city lights of Swift Current, but at night there was nothing. No cars. No noise. Nothing. Tom Wickenheiser would stand in his backyard and spray water from a hose, back and forth, over and over, building a rink. He was doing what so many Canadian fathers of so many Canadian hockey players—Orr and Howe, Gretzky and Lemieux, and the rest—had done, providing not only the opportunity for winter fun but also laying out the slippery magic carpet that every once in a while carries a kid to fame, fortune and large arenas around the world.

> There was one difference. Wickenheiser's rink was for his daughter, Hayley. There was no place the magic carpet could go.

"There was a time, I forget exactly how old Hayley was, when I sat her down," Tom says. "I tried to explain life. She was a good athlete in all sports—softball, volleyball, basketball. I told her these were sports with an upside. She probably should concentrate on them. Hockey, I said, really didn't have a future. She said she didn't care. She wanted to play hockey."

Contrary to what Tom Wickenheiser said, hockey did have a future for women—and his daughter helped create it. Over 23 years with the Canadian national team, Hayley Wickenheiser won four Olympic gold medals and seven world championships. She retired as Team Canada's top scorer, with 379 points in 276 international games. More importantly, she was the face of the sport. When she finished her career, tens of thousands of girls and women were playing hockey across Canada.

At her retirement, Gretzky saluted her accomplishment: "You've opened so many doors for so many young girls."

Photograph by PETER READ MILLER

SID THE KID

MELLON ARENA, PITTSBURGH | *November 27, 2007*

HOW DO YOU solve a problem called Sidney Crosby? This was the question *Sports Illustrated* addressed in its February 29, 2016, issue. Michael Farber stated the conundrum:

> On the one hand, he has been an exemplar on the ice, a generational player and a worthy ambassador for the game. Like Wayne Gretzky. On the other hand, unlike Gretzky, he has not been a crossover star who is part of the daily sports conversation.
>
> The faults, if you find them, are not in the star but in ourselves. The expectations were always overblown for a hockey savant the likes of which seem to come along in Canada every seven or so years (Orr, Lafleur, Gretzky, Lemieux, Lindros, Crosby, McDavid). Crosby has always been graded on the Gretzky Curve, which works against him as a player and as an NHL flag bearer. If Gretzky could peer around corners, Crosby is a hard-driving, heavy-traffic player, more a workman than a visionary. And while Crosby has excited hockey fans, he hasn't necessarily inspired hockey converts. Now in his 11th season—it began with a five-game pointless streak and has included a seven-game goal streak, each matching the longest of his career—he is an enigma in plain sight. His name comes with appreciative nods and also a "Yes, but...."

When Farber wrote his analysis, Crosby's statistics showed signs of a scoring decline, perhaps an end-of-career slide. "Crosby still has years to change the plot," Farber added. "He may never score like Gretzky or lead like Mark Messier or be a godlike figure like Jean Béliveau, but a few more Stanley Cups or Olympic gold medals will sand off the corners and burnish a reputation to a lustrous glow. Of course, given the career arc of elite scorers, can Crosby's best hockey really lie ahead?"

The answer was yes. Later that year, Crosby led the Pittsburgh Penguins to another Cup and then repeated in 2017, a season in which he was the league's top goal scorer. After turning 35 in 2022, he had three seasons in a row of more than 90 points. Sid the Kid definitely changed the plot.

Photograph by HEINZ KLUETMEIER

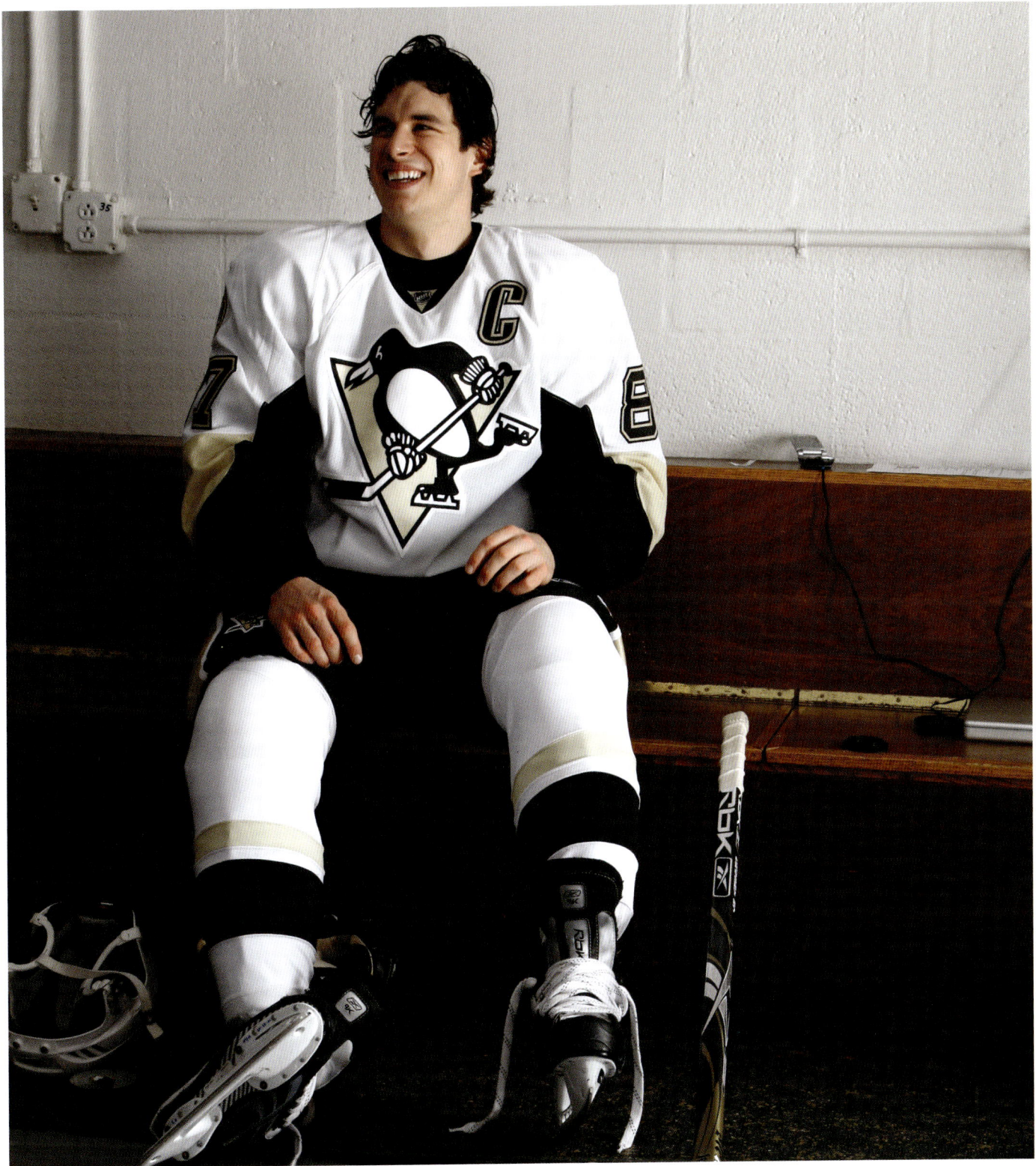

THE ICE MACHINE

JOE LOUIS ARENA, DETROIT | *June 2, 2008*

IT IS A miraculous machine. The scars of battle are wiped away, leaving behind a surface that is fresh, clean, gleaming. Hockey players agree that there is no greater pleasure than gliding across the ice after its work is complete. Spectators young and old find themselves transfixed by the machine's methodical path.

"There are three things in life people like to stare at," Charlie Brown once said: "a flowing stream, a crackling fire and a Zamboni clearing the ice."

Minnesota songwriter Martin Zellar expressed the longing of many a hockey fan in his 1990 song "Zamboni," performed by his band the Gear Daddies. The song's chorus is now heard in arenas around the world: "I wanna drive the Zamboni."

In truth, the Zamboni's origins were not connected to hockey. The Zamboni brothers opened their Los Angeles–area rink at the height of the figure skating craze inspired by Sonja Henie. Production of ice skates doubled in the United States in the late 1930s, as millions of young girls hoped to follow the Norwegian champion's path from the Olympics to Hollywood stardom. When Iceland opened in Paramount, California, in 1940, it was the largest rink in the country. But with 20,000 square feet of ice, it took five men over an hour and a half to clean the rink. The middle Zamboni, Frank, went to work right away to find a mechanized solution.

Nine years later, Frank Zamboni applied for a patent for his "Ice Rink Resurfacing Machine." Henie was one of his first customers, buying two for her traveling ice show. Chicago Black Hawks owner Arthur Wirtz bought one as well, although he quickly soured on the contraption. Fans tended to stay in their seats between periods to watch it rather than buying concessions.

Frank Zamboni himself never cared for hockey, and he could barely stand on skates. Nevertheless, his invention has brought more joy to hockey fans than any highlight-reel goal. Just mention a Zamboni and people smile. "I can only think of one other machine whose name does that," Frank's son Richard told *Sports Illustrated*, "and that's a Jacuzzi."

Photograph by BRUCE BENNETT STUDIOS

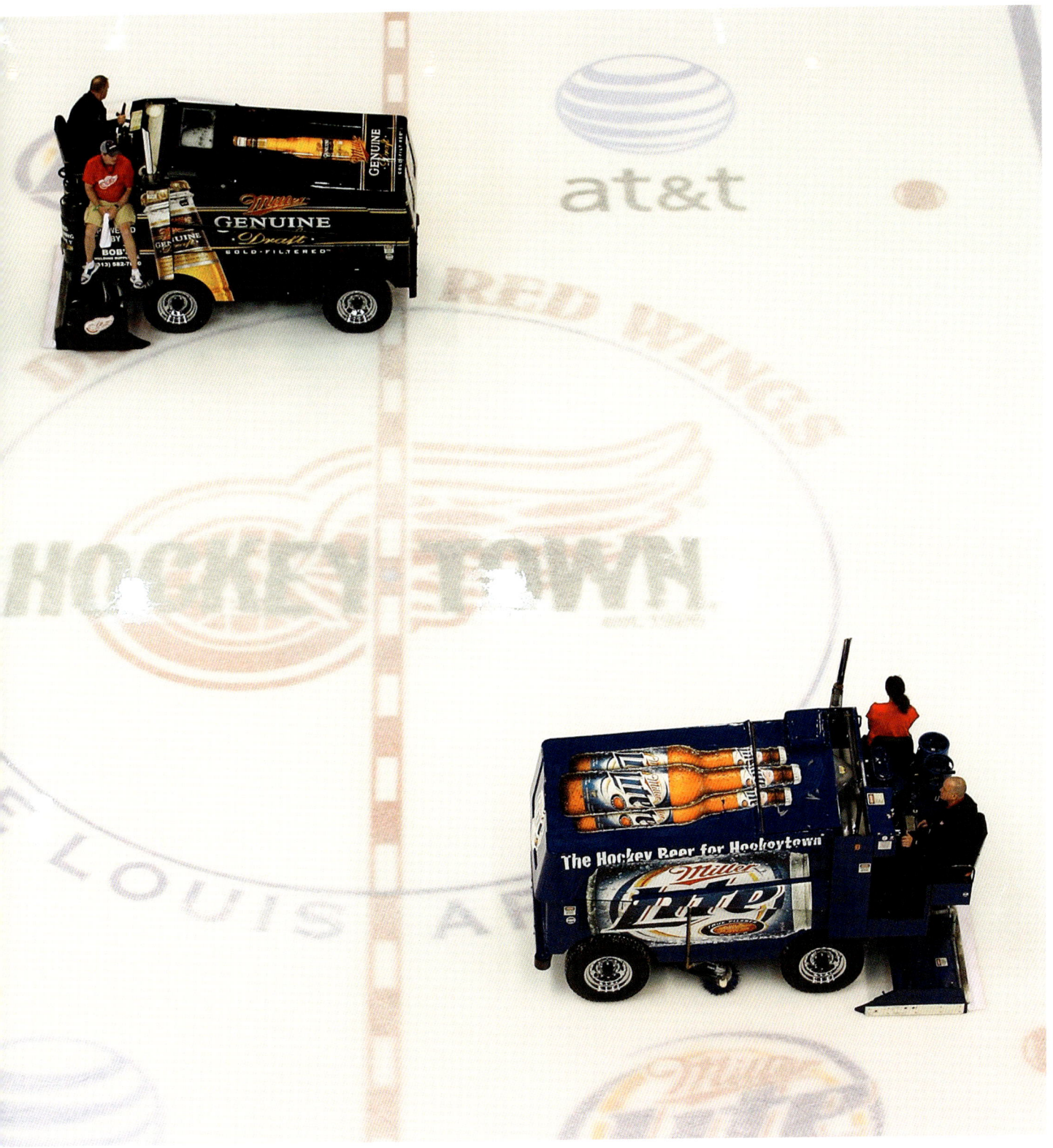

GOOD ENOUGH

MELLON ARENA, PITTSBURGH | *June 4, 2008*

THE PUCK WOBBLED in the blue paint like a time bomb. The clock above the glass gasped its final breaths. Marián Hossa lunged. Chris Osgood lunged back. Doc Emrick made the call: "Save, Osgood!"

And then, suddenly, the horn blared, the gloves flew and Pittsburgh's Mellon Arena fell silent. The Detroit Red Wings were Stanley Cup champions.

For Osgood, this was more than just the final save of the season. It was the exclamation point on a redemption story that had been a decade in the making. Once cast off from Detroit, replaced by Dominik Hašek, claimed on waivers by the New York Islanders, traded to St. Louis and presumed done for good, Osgood had fought his way back. He'd started the 2008 playoffs as a backup, but when Hašek faltered against Nashville in the first round, Detroit coach Mike Babcock turned to the 35-year-old veteran.

Osgood seized his chance and refused to relinquish the net. He posted a remarkable 1.90 goals-against average in a sweep of the Colorado Avalanche and a six-game win over the Dallas Stars, silencing doubters and reminding everyone of the clutch goaltender he had always been. In the first two games of the Final, he posted back-to-back shutouts against the Penguins. But his defining moment came in Game 6, with the home team pressing to force overtime.

In the final seconds, with Pittsburgh down 3–2, Sidney Crosby ripped a shot that clipped Osgood's glove and dribbled behind him. Hossa crashed the crease, reaching ahead with his stick. Osgood sprawled across the ice, blocking the puck's path. The disc slid past the post as the horn sounded.

"It was chaotic that last 40 seconds," Osgood said later.

"When I saw the puck and looked up and it was 0.0 on the clock, I was a pretty happy man," said Henrik Zetterberg.

The last-second save was the culmination of a remarkable comeback—and a remarkable dynasty. Detroit's fourth title in 11 years was brought home not by one of its brilliant Europeans, not by a high-profile trade acquisition or multi-millionaire free agent, but by the old hand everyone thought was done.

Photograph by DAVID E. KLUTHO

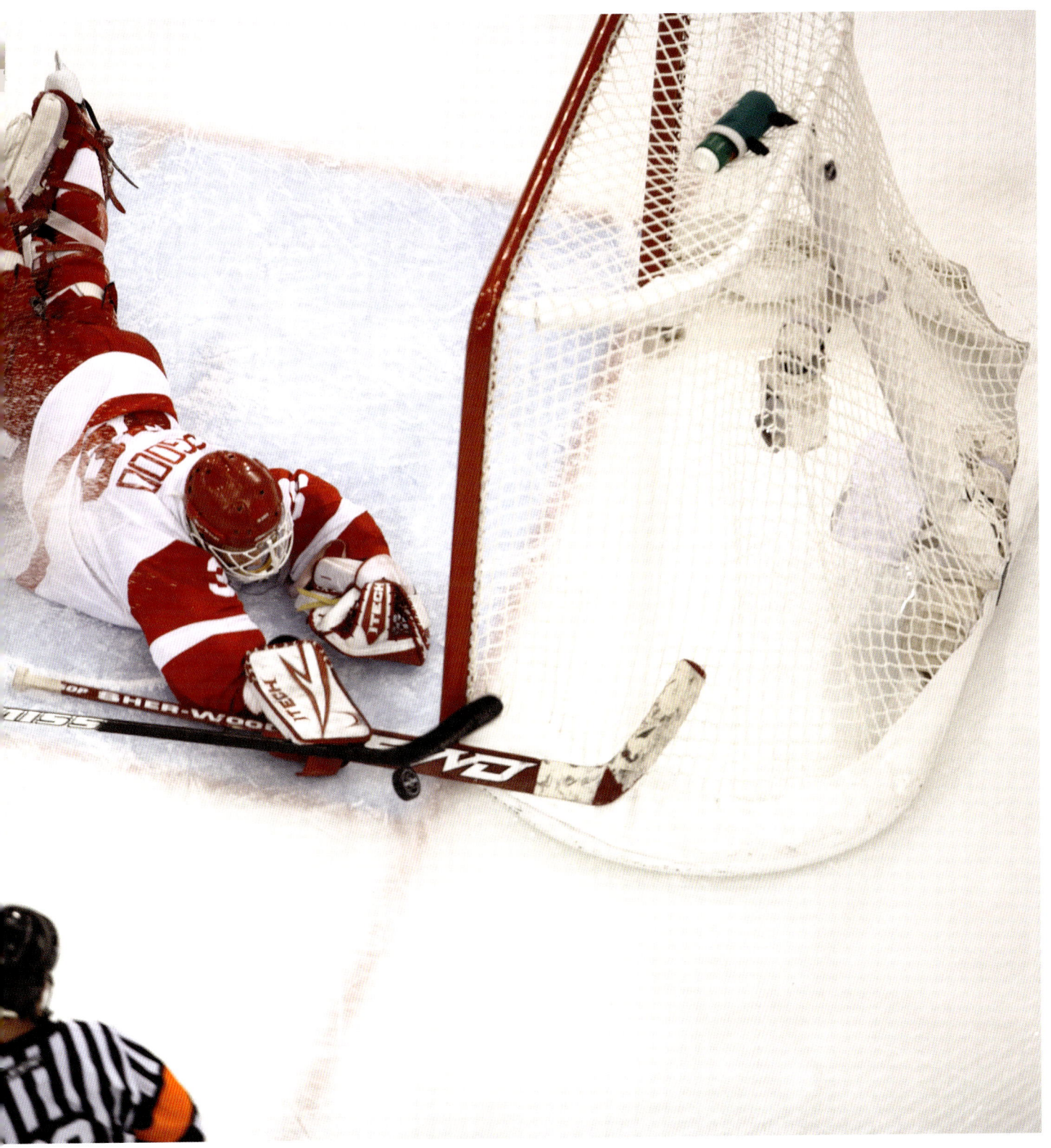

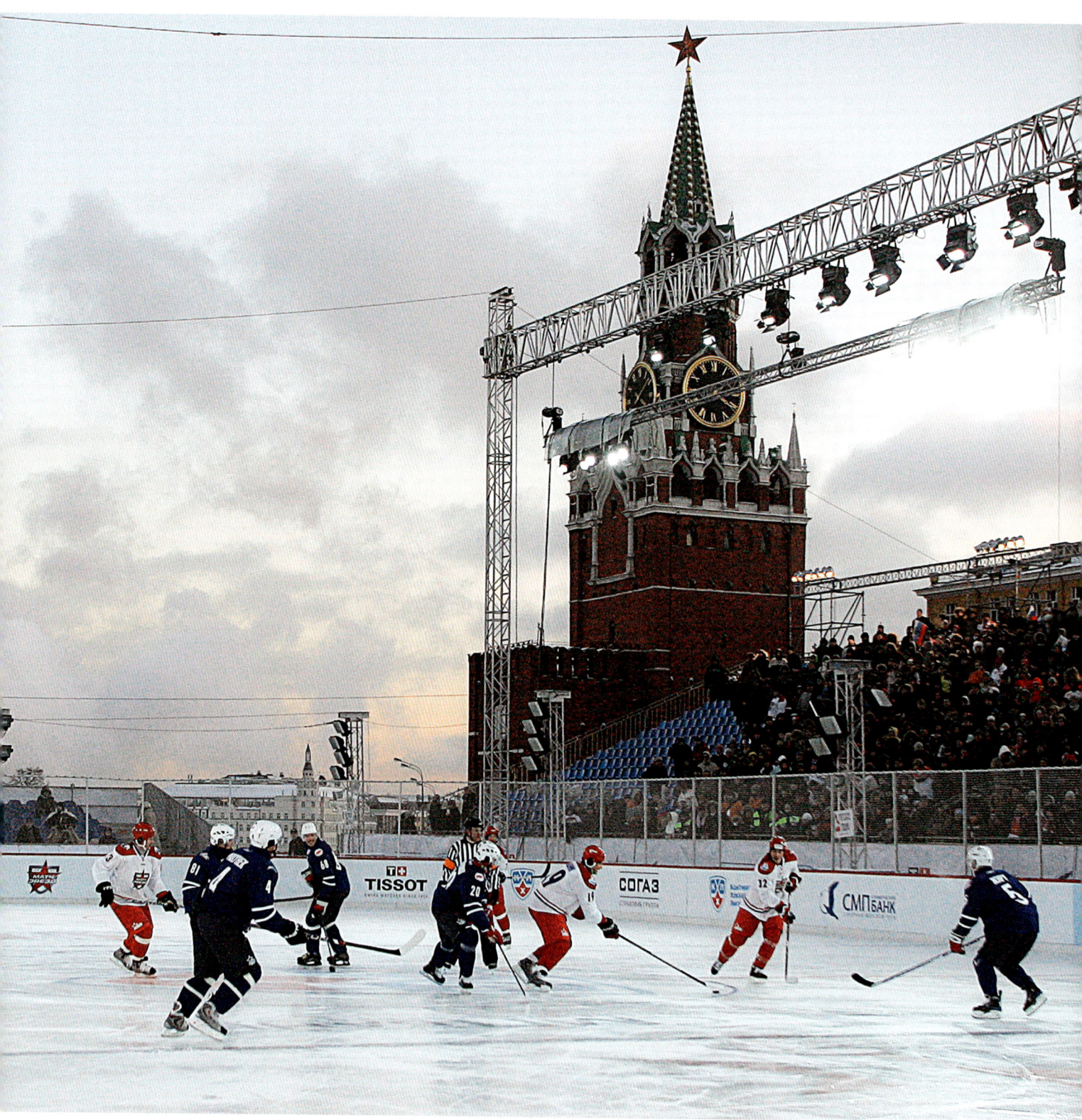

THE KONTINENTAL HOCKEY LEAGUE

RED SQUARE, MOSCOW | *January 10, 2009*

THE KONTINENTAL HOCKEY League began play in 2008 with 24 teams spread throughout Russia as well as in the capitals of Latvia, Belarus and Kazakhstan. The KHL imported many of the features of North American sports: giant fuzzy mascots entertaining kids at rinkside, cheerleaders shaking poms-poms on arena steps and players skating through clouds of dry-ice fog for pregame introductions.

The Russian league also adopted the NHL's practice of holding marquee games outside. This photo shows the league's first all-star game on Moscow's Red Square. Selected players were organized into teams representing Russia and the rest of the world. With financial backing from Gazprom and other energy companies, KHL teams had signed National Hockey League veterans from Russia and Europe, as well as a handful of North American journeymen. For the game on Red Square, former Ottawa Senators and New York Islanders All-Star Alexei Yashin captained Team Russia, while the international squad was led by the KHL's biggest star, Jaromír Jágr.

According to the league's founders, signing players like Jágr and Yashin was a key strategy. Sports Minister Slava Fetisov, the former Soviet captain who won the Stanley Cup with the Detroit Red Wings, expected all the best Russian and European players to play in the KHL. By contrast, the NHL would be left with only Americans and Canadians. The KHL would expand to 60 teams, spread from Western Europe to East Asia. Just as in international politics, Russia's hockey league would counter the wealth and power of America.

Fetisov had the idea for the KHL, but the person who took credit for the league was his boss. "I did not just support the KHL," Vladimir Putin told a Moscow newspaper. "I was the initiator."

With Russia's president claiming to be its founder and Russian oil money bankrolling teams, the Kontinental Hockey League was about far more than hockey. The league aimed to extend the Kremlin's influence across Russia and into neighboring countries. Yet the KHL was never a serious threat to the National Hockey League. Like Putin's Russia, the KHL had the shiny facade of a modern Western operation and the rusty gears of an old Soviet machine.

Photograph by AFP

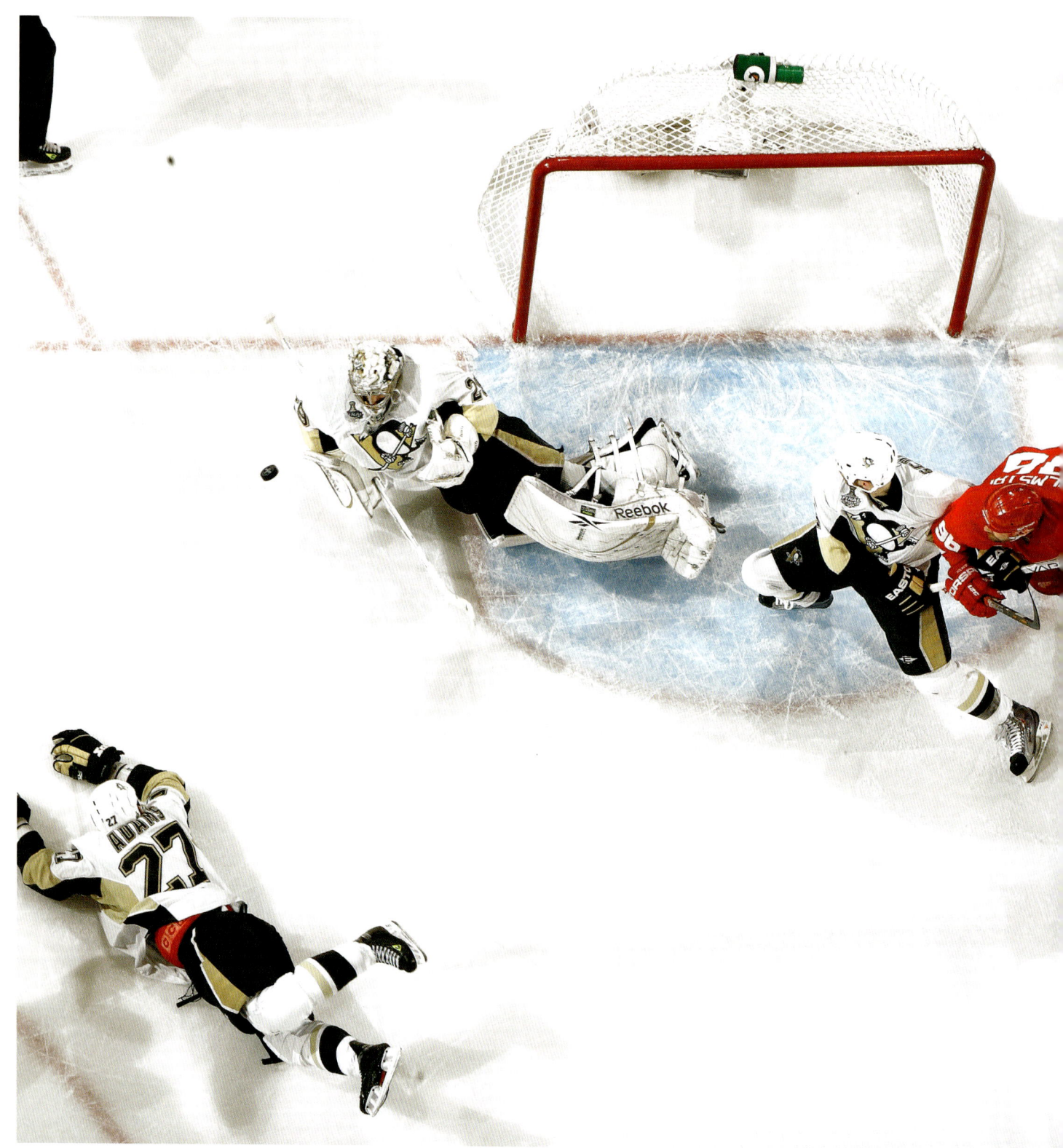

FLOWER POWER

JOE LOUIS ARENA, DETROIT | *June 12, 2009*

ONE YEAR LATER: the same two teams, the same stakes, a different setting and a more high-pressure situation—Game 7 of the Final, closing seconds, Pittsburgh holding a 2–1 lead and facing off in their own end.

Detroit won the draw, and the puck went back to the point. Brian Rafalski took a shot, but it was knocked down in traffic. The puck found the stick of Henrik Zetterberg, who took a quick wrister from the right faceoff dot. Marc-André Fleury kicked the puck to the left circle. Nicklas Lidström raced forward and fired high toward the open net. Fleury lunged across the crease. The goalie's right shoulder sent the puck toward the corner. Lidström chased the rebound, but Pittsburgh's Craig Adams stretched across the ice to block his path to the goal.

And then, suddenly, the horn blared, the gloves flew and Detroit's Joe Louis Arena fell silent. The Pittsburgh Penguins were Stanley Cup champions.

Gary Bettman handed the Cup to Sidney Crosby, the youngest captain ever to lift the trophy. Though a knee injury kept him on the bench for much of the third period, Crosby's leadership throughout the playoffs was undeniable. He finished with a playoff-leading 15 goals plus 16 assists, and despite "middling numbers" in the Final, he displayed an unyielding work ethic. Four years into his career, he capped Pittsburgh's rebuild from the losing seasons of the early 2000s. As co-owner Mario Lemieux said after the game, through tears of joy, "When you have Sid, anything is possible."

But the image etched in Pittsburgh lore was Fleury's sprawling denial of Lidström. After hoisting the Cup with Pittsburgh in 2009, Marc-André Fleury's career became a masterclass in resilience and reinvention. The acrobatic Fleury backstopped the Penguins through highs and lows, eventually ceding the crease to Matt Murray during their 2016 and 2017 Stanley Cup runs. Fleury found new life in Vegas, guiding the expansion Golden Knights in the Final in their inaugural season. The Flower earned three All-Star nods and a Vezina Trophy in Vegas. He finished his career in 2025 with Minnesota. His 575 wins rank second all time.

Photograph by DAVID E. KLUTHO

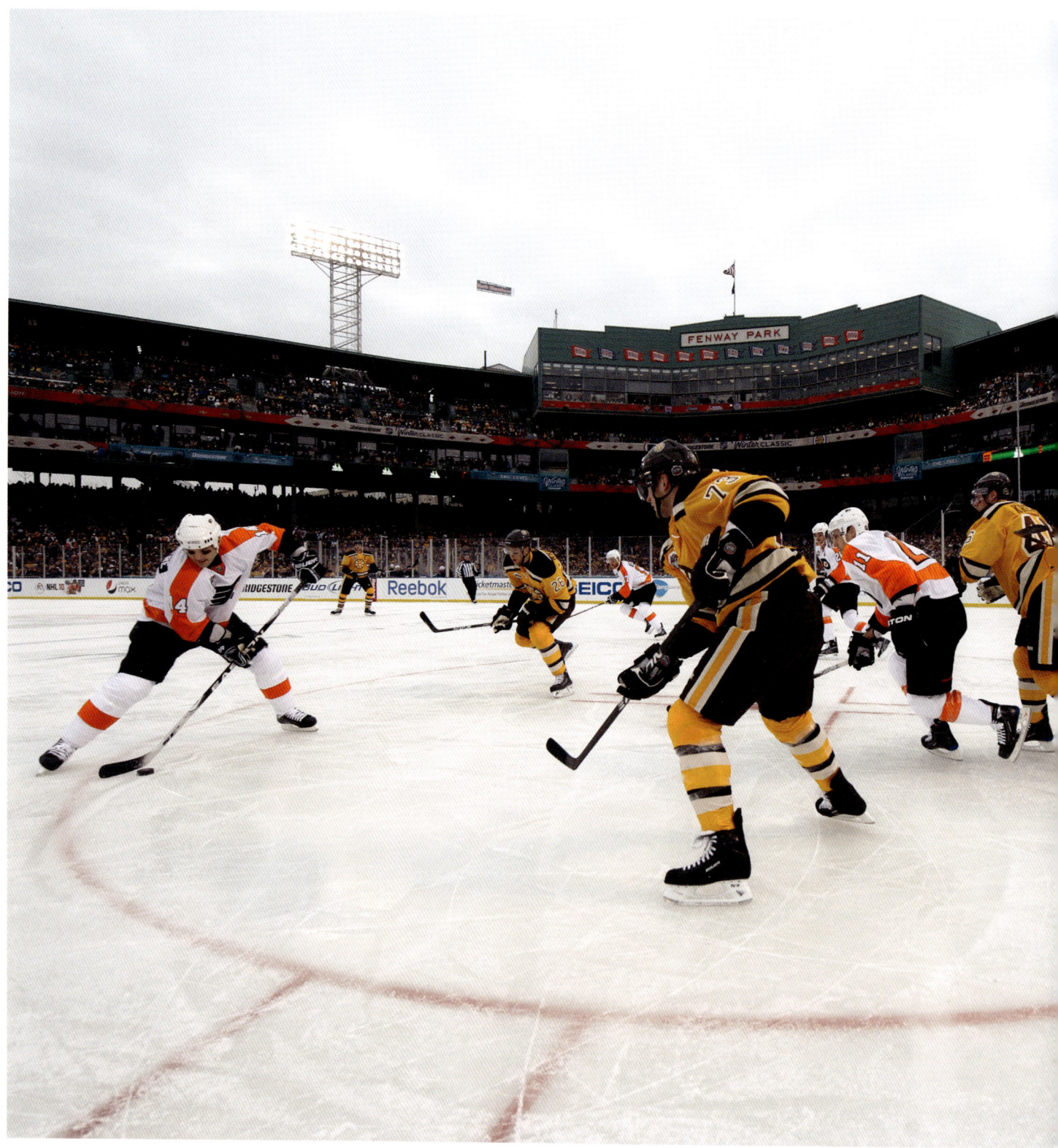

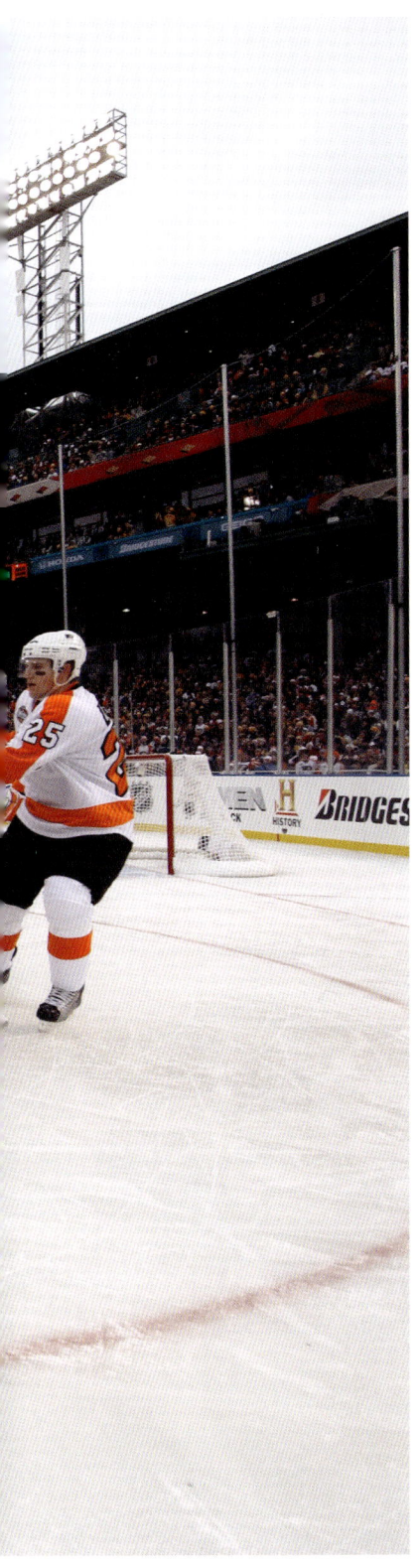

THE WINTER CLASSIC

FENWAY PARK, BOSTON | *January 1, 2010*

SIDNEY CROSBY STILL recalls the snowflakes drifting in Buffalo on that New Year's Day, the bare-chested fans at Ralph Wilson Stadium braving sub-freezing temperatures, the buzz in the chilly air that made it feel like both a Stanley Cup Final and a neighborhood shinny game.

"It was like this perfect mix between hockey being pure outside, combined with your dream of playing in the NHL," Crosby told ESPN's Greg Wyshinski. Since that first game in 2008, he and the Pittsburgh Penguins have played outdoors another five times, in both Winter Classic and Stadium Series matchups. But according to Crosby, "nothing matches that feeling coming out of Buffalo."

The Winter Classic has become an annual pilgrimage to the sport's origins, a captivating outdoor spectacle cherished by players and fans alike. For players, the Winter Classic rekindles the joy of pond hockey, even if the pond is surrounded by skyscrapers, stadium lights and tens of thousands of spectators.

Fans have embraced the event with unbridled enthusiasm, turning football and baseball stadiums into cathedrals of cold-weather devotion. Storied venues from Fenway Park and Wrigley Field to Notre Dame Stadium and Michigan's Big House have provided unforgettable backdrops. Even in warm-weather locales like Dallas, where more than 85,000 fans packed the Cotton Bowl, the Winter Classic has shown that outdoor hockey has an allure in any climate.

The Winter Classic's appeal extends beyond ticket sales. Television audiences have consistently delivered some of the league's highest regular-season ratings, with millions tuning in despite competition from college football bowl games.

And then there's the gear. Winter Classic jerseys have become a must-have for hockey faithful. In 2023, when the Penguins played the Boston Bruins at Fenway Park, jerseys accounted for 72 percent of total merch sales. Adidas and the NHL lean hard into history, sometimes faithfully, sometimes with bold reinterpretations. The Penguins' 2023 yellow "P" jersey paid homage to Pittsburgh's 1920s NHL team, the Pirates. Chicago's 2024 red sweater with white and black stripes gave a modern polish to early franchise glory.

With its outdoor venues and retro sweaters, the Winter Classic is hockey history come to life. The nostalgia business has never looked better.

Photograph by DAVID E. KLUTHO

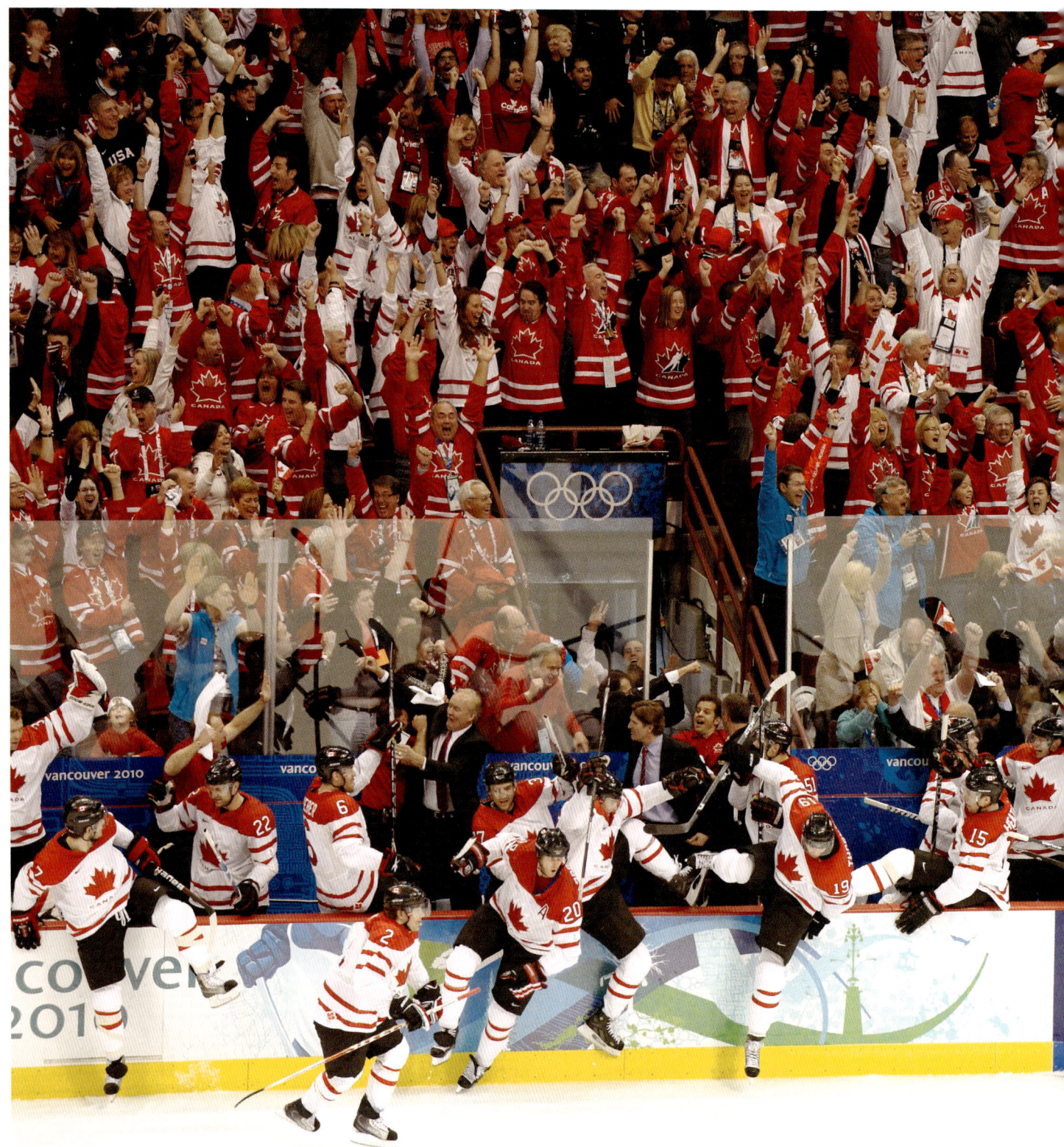

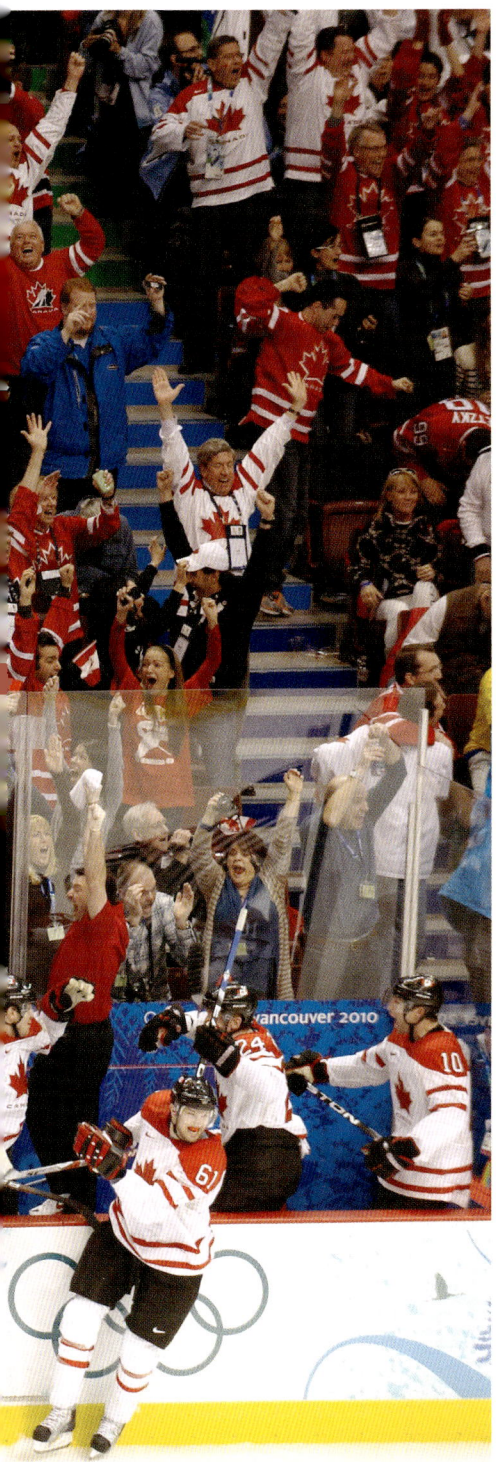

O CANADA!

CANADA HOCKEY PLACE, VANCOUVER | *February 28, 2010*

IT WAS A goal for the new century. Sidney Crosby delivered on the home ice of the 2010 Vancouver Winter Olympics, claiming the gold medal for Canada in a 3–2 overtime win over their rivals to the south. *Sports Illustrated*'s Michael Farber summed up its significance for hockey's homeland:

> Crosby had earned a standing O Canada, but the open secret of these Olympics was that he had been unexceptional. He had not scored a point in the two previous games…. Team Canada general manager Steve Yzerman would later praise Crosby for doing all the little things, but some people are destined to do the big things on the biggest stage….
>
> The decisive play started along the boards when Crosby chipped the puck past U.S. defenseman Brian Rafalski to Jarome Iginla. Crosby jumped off the wall, wheeled toward the net and, as he left Rafalski a stride behind, screamed, "Iggy! Iggy!"
>
> "He was yelling pretty urgently," Iginla said. "There are different pitches of yell. You could tell he had a step." Iginla…slipped a pass onto Crosby's stick for the wrist shot heard, at the very least, from British Columbia to Newfoundland.
>
> For a nation that never has been humble about its hockey ambitions, this was, in Canadian terms, a Paul Henderson where-were-you-when? In the U.S., defining events have more gravitas—the moon landing, 9/11—but it is a reflection of Canada's role in the world that its frozen-in-time moments of the last half-century involve frozen water. Henderson scored the game-winner against the Soviet Union in Moscow in the finale of the 1972 Summit Series, a goal that stopped time. Now at 2:53 PST in the most-watched hockey game in North America since the Miracle on Ice in 1980—it drew 27.6 million viewers on NBC and a staggering 16.6 (about half the country) on CTV in Canada—Crosby had done the same. He had written a new story for those who had experienced "Henderson scores for Canada!" only through the gilded memory of their parents.

Photograph by ROBERT BECK

THE GOAL OF THE DECADE

WACHOVIA CENTER, PHILADELPHIA | *June 9, 2010*

GAME 6 IN Philadelphia was tied 3–3. Overtime carried a half-century of frustration. Chicago had a 3–2 series lead, and the Blackhawks faithful hoped for an end to years of heartbreak. This was a championship-or-bust season: the roster was loaded, and the salary cap was about to break it apart. Anything less than the Stanley Cup would only reopen the wounds of 1971, and 1973, and 1992.

Just over four minutes into the extra frame, Patrick Kane took the puck along the left boards, cut toward defenseman Kimmo Timonen, and snapped a shot that slid under goalie Michael Leighton's pads. Kane flung his gloves in the air as he bounded to center ice.

"It didn't seem like there was much reaction from anyone, so I think that's why I celebrated the way I did," Kane recalled. "I went kind of crazy, threw the gloves off, skated down the ice."

There wasn't much reaction because nobody was sure Kane had scored. The red light never went on. The puck had just disappeared.

On replay, the goal was confirmed. The Blackhawks were champions for the first time since the Kennedy administration.

But the story didn't end on the ice. The six-ounce piece of vulcanized rubber vanished in the chaos, spawning one of hockey's strangest whodunits. The Hockey Hall of Fame wanted it. The CEO of Harry Caray's Restaurants offered $50,000 for it. Theories flew: Chris Pronger was swiping pucks earlier in the series; grainy video showed linesman Steve Miller bending toward something black on the ice.

FBI photo analysis, fan-shot video and countless interviews couldn't pin it down. Even 15 years later, no one had come forward with definitive proof of the puck's whereabouts.

As for the goal itself, Kane's phantom snipe was dubbed Goal of the Decade by the NHL. It was certainly the most important in Blackhawks history.

Photograph by BILL SMITH/NHLI

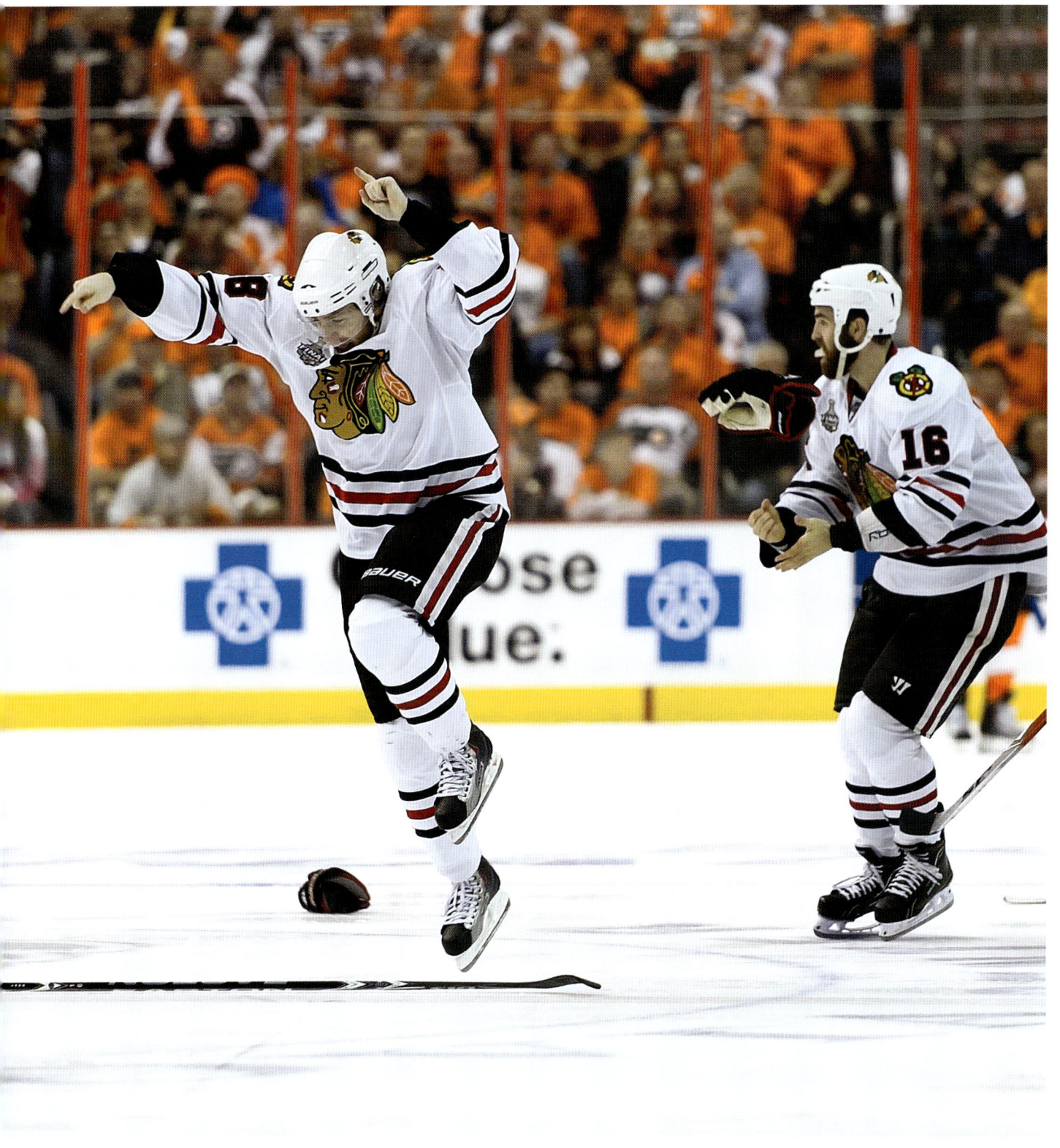

HAVE CUP, WILL TRAVEL

CROWN MOUNTAIN, BRITISH COLUMBIA | *July 19, 2010*

THE STANLEY CUP'S long life has been full of adventure. In 1907, when it was still just a cup, the trophy was left at a photographer's house by the Montreal Wanderers. Someone turned it into a flower pot. Montreal Canadiens owner Leo Dandurand and a few players on the 1924 team left the Stanley Cup on a Montreal street curb when they had to push their stalled Model T.

The Cup made its first lap around a rink in 1950 at Detroit's Olympia Stadium. After a nail-biting series, Red Wings captain Ted Lindsay decided the Wings' faithful deserved to see the trophy. "I just saw the Cup sitting there, so I just went over and picked it up," Lindsay recalled. "I wasn't starting a tradition. I was taking care of my fans."

With the Cup in the winning team's possession over the off-season, players sometimes brought it on unapproved wanderings. In 1978, Guy Lafleur masterminded a plan to steal the Cup, complete with duplicated keys and a stolen car. He drove the trophy home to tiny Thurso, Quebec.

The Cup had its wildest outings with the New York Rangers in the summer of 1994. After 54 years, New Yorkers were eager to get reacquainted with Lord Stanley's silver bowl. It made the rounds from bar to nightclub to racetrack to firehouse to a Bronx nursing home. After its summer of fun in the Big Apple, the Cup needed some repair work. It also needed a chaperone. The following year, when the New Jersey Devils won, a newly established Keeper of the Cup accompanied the prize as each member of the team was allowed to have it for a day.

The Cup's travels have been more regulated since 1995, but it still has its share of escapades. In 2010, Andrew Ladd brought it to the top of Crown Mountain, north of Vancouver, to celebrate Chicago's championship. Finnish players have been known to bring it into the sauna. Of course, the silver bowl has held a variety of delicacies, from poutine to caviar. On two occasions, Lord Stanley's Cup has even served as a baptismal fount.

Photograph by AP PHOTO/THE CANADIAN PRESS, MARK L. JOHNSON

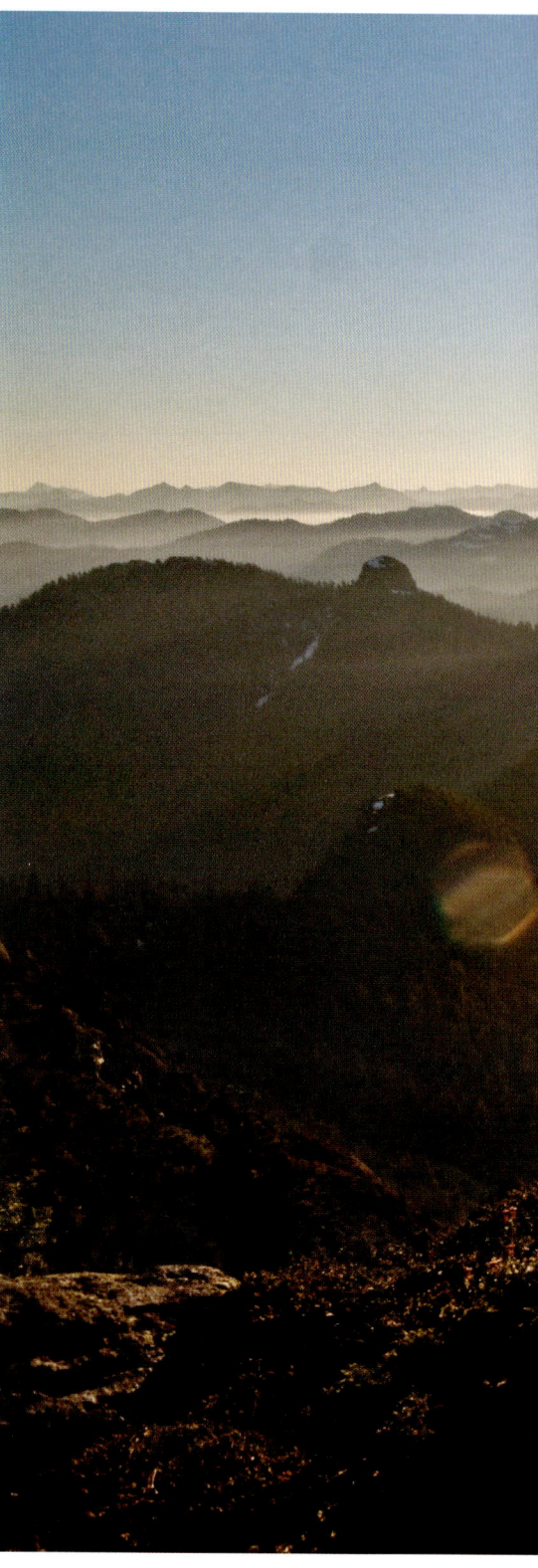

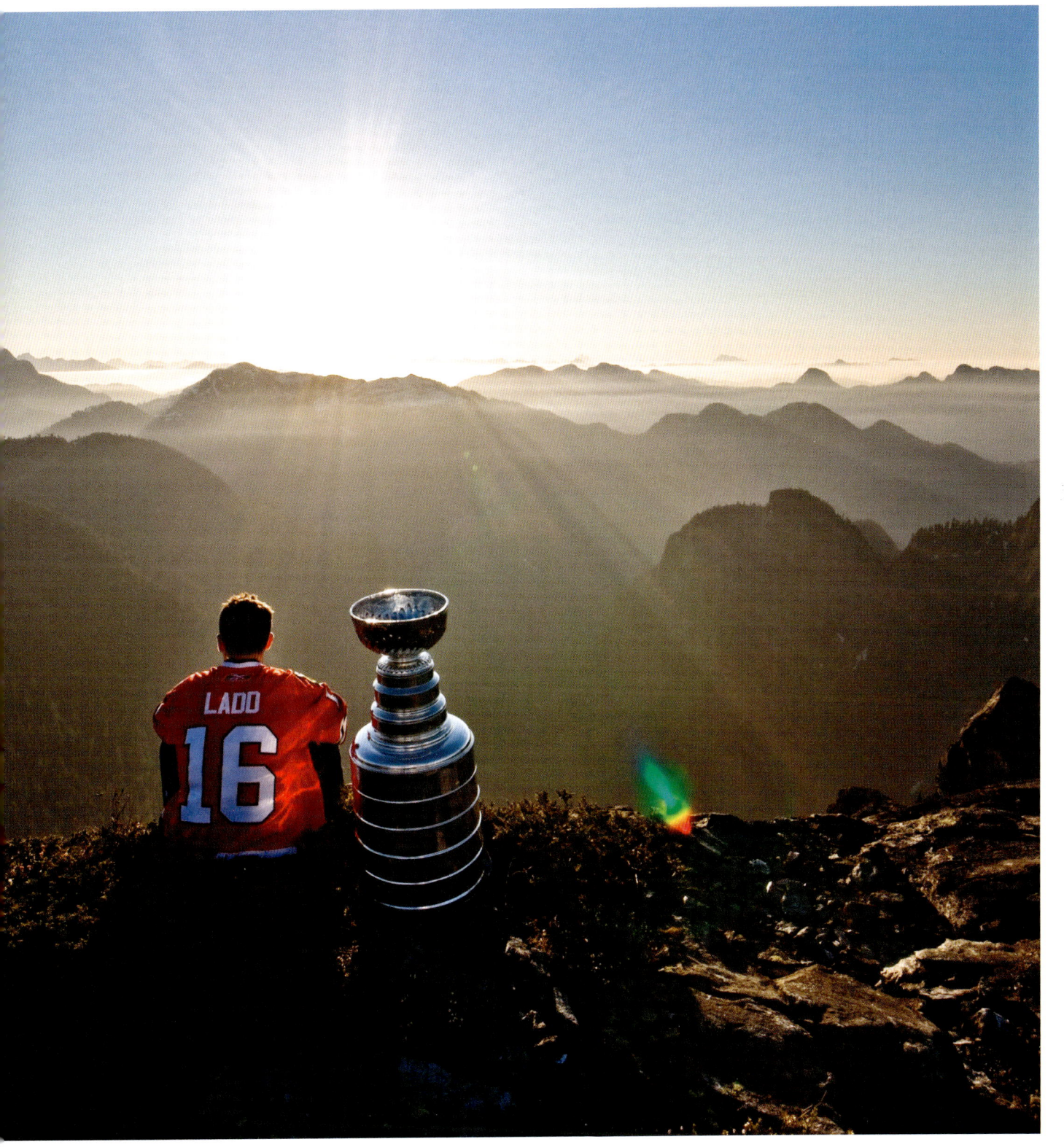

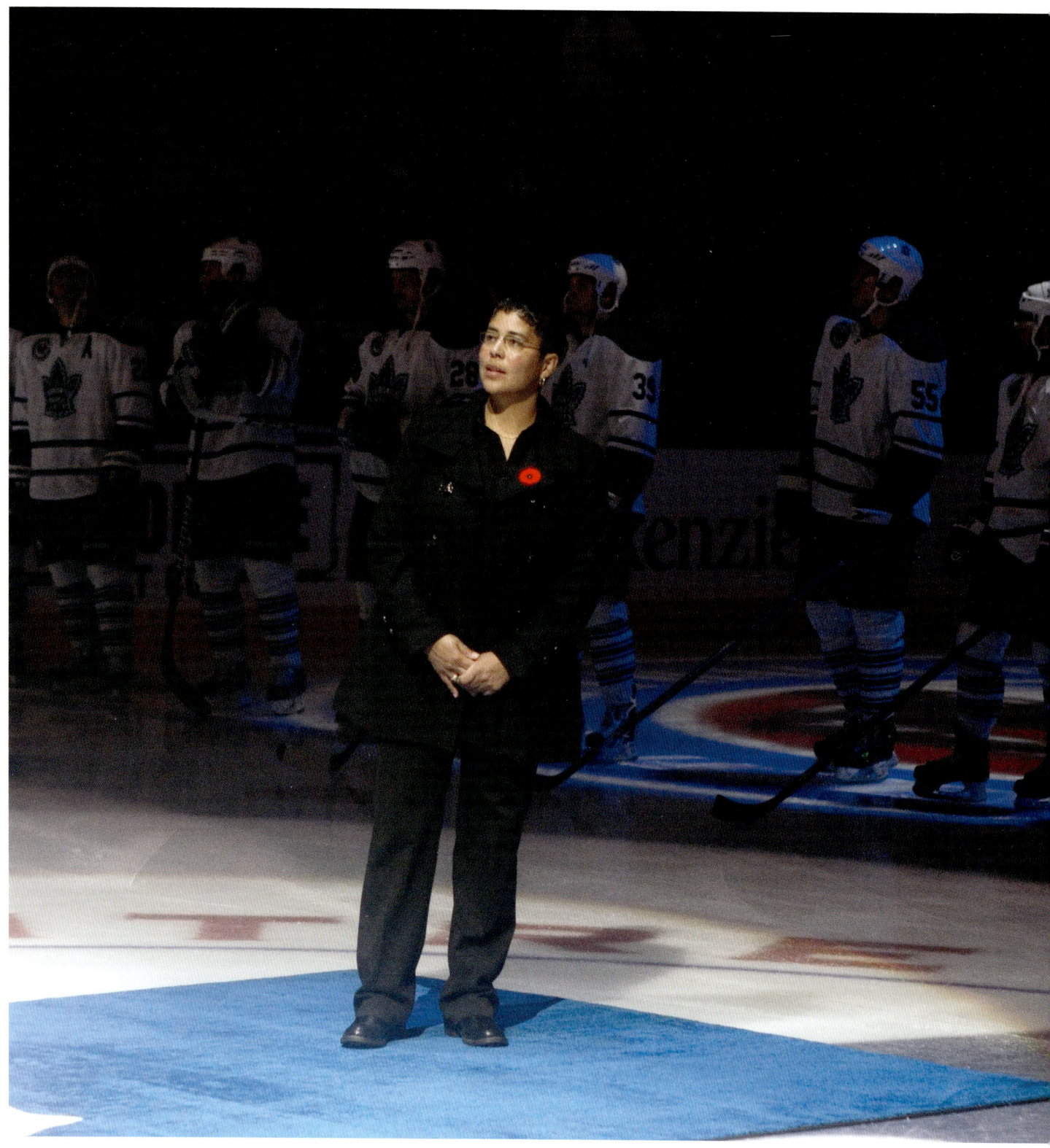

"THE WAYNE GRETZKY OF WOMEN'S HOCKEY"

SCOTIABANK ARENA, TORONTO | *November 6, 2010*

LONG BEFORE WOMEN'S hockey became a spotlight event of the Winter Olympics, Angela James was redefining the game. A fierce competitor from Toronto's working-class Flemingdon Park neighborhood, James was so dominant as a teenager she faced women twice her age in a senior league.

"I remember getting the snot literally knocked out of me," she told Canada's Sportsnet. "Then, finally, I grew. It was like, 'OK, revenge for all these years that you guys beat up on me.' From that point, hitting was part of the game—and I loved it."

As a student at Toronto's Seneca College in the early 1980s, James posted video-game numbers: 50 goals and 73 points in just 14 games, earning her the moniker "The Wayne Gretzky of Women's Hockey." Those who knew her style—rugged, relentless and utterly unafraid—likened her more to Gordie Howe. "She hit people to another country," said former teammate Cassie Campbell-Pascall.

James was a force in international hockey. In her debut at the 1990 IIHF World Championship, she led Canada to gold with 11 goals, a record that stands today. She won three more world titles in 1992, 1994 and 1997, often taking over games single-handedly.

Yet her career was not without heartbreak. In 1998, she was cut from Canada's first Olympic team. At the time, James was unknowingly battling Graves' disease, which sapped her strength. "I believe to this day she should have made that team," said Campbell-Pascall, who played for Canada at Nagano.

James returned to the national squad in 1999, scoring the shootout winner in her final international game. By then, she had cemented her legacy as a scorer and a trailblazer. In 2010, she joined Cammi Granato as the first two women inducted into the Hockey Hall of Fame. After Grant Fuhr, she was the second Black player to be enshrined.

Campbell-Pascall believes that James's absence from the Winter Olympics cost the hockey world a chance to see James on the biggest stage. "People would have known her name," she said.

James, however, insists she has no regrets. "I did everything I needed to do," she said.

Photograph by AP PHOTO/THE CANADIAN PRESS, CHRIS YOUNG

THE BIG CHILL

MICHIGAN STADIUM, ANN ARBOR | *December 11, 2010*

THE UNIVERSITY OF Michigan campus has plenty of houses that Yost built. The Wolverines men's hockey team has played in them all. In 1925, wearing his hat as university athletic director, Fielding Yost bought the Ann Arbor rink where the team played in its first seasons. Yost had the open end walled off, artificial ice installed and stands built around the rink. The Coliseum served as the hockey team's home for 50 years.

The Wolverines won the first national championship in hockey in 1948 and then took six more titles in the 1950s and '60s. By the '70s they had outgrown Yost's Coliseum, so they moved across town to Yost's Field House, the 8,000-seat arena he had constructed for the basketball team. Another two national championship banners were raised in the '90s.

By the 2000s, over 60 teams were playing Division I men's college hockey. National powerhouses like Minnesota, Wisconsin and Denver drew big crowds and sent their best players to the NHL. But none could pull off Michigan's next feat.

On December 11, 2010, the Wolverines hockey team stepped onto the ice at Yost's most famous house, the biggest one: Michigan Stadium. Their opponents were cross-state rivals Michigan State. The two teams had played outside once before, at Michigan State's Spartan Stadium, in 2001. Over 74,000 fans had watched a 3–3 tie in that game. For the outdoor rematch, you could have fit the whole State crowd inside the Big House, with enough leftover space for a Red Wings sellout.

Although it was dubbed the Big Chill at the Big House, the game was played in a tropical 40 degrees. In any event, there was plenty of body warmth to go around. The official count put attendance at 104,173—the biggest crowd ever to watch a hockey game. The NHL made a run at the attendance record in 2014, organizing a Winter Classic game between Detroit and Toronto at Michigan Stadium. Guinness sent its world-record watchers to make the final count. Fittingly, the Maize and Blue kept the record in their own house. Yost would be proud.

Photograph by LEON HALIP/GETTY IMAGES

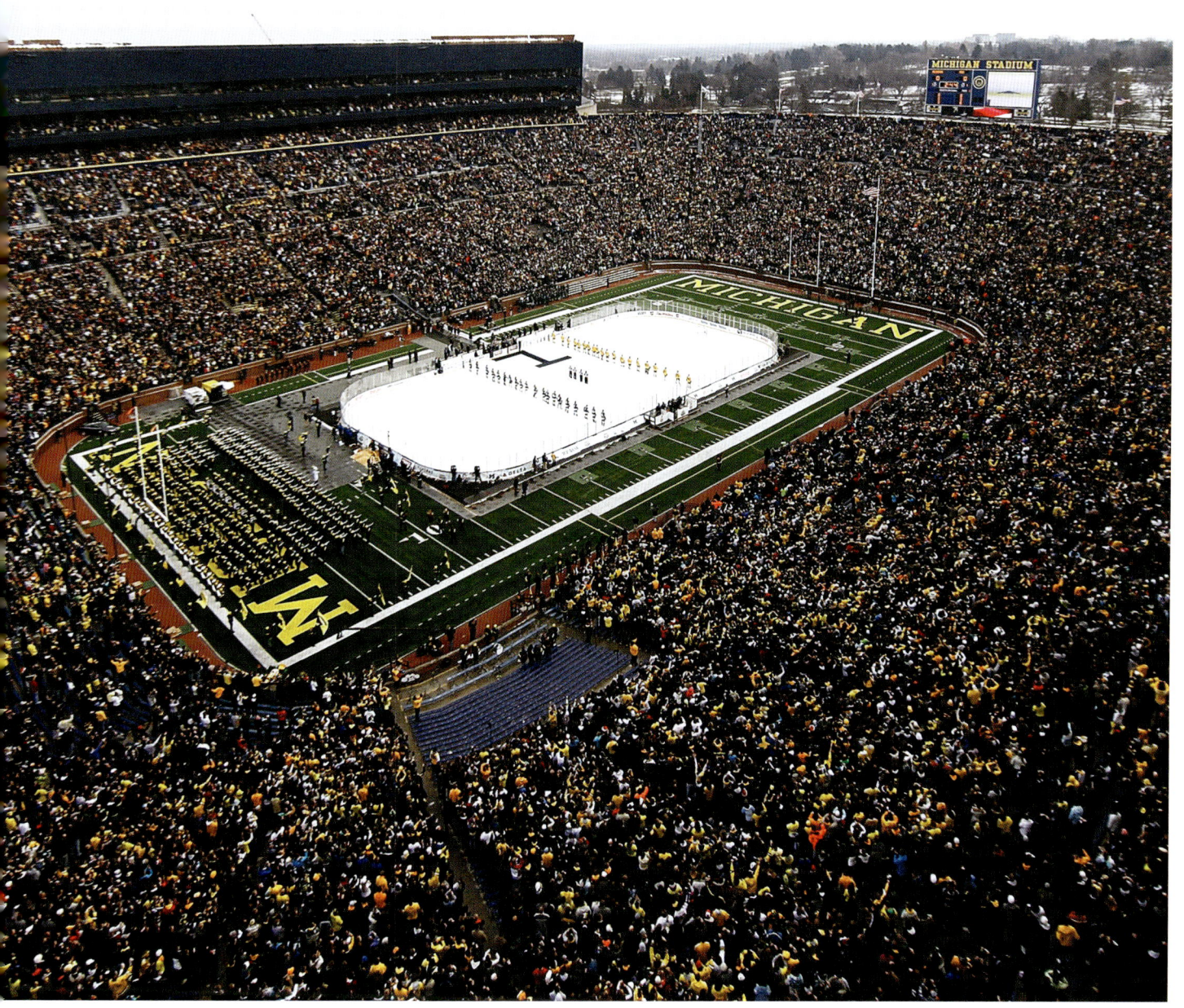

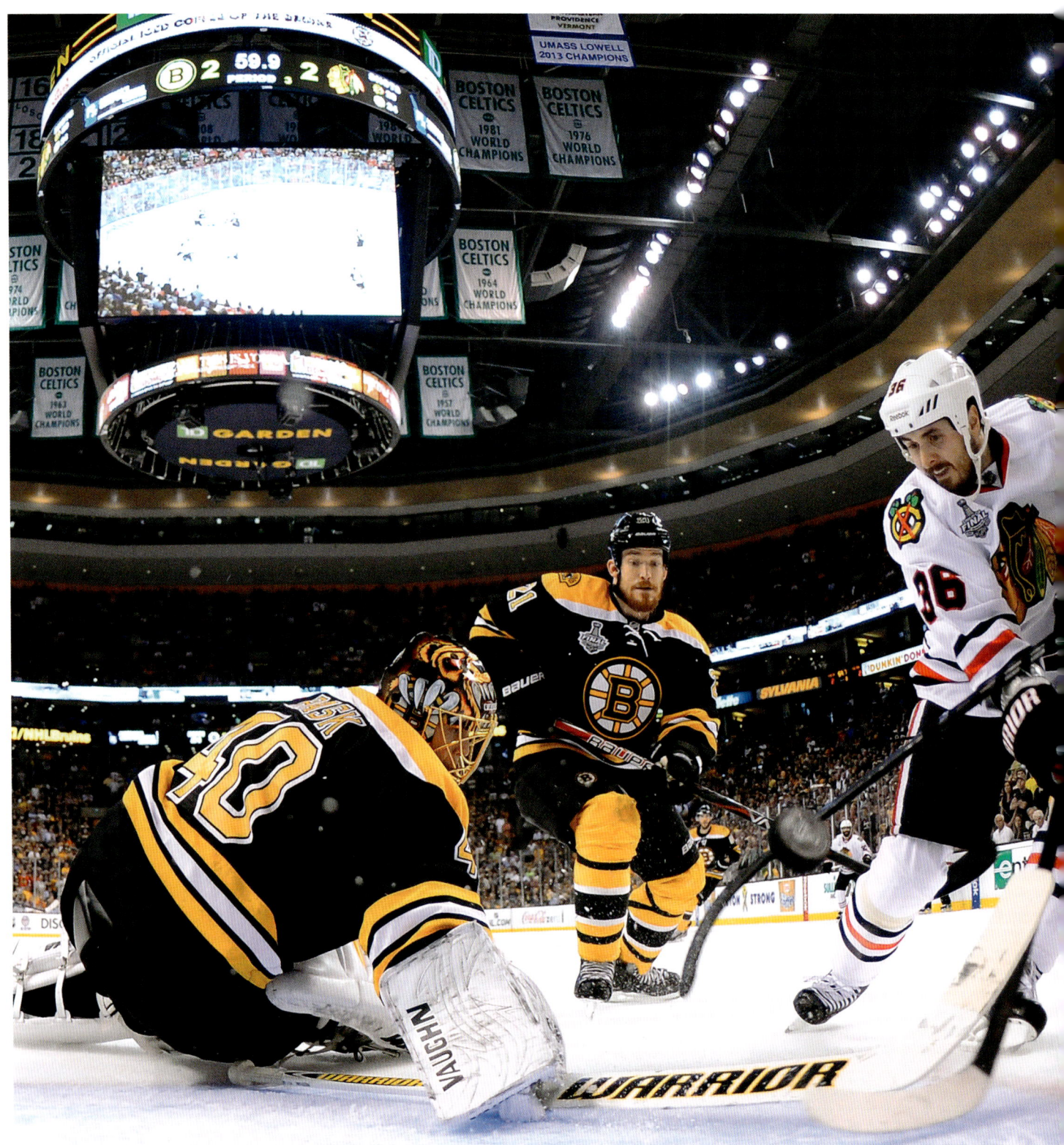

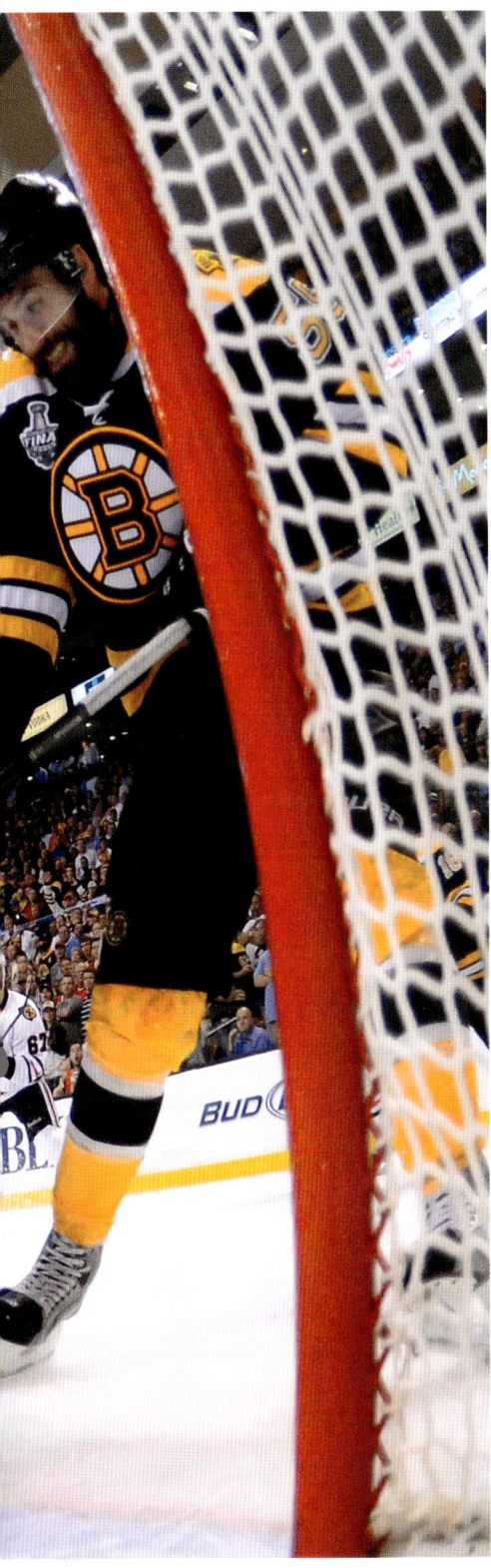

17 SECONDS

TD GARDEN, BOSTON | *June 24, 2013*

THE SEASON THAT almost didn't begin ended with a Stanley Cup Final that will live forever. In six thrilling games (with three going to overtime), the Chicago Blackhawks beat the Boston Bruins for the team's fifth Stanley Cup championship and second in four seasons. The stunning conclusion came in the last two minutes of Game 6. Bryan Bickell and Dave Bolland scored goals 17 seconds apart to erase a 2–1 Boston lead and bring the Cup back to Chicago. Brian Cazeneuve gave an account in the July 1, 2013, issue of *Sports Illustrated:*

> The 2013 Stanley Cup Final was a triumph not just for Chicago. Five months ago, as the NHL crawled out of the rubble of its third lockout in two decades, nobody—not the owners, not the players and certainly not commissioner Gary Bettman or union chief Donald Fehr—could have drawn up anything as perfect as this series, a marquee matchup between two Original Six franchises that turned out to be one of the most competitive and compelling finals in recent memory. In six games and more than 435 minutes of hockey, including an exhausting triple-overtime opener in Chicago, neither team ever had more than a two-goal lead…. The cuticle-shredding drama and fierce pace of play all added up to exactly what the NHL needed in a year that began with the hockey world facing the possibility of a season lost to a labor stoppage….
>
> The action was so relentless—and the casualties were piling up so fast—that after Game 2, Boston winger Jaromír Jágr, 41, joked that he was becoming concerned for the fans. "If you have a bad heart, you might get a heart attack," Jágr warned. "For young people it's pretty exciting to watch. Old people, don't watch it."
>
> At least by NHL standards, plenty of fans did watch, though. Ratings on NBC and the NBC Sports Network were robust: the games averaged 5.4 million viewers per game, the best in nearly 20 years. "It's only fitting," said Blackhawks winger Patrick Sharp after Game 4, "that two of the oldest teams would give people a series for the history books."

Photograph by BRIAN BABINEAU/NHLI

KNIGHT MOVES

GRAND SUMMIT HOTEL, PARK CITY, UTAH | *October 2, 2013*

AS SOON AS Hilary Knight could skate, around age six, she started to play hockey against boys. She had her hair cut short, so opponents wouldn't recognize her as a girl. Yet from the very beginning, Knight knew where the sport could take her. When she was in second grade, she wrote and illustrated a book called "The Magical Hockey Stick," about a little girl who goes to the Olympics.

Knight has played in more Olympic games than any member of Team USA, winning a gold medal, in 2018, and three silvers. She first skated for the national team when she was 17. In 2025, at age 35, she captained the Americans to a title at the world championships. Knight was the tournament's third-leading scorer.

Knight stands out not only for her play on the ice or her longevity. One of her longtime teammates, Kendall Coyne Schofield, told The Athletic in 2022 that Knight's legacy goes beyond awards, goals and the medals: "It's who she is as a person and what she's fought for and how she's changed this game forever. It's the fight that she has within her to leave this game better than when she entered it as a little girl."

In 2017 Knight and her teammates challenged the sport's governing body in the United States, USA Hockey, to support the women's national program on a level more equal to the men's. The players threatened to boycott the world championships, and they won. Their success opened Knight's eyes as to what could be achieved in challenging the status quo in women's sports.

"We were told we couldn't do this by so many people, and then we did it collectively," she said. "It gave me this confidence and empowerment to start thinking about things a little differently."

Something different might be assembling an all-women ownership group for a pro team or two. This was one of the ideas Hilary Knight had for her future. But it will have to wait until her playing days were over.

Photograph by AP PHOTO/CARLO ALLEGRI

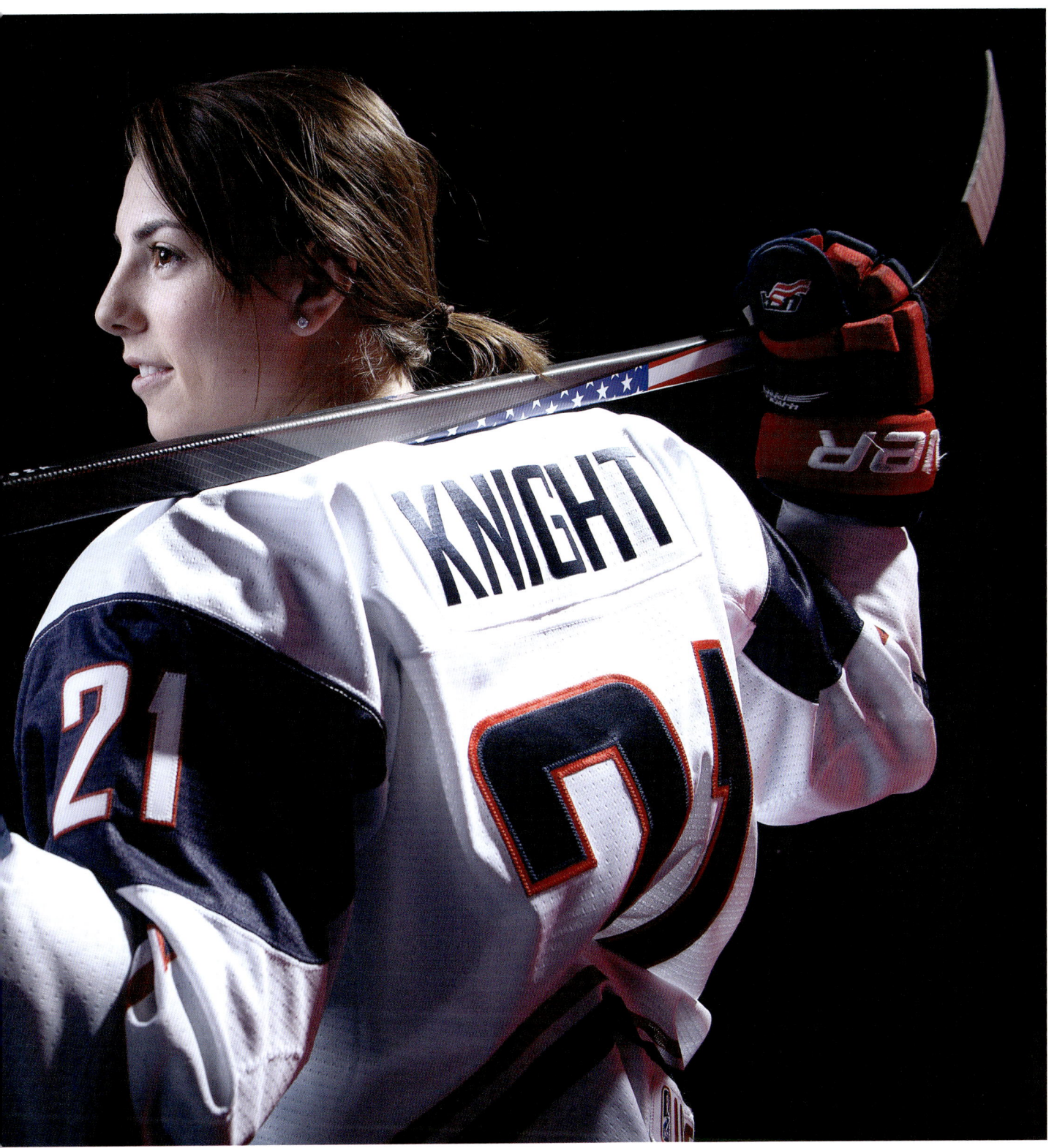

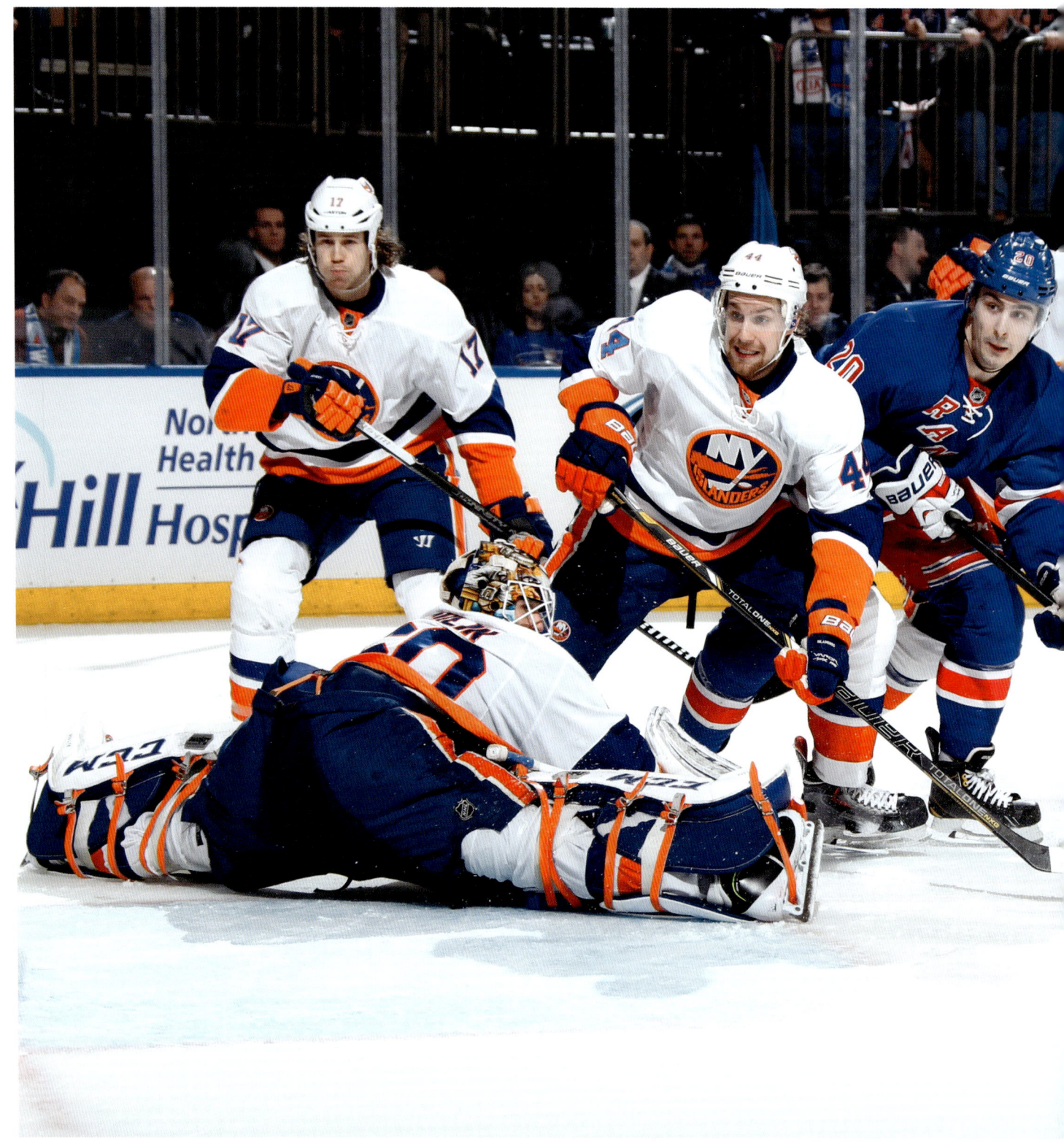

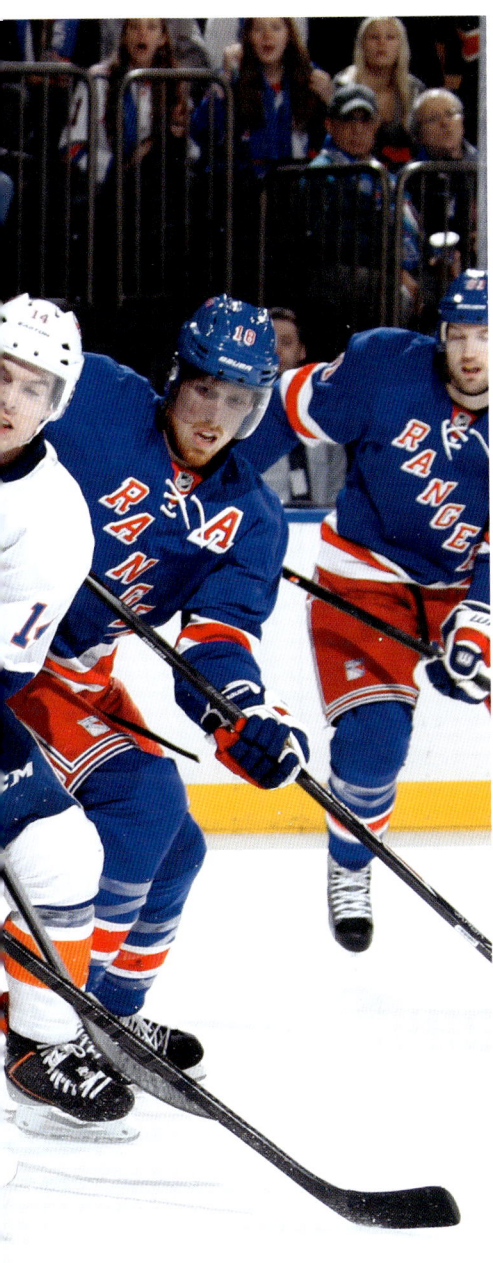

BITTER RIVALS

MADISON SQUARE GARDEN, NEW YORK CITY | *January 21, 2014*

LEAVE IT TO New York's Islanders and Rangers to turn Christmas cheer into a brawl.

In December 2003, the Isles hosted a seemingly harmless holiday promotion at Nassau Coliseum: wear a Santa suit to their game against Philadelphia, get a free ticket and parade across the ice between periods. But a lighthearted nod to the season became a reminder that the Rangers-Islanders rivalry doesn't take holidays off.

Roughly a thousand Saint Nicks flooded the rink after the first period. That's when two imposters mingling among the Kringles peeled off their red Santa jackets to reveal blue Rangers jerseys. In seconds, jingle bells turned into boxing bells. Santas tackled Santas, beards flew and jerseys were torn away like wrapping paper. The melee lasted six minutes. Isles forward Arron Asham scored the fight with one word: "Awesome."

Born in 1972 when the expansion Isles landed in the Rangers' territory, the New York rivalry is fueled by geography, pride and decades of playoff clashes. Yet it's hardly the only rivalry in the NHL capable of spontaneous combustion.

The Battle of Alberta between Calgary and Edmonton is an old-fashioned Western showdown, Canadian style. In the late '80s, their early round playoff series determined who would eventually win the Stanley Cup. In 2020, the rivalry fueled a full-line brawl and goalie fight.

The Detroit-Colorado rivalry dominated the late '90s and early 2000s. Sparked by the 1996 hit on Detroit's Kris Draper by the Avs' Claude Lemieux, the rivalry featured crunching checks, brutal fights and high-stakes playoff battles. "Fight Night at the Joe" in 1997 cemented its legendary status. Though conference realignment cooled tensions, the rivalry remains iconic.

Hockey's eternal grudge match pits the Boston Bruins against the Montreal Canadiens. Rocket Richard's unforgettable series-winning goal in 1952—darting through defenders with a bloodied face—engraved Montreal's mythic edge. The '70s brought a standoff between two dynasties, with the Canadiens' grace matching Boston grit. Decades later, the venom hadn't faded. In 2014, Bruin Milan Lucic flipped off Canadiens fans at the Bell Centre on his way to the penalty box, giving a modern exclamation point to nearly a century of snarl.

Photograph by SCOTT LEVY/NHLI

THE SPECIALIST

BOLSHOY ICE DOME, SOCHI, RUSSIA | *February 15, 2014*

THERE WERE ECHOES of Lake Placid. But this was a group-stage match rather than a showdown for gold. And Team USA would go home without any medal, ultimately losing to Finland in the bronze-medal game. Nevertheless, the 2014 Winter Games in Sochi hold a place in American hockey lore. This was due to one man: T.J. Oshie. Just 27 years old, the St. Louis Blues forward from Warroad, Minnesota, faced the full weight of U.S. hopes and Russian pride. By the end, he'd transformed from solid NHLer into American folk hero.

Led by Pavel Datsyuk, Alex Ovechkin and other NHL stars, Russia was aiming for gold on its home ice. Vladimir Putin was in the crowd for the preliminary-round game at the Bolshoy Ice Dome. Pavel Datsyuk's second goal, coming in the third, sent the game into overtime. Goalies Jonathan Quick and Sergei Bobrovsky stopped late shots by Ovechkin and Patrick Kane, and the game went to a shootout.

After the first three rounds, goals by Oshie and Ilya Kovalchuk kept the teams deadlocked. Under international rules, once the initial three shooters were done, coaches could reuse players. Russian alternated Datsyuk and Kovalchuk. Team USA coach Dan Bylsma kept going back to his specialist. Even when Oshie was stopped twice, Bylsma sent him back on the ice.

Four goals on six attempts. The game-winner came in the eighth round, another five-hole dagger past Bobrovsky, capping a display of stickhandling sorcery and unflappable composure. "I was running out of moves there," Oshie laughed afterward.

His teammates were less casual: "I've never seen anything like it," said New York Rangers defenseman Ryan McDonagh.

Oshie insisted he would have traded the moment for an Olympic gold medal. "You always dream of scoring the big goal," he said, "but the medal's what you hang on your wall."

Few moments in hockey history can match Oshie's shootout heroics for drama, skill and individual composure. He later won the Stanley Cup with Washington and played in one All-Star Game. But T.J. Oshie will be remembered for one night in February 2014, when he thrilled fans across America.

Photograph by DAVID E. KLUTHO

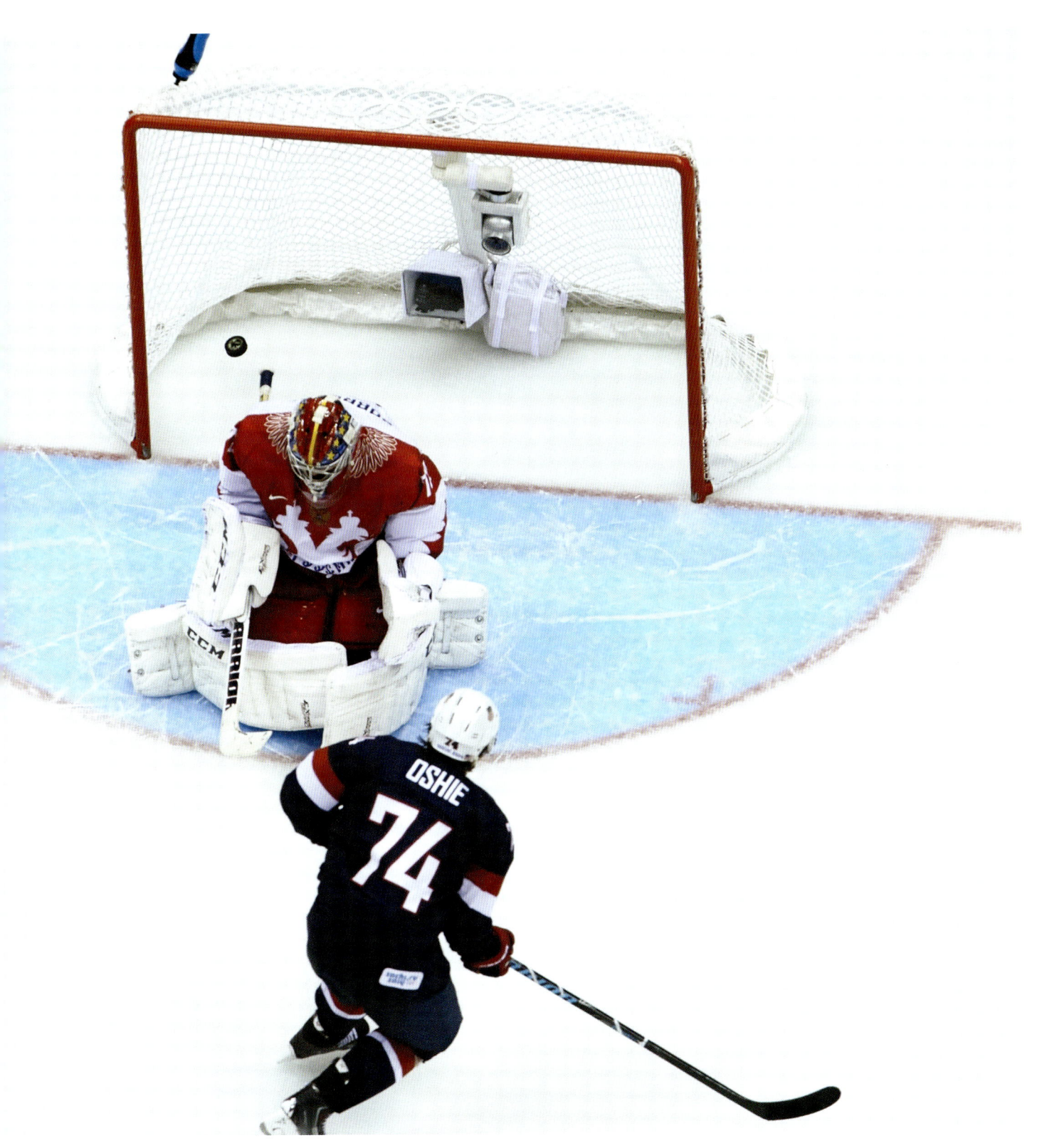

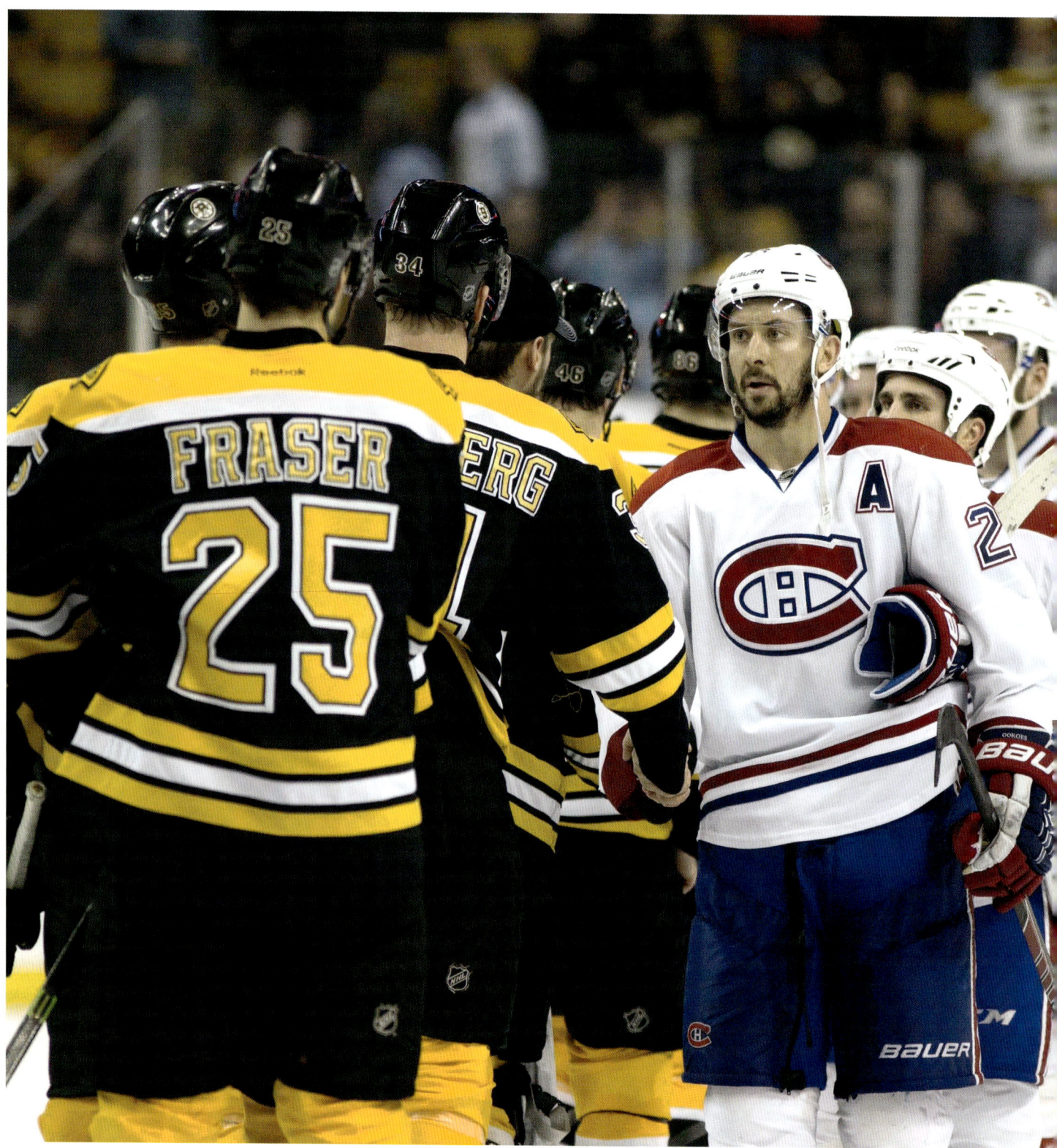

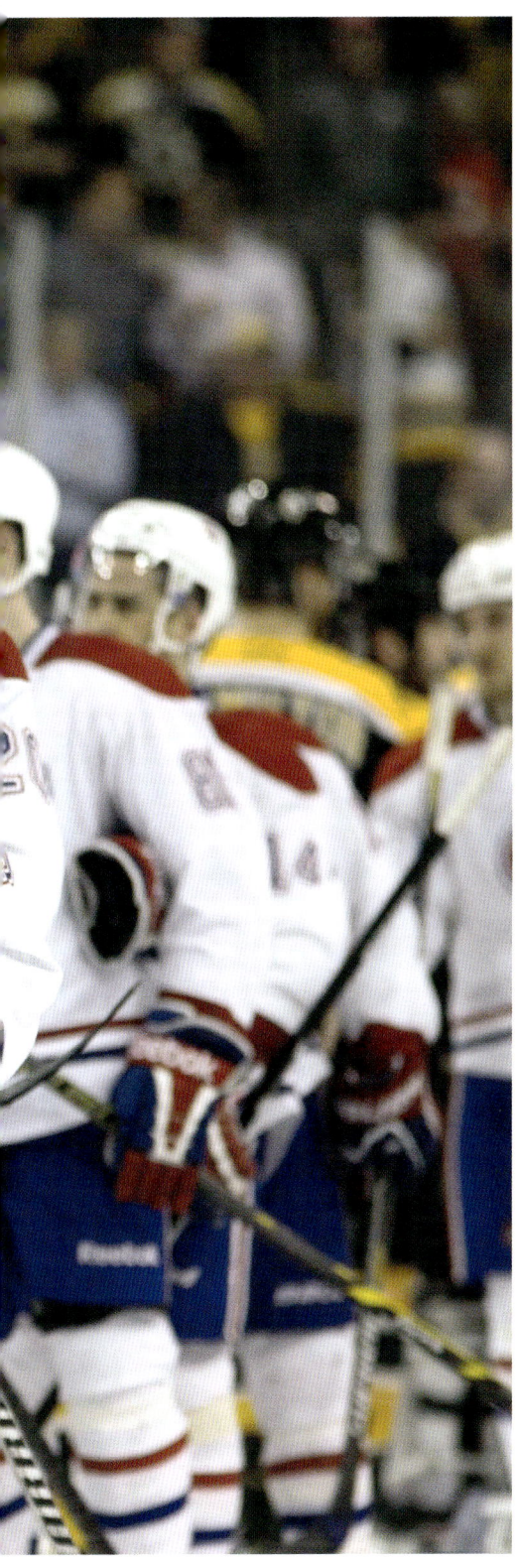

A GRAND TRADITION

TD GARDEN, BOSTON | *May 14, 2014*

HOCKEY BEGAN AS rugby on ice. The winter game adopted features of the older sport: for example, the early rule against forward passes or the practice of punting the ball away (i.e., hockey's dump and chase). Hockey also inherited some of rugby's virtues. Still today, rugby teams have a drink-up after a match, holding to the tradition that you respect your rivals even after pounding them. Hockey contents itself with a handshake.

It is one of the sport's most enduring rituals. From peewees to beer leagues, players line up after each game to shake hands and exchange salutes of "Good game." In the NHL, the tradition is limited to the deciding game of a playoff series, when mutual appreciation can shine through bruises, stitches and exhaustion. Television cameras linger on the postgame exchanges: former teammates greeting each other, goalies speaking the secret code of their brotherhood, younger players showing respect to veterans (and vice versa).

There have been tense moments. After the Montreal Canadiens took a hard-fought, seven-game series from Boston in the 2014 playoffs, the Bruins' Milan Lucic had a few extra words for Dale Weise: "I'm going to f------ kill you next year." But those who violate the code of the handshake line are typically called out. Evander Kane was widely criticized for skipping the handshake after the Edmonton Oilers lost the 2025 Final to the Florida Panthers.

Meanwhile, Florida coach Paul Maurice explained that his refusal to join the handshake line came out of respect. "There's something really kind of beautiful about just the camera on those men who played shaking hands," he said.

The ritual can indeed be beautiful. The handshake line after the 2025 Western Conference semifinals showed that. Before Game 6 between Winnipeg and Dallas, the Jets' Mark Scheifele received news that his father had unexpectedly passed away. With his team down 3–2 in the series, the veteran forward and alternate captain decided to play. Scheifele scored a goal, but Winnipeg went down in overtime. After the game, the handshake line moved more slowly than usual as one Dallas player after another consoled one of their own.

Photograph by DAMIAN STROHMEYER

THE COMMISSIONER

STAPLES CENTER, LOS ANGELES | *June 4, 2014*

IT IS ONE of the NHL's great traditions, like playoff beards and hats on the ice, stick taps and three stars. Each spring, after the championship has been decided, the keepers of the Stanley Cup carry the trophy to center ice. With gloved hands, they set the Cup carefully on its pedestal. Commissioner Gary Bettman steps forward to summon the winning team's captain. And then it begins.

The booing. Even when the Cup is being awarded on a team's home ice, fans turn in an instant from cheering their victors to howling the league's top executive.

The tradition began soon after Bettman took over as commissioner in 1993. He was blamed for the 1994–95 lockout, which delayed the start of the season until January. In Canada, he was the scapegoat for the departure of the Quebec Nordiques and Winnipeg Jets. Especially among Canadian fans, Bettman exemplified all that is wrong with the NHL. The highest-grossing film ever made in Canada, the 2006 comedy *Bon Cop, Bad Cop*, featured a ruthless caricature of the commissioner, played by a 4'7" actor in a cheap wig.

"Gary codifies the ugly American," the film's creator, Kevin Tierney, told *Sports Illustrated*, "a greedy f--- who stole our game and put it in s---faced American towns where they don't care."

For all the hate Bettman endures, the fact is he has made the NHL bigger, stronger and richer. The league has added eight franchises during his tenure, while revenue has risen from $400 million in the early '90s to $6.3 billion in 2024. Owners make more money, and so do players: average salaries have risen steadily.

And while it might be difficult for Canadian fans to accept, Bettman has been an advocate for teams in hockey's homeland. For a decade, the league transferred money to the Edmonton Oilers, Calgary Flames, Ottawa Senators and Vancouver Canucks, enabling those franchises to survive the Canadian dollar's decline.

The NHL hits new records for revenue each season, and new records for attendance. In 2024–25 over 23 million fans went to games. Fans can boo all they want, but Bettman must be doing something right.

Photograph by DAVID E. KLUTHO

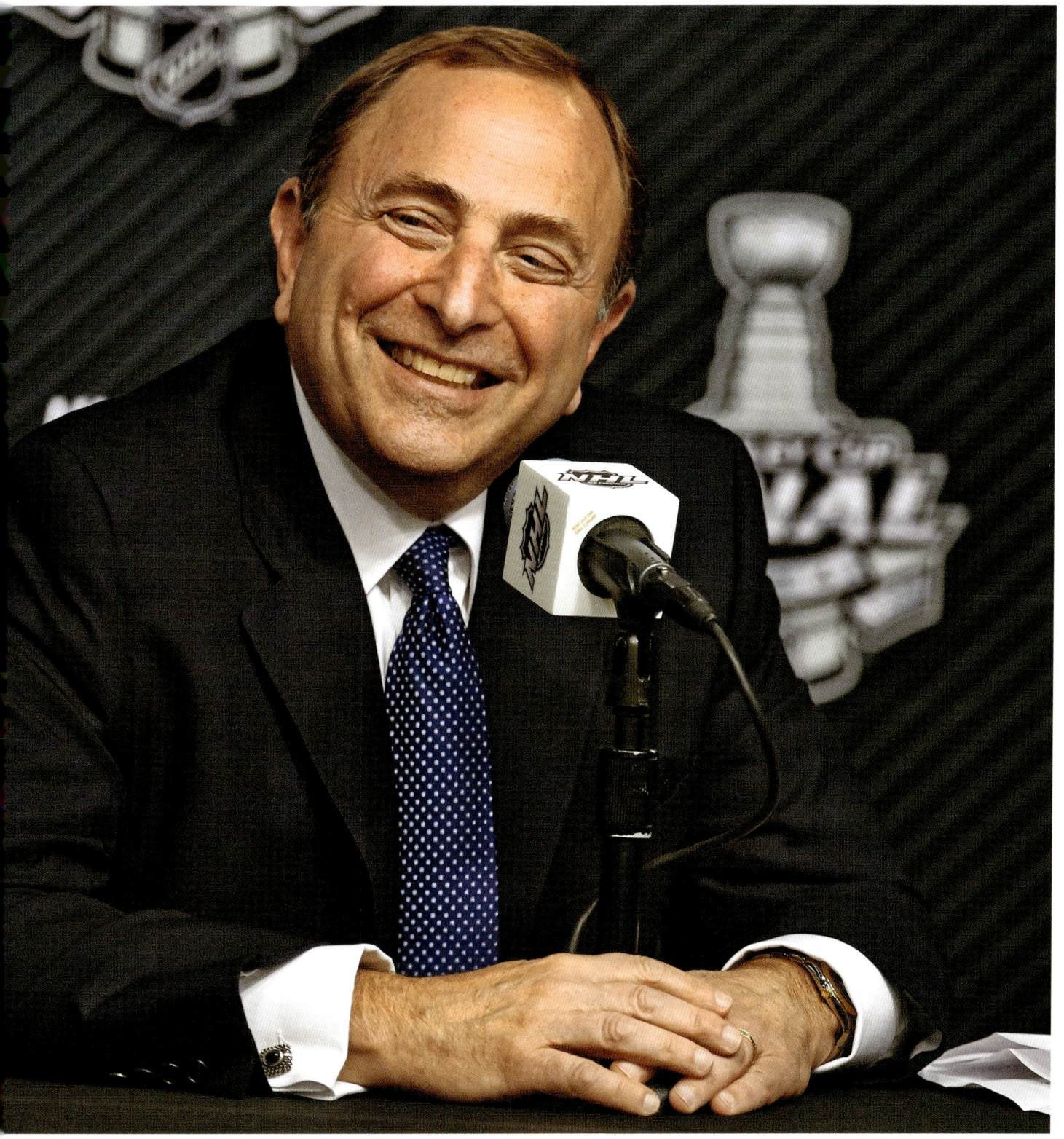

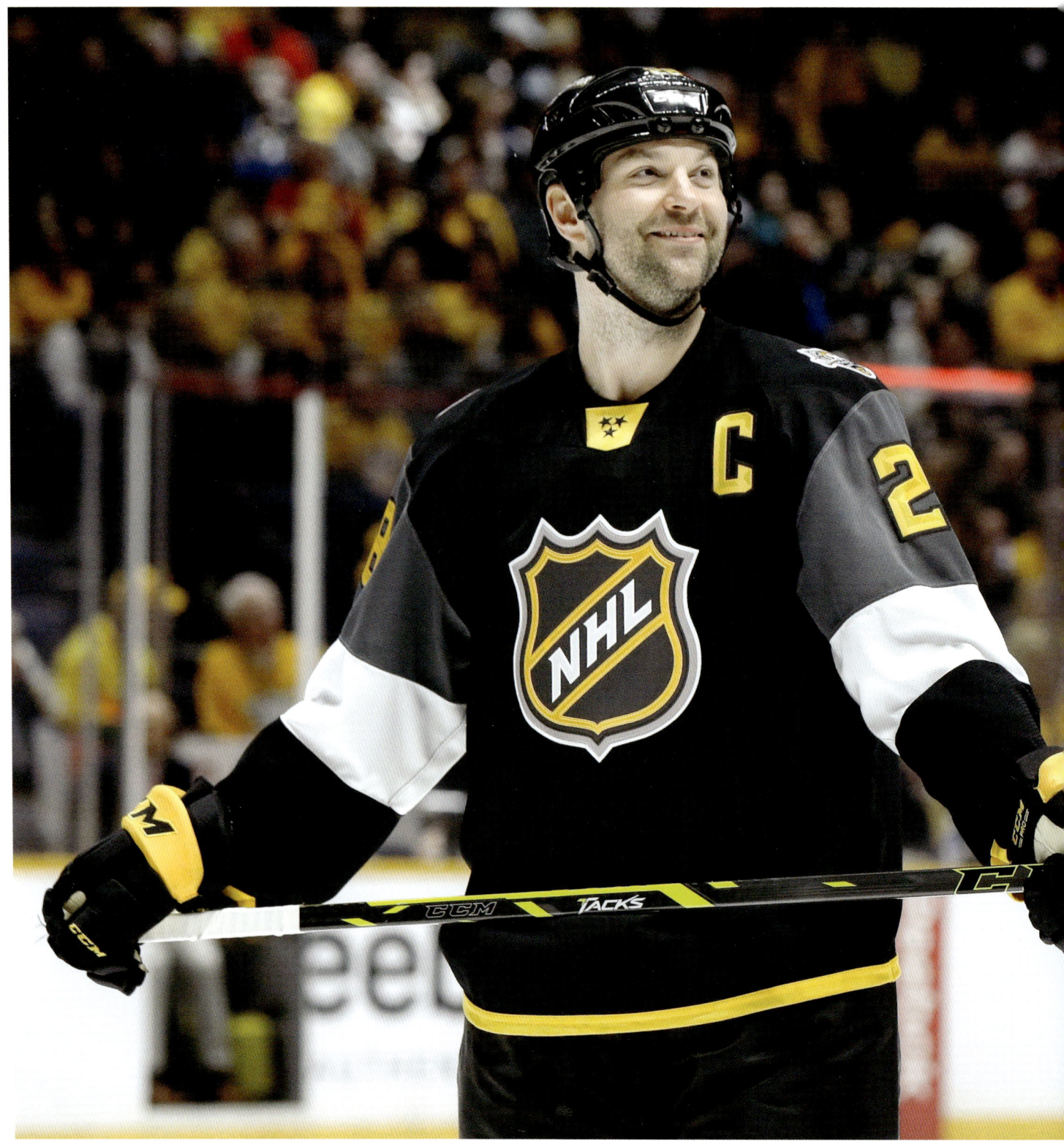

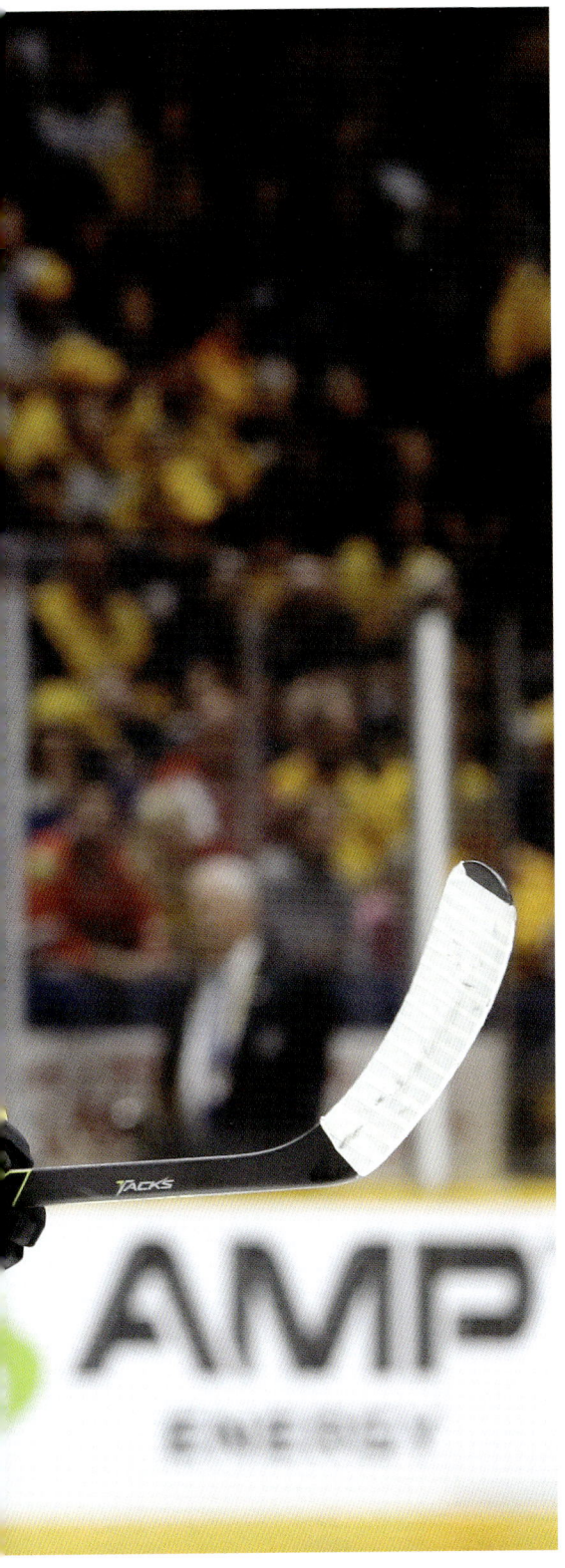

GREAT SCOTT!

BRIDGESTONE ARENA, NASHVILLE | *January 31, 2016*

IT HAD ALL the makings of Hollywood. Veteran enforcer John Scott, a player known more for his fists than his finesse, found himself the improbable captain of the Pacific Division team at the 2016 NHL All-Star Game. This was no ordinary All-Star selection; it was a fan-driven movement, a groundswell of support for "a guy like me," as Scott himself put it.

Scott's whole career had been unexpected. He played college hockey at Michigan Tech but spent the long bus rides studying toward an engineering degree. A free-agent stint in the AHL led to an entry-level contract with the Minnesota Wild. Seven seasons later, when he was in Arizona, he had five career goals, to go along with over 500 penalty minutes. His All-Star candidacy started as an internet joke, sparked by a podcast quip. It snowballed into a grassroots campaign that vaulted him past the league's superstars.

The NHL wasn't thrilled about the fans' choice. Weeks before the event, Scott was traded to Montreal, who promptly sent him to their AHL affiliate in Newfoundland. Many suspected the league hoped to erase him from the All-Star lineup. But after public backlash, the NHL relented. The enforcer who was told, "Guys like you don't get to play in games like this," was officially in.

What happened in Nashville turned the joke into legend. In the 3-on-3 tournament format—designed for speed and skill—Scott scored twice in the semifinal against the Central Division. His Pacific Division squad went on to win the championship 1–0 over the Atlantic, earning each player $90,000. In a moment that summed up the weekend's magic, Scott's teammates hoisted him on their shoulders as chants of "MVP! MVP!" filled Bridgestone Arena.

Fans on social media demanded Scott be named Most Valuable Player. The league, bowing to overwhelming sentiment, made it official.

Scott's All-Star weekend was a celebration of the underdog, a moment when a grinder got to shine. His helmet from that memorable weekend now resides in the Hockey Hall of Fame, a permanent tribute to the journeyman who became an All-Star MVP.

Photograph by AP PHOTO/MARK HUMPHREY

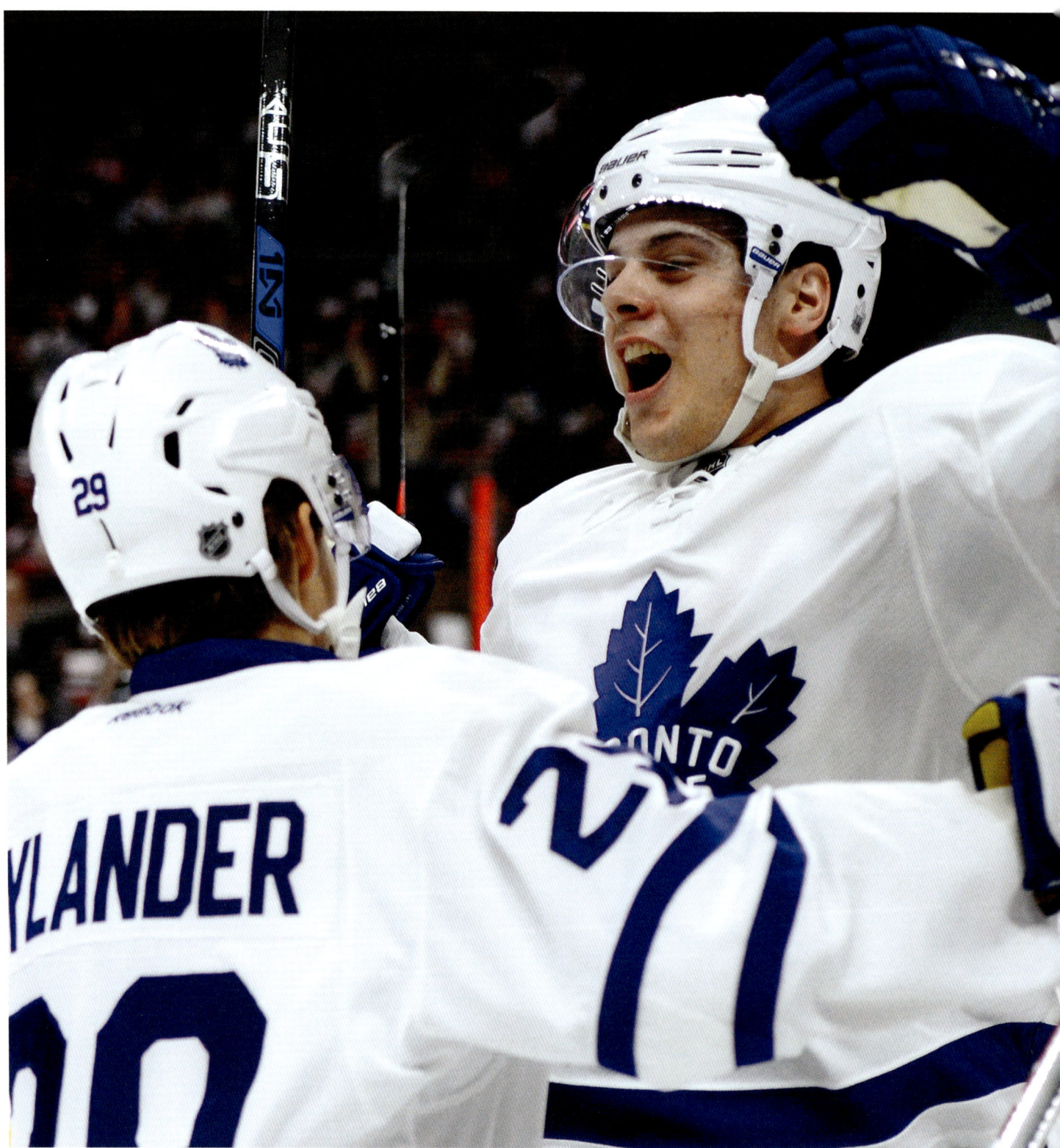

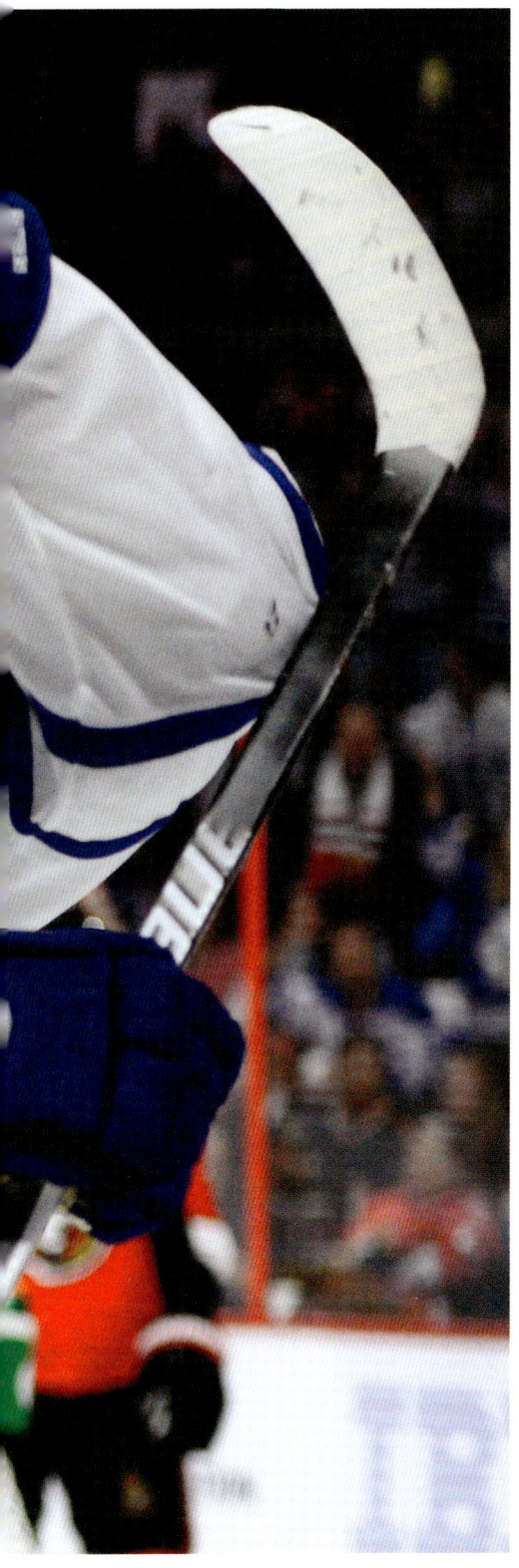

A STAR IS BORN

CANADIAN TIRE CENTRE, OTTAWA | *October 12, 2016*

AUSTON MATTHEWS HAS been compiling firsts throughout his career. Even before he arrived in the NHL, he was getting attention for his notable accomplishments. Matthews was the first American player from a Sun Belt state to be top pick in the draft. And he was the first North American teenager to build his skills by playing pro hockey in Europe. In 2015–16, the season before the Toronto Maple Leafs selected him, he played in the Swiss league for the Zurich Lions.

"No one had ever done this before," teammate Ryan Shannon told *Sports Illustrated*. The Lions' veteran American paused, then added: "That'll be a common storyline throughout his career."

The storyline continued in Matthews's debut for the Leafs, against the Ottawa Senators on October 12, 2016. Scores of Toronto fans trekked to Ottawa to see their new first-line center, the Arizona kid who had honed his game in Switzerland. Matthews did not disappoint.

Matthews scored his first goal midway through the first period, giving Toronto a 1–0 lead. A few minutes later, he stickhandled through three Sens and fired a dart past goalie Craig Anderson. He got the hat trick early in the second period. Then, in the last seconds of the period, Matthews did something no NHL rookie had ever done—he scored his fourth goal in his first game.

Matthews's debut caught the attention of NBC Sports executive producer Sam Flood. "We should do more," he wrote in an email to Gary Bettman the next morning.

"We're thinking the same," the commissioner replied.

SI's Alex Prewitt reported on the new strategy hatched by the network and the league:

NBC Sports soon received permission to flex Toronto's home opener, an eventual 4–1 win over Boston, into its Saturday-night prime-time slot. Though such moves are more commonly reserved for spring's playoff push, Matthews's instant stardom was too juicy to ignore. "This is purely based on a player," Flood says. "There's no other reason we're doing this than Auston Matthews."

One more first: a rookie getting a network to change its programming after a single game.

Photograph by SEAN KILPATRICK/THE CANADIAN PRESS

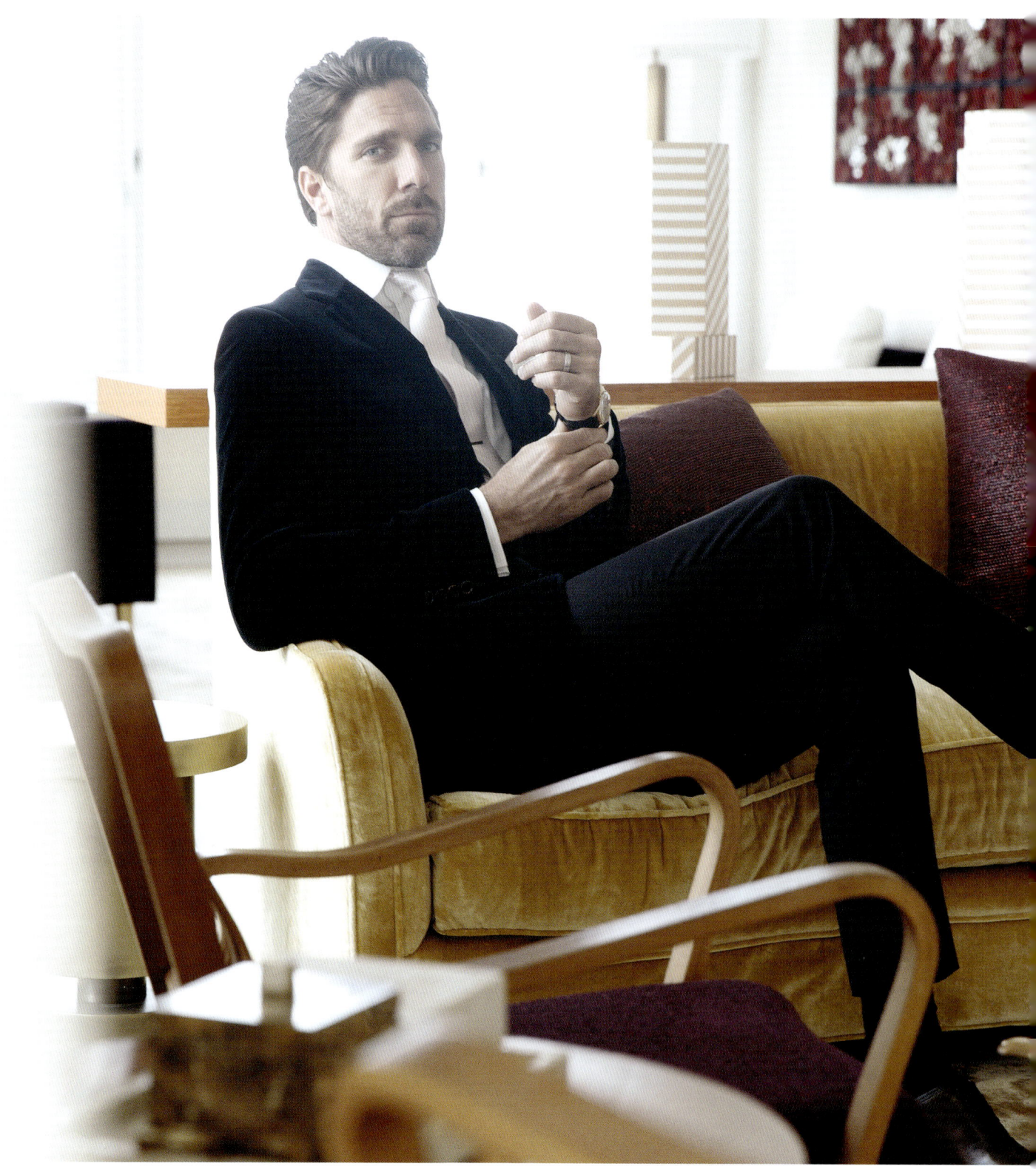

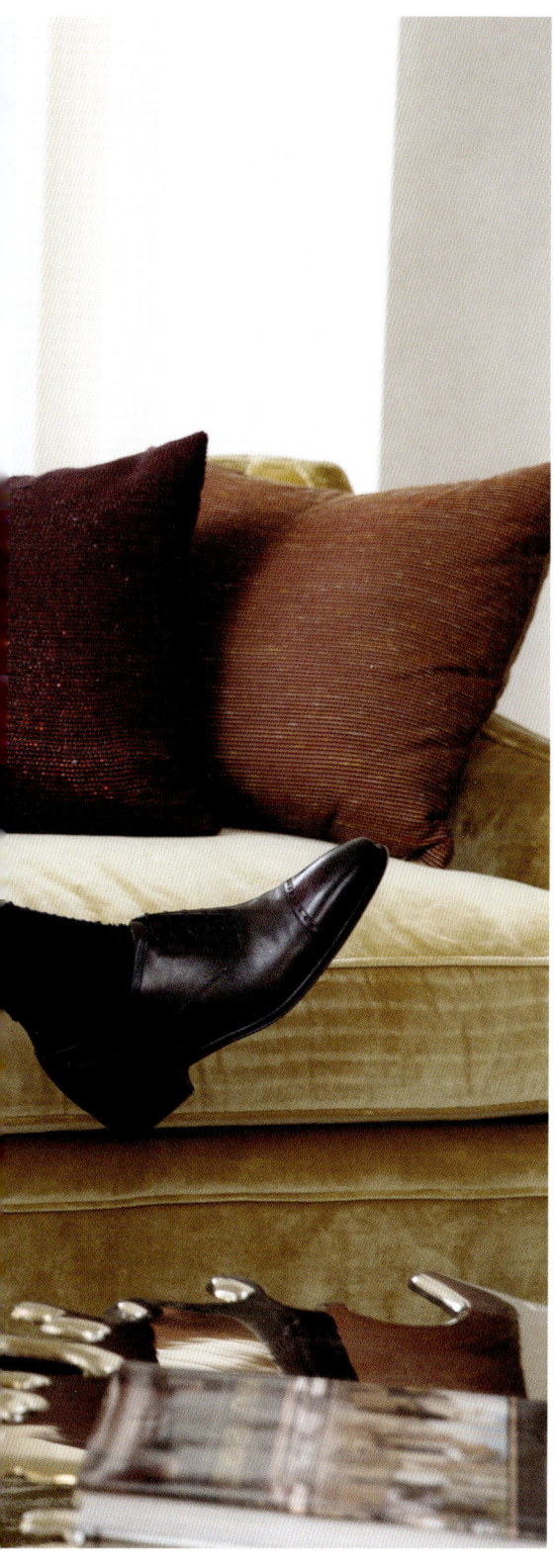

KING HENRIK

30 PARK PLACE, NEW YORK CITY | *Circa 2017*

HENRIK LUNDQVIST WAS more than a pretty face. In his first season, the Swedish goalie won 30 games for the New York Rangers, earning his nickname "The King." Another six consecutive seasons with more than 30 wins followed, something no netminder had accomplished at the start of his career.

The 2012–13 lockout interrupted Lundqvist's run of 30-win seasons. (He still won 24 in the shortened campaign.) He then started a new streak the following year, notching another four straight seasons with more than 30 wins. Lundqvist and the Rangers reached the Stanley Cup Final during that stretch, losing to the Los Angeles Kings in 2014. He won Olympic gold with Tre Kronor in 2006.

The King's reign was undisputed in one realm of the hockey world: fashion. Hailing from a mountain village in northwestern Sweden, Lundqvist showed he belonged in Midtown Manhattan with his tailored suits, flawless hair and precisely trimmed beard. He was a regular member of *Sports Illustrated*'s Fashionable 50. In 2017, *SI*'s Jamie Lisanti queried the King about his attire:

When you first came here and first started playing on the Rangers, did your style fit in with New York?

I think it fit in with New York but it didn't really fit in with hockey. I remember all of the older guys, they were making fun of my suits, my skinny ties and my skinny jeans. But for New York, it blended in right away. But now you see a change a little bit in hockey with the younger guys, they care a little more about fashion….

It's a big difference now than 12 years ago when I got here. Hockey is very old school and traditional when it comes not only to the game, but everything around the game. Now it's changing with the younger guys—they care a little more about fashion…. It's moving in the right direction.

Photograph by TAYLOR BALLANTYNE

THE MISSIES

BEFORE THE 2010 Winter Olympics, *Sports Illustrated*'s Gary Smith visited the Lamoureux family of Grand Forks, North Dakota. The youngest of Pierre and Linda's six children, twins Jocelyne and Monique, were linemates for Team USA. In the February 1, 2010, issue, Smith showed readers how their only daughters, known around the house as the Missies, were prepared for their Olympic moment after years of playing against their older brothers:

There are girls on their team! Every rink they entered, the moment that cry was raised, the stakes went up, and humiliation, like a scythe, hovered overhead. Above opposing boys who got flattened by the twins and then serenaded by players on both sides, "You got freight-trained by a girl!" Above the twins' teammates, not to mention their parents, who had to watch two girls dominate play and playing time. Above the twins themselves, who had to keep proving they belonged, physically and emotionally, or get jeered off the ice….

They led their boys' 12-year-old hockey team, the Wheatkings, to the state championship, Mo scoring twice and Jocelyne blanking Grafton for two periods of the final in goal, then switching to forward and scoring on her second shift. But at 13 the Missies were becoming targets of punctured adolescent male pride…so, at last, entering ninth grade, the twins accepted scholarships to Shattuck–St. Mary's Prep, the Minnesota private school where Sidney Crosby had played. They left home at a young age just like their brothers and with trepidation entered the no-checking world of female hockey.

The girls at Shattuck had never seen anything like it: The twins hit the ice at 6:15 for 7 a.m. practices, hit the weight room seven days a week when only two were required…. They were so damn humble and yet shoved everything so close to the edge, or beyond it—as Mo would rue, "Some things we learned in boys' hockey have really come back to bite us in the ass in girls' hockey."

Photograph by ED JONES/AFP

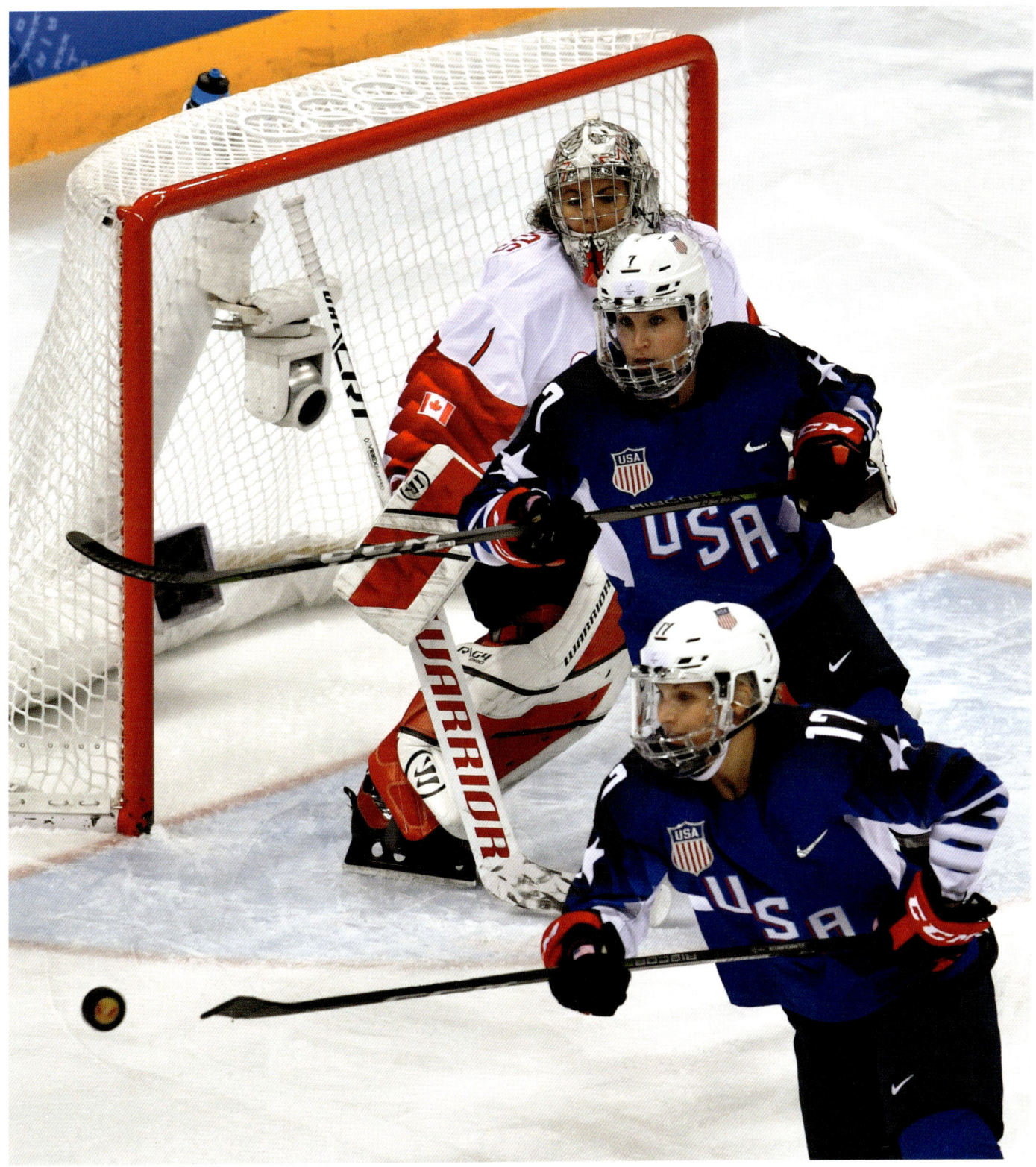

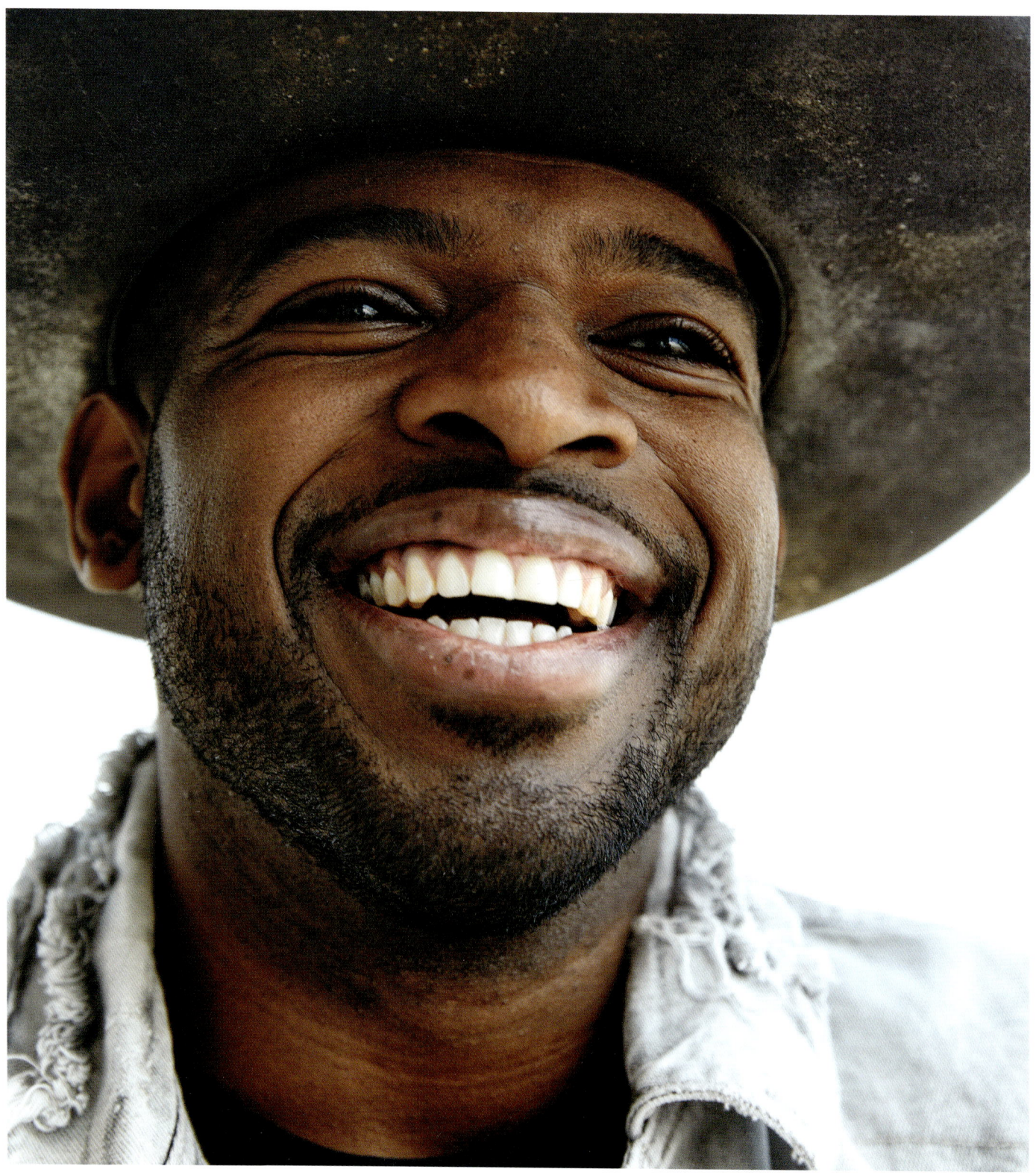

THE SUBBANATOR

FOUR SEASONS PRIVATE RESIDENCES, NEW YORK CITY | *May 29, 2018*

THE MANY SIDES of Pernell Karl Subban were documented in *Sports Illustrated* over the defenseman's 13-season career. Here was *SI*'s assessment in the December 20, 2010, issue during Subban's rookie season, in the lede to an article titled "Montreal's Mighty Mouth":

Rookie defenseman P.K. Subban has talent to burn, but so far he's made his mark more as a trash-talker. After a recent benching, can he learn to channel his passion into better play on the ice?

Four years later, after Subban won the Norris Trophy as hockey's best defenseman, *SI*'s Brian Cazeneuve highlighted his play rather than his chirping:

P.K. Subban doesn't merely play hockey games; he grabs them by the throat. No matter what happens in this series with the [Boston] Bruins, nobody has been more pivotal in the first two rounds of the NHL playoffs than Subban, who is in the middle of everything—mostly to positive effect but sometimes decidedly not. Through Sunday the reigning Norris Trophy winner led all defensemen in points (12), giveaways per game (1.7) and attention drawn. He has been on the ice for 11

of Montreal's 13 goals and has been the fulcrum on which momentum has tilted. "When he's going, he changes your game," said Bruins forward Milan Lucic. "He does so many things."

In 2016 *SI* reported on the stunning trade that sent Subban to Nashville. Alex Prewitt quoted the Preds' big-name addition, who saw the move as motivated by more than on-ice performance. "People said it was a hockey trade," Subban said. "I think it's the furthest from that. I think it was a personality trade."

As a veteran, Subban drew more attention for his off-the-rink attire, earning him a perennial spot among *SI*'s Fashionable 50. The 2017 rankings placed him at Number 15. Jamie Lisanti profiled the style icon:

His killer (and colorful) suits and extensive hat collection have become as unmistakable as his bow-and-arrow pantomime on the ice. "My style is true to who I am and definitely different," Subban says. "I'm always looking for things that are uncommon and unique."

Photograph by TAYLOR BALLANTYNE

SERIOUS SKILLS

SAP CENTER, SAN JOSE | *January 25, 2019*

ALL-STAR WEEKEND HAS become one of the NHL's most popular events. A highlight of the weekend is the skills competition, held the night before the midseason All-Star Game. The best players in the world compete against each other in events that test their shooting, passing, skating and goaltending skills.

Like Larry Bird talking trash and hitting threes at the 1988 NBA All-Star Three-Point Contest, some of the NHL skills performances have become the stuff of legend. Zdeno Chára's 108.8-mph rocket at the 2012 competition is still jaw-dropping, as is Patrick Kane's Superman deke in that year's breakaway competition.

The fastest skater contest has been part of the competition since 1990. Early winners Paul Coffey and Sergei Fedorov are now in the Hockey Hall of Fame, while Connor McDavid has owned the event during his career. He won the event a record three consecutive years and won again in 2024.

But perhaps the most memorable performance is not McDavid's record-setting sprint of 13.02 seconds in 2017. Instead, it's the one that came two years later. During the 2019 competition at San Jose's SAP Center, Kendall Coyne Schofield skated first—and set the pace for other players to beat. Wearing the jersey of the U.S. women's national team, she circled the rink in 14.346 seconds. Her top speed was 23 miles per hour. In the eight-person field, Coyne Schofield finished seventh.

Three other women took part in skills events that year: Renata Fast and Rebecca Johnston of Team Canada, and American Brianna Decker. Their performances were billed as "exhibitions," not eligible for the final standings, unlike Coyne Schofield, who competed as a last-minute replacement. If these women had been included as full contestants, the final standings of one event would have different. Officially, Leon Draisaitl's name is etched as the winning of the 2019 passing competition. In fact, Brianna Decker finished with a time three seconds faster than the Edmonton Oilers forward.

Competing against the best male players in the world, the best women players showed their skills were up to the challenge.

Photograph by EZRA SHAW/GETTY IMAGES

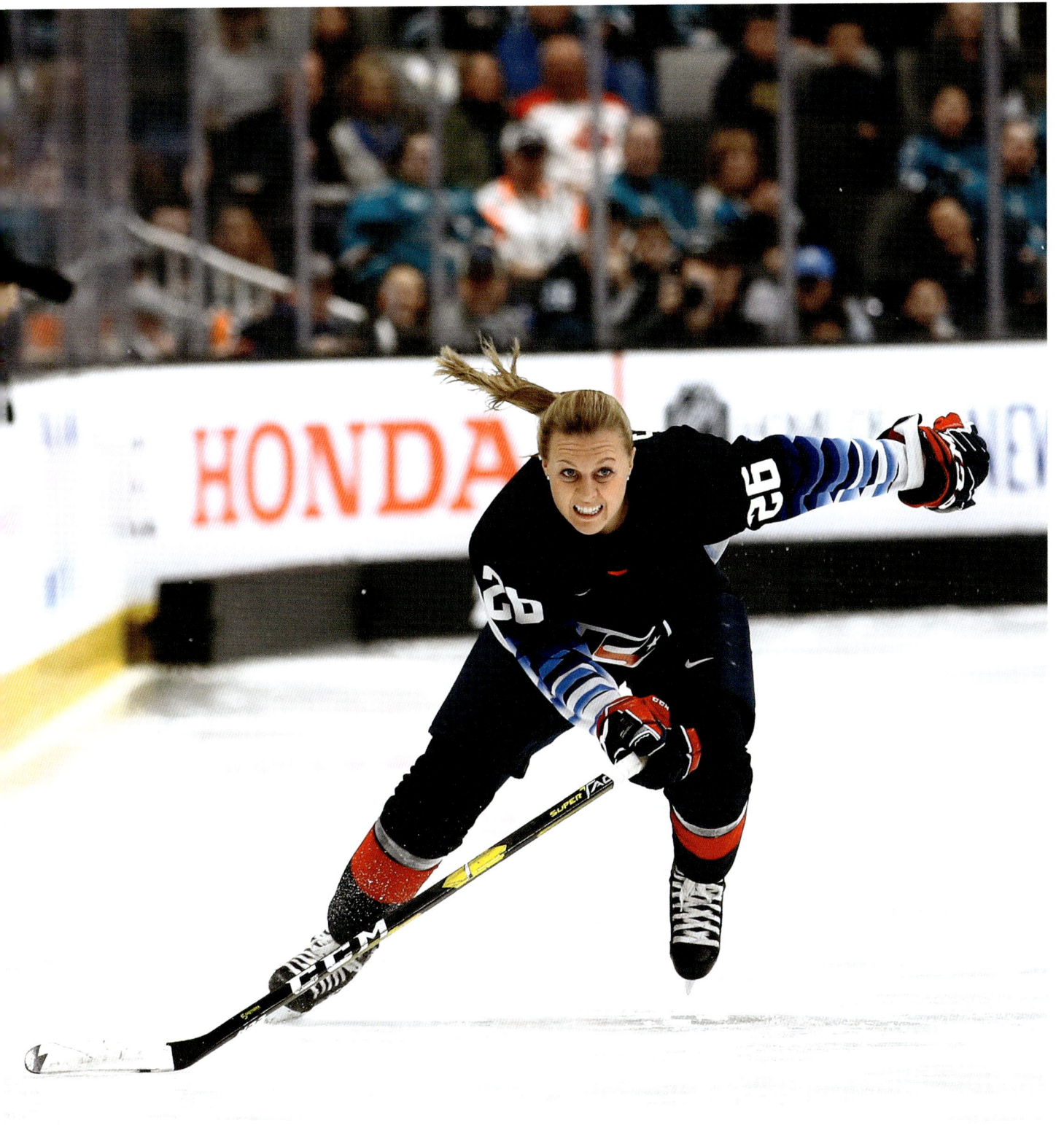

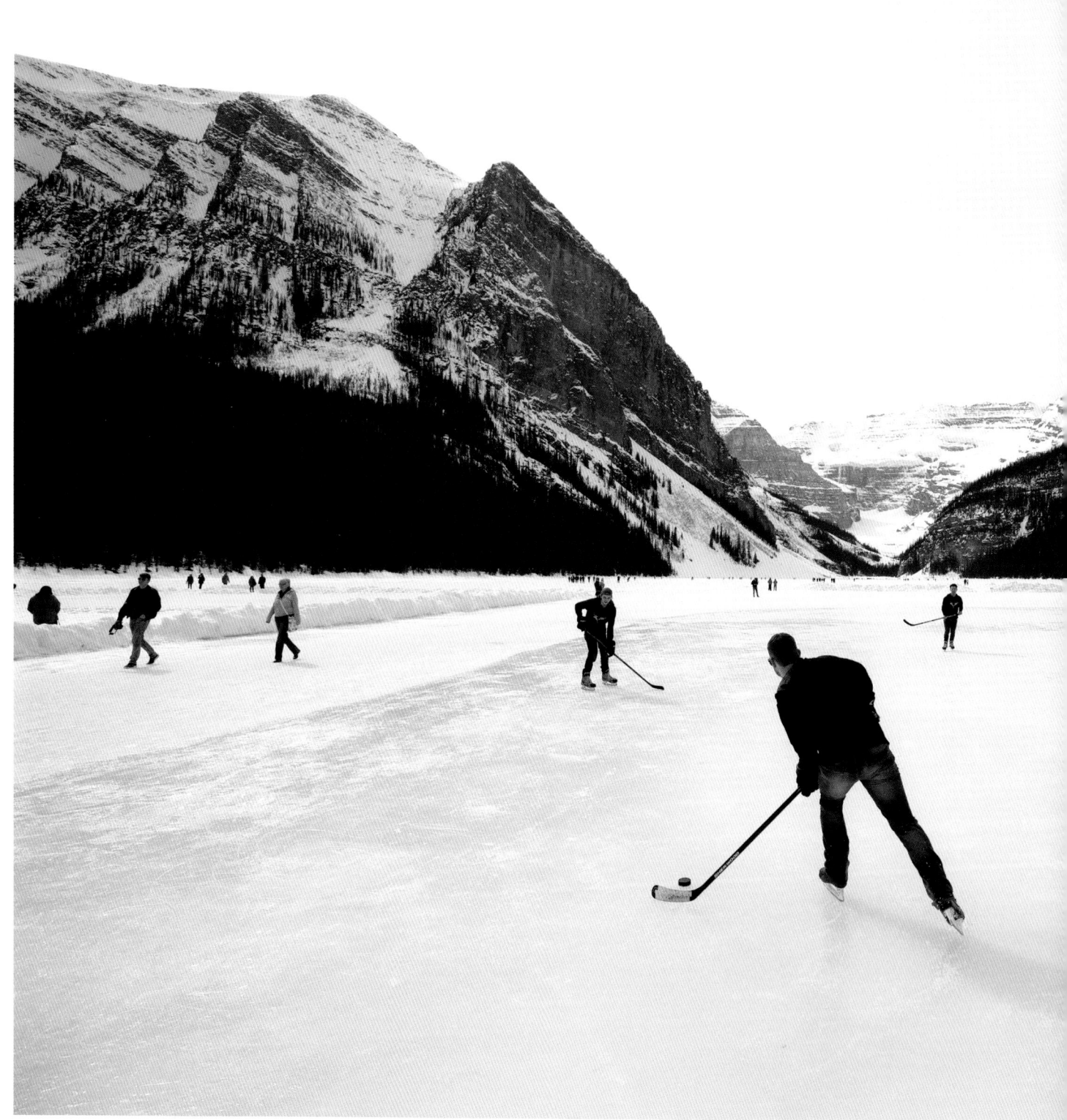

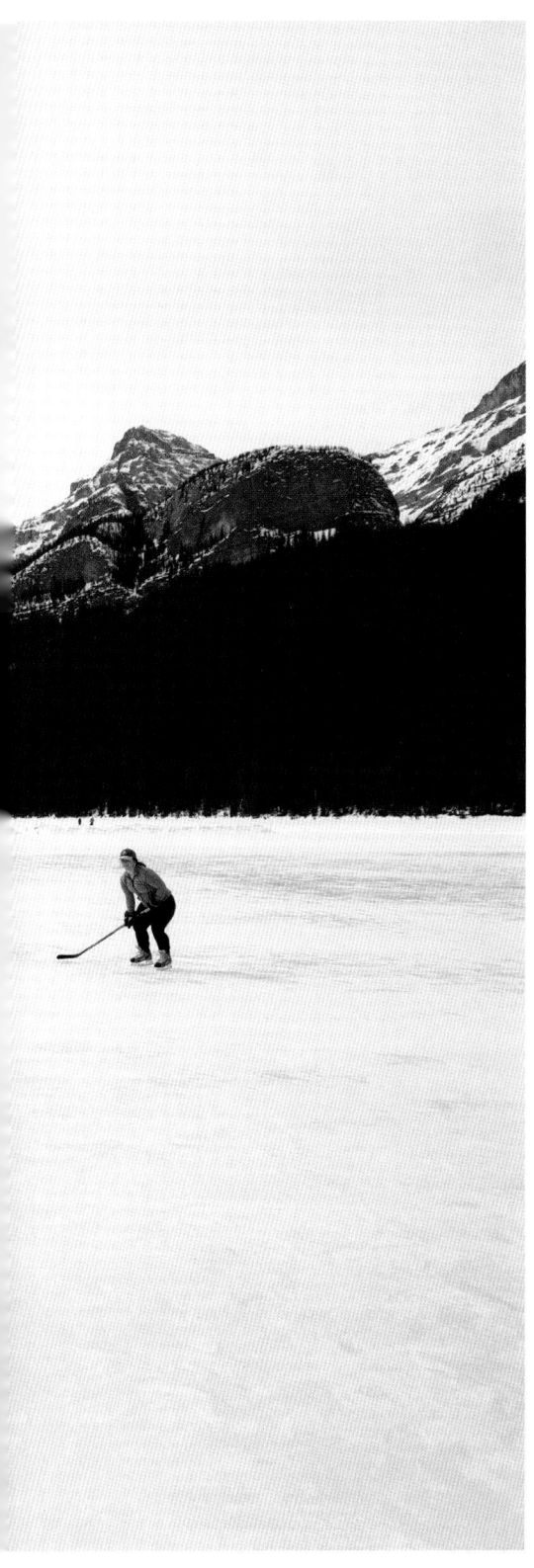

VANISHING ACT

LAKE LOUISE, ALBERTA | *March 23, 2019*

"THE SENSATION OF the skate blades cutting into crisp outdoor ice, the crunching sounds of ice chips flying tidy arcs," recalled Bobby Orr in his memoir. "These are sights and sounds and feelings that are forever lodged deep in my mind."

As hockey has become more expensive to play, as competition—even at the youngest levels—has become more intense, many people have yearned to go back to the simple game remembered by Orr and others. They have gone outside.

In 2002, the local association of Plaster Rock, New Brunswick, organized the first pond hockey tournament on the frozen Tobique River. The inaugural champions were the hometown Tobique Puckers, who bested a field of 40 teams from the area. Word spread in the following years. Four-person squads brought their skates from Arizona, England, the Cayman Islands, even Singapore. Meanwhile, other communities in frostbitten climes started their own tournaments. Today, there are more than a hundred pond hockey events in the United States, Canada and Europe, all claiming to bring hockey back its icy roots.

Part of this nostalgia for hockey in the winter air comes from the awareness that winter itself is disappearing. In Brantford, Ontario, where young Wayne Gretzky learned to skate on his backyard rink, average winter temperatures have risen and the window for outdoor skating has narrowed. According to environmental scientists, southern Ontario has lost a quarter of its skating days in recent years. They expect the number to drop by another third by century's end.

In *Sports Illustrated's* April 22–29, 2019, issue Stanley Kay asked what will happen when hockey is a game played only inside a giant refrigerator, on a surface made by machines:

> Winter sports, unlike the glaciers of Glacier National Park or ash trees of the Northeast, aren't going away anytime soon. The NHL plays its games in climate-controlled arenas, and competitive skiing often relies on artificial snow. But as climate change forces communities like Brantford to consider forfeiting their beloved winter pastimes, we'll have to reckon with an existential question: What will we lose if we can't play sports where they're meant to be played?

Photograph by TODD KOROL

STILL SEARCHING

ENTERPRISE CENTER, ST. LOUIS | *January 24, 2020*

MARIO LEMIEUX CAPPED his seventh season with the Stanley Cup. Wayne Gretzky lifted the Cup after his sixth. Bobby Orr won it in four, as did Sidney Crosby.

Connor McDavid played his 10th NHL season in 2024–25. In his first decade, he won the Art Ross Trophy five times and the Hart Trophy three. But he didn't win the Stanley Cup. Two years in a row, he was the playoffs' top scorer in leading the Edmonton Oilers to the Final. Two years in a row, Florida sent him home without hockey's greatest prize.

Drafted first overall by Edmonton in 2015, McDavid was hailed as the player of his generation. Even a fractured collarbone couldn't hinder his rookie magic; he scored 48 points in just 45 games, proving he was built for the spotlight.

The following season, McDavid was named captain at age 19—the youngest in NHL history. He responded by leading the league with 100 points and sweeping the postseason awards. In 2021, McDavid joined Gretzky as the only players ever to be the unanimous choice for MVP. In 2023, he missed another unanimous selection by one vote.

Yet, for all the individual accolades, McDavid's reputation remains tarnished. Even being named playoff MVP in 2024 cannot silence the doubters. McDavid himself expressed his frustration after the decisive Game 6 loss in 2025. "We kept f------ trying the same thing over and over," he said in the postgame press conference. "Just banging our heads against the wall."

Perhaps recognizing he had crossed a line, McDavid then offered the proper platitudes: "They're a heck of a team. They're the Stanley Cup champions back to back for a reason."

Critics argued that McDavid's tendency to pass first made him predictable in clutch moments. Others pointed to the Oilers' lack of roster depth, especially compared with the Panthers. In any case, McDavid was saddled with pressure as he entered his second decade in the league.

Will he secure his legacy as a graybeard, like Ray Bourque and Alex Ovechkin?

Or is Connor McDavid destined to be the greatest of the greats who never lifted the Cup?

Photograph by JAMIE SQUIRE/GETTY IMAGES

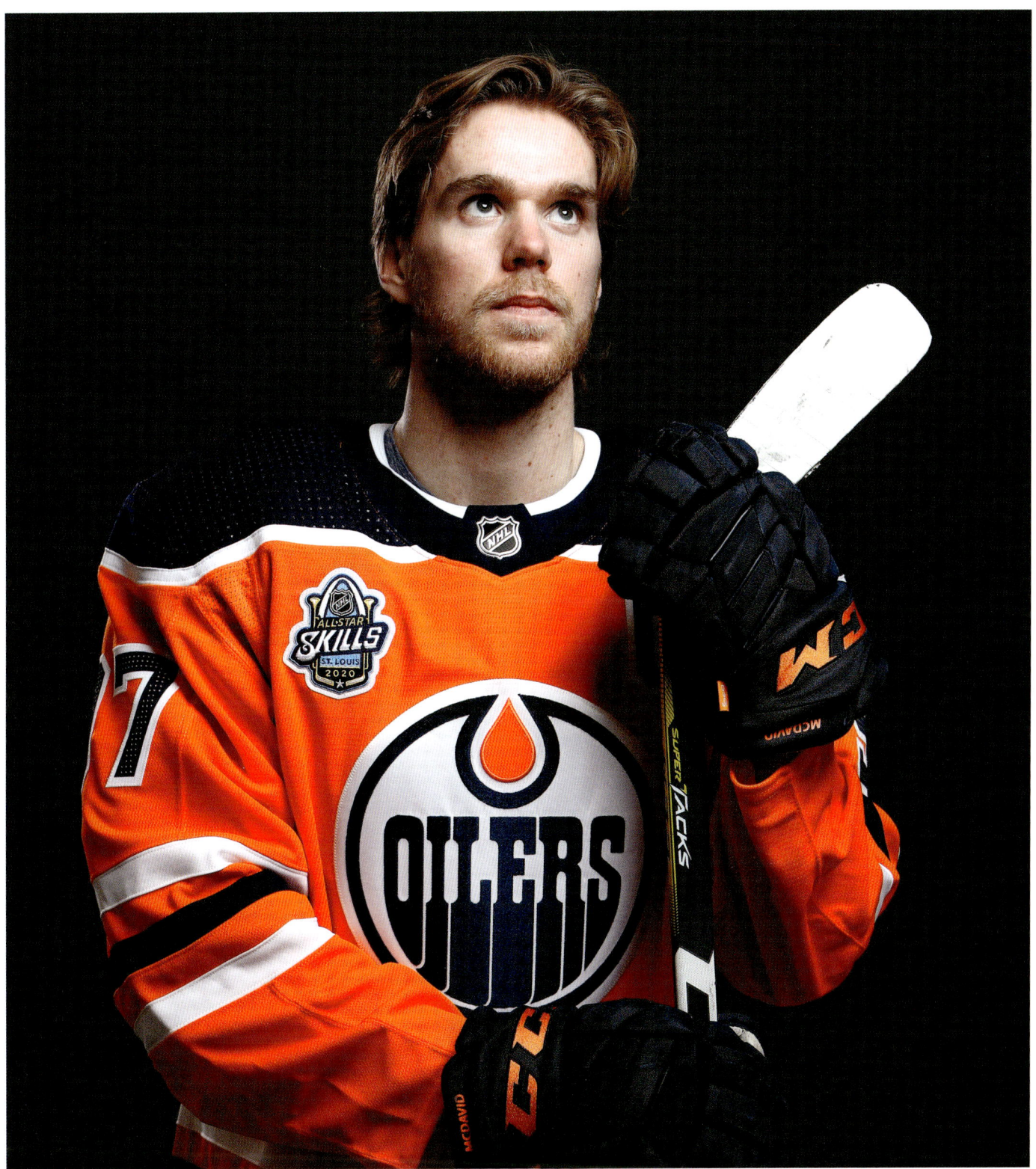

IN CASE OF EMERGENCY

SCOTIABANK ARENA, TORONTO | *February 22, 2020*

OF ALL THE peculiar rules one can find applied to professional sports, perhaps none are as unusual as the NHL's Rule 5.3. It states that in the event a team's active goaltenders are injured or otherwise unable to perform, an emergency backup goaltender (EBUG) shall be pressed into service. That means that in every arena at least one person—be they a minor-league goaltender, a weekend warrior or a Zamboni driver with playing experience—can, at a moment's notice, be asked to shed their civilian clothes and don a pair of goalie pads.

The latter is exactly what took place the night of February 22, 2020, in Toronto. During a game between the Carolina Hurricanes and Toronto Maple Leafs, the road team's goaltending duo, James Reimer and Petr Mrázek, were both injured before the second period had ended. Into the crease stepped David Ayres, a 42-year-old Ontario native and the building operator at Ricoh Coliseum, where his duties included occasionally driving the Zamboni. Despite minimal experience or time to prepare, Ayres stopped eight of the 10 shots he faced as the Hurricanes held on for a 6–3 victory. Ayres became the first EBUG in history to be credited with a win, and also became the oldest to win his NHL regular-season debut.

EBUGs have only been called into duty six times in an NHL game. Indeed, Ayres's triumph may be the last of its kind: the league's new collective bargaining agreement, scheduled to take effect for the 2026–27 season, requires that every team employ a full-time, travelling replacement.

Photograph by KEVIN SOUSA/NHLI

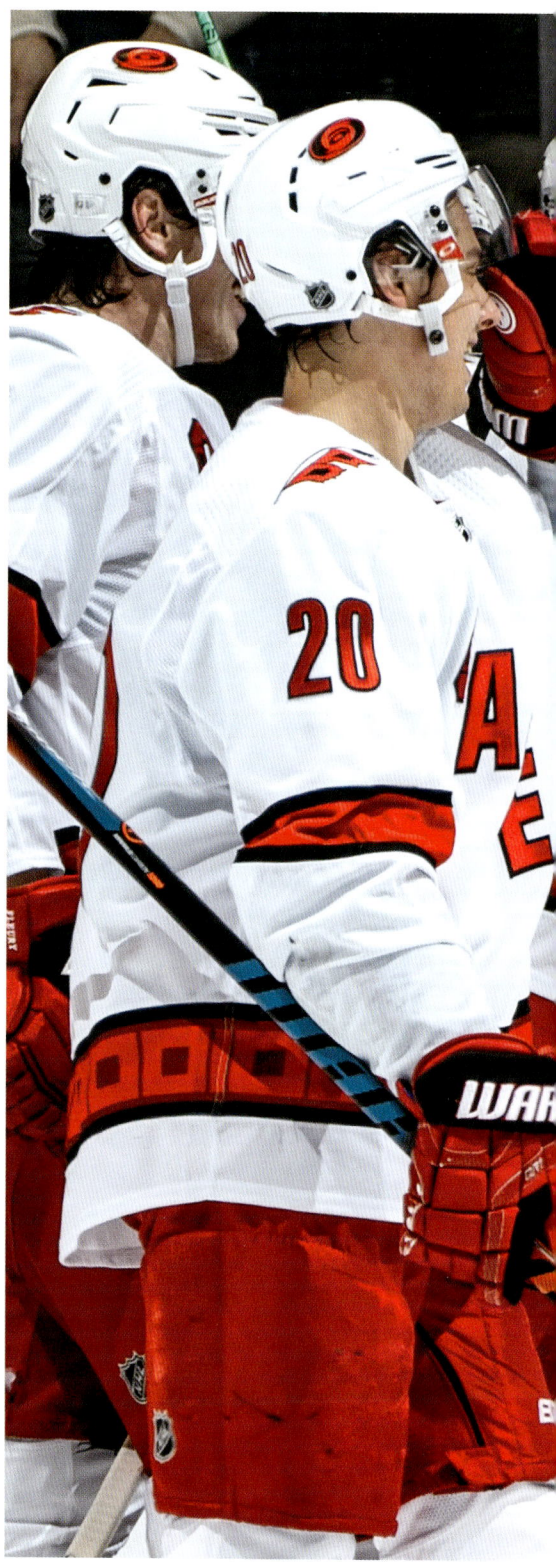

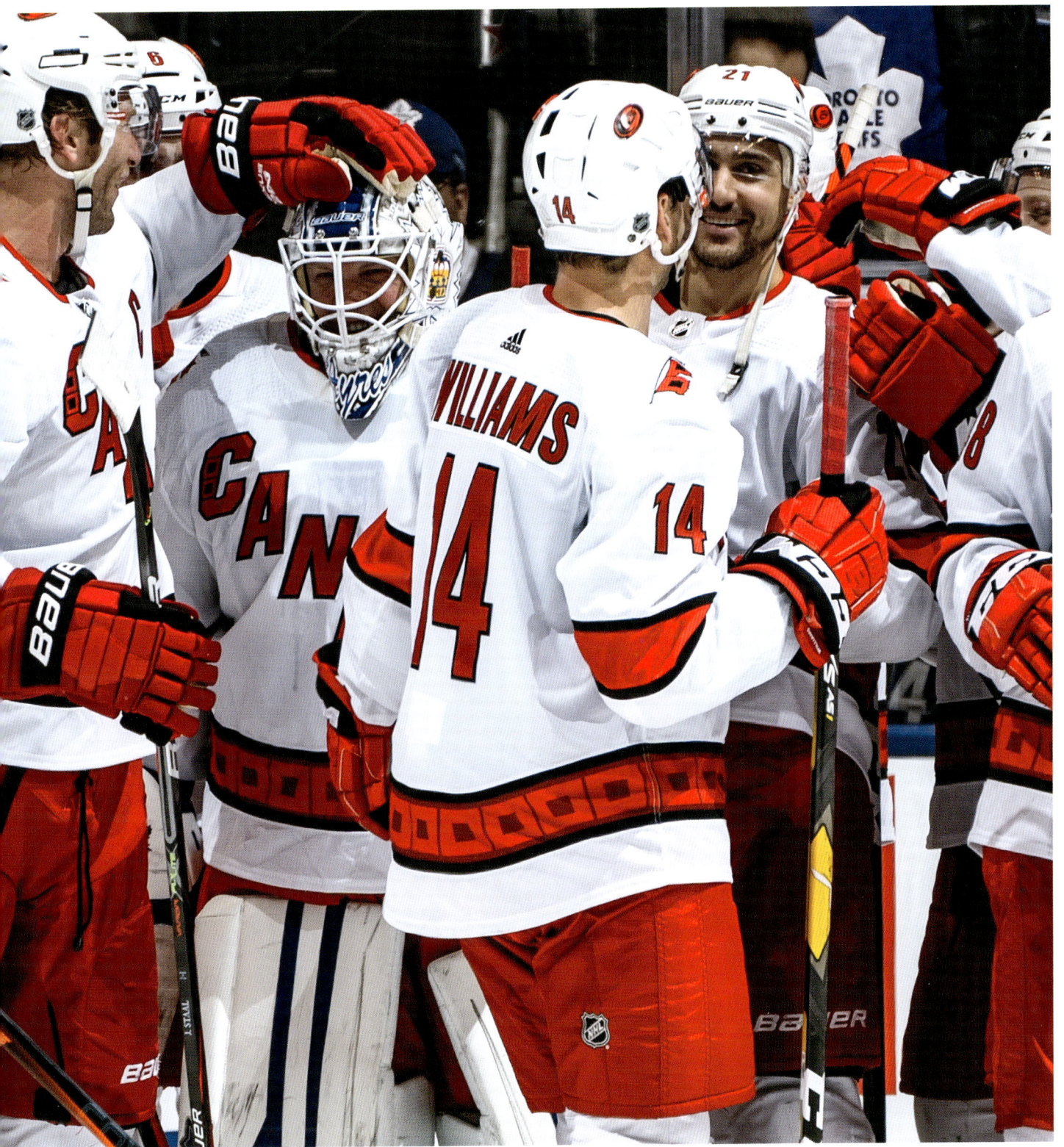

THE BUBBLE

ROGERS PLACE, EDMONTON | *September 19, 2020*

IN MARCH 2020, the COVID-19 pandemic forced sports across the globe to shutter, and hockey was no exception. NHL commissioner Gary Bettman's carefully chosen word "pause" kept hope alive that the season would resume. But the road back to the ice would require unprecedented creativity, cooperation and sacrifice.

The pause froze the standings after teams had already played 68 to 71 games. Behind the scenes, the league quietly began planning for a radically different postseason, one that would require sealing off players from the outside world.

Just over two months later, the NHL and NHLPA hammered out a bold "Return to Play" plan: a 24-team postseason tournament in two Canadian "bubble" cities, Toronto and Edmonton. The regular season was scrapped, and points percentage from March determined seeding. In August, 16 teams played best-of-five qualifying rounds, with the winners going on to face the top four seeds in each conference in traditional best-of-seven series, all played without fans. Players, coaches and staff lived under strict quarantine rules, undergoing daily testing. Over nine weeks, more than 33,000 tests were administered. The league reported zero positive cases.

The last two teams standing were Tampa Bay and Dallas, battling in Edmonton's empty Rogers Place. It was the first Final between two Sun Belt franchises. It was also the first Final played in a single arena since 1928, when the New York Rangers had to stay on the road in Montreal while the circus took over Madison Square Garden.

In Game 6, Andrei Vasilevskiy slammed the door on Dallas with a 22-save shutout, sealing Tampa Bay's 2–0 win and the second Stanley Cup title in franchise history. When Bettman handed the Cup to Steven Stamkos, his words carried extra weight: "This Stanley Cup run will go down in the record books as perhaps the hardest run of all times. You guys should all be incredibly proud."

The league was so successful in keeping its players and coaches healthy that one of the game's honored rituals went forward, despite the pandemic. At the end of the game, players from both teams lined up, took off their gloves and shook hands.

Photograph by DAVE SANDFORD/NHLI

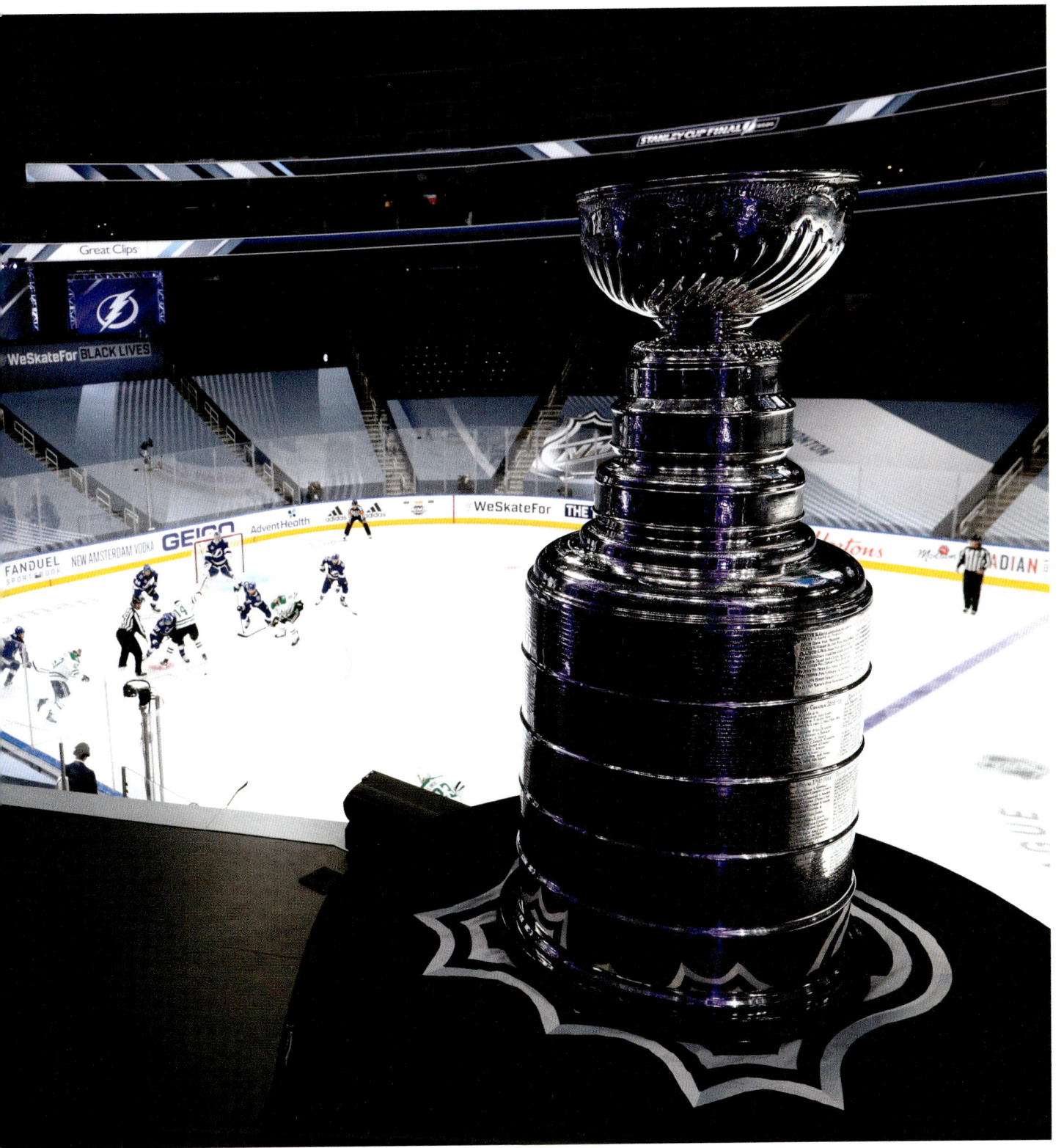

A STRONG START

TSONGAS CENTER, LOWELL, MASSACHUSETTS | *May 29, 2024*

IF THERE IS a textbook on how to start a sports league, the first chapter should be dedicated to the Professional Women's Hockey League. With packed arenas, brilliant social media and corporate sponsorships, the new league showed that pro women's hockey was a winning business.

From the start, the league's principal investors, sports icon Billie Jean King and Los Angeles Dodgers owner Mark Walter, cooperated with players to establish a stable, well-funded structure. Unlike previous attempts at pro leagues, the PWHL hired over 100 people to manage merchandising, endorsements and media. At the same time, the league kept its scope limited to just six franchises: Boston, Minnesota, Montreal, New York, Ottawa and Toronto. In a move that worked brilliantly, the teams had no nicknames. Each city name was stitched diagonally across every sweater, in the same font with different colors. The brand was the PWHL, not the individual teams.

On New Year's Day 2024, the league played its first game, between Toronto and New York. Broadcast on Canadian television, the game drew more viewers that day than the NHL Winter Classic. Attendance records for women's hockey fell one after another throughout the season. The biggest crowd was over 21,000 in Montreal, for a late-season matchup against Toronto.

But it was PWHL Minnesota who engraved their names into history as the first champions. After finishing fourth in the regular season, Minnesota dropped the first two games against top-seeded Toronto before winning three straight to take the series. The final against Boston also went the full five games, after Boston won a double-overtime thriller in Game 4. A shutout on the road sealed the title for the State of Hockey. Minnesota-raised Taylor Heise, who had been the top overall pick in the league's first draft, was named its first playoff MVP.

At the same time the final was being played in Boston and St. Paul, PWHL leaders were in New York to receive a sports-business award. Industry professionals commended the league for its record-breaking attendance, social engagement and business partnerships. "I've waited my entire life for moments like this," said Bille Jean King as she accepted the award.

Photograph by M. ANTHONY NESMITH/ICON SPORTSWIRE

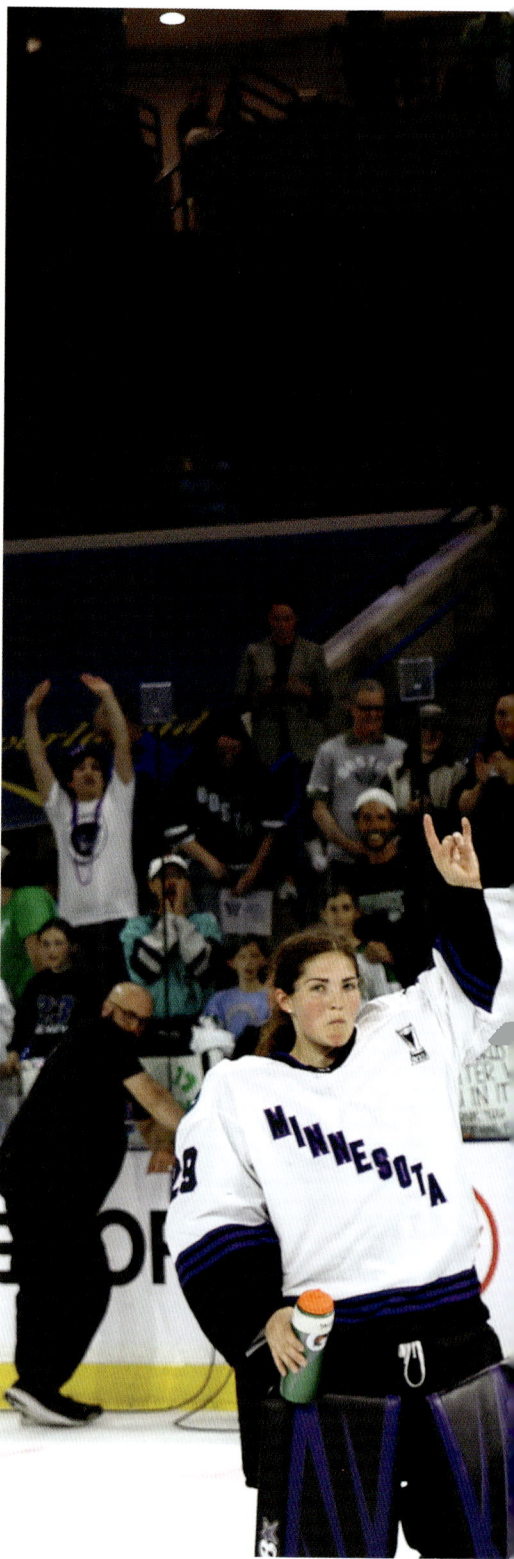

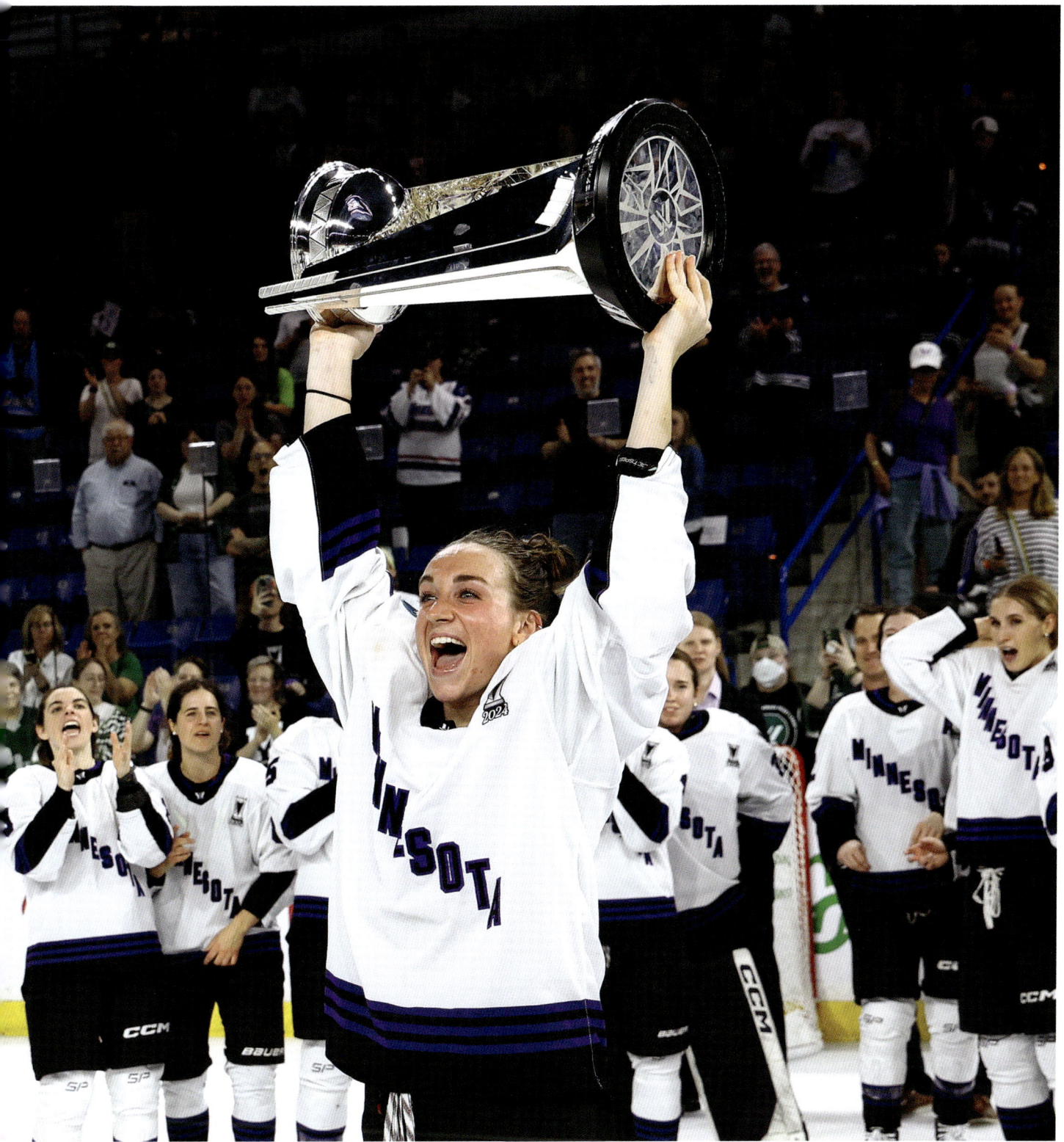

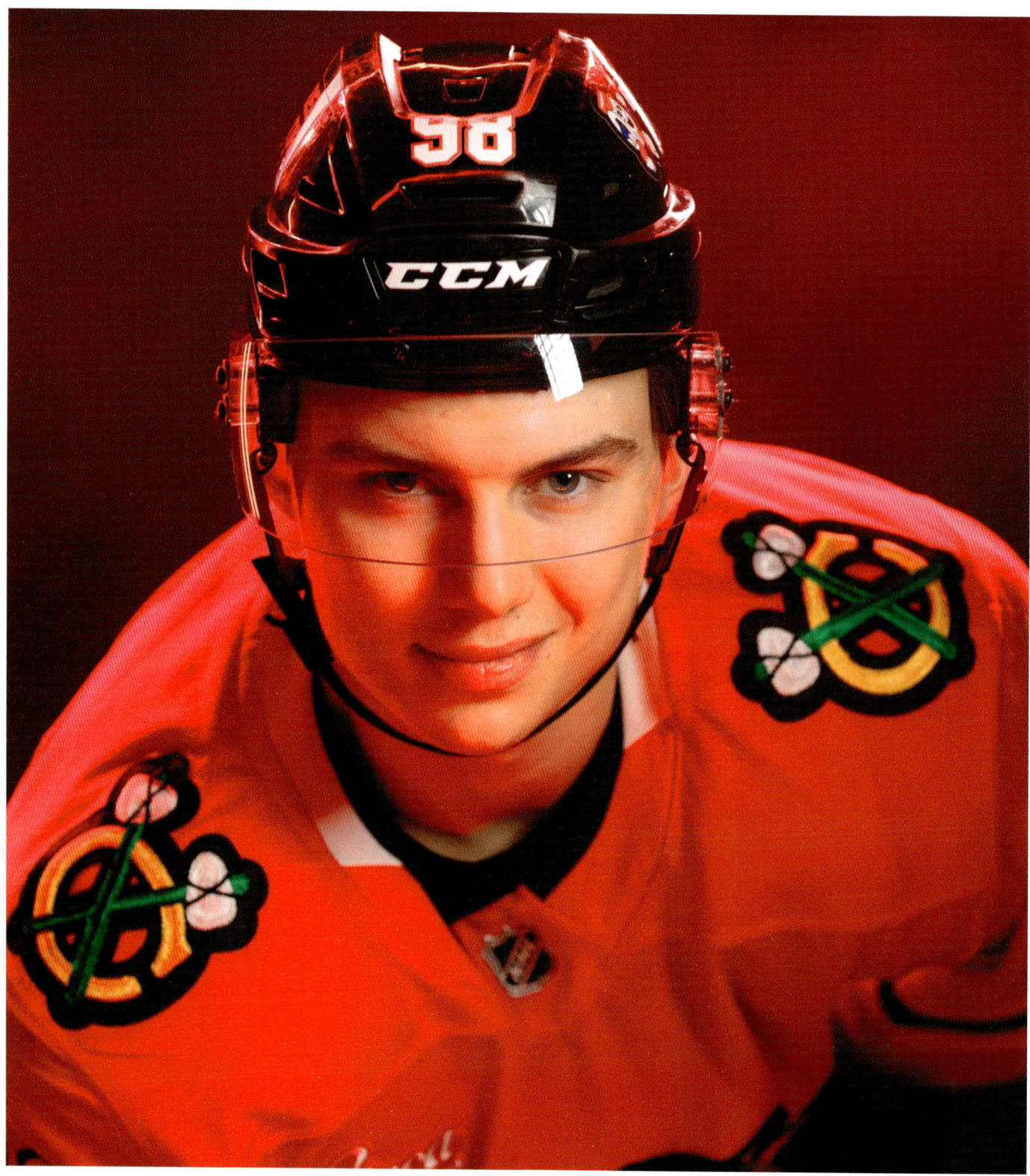

THE NEXT BIG THING

FIFTH THIRD ARENA, CHICAGO | *October 24, 2024*

CONNOR BEDARD WAS in distinguished company by the age of 13. Like Orr, Lafleur, Crosby and McDavid, he was the next teenage prospect to be christened the player of his generation, the future of hockey.

Bedard was given special permission to enter Canada's major junior ranks a year early. He averaged over two points per game in three seasons in the Western Hockey League. At the 2023 World Junior Championships, he averaged more than three points per game, leading Canada to the gold medal. When the NHL Draft opened later that year, there was no question whose name would be called first.

Bedard's debut season with the Chicago Blackhawks was shortened by a broken jaw, but he still tallied 61 points in 68 games and earned the Calder Trophy as the top rookie. He also assembled a highlight reel of dekes, passes and snipes. To understand how a teenager could get the better of seasoned pros, *Sports Illustrated* interviewed skills coach Tim Turk, who had worked with Bedard during his years in juniors:

Turk has worked with NHL players for 29 of his 35-year coaching career. But there was something about this kid, particularly with his wrist shot, that was like nothing he'd ever seen before. "It looked like a cowboy drawing his gun out of his holster in a gunfight," Turk says.

Turk saw that Bedard's shot was not only fast; it was unconventional. This was partly because the right-hander had broken his right wrist when he was 13. Bedard spent three months living left-handed. He practiced shooting and stickhandling exclusively with his off-hand. When the cast came off, Bedard could power shots with his left hand while the right acted as a fulcrum on the stick—the opposite of most right-handed shooters.

As Turk recognized, a lefthanded shot coming from a righthanded player was confusing even in the NHL. "When it gets in close like that, it creates all these different types of deceptions," he said. For young players aspiring to be the next future of hockey, Turk warned that it wouldn't be easy to copy Bedard's gunslinging. "It's just too hard to mimic him."

Photograph by JEFFERY A. SALTER

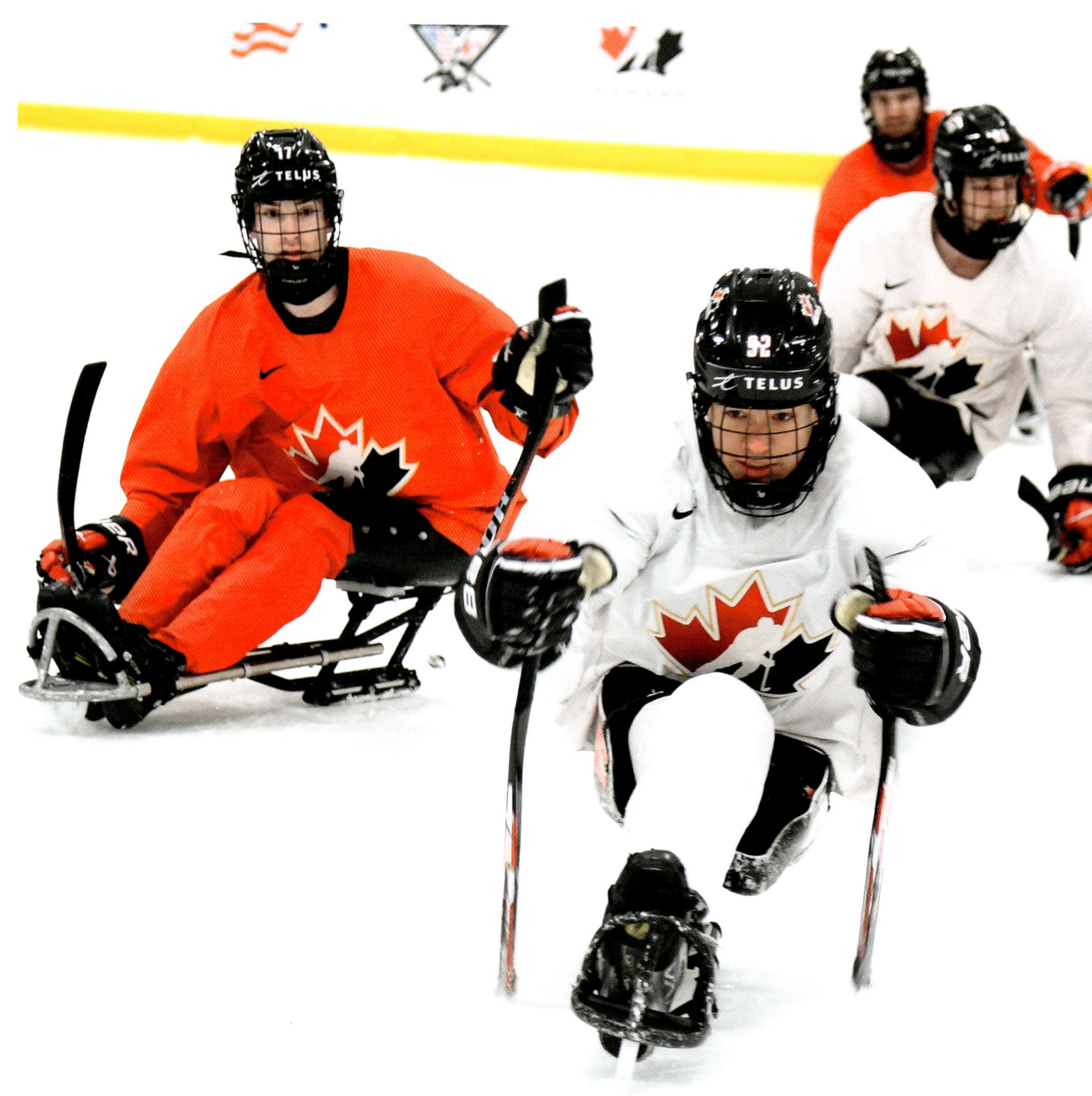

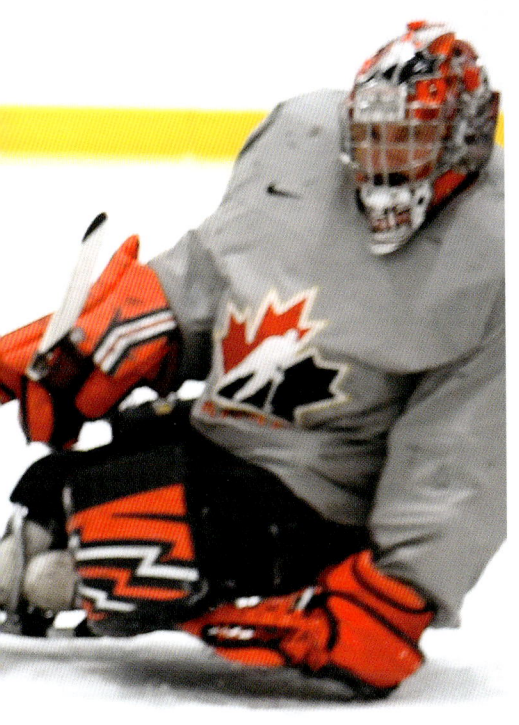

HOCKEY IS FOR EVERYONE

KASABUSKI RINK, BOSTON | *February 18, 2025*

ON A FROZEN Swedish pond in the early 1960s, Bengt-Gosta Johansson and a few friends strapped themselves into crude wooden sleds, grabbed broom handles and whacked a puck toward cardboard-box goals. Johansson, who lost his legs in a motorcycle accident at 15, would play the sport he helped invent for another four decades.

"I was born for it," he told an interviewer.

The sport barely survived its infancy. A loosely organized league of five teams, composed of disabled and able-bodied players, played a few games each winter in the '60s. By 1976, the game was big enough to go global, debuting as an exhibition at the first Winter Paralympics. It was not until 1994 that sled hockey, also known as sledge or para ice hockey, became an official event. Johansson, who had participated in Summer Paralympics in wheelchair marathon and volleyball, led the Swedish team to gold at Lillehammer.

If Johansson represents the sport's origins, Marine Gunnery Sergeant Ralph DeQuebec shows its promise. Nearly killed by an IED explosion in Afghanistan in 2012, DeQuebec lost both of his legs above the knees. During his long recovery at Walter Reed Hospital, another wounded soldier suggested that DeQuebec try sled hockey. Roughly a year after the explosion in Afghanistan, he gave the sport a try. He spent most of the time trying to stay upright.

The learning curve was steep—standard equipment is now a narrow sled balanced on twin blades and short sticks tipped with picks. But the camaraderie was immediate. DeQuebec came back the next week and took private lessons. The former high school football player also had to learn the rules and strategy of hockey. Playing *NHL 14* on his Xbox helped with that.

When *Sports Illustrated* profiled DeQuebec in 2016, he hoped to make the U.S. national team as a defenseman. He was selected in 2017 and went on to win gold at the 2018 and 2022 Paralympics. More important than medals was the renewed sense of purpose he gained.

"I finally found something that I wanted to wake up for every day," he said.

"It brought out who he was before his injury," added his wife, Katie.

Photograph by STEVE BABINEAU/NHLI

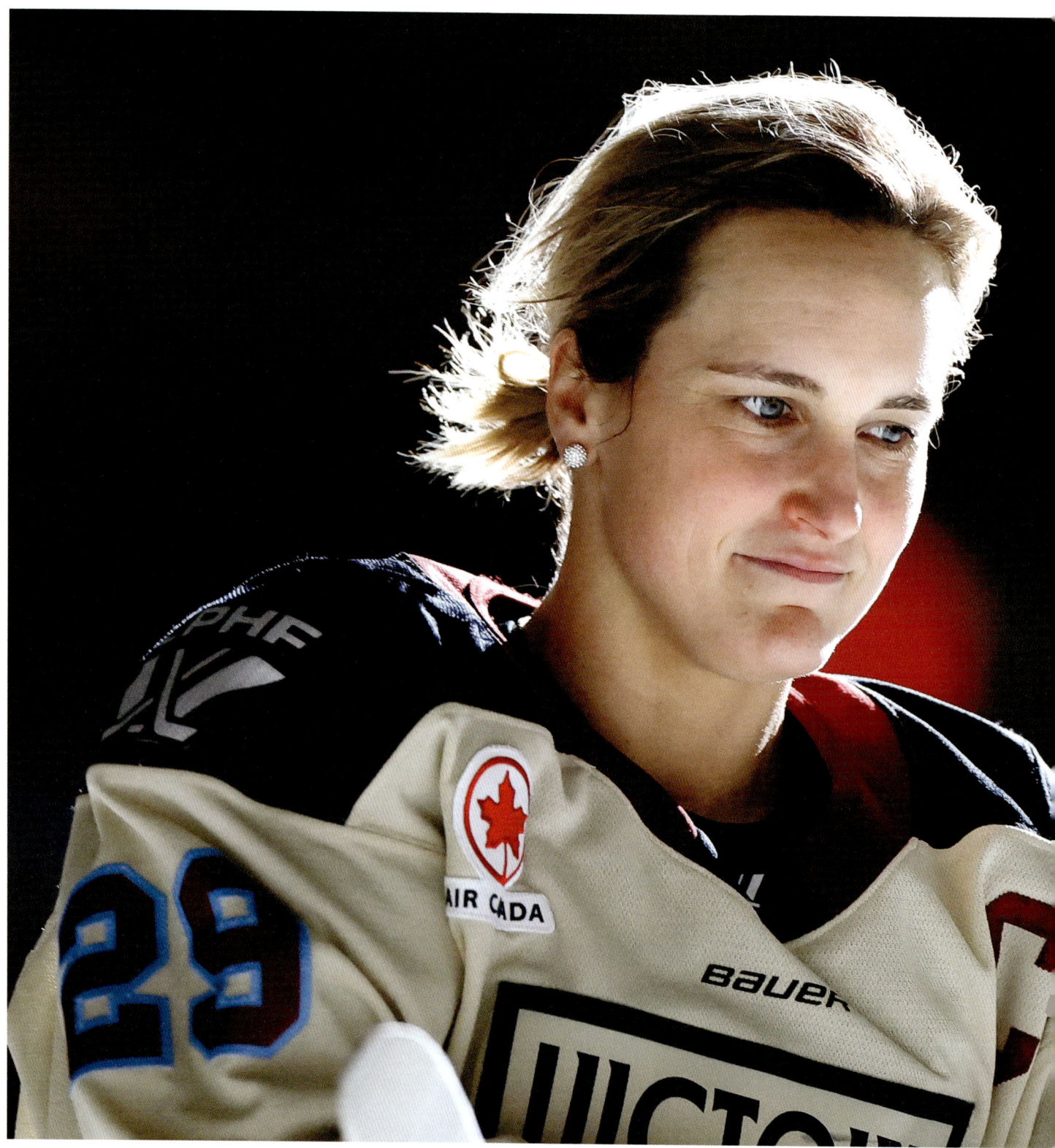

CAPTAIN CLUTCH

COCA-COLA COLISEUM, TORONTO | *March 6, 2025*

MARIE-PHILIP POULIN HAS accomplished something no other player has done.

At the 2010 Vancouver Games, the 19-year-old Poulin made her Olympic debut for Team Canada. In the final game, inside an arena awash in maple-leaf red, Poulin scored two first-period goals against the Americans. The Canadians shut down their rivals for the rest of the game, sealing Canada's third straight gold in Olympic women's hockey.

Four years later, at Sochi, Canada met Team USA again for the gold medal. Poulin had only one goal in the previous four games, but she found her touch when it mattered most. Late in the third period, Canada was trailing 2–0. With just under four minutes left, Brianne Jenner scored to make it 2–1. At the one-minute mark, goalie Shannon Szabados went to the bench. Just seconds later, Poulin scored the game-tying goal.

In overtime, a flurry of penalties on both teams gave Canada a four-on-three advantage. Passing crisply around the American's penalty killers, the Canadian skaters looked for an opening. Laura Fortino found Poulin in the slot. She snapped a quick shot past the sprawling goalie. Canada had its fourth straight gold.

Poulin scored again in the 2018 final, at Pyeongchang. This time, however, it was the Americans' turn for heroics. Monique Lamoureux's goal late in the third period evened the score, and then her sister Jocelyne won the game in the shootout.

At the 2022 Beijing Games, Poulin captained the Canadians to another gold-medal faceoff with the Americans. One of the top scorers in the tournament, she was again the difference-maker in the final. She assisted on Sarah Nurse's opening goal, then added two goals of her own. The U.S. closed the gap in the third but the Canadians held against the last-minute pressure.

Once more, Canada's women skaters had Olympic gold. Once more, Poulin had the golden goal. No hockey player, male or female, has scored the game-winning goal in three Olympic finals.

Photograph by MICHAEL CHISHOLM/GETTY IMAGES

THE RECORD BREAKER

UBS ARENA, ELMONT, NEW YORK | *April 6, 2025*

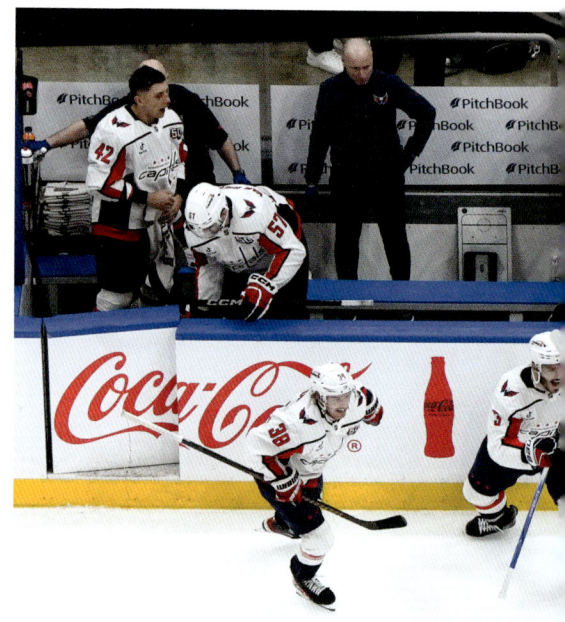

EVEN ALEX OVECHKIN thought the record was unbreakable.

"No. I don't think somebody will beat this record," the Washington Capitals forward told Canada's Sportsnet in 2016.

At the time, he had already passed the 500-goal mark in his career. But Ovi knew that reaching Wayne Gretzky's record of 894 demanded years of consistent production, something that would be harder as the seasons piled up.

"I'd have to have six seasons of 50 goals," he added. "I don't know if I'm going to be able to skate in six seasons."

Ovechkin was correct that six seasons of 50 goals was a big ask. Instead, he averaged 41 goals over eight years. Breaking the Great One's record was a relentless pursuit. Right at the end, when he was just 26 goals away from immortality, Ovechkin went down with a fractured fibula. He was out for only 16 games. In the first five games after his return, he scored four goals.

The record fell on April 6, 2025, on the road against the New York Islanders. When the Capitals got a power play in the second period, the crowd at UBS Arena got to its feet in anticipation of a scoring chance for Ovechkin. The 39-year-old fired a shot past Ilya Sorokin for goal 895. Ovi thrust his arms in the air and immediately dove head first onto the rink at center ice.

As the game was paused to commemorate the moment, Gretzky went to the ice to congratulate the NHL's new goal-scoring record holder. When the Great One retired, in 1999, the conventional wisdom was that his records would remain untouched. But his mark of 894 goals had been amassed in two distinct periods: in his first 10 years, he averaged a Gretzky-esque 63 goals per year; in the next 10 years, his output dropped to the more human level of 26 per year. By contrast, Ovechkin tallied an average of 48 goals in his first decade and 42 goals per season in the second. He reached 895 goals by steady production over 20 years.

Endurance and consistency. This was how to achieve the impossible.

Photograph by JESS RAPFOGEL/NHLI

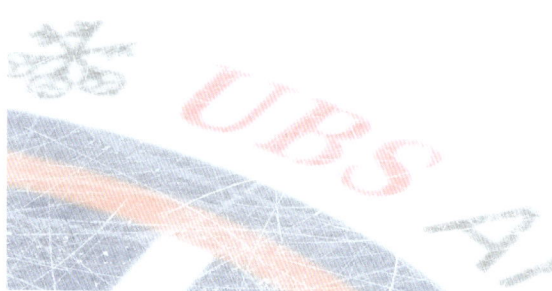

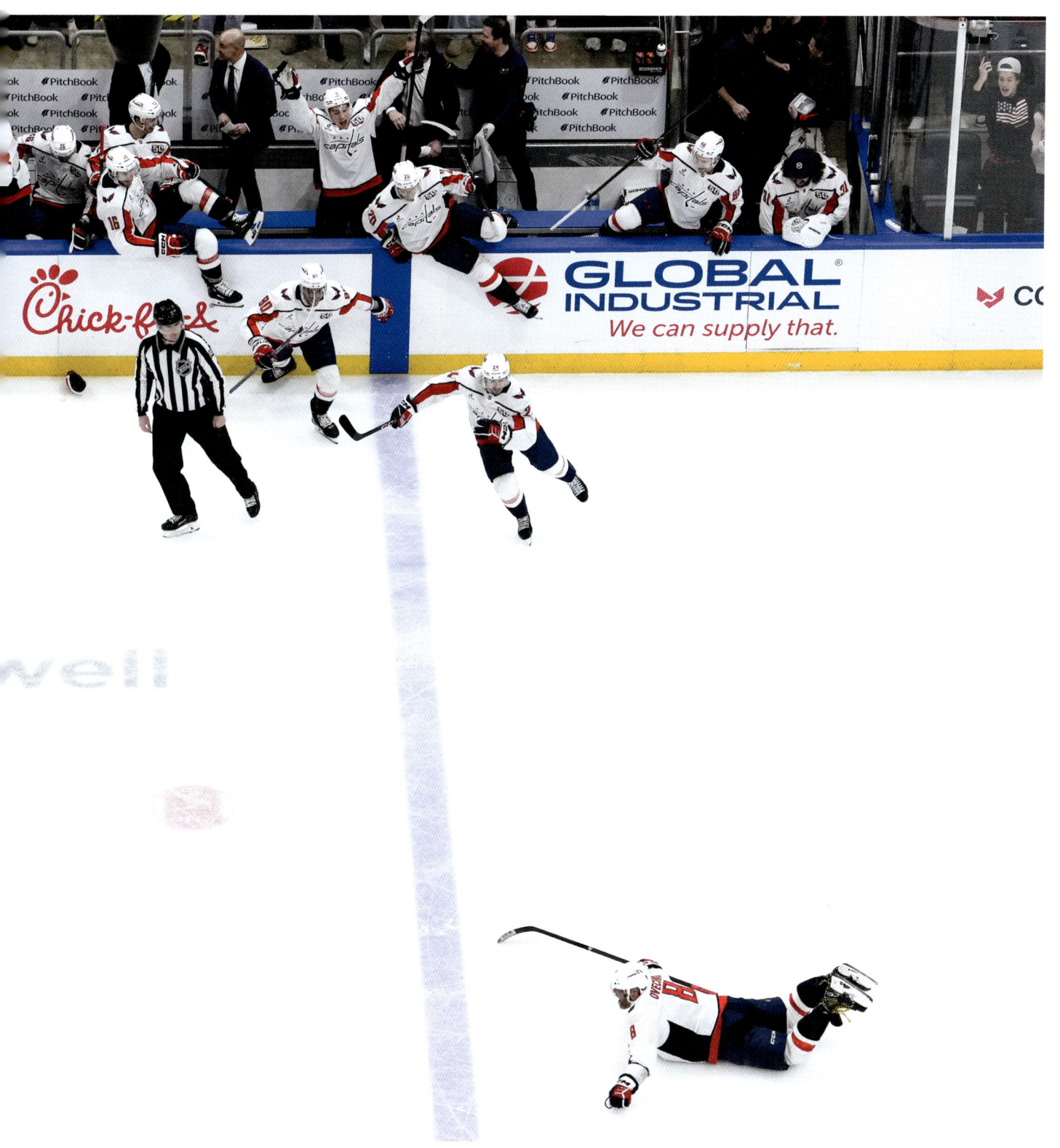

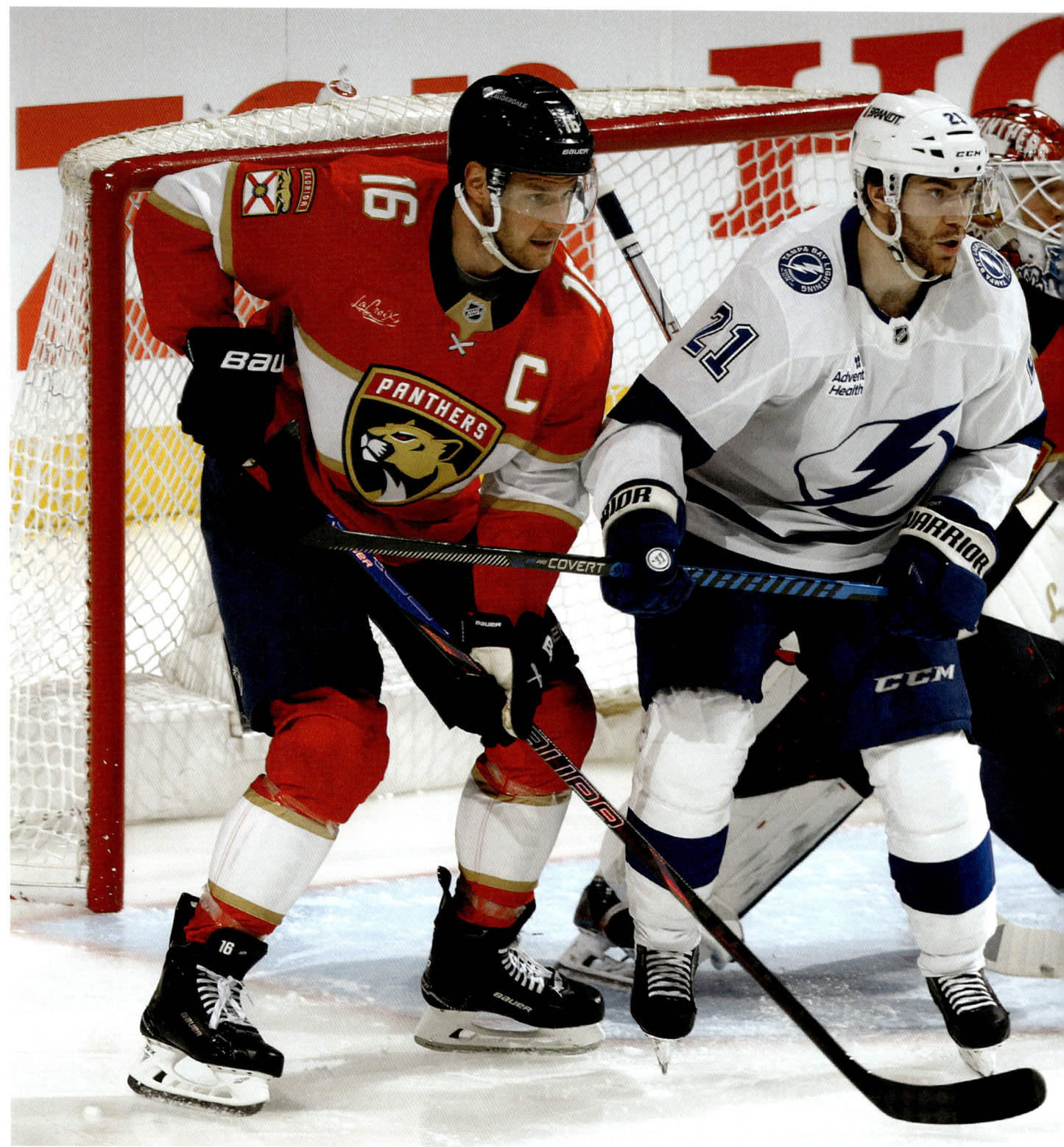

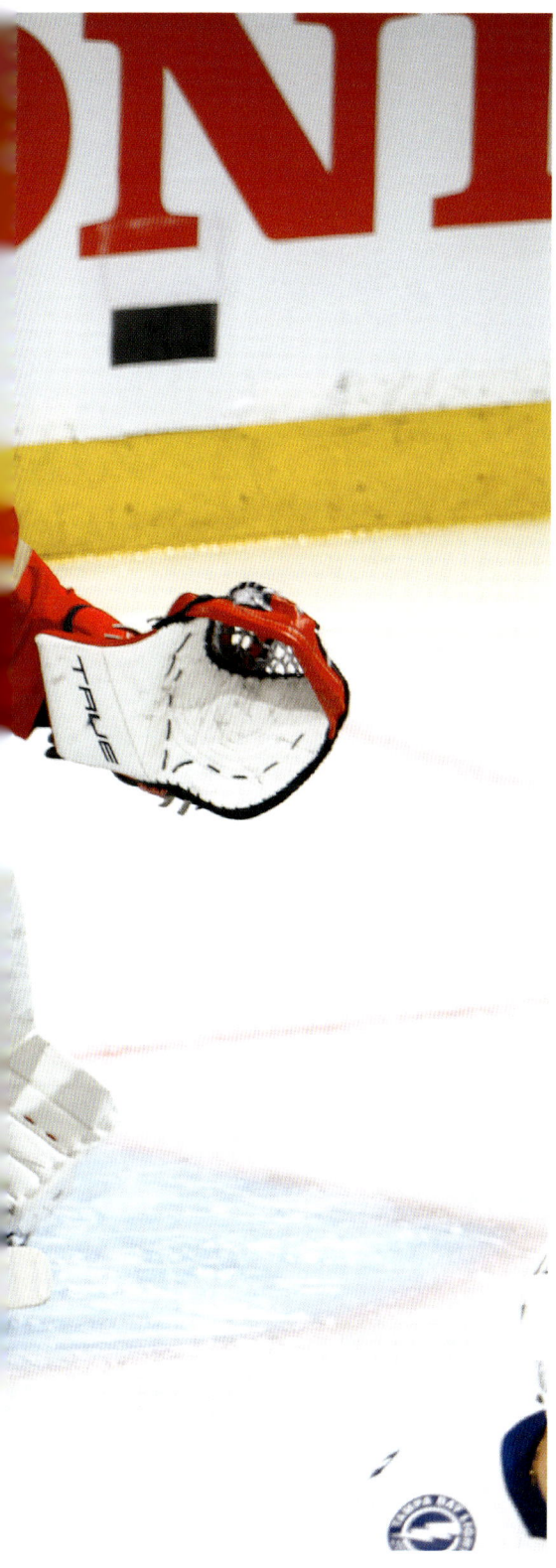

FUN IN THE SUN

AMERANT BANK ARENA, SUNRISE, FLORIDA | *April 26, 2025*

LIKE THOUSANDS OF Canadian snowbirds who head to warmer climes each winter, Lord Stanley's silver Cup bathed in the sunshine of the American South for much of the 2020s.

Tampa Bay won the Cup twice to start the decade, then the Florida Panthers beat the Edmonton Oilers twice, in 2024 and 2025. Each team also reached the Final in the season in-between: the Lightning lost to the Colorado Avalanche in 2022, while Florida fell to the Vegas Golden Knights the following year.

The 2023 playoffs also marked the first time in NHL history when all four teams in the semifinals came from the Sun Belt: Vegas, Florida, Dallas and Carolina. Clearly, the NHL's southern strategy has been a success. In 2024–25, Tampa Bay and Florida were among only five teams to top 19,000 per game in average attendance, joining Original Sixers Montreal, Detroit and Chicago. Likewise, the Stars, Canes, Knights and Nashville Predators each averaged over 17,000 per game.

With packed arenas, the Lightning and Panthers have the revenue to use every cent of the salary cap. In addition, these teams have an additional financial advantage, thanks to Florida being a no-tax state.

As Dom Luszczyszyn of The Athletic reported after the Panthers won their second consecutive championship, the Florida teams were able to net discounts on cap hits that allowed them to build deep rosters. "We're in the midst of a no-state tax dynasty," he wrote.

The Panthers took special advantage of their state's no-tax status by paying new players hefty signing bonuses rather than big salaries. Aleksander Barkov, Matthew Tkachuk, Brad Marchand and other Panthers shared the same contract structure: $1 million in base salary with the rest of the deal paid in signing bonuses. Because these bonuses were taxed in the player's state of residence, Florida, they could take full advantage of the tax breaks.

"This isn't Florida's entire advantage," Luszczyszyn admitted, "far from it." But tax laws give some explanation as to why the NHL's future dynasties will likely be found in the Sun Belt rather than hockey's tradition homeland.

Photograph by JOEL AUERBACH/GETTY IMAGES

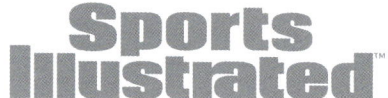

THE STORY OF

Hockey

IN 100 PHOTOGRAPHS

Library of Congress Cataloging-in-Publication Data available upon request.

This book is available in quantity at special discounts for your group or organization. For further information, contact:

Triumph Books LLC
814 North Franklin Street,
Chicago, Illinois 60610
(312) 337-0747
www.triumphbooks.com

Printed in U.S.A.
ISBN: 978-1-63727-928-1